For Donald. a sharing of the
wealth of bodies &
knowledge.
Love Barbara
Fall
1996

Penguin Handbooks

The Penguin Guide to Ancient Egypt

William J. Murnane was born in New York in 1945, but moved to
Venezuela soon afterwards. Somehow missing a vocation for Latin
American archaeology, he returned to study in the United States
and specialized in ancient Egyptian at the Oriental Institute of the
University of Chicago. Shortly before receiving his doctorate in
1973 he joined the staff of the Institute's Epigraphic Survey in
Luxor, an arrangement that permits him to avoid the winters in
Chicago and to travel widely within Egypt. In addition to scholarly
articles, reviews and a monograph, he has written *United with
Eternity*, a guide to the temples of Medinet Habu in Western Thebes,
and has been entrusted with the first comprehensive publication of
the reliefs and inscriptions in the great hypostyle hall at Karnak.

THE PENGUIN GUIDE TO
ANCIENT EGYPT

WILLIAM J. MURNANE

PENGUIN BOOKS

Penguin Books Ltd, Harmondsworth,
Middlesex, England
Penguin Books, 40 West 23rd Street,
New York, New York 10010, U.S.A.
Penguin Books Australia Ltd, Ringwood,
Victoria, Australia
Penguin Books Canada Limited, 2801 John Street,
Markham, Ontario, Canada L3R 1B4
Penguin Books (N.Z.) Ltd, 182–190 Wairau Road,
Auckland 10, New Zealand

First published 1983
Published simultaneously in hardcover in Great Britain by Allen Lane
This paperback edition reprinted 1984, 1985

Printed in the United States of America by
R. R. Donnelley & Sons Company, Harrisonburg, Virginia
Set in Palatino

Designed by Patrick Yapp

FRONTISPIECE: Temple and Sacred Lake at Karnak

Contents

List of Text Figures

List of Maps

List of Photographs

Photographic Acknowledgements
Bildarchiv Foto Marburg: page 60; Boston Museum
of Fine Arts: pages 186, 260–61, 320; Cairo
Museum: page 54; Cash, J. Allan: pages 27, 96;
Dickins, Douglas: page 300; Halliday, Sonia: pages
16–17; Harding, (Robert) Associates: page 206;
Holford, Michael: pages 2–3; GEKS: page 224;
Metropolitan Museum of Art: pages 162, 278;
Philadelphia, University Museum: page 180; Sheridan
Photo Library: page 102; Yale University Art
Gallery: page 90; Wood, Roger: pages 44, 66,
80–81, 145, 336.

The hieroglyphic characters on pages 67, 82, 163 and
166 are taken from *Egyptian Hieroglyphic Printing Type*
by Alan H. Gardiner, courtesy of Oxford University
Press.

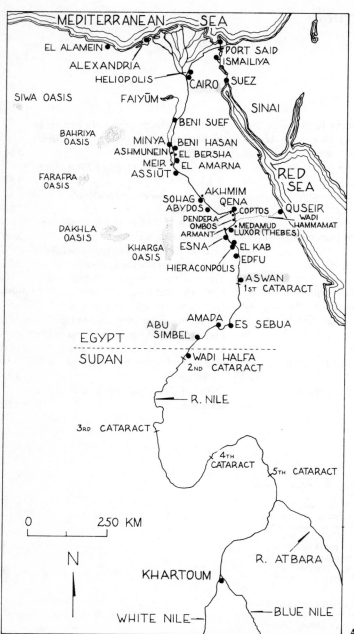

Ancient Egypt and Nubia

Preface

Visiting Egypt today is a very different proposition from what it was nearly a century ago, when Karl Baedeker first compiled his classic guide to the Nile Valley. Travel is no longer an exclusively leisured pursuit, and ever increasing numbers of tourists are able to spend two or three weeks on holiday in Egypt. The hallmarks of mass travel are everywhere: large groups are hustled around the country with a dispatch that sometimes borders on frenzy. Services are tailored to this easily managed majority. It is a melancholy fact that visitors will see less, and see it more superficially, than in their grandfather's day. The individual traveller will thus find his choices restricted, not only in accommodation, but also in the range of sites that can be easily seen.

The writer of a modern guidebook is thus caught in a dilemma. He could limit his remarks to those monuments kept open by the authorities, knowing that most visitors will get no further. To do so, however, would be wilfully to ignore much that is important and potentially of interest to visitors. Internal conditions change, sites are re-opened, and many places off the beaten track can in fact be seen if the proper arrangements are made.

I have tried to steer a middle course in this book, devoting most of my attention to sites that tourists will surely see. Sections of such areas which are now closed to the public (for example, many of the Theban tombs) are included, to the extent that their interest justifies the hope that they may eventually become more accessible. Elsewhere, my coverage is less comprehensive than

Baedeker's. Some sites, though important in antiquity, are so poorly preserved today that they are scarcely worth mentioning. In yet other places, the undoubted interest of what remains is compromised by such factors as difficulty of access or generic similarity to neighbouring monuments, so with regret I have left them out. The measure of a guidebook ultimately lies in its usefulness to its readers: let them decide.

Some visitors may come to Egypt with specific interests in mind. For them, as well as for those readers who simply want to place the monuments within the framework of their times, this book is organized in two sections. Part One will provide an introduction to the land and its antiquities, each chapter covering, in selective fashion, one aspect of ancient Egypt. Since only the essential background can be supplied in these pages, such topics as the development or the decipherment of Egyptian writing have been dealt with summarily or not at all, though I have tried to suggest other books (many of them available as paperbacks) to fill these gaps. Entries in SMALL CAPITAL LETTERS preceded by the symbol ▷ will relate the introductory material to the site descriptions that will follow in Part Two. Such a device is hardly original with me, and readers of this guidebook will no doubt recognize the influence of E. M. Forster's graceful contribution to the genre, *Alexandria: a History and a Guide*, a model I acknowledge with gratitude.

Since this book is by definition a guide to ancient Egypt, the Islamic monuments must perforce be excluded. To describe them adequately would swell this guide far beyond its present limits; besides, they really deserve a volume to themselves. This leaves us, however, with an awkward problem: what to do with the Christian antiquities. They are comparatively few, and not many visitors journey to Egypt expressly to see them. Especially in Cairo, however, they have a certain claim on our attention, and many of them show affinities with the Pharaonic past that can shed some light on earlier monuments. In the end I decided to include them, particularly when they impinge on pagan remains nearby.

Site descriptions have been given throughout in hopes that they will provide orientation, but without so much detail as to deter the reader from using his own eyes. More extensive descriptions of individual themes are provided in the first part (see especially Chapters 2 and 6). The maps and plans, similarly, are supplied for the reader's convenience and have no pretensions to strict proportional accuracy. I am grateful to Thad Rasche, W. Raymond Johnson and Paul Hoffman for their patience and skill in executing them.

Finally, readers should be aware that the Egyptian monuments are more delicate than they seem. Many of them have deteriorated shockingly over the last 150 years owing to both their innate instability and the carelessness of man. Visitors can avoid contributing to their decline by treating the Nile Valley as an open-air museum: look, but please don't touch.

I would like to thank collectively all those friends and colleagues who, by criticism or the stimulus of their conversation, helped in the formation of this book. And I am particularly grateful to John Ross, who first encouraged me to write it.

William J. Murnane
London, 1982

PART ONE

1. The Land and the River

'Land acquired by the Egyptians, the gift of the river' — the discovery of Egypt begins aptly with Herodotus' classic description. The map abets this impression, for the narrow strip of land that hugs the course of the Nile widens only when the river itself divides into several channels as it approaches the sea. But this is only a beginning: the ancients themselves saw their country as an amalgam of two contrasting elements, 'Black Land' and 'Red Land', and without the desert the river valley is cut off from some of its most precious resources. The desert, far from being a void, is the natural setting for Egyptian civilization. It is here, moreover, that the development of the land is most clearly seen.

About fifty million years ago, most of Egypt was under water. The Mediterranean Sea stretched across North Africa, covering Egypt and Libya down to the twenty-third parallel, south of modern Luxor. By then, the land had already undergone a long and complex 'history' that is reflected in the contemporary Egyptian countryside. The bed of this prehistoric bay is formed of three layers of stone that illustrate this process. The oldest deposits are the metamorphic and igneous rocks — diorite, granite, quartz — that are mostly found south of the Second Nile Cataract, though there are major outcroppings at Aswan and in the eastern desert (e.g., the quarries of the Wadi Hammamat) where the upper layers have been worn away. The middle layer consists of sandstone

and is found on the surface in southern Upper Egypt and in Nubia. The sedimentary limestones, shales and clays that form the top layer are found exposed in the oases of the western desert and in the northern part of the river valley: a slight tilting of the land during the Eocene Period (50–40 million years ago) allowed the waters of the ancient bay to drain slowly into the sea, but the northern end of the country was submerged longer than the south and was thus overlaid with a thicker and more permanent crust of limestone. It is this stone, then, which forms the surface of the desert between the apex of the Delta and the town of Es-Sebaiya in Upper Egypt, at which point the 'Nubian' sandstone definitely emerges on the surface. These events (much simplified in this telling) have fixed the geological character of Egypt through historic times down to the present.

The river's role in shaping the environment is a comparatively recent development. Drainage of water off the African highlands was, during the Eocene, neither seasonal nor the only source of moisture to the land. The meandering course of the sea-bound waters was augmented by frequent rainfall, and the traveller, airborne over the eastern desert, can follow the channels (*wadis*) carved by this water action. Gradually, an important change took place. During the Miocene Period (26–8 million years ago), a further rise in the level of the land was accompanied by enough vertical erosion in the plain to form an enormous gorge, between six and

OVERLEAF Egyptian landscape — the Nile, the cultivation, and the desert hills beyond

nine miles wide. For the first time, the river was confined to what is roughly its present bed.

As the new channel bored into the bed of the prehistoric bay, it exposed geological strata that appear today as sudden and dramatic features in the landscape. The limestone hills of Mokkatam that overlook modern Cairo were formed thus, as was the sandstone outcropping that erupts north-west of Cairo at Abu Rawash. Gebel Silsila, today the last great sandstone mountain before the complete takeover of the limestone strata some sixty-four kilometres downstream, was then a cataract. A slower, less spectacular, but more significant development took place during the ensuing Pleistocene Period (2,500,000–16,000 years ago): as masses of loose debris were deposited near the valley's centre, they formed terraces, apart from the harder deposits by the sides of the gorge. The river valley's typical profile, with its separation of the cultivable lowlands from the high desert, had begun to emerge.

The river as described above was the ancestor of what today is called the White Nile. These waters, flowing down from Lake Victoria, are the most consistent contributors to the Egyptian Nile throughout the year, but they provide none of the seasonal flooding and little of the topsoil that are the foundations of Egypt's agricultural success. These come instead from two other branches, the Blue Nile and the River Atbara, both of which carry run-off water from winter rains on the Ethiopian plateau. The Blue Nile meets the White at Khartoum: so violent is the summer flood that the White Nile is backed up and the torrent, at its peak in September, has risen from 7,000 to 350,000 cubic feet of water *per second*. Until fairly recently, these waters were the source of the yearly rise of the Nile in Egypt, the flooding that made basin agriculture possible. But this phenomenon, once more, was a comparatively late development. The channels that connect the main Nile to the Ethiopian drainage system were formed only between thirty thousand and twenty-five thousand years ago, and a concurrent drop in rainfall now gave the Nile its dominant role in supplying the valley's moisture. An equally important side-effect was the seasonal deposit of silt from the flood waters: this 'gift of the Nile', along with further erosion of the river banks, began to build up a bed of fertile soil throughout the valley, and as these deposits swirled and eddied in the seasonal flood they came to form the levees and basins that later came into play as sites for human settlement and agricultural development. The historic Egyptian countryside was in the making, but it was not yet fully recognizable: the river was twice as wide at the beginning of human prehistory as it is today, and the climate was moister. The valley's edge branched off into lakes and marshes that have for the most part vanished today: the ancient swamp in the Kom Ombo basin has long since dried up, for instance, and only Lake Qarūn remains of the once extensive Lake Moeris. But the borders of the Nile Valley had been formed well before the start of human history in Egypt.

About sixteen kilometres north-west of Cairo, the Nile divides into two branches and begins its final journey to the sea. The western arm, called the 'Rosetta', proceeds in a north-westerly direction and debouches some fifty-six kilometres east of Abukir, while the other, the 'Damietta' branch, goes north-north-east to a mouth near the western edge of Lake Menzala. In antiquity, however, the Delta's topography was more complicated, with no fewer than seven river branches. The dispersion of the flood over this area resulted in a silt deposit covering roughly 15,000 square kilometres, with a depth of between ten and forty metres. It is this triangular delta, which reached its present dimensions about 4000 B.C., that forms the bulk of historic Lower Egypt. ▷ MODERN COASTLINE = TAPOSIRIS MAGNA, Chapter 11, p. 144.

The only landform to disrupt the symmetry of the Nile Valley below the Delta is the Faiyūm. On a map or from the air it appears as a westward bulge, starting some twenty-five kilometres west of the river and extending over an area of 4,500 square kilometres. The entire depression was probably created by combined water and wind erosion during the early Pleistocene (starting about two and a half million years ago) and was at first covered by a vast lake fed seasonally by the overflow from the Nile. What is left of this, the Lake Moeris of the ancients, is confined to the north-west corner of the modern Faiyūm: called Lake Qarūn, it is fed by a branch of the river called the Bahr Yusuf ('Joseph's River') that leaves the main channel near Assiūt. Although archaeological evidence shows that the Faiyūm was inhabited from late Palaeolithic times, at least, the area's agricultural potential was not thoroughly exploited until the Middle Kingdom. At that time, the efforts of the kings of the Twelfth Dynasty to clear the Bahr Yusuf channel and reclaim unused terrain increased the amount of cultivable land by roughly four and a half times, to 450 square kilometres. By the New Kingdom, population density in the Faiyūm was already higher than in the Nile Valley. Ambitious land-reclamation projects under the Ptolemies once more increased the extent of arable land to a maximum of 1,300 square kilometres, and during the Byzantine period it is estimated that there were 198 towns, with over 300,000 people living in the Faiyūm alone. The pattern continues today, for the area's rich vineyards and its plantations of flowers and fruit trees make it one of the most agreeable spots in Egypt. ▷ THE FAIYŪM, Chapter 14, pp. 183–5.

The majority of Egyptians seldom strayed far from home: thus an ancient writer could evoke the extreme improbability of 'a Delta man [who] sees himself in Aswan, or a man of the marshlands in Nubia'. The Egyptian peasant's ties with his home territory may have been encouraged by the physical setting, for although the river valley is long, its limited width – usually less than twenty kilometres, and as little as two between Edfu and Aswan – is nearly always within one's range of vision. No matter where one is in Upper Egypt, the enclosing hills and the desert never seem far away. The Delta, by contrast, is almost unnervingly open and unlimited to someone accustomed to the easily grasped confines of the upper Nile Valley. In earlier historic times, the north was wilder and more untamed than the rest of Egypt. Only two-thirds of the Delta seem to have been populated during the Old Kingdom and – judging by the number of estates carved out of Delta land to serve the mortuary cults of high officials – virgin territory was freely available. The moister climate of pre-Dynastic times also encouraged a lusher concentration of plant and animal life in the Delta than in the rest of Egypt: the area was a favourite hunting ground, renowned as the haunt of hippopotamus and crocodile and for its rich catches of birds and fish. Even when fully developed, the Delta remained a land of gardens and vineyards, with cattle-grazing a main occupation in several areas. In later antiquity, as Egypt's horizons widened, Delta harbours gained importance as conduits for trade and other foreign ventures. The land, however, never did lose its unsettled aspects. Separatist movements (as in the Second and Third Intermediate Periods) periodically arose from there, and the land was notoriously a haven for migrant Libyans and Asiatics who either settled or sojourned briefly in Egypt. As late as the Ptolemaic period, new colonists could still find homes in the Delta, but the area was practically deserted during the Middle Ages. The change from basin cultivation to a system of perennial irrigation, begun in 1802, may have brought to the Delta a permanent prosperity at last. ▷ THE DELTA, Chapter 11, pp. 129–33.

The river is the inescapable hub of all activity. For millennia the main artery of communication, it was also the supreme arbiter of life and death – of high and low Niles, of prosperity and famine. In early times, when the southlands were still unfamiliar territory, men had believed that the flood originated in two caverns in the Aswan Cataract area. The lord of that region, the ram god Khnum, was venerated as the power which controlled the yearly overflow. Later, in the New Kingdom, yearly sacrifices to the Nile were offered downstream, at Gebel Silsila, 'so that there might be no scarcity of water'. But there were other, more practical ways by which the authorities could control the inundation. Large well-like gauges, called Nilometers, were set up at Aswan and Memphis to measure the strength and timing of the rising waters. Egyptian expansion into Nubia later permitted the establishment of subsidiary Nilometers at the Second and Fourth Cataracts, giving farmers greater latitude in preparing for extremes in the Nile flood each year. ▷ NILE SHRINES AT GEBEL SILSILA, Chapter 20, pp. 313–16; NILOMETER ON ELEPHANTINE ISLAND AT ASWAN, Chapter 21, p. 324.

The flood and its aftermath were the central verities of life in ancient Egypt. The Egyptian civil year was itself divided into three seasons entitled 'Inundation', 'Seed' and 'Harvest': each of these consisted of four months, all thirty days in length, with an additional five epagomenal ('extra-yearly') days added at the end of the harvest season to bring the seasons into line with the solar year. The resulting year of 365 days fell short of the true solar year by one day in every four years, however, so the coincidence of the growing seasons with the months that bore their names was steadily, if slowly, undone. People in the second millennium B.C. were already complaining that 'winter is come in summer, and the months come about turned backwards', and by 238 B.C. the chaos became so acute that, in the Decree of Canopus, the timing of certain feasts was adjusted 'so that the seasons of the year may coincide wholly with the present settlement of the world, that it may not happen that one of the popular festivals that ought to be held in winter comes to be held in summer owing to the star changing one day in the course of four years ... as formerly happened and would still happen if the year continued to consist of 360 days plus the five additional days that are customarily added to it!'[1]

Despite problems of this sort – which, incidentally, were allowed to persist over the length of Pharaonic history, a period of nearly 3,000 years – the ancient Egyptians did very well by the river. The floodwaters, beginning to rise in Upper Egypt by August and reaching the northern end of the country four to six weeks later, provided the moisture essential for planting. They also flushed harmful salts out of the soil and deposited fresh layers of silt to renew tired land. A

1. The 'star' in question is the Dog-star, Sirius (called Sopdet or Sothis by the Egyptians), whose rising traditionally signalled the start of the Inundation, and which would fall one day later in the civil calendar every four years, owing to the discrepancy of one-quarter day between the calendar and the solar year. The problem was conveniently resolved only with the adoption of the 'Julian' calendar (an adjusted form of the Egyptian system); the later modification of this calendar (called the 'Gregorian') is the one used in the western world today.

system of canals brought water to fields which were normally out of the inundation's reach, and when the waters receded (usually by late October) a remnant was conserved in reservoirs, to be released when most needed during the growing season. The back-breaking labour — planning, administering and executing the work needed to sustain basin agriculture under these conditions — was handsomely rewarded: the fertile soil yielded as many as three and four crops per year on some vegetables (and it still does), while Egypt's intensive cultivation of emmer and wheat made her renowned — and, later, abused — as the breadbasket of the Mediterranean world. The pattern is different today. Cash crops such as sugar-cane and cotton replaced basic foodstuffs in the nineteenth century, so that Egypt must now import food for its people. The most devastating change, however, is the loss of the inundation: with the completion of the Aswan High Dam in 1972, the flood is now stopped at the First Cataract and a system of perennial irrigation has replaced the ancient basin agriculture throughout the Nile Valley. ▷ ASWAN HIGH DAM, Chapter 21, p. 331.

But the river remains, even in this age of air and rail travel, a vital avenue of communication. The ever-present 'cool breath of the north wind' facilitates travel upstream, while boats journeying in the opposite direction can usually float with the current. In funerary scenes in tombs at Saqqara, boats shown making the ritual pilgrimage to Abydos use sail on their journey southward against the current, and in the Luxor Temple we see the gods' barges with their sails unfurled as they are pulled against the current with tow-ropes from the shore. This simple system is made possible by the fortunate concurrence of the river's direction and the wind: only at the great bend between Qena and Nag Hammadi, where the river flows from east to

west, is it necessary to employ a painfully slow method of tacking from one side of the river to the other in order to make any headway against the current. The Nile is navigable only in certain channels, however, and anyone rash enough to depart from them runs the risk of running aground. The modern traveller suffers no more than inconvenience, for crocodiles have long since ceased infesting the river in Egypt and one must go far into the Sudan to catch a glimpse of one of these 'dread lords of the shallows, who cannot be approached'.

During Pharaonic times, the river was thronged with travellers officials journeying on government business, cargo vessels laden with produce, and local transport ferrying people across the Nile. In many parts of Egypt, particularly where the cultivated land is narrow or non-existent on one side of the river, the cemeteries were located in the deserts across from the towns, so the normal traffic between banks would be periodically swelled by the funeral cortèges bearing mourners on the deceased's last journey. Complaints about ferrymen and their extortionate charges are a commonplace in ancient literature: perhaps this was the expected stereotype. Just as frequently, though, we hear of local people whose boats have been seized by crown agents to expedite deliveries for the state. Abuses of this sort were as endemic as they were illegal, and reforms were never more than temporarily effective.

A more successful field of government intervention lay in building canals, both for irrigation and for transport purposes. The modern Suez Canal was roughly anticipated by Necho who, in about 600 B.C., built a canal that ran from the Bubastite arm of the Nile, through the Wadi Tumilat and thence through the Bitter Lakes area to the Gulf of Suez on the Red Sea. That few of these ancient engineering feats can be seen today

— and these but the barest traces — is due not to their insignificance but rather to natural factors that, together with the lack of proper maintenance, caused them to be quickly sanded up and abandoned. The immense prestige of Necho's achievement did not prevent the ruin of his canal during the later Persian occupation of Egypt, and though it was cleared and re-opened by Ptolemy Philadelphus in 280/279 B.C., it has effectively disappeared today.

Beyond the valley's edge stretch the deserts. Their barren appearance is deceptive, for since the beginning of human history they have been intimately involved with the life of the Nile Valley. The climate during late prehistoric times was still moist enough to support a varied wildlife in the steppes beyond the cultivation: the evidence of rock drawings shows them to have been frequented by elephants, giraffe, ostrich, gazelle, wild asses and cattle, hippopotamus, rhinoceros and lions. Wetter conditions also favoured human occupation far from the Nile Valley and facilitated contacts with the western oases, themselves inhabited from earliest times. But when rainfall became scarce after 2900 B.C., and virtually ceased after the start of the Middle Kingdom (c. 2040 B.C.), deforestation and the concurrent drying out of the steppe led to a contraction in the areas capable of supporting life. The abandonment of the earliest settlements along the valley's edge (at Hieraconpolis, Armant and Abydos, now far into the desert) is symptomatic. The oasis dwellers, too, became more isolated from the mainstream of Egyptian society, though they were never cut off altogether. At the same time, most of the animals listed above either disappeared or became rare: only certain types of gazelle and related animals, herds of wild asses and cattle, and a few of the big cats survived into historic times. ▷ GEBEL EL-KHASHAB, Chapter 10, p. 106.

Even so, the uplands continued to play an important part in Egypt's economic life. Trade routes took the ancient Egyptians deep into the deserts. The search for precious stones, metals and other materials for buildings and statuary continually brought expeditions to the remotest fringes of the land. The quarries of the Wadi Hammamat, for instance, were regularly exploited for diorite, schist and greywacke, and from other sites in the eastern desert came garnets, steatite, onyx, agate, rock crystal and chalcedony. The Wadi Hammamat was also the main road from Coptos to the Red Sea ports that served Egypt's trade with the rest of Africa. The destination of these missions was the land of Punt. Located on the coast of Ethiopia, Punt supplied a variety of its own products (for instance, incense trees), but it was mainly of importance as a contact point between Egypt and central Africa: episodes from a notable expedition during the Eighteenth Dynasty are portrayed vividly in a well-preserved relief from Queen Hatshepsut's mortuary temple at Deir El-Bahri. ▷ DEIR EL-BAHRI, PUNT RELIEFS, Chapter 18, p. 259.

The ancient Egyptians ranged far and wide after their country's mineral wealth. Amethyst and cornelian could be found at Aswan and in the Nubian deserts. Costly expeditions penetrated into the Sinai to mine turquoise, vital to the ancient jeweller's art. Copper, for the more sophisticated tools, was mined in the Sinai and the eastern desert. And almost everywhere, it seemed, there was gold. 'Let my brother send gold in great quantity,' an Asiatic king would write to Pharaoh Amenhotep III, 'for in my brother's land gold is as plentiful as dust.' The gold mines of the Egyptian deserts were exploited from earliest times. The famous 'gold of Coptos' came from the deserts bordering on the Wadi Hammamat. Another source, the rich Barramiyah mines in the desert east of

Edfu, may have played a role in the early dominance of the kings of Upper Egypt: a tangible record of their exploitation is the small temple at Wadi Mia, built by Sety I to commemorate his re-opening of the wells that made work in the district possible. And, as the Egyptians pushed into Nubia, they were able to command that country's rich resources of gold, thus becoming a major commercial power. Few substances found in nature seem to have gone unused in Pharaonic Egypt: exceptions are the porphyry, beryls and emeralds which would be exploited during the Roman occupation. ▷ WADI HAMMAMAT, Chapter 16, p. 222; WADI MIA, Chapter 20, p. 308.

The western desert was Egypt's gate to west Africa – to the five great oases and thence to Libya and the lands to the south. The oases themselves – large depressions that owed their moisture to flowing springs – produced raw materials that were highly prized in the Nile Valley. Kharga, Dakhla, Bahriya and Farafra produced notable wines, and Siwa, the most westerly of the oases, was renowned for its dates and (much later) for its oracle. The oasis closest to the Nile Valley – the Wadi Natrūn, located at the western edge of the Delta – was the main source in antiquity for natron, a soda-like substance used as a detergent and a preservative in mummification. The introduction to the *Tale of the Eloquent Peasant*, a moralizing social tract set in the First Intermediate Period, contains a long list of plant products exported from the Wadi Natrūn into Egypt, thereby indicating a level of moisture that is much reduced today ▷ WADI NATRŪN, Chapter 11, p. 133; WESTERN OASES, Chapter 22, pp. 345–9.

Between the oases were the steppes that connected Egypt with her western possessions and with southern Africa: a modern survivor among these caravan routes is the *Darb el-Arbayīn*, 'the Road of the Forty (Days)', that runs from Assiūt to Darfur. Though lacking in the mineral wealth of the eastern desert, the western steppes were favoured hunting grounds for gazelle, antelope and other, smaller mammals during the Old and Middle Kingdoms. Herds of wild bulls were still to be sighted as late as the Eighteenth Dynasty, when no fewer than ninety-six animals were bagged by Amenhotep III in the 'district of Shetep'.

The world of ancient Egypt depended on the interaction of the river valley with its surrounding deserts. The Egyptian peasant's view of his country stopped, however, at the desert's edge. Reality was seen in terms of complementary, often opposing parts that were brought into harmony with one another. The duality, 'Black Land' and 'Red Land', defined the character of Egypt and not-Egypt respectively. Inside the river valley were 'The Two Lands' which, in historic times, were *Shemau* and *To-Meḥu*, or Upper and Lower Egypt. The boundary lay in the neighbourhood of Memphis, south of modern Cairo, and in earliest Egyptian history the Two Lands were themselves divided into districts called 'nomes' – sixteen in Upper Egypt and ten in the Delta lands of Lower Egypt. Some of them must have begun as natural basins used by the earliest farmers once the rhythm of the inundation had been learned; and the focus for community action found in such a setting may well have paved the way for the development of the separate kingdoms that arose during Egypt's prehistory.

During the Old Kingdom, most of the nomes had already reached the rough geographical limits they would retain until the end of Egyptian civilization. Some were organized under the aegis of a local deity (for instance, Bat of the seventh Upper Egyptian nome, or Neith of Sais in the Delta). Others, where social groupings may have been more complex, had various communities grouped under one standard that encompassed the nome as a whole: the worshippers of Sobek the crocodile, the rabbit goddess Wenut and other divinities, including the great gods Amun and Montu, for example, were gathered together in the Theban nome under the standard of the *Was*-sceptre. Parts of the country that originally lay outside the nome system — the territory around Memphis and the district of Thinis in Middle Egypt (homeland of the First Dynasty), as well as parts of the east Delta and the districts south of El Kab and Hieraconpolis to the First Cataract — were gradually integrated into the rest of the country. Some of the nomes either absorbed their less viable neighbours or were subdivided into smaller units: the ancient territory of Neith, for instance, was split into the fourth and fifth Lower Egyptian nomes; while the twelfth nome of Upper Egypt was administered by the adjacent tenth nome, once it had exhausted the gold in the eastern desert that was its economic *raison d'être*. Borders were fluid, especially in the Delta,

and the threat posed by powerful nomarchs sometimes moved the crown to try alternative forms of organization: the nomes were deprived of their political status, for instance, by Senwosret III, who re-organized the country into three districts governed by his own officials. Later, during the New Kingdom, the Two Lands would be administered by the viziers, also crown appointees. Nevertheless, the nomes were too fixed a part of the Egyptians' mental landscape to fade away altogether. Their influence on provincial government has long outlasted the Pharaohs.

Such was the ancient kingdom of the Nile. Beyond — south of the First Cataract, and to either side of the river valley — lay the 'plains and hill countries, the foreign lands that know not Egypt'. Egyptian statecraft is not to be despised; but it was due mainly to the accidents of her location and natural resources that Egypt was able to develop her distinctive civilization for so long under her own initiative.

2. People, Professions and Leisure

To visit Egypt is to become aware of the old mirrored in the new. Rural life seems much the same as in ancient times, despite such improvements as electricity and the pervasive influence of Islam. The physical character of the ancient people has survived basically unchanged across the millennia, and observers of the modern Egyptians find many customs and even mental attitudes that would be quite at home in the ancient world.

Daily life in ancient Egypt is most sharply evoked in the decoration of officials' tombs. Both at Thebes (Luxor, West Bank) and Memphis (Giza, Abusir, Saqqara) we find carved and painted scenes illustrating almost every aspect of work and leisure under the Pharaohs. To some extent, these scenes reflect the ancients' belief that they could 'take it with them', projecting an ideal of the good life into the world beyond death. But their main *raison d'être* was practical. People knew that the endowments that supported their mortuary cults would in time be diverted elsewhere, so the reciting of a spell ('A thousand of bread, beer, oxen, fowl, everything good and pure' for the tomb owner) took the place of the offerings themselves. Creating a picture of these offerings, of the servants who presented them and, ultimately, of the means of production that brought them into being were all logical extensions of the same concern, that is to guarantee these materials for the tomb owner's use for ever. A wide variety of rather humdrum activities thus came to be illustrated in most private tombs. The selection of what was shown (and how it was shown) was often arbitrary, and it was quickly conventionalized: current practice sometimes left these stereotypes behind. Often, however, these scenes illuminate processes that are otherwise obscure or unknown; and they have the additional merit of showing the ancient Egyptians as they saw themselves.

Farming

Since the principal business of Egypt was (and is) farming, agricultural scenes bulk large in the tombs. Most of them illustrate the cultivation of grain, for cereals such as barley, emmer and winter wheat were staples of Egyptian diet and also the basis of the economy. The Pharaohs' harvest tax, and the rations in kind that the state paid its employees, consisted largely of grain and its products, for instance, bread and beer. Later, when Egypt was ruled by Rome, its vast exports of grain were absorbed by the vine-growing lands of Italy, where production of cereals did not meet the demand. Egypt today is in much the same position, having to import foodstuffs in order to cultivate its cash crops of sugar and cotton.

Most of the land in ancient Egypt was farmed for the crown, the temples and other great landowners. The temples were particularly large landlords, owning land not only in their immediate locality but all over Egypt. The temple of Amun at Thebes, for instance, was given 1,500 square kilometres of territory during Ramesses III's reign alone; even if much of this consisted of grants renewed from previous reigns, the figure still represents about ten per cent of the cultivable land at that time. Private holdings were on a smaller scale, but even during the Old Kingdom some very lowly people could (and did) own land: during the Fourth Dynasty, an official named Metchen purchased from numerous small freeholders land equal to one-hundredth of the cultivable land in Egypt; in the eleventh century B.C., the High Priest of Amun, Menkheperrē, bought a tract of land for his god from an extended family, each of whose members received a portion of the price. Wealthy farmers could even rent land, but cultivators generally did not own the land they worked and enjoyed, at most, a tenant's status.

Practically all aspects of farming are illustrated in the tombs. One of the rarer episodes is the issuing of seed, shown in an Old Kingdom tomb at Giza (G 6020[7])[1]: behind the tomb owner's chair, a man is seen scooping the seed up from a heap, while a scribe records the transaction; two other tenants are seen leaving at the right, their grain scoops on their heads. By this time, the waters of the inundation would have receded and the muddy fields dried out, for the next step to be shown is the preparation of the ground for ploughing: the compacted clods of earth are broken up with mallets, while other men cut down trees, scrub and the grass that has sprung up since the last harvest (Th 52[1]; 57[5]; 60[5]).

Now the work of ploughing can begin: men with hoes lead the way, marking out the furrow for the ploughman who follows with his team of oxen dragging a wooden plough. Behind the ploughman are men with bags of seed (usually slung over their shoulders) who drop the seedlings into the open furrows. During the Old Kingdom, the seed was next trampled into the ground by a team of rams (G 6020[7]; 7530–40[4]; Ti [14]; Nefer [1, upper right]). This episode is omitted in most New Kingdom tombs (e.g. Th 52[1]; 57[5]; 60[5]; 69[1] – the latter with a delightful vignette showing two girls, first quarrelling, then making it up, with one pulling a thorn from the other's foot); but the technique must still have been in use, for Herodotus saw pigs trampling in the seed when he visited Egypt during the sixth century B.C.

The next group of scenes is concentrated around the busy season of the harvest. While the grain was still standing in the field, state agents measured the yield for each farm and calculated the tax expected from each cultivator: this is shown most simply by a procession of men – the scribe and his associates – moving along a background of unharvested grain (Th 38[2]), but a more elaborate example (Th 69[1]) shows them stretching a knotted cord along the field's length, each interval between knots being counted as one unit for taxing purposes. The tax was thus shrewdly based on the most promising prospects of the harvest, and with the landlord's share varying between one-third and one-half of the crop, the burden of bad years was shifted inexorably on to the farmer.

Under such conditions, it is not surprising that peasants sometimes found themselves unable to pay their dues, and punishment of defaulters is a theme frequently sounded in the tombs of Egypt's upper classes. The unfortunates are often shown bound and

OPPOSITE Grape harvest, tomb of Nakht (Luxor, West Bank)

1. In the references to private tombs which follow, the tombs at Saqqara (Chapter 13) – which have no comprehensive numbering system – are listed by name of the tomb owner (e.g., Idut). Elsewhere, G = Giza (Chapter 12); BH = Beni Hasan and EA = El Amarna (both in Chapter 15); Th = Thebes (Chapter 19); EK = El Kab (Chapter 20); and A = Aswan (Chapter 21).

waiting, while the scribe reports to the master (*Nefer* [1]; *Kagemni* [4]); elsewhere, we see culprits stripped and bound to whipping posts (*Mereruka* [6]). One New Kingdom example (Th 69 [1]) shows a man being beaten, while a woman (his wife?) kneels and begs for mercy. The infrequency with which this episode is shown in later tombs is, alas, no reflection of a gentler age, as this excerpt from the records of a trial during the reign of Ramesses XI makes clear:

The scribe Paōemtauōme (the son of Pewerō) was brought in. He was given the oath not to speak falsehood, and he said: 'As Amun endures and as the Ruler endures, if I be found to have had anything to do with the thieves, may I be mutilated in my nose and ears, and [then] be impaled!' He was examined with the stick, and was found to have been arrested in place of the measurer Paōemtauōme, the son of Kaka ...

The harvest was a festive occasion in ancient Egypt, and its episodes are well represented in the tombs. Reaping, the first step, is performed by men with sickles working in the open field; women and children are employed to glean the stray corn. During the Old Kingdom, the grain was stuffed into bags and laden on to donkeys for its trip to the threshing floor (G 6020[7]; *Akhethotep* [1]; *Ti* [14]), but in the Middle and New Kingdoms the baskets of grain were slung on poles and carried off by the field-hands themselves (Th 57[2]; 60[4]; 69[1]): an elaborate version of this scene shows a man using his carrying pole to force the grain down into the basket (Th 52[1]).

Next, to separate out the chaff and other impurities, sheaves were placed on the ground and trodden continuously by work animals, either by donkeys (*Ti* [14]) or oxen (*Akhethotep* [1]; Th 57[2]; 60[4]) or even by the workmen themselves (Th 69[1]). Winnowing, the next step, also took place on the threshing floor (Th 217[3]): young women scoop up the trodden grain into shallow bowls and toss it into the air, the lighter chaff being borne away by the wind (Th 57[5]; 60[4]) as other women sweep the fallen grains back into the pile. One outstanding example (Th 52[1]) skilfully suggests the heavy atmosphere, laden with dust and chaff, against the painted background. The popular thanksgiving for the harvest is conveyed in nearly all New Kingdom sequences by vignettes in which the tomb owner and his associates make offering to the serpent goddess Ernutet. But the official culmination of the harvest consisted of yet another assessment in the presence of the scribe (G 6020[7]; Th 52[1]; 69[1]), after which the grain was borne off to granaries — long, domed buildings with stairs leading to the roof, where the grain was poured into silos below (*Mereruka* [13]; Th 60[1]). From here the grain was transferred to other depots around the country, usually by boat (Th 57[3]; EK 3[2]).

The many other crops cultivated by the ancient Egyptians are shown less frequently in the tombs. Flax — the basis of Egypt's important linen industry — is often seen being harvested with grain: the plants are dark green, and in one instance the field-hands are next seen stripping away the stalks with the aid of a forked stick set up on the ground (Th 69[1]). Many fruits and vegetables — onions, lettuce, beans, melons, dates, figs and pomegranates, as well as flowers — were grown in garden plots: we see men bringing water jars to a lettuce patch (*Mereruka* [2]) and picking fruit (especially figs: G 60206[6]; Th 188[2]; 279[7]; BH 3[2]).

During the New Kingdom, a labour-saving device was introduced to help water the outlying fields and gardens. Known by its Arabic name, the *shadûf* consists of a pole balanced on a frame: the operator dips the container mounted on one end into the water, then uses the weight attached to the pole's other end to lift the container up to the feeder canal that carries the water to the fields. The introduction of the *shadûf* increased the amount of land under cultivation by ten or fifteen per cent, and the instrument is still widely employed in the Nile Valley. Although it first appears in the tombs during the later Eighteenth Dynasty (Th 49[7]; cf. 217[1]) it may have been invented even earlier.

Viticulture

Although Greeks dismissed the Egyptians as a nation of beer guzzlers,[2] the vine was both known and appreciated from earliest times. Grapes are first seen being picked during the Old Kingdom, normally from rather stylized arbours (G 6020[6]; *Ptahhotep* [4]; cf. Th 15[6]), though sometimes a more formal pergola is suggested (Th 49[7]; 90[5]). The fruit is next dumped into a trough and is trodden in the time-honoured fashion to produce grape juice, the men holding on to a pole slung across the trough or on to ropes suspended from it. In some Old Kingdom examples the pace is set for them by musicians who sit beside the trough and mark out a rhythm with castanets (*Mereruka* [13]; *Nefer* [1]). In some New Kingdom examples, the trough itself is equipped with runnels pierced into its sides, allowing the grape juice to drain into buckets placed below (Th 49[7]; 52[5]). In the following episode, we see the crushed grapes being strained through a bag placed over a vat: two men tug the poles attached to either end of the bag, while extra tautness is supplied by a man who balances himself between the tops of the poles and pushes with his hands and feet (G 6020[6]; *Mereruka* [13]; *Ptahhotep* [4]). An odd variant of this scene (*Nefer* [1])

finds a baboon instead of the balancing man (perhaps reflecting a private joke that died with the tomb owner).

Wine making can now begin. The juice is poured into jars (G 6020[6]; Th 49[7]; 81[6]) which are next sealed with mud stoppers in the presence of the ubiquitous scribe (Th 56[6]; 81[6]; 90[5]), and stored for later use. The great centres of Egyptian viticulture were found in the Delta and the western oases, but an arbour seems to have been *de rigueur* in any wealthy man's garden. Even today, a few vines are still to be seen in Upper Egypt.

Animal husbandry

Stockbreeding vied with agriculture in its importance in Egyptian rural life. Scenes of milking (G 6020[4]; *Kagemni* [3]; *Ti* [18]; *Nyankh-Khnum and Khnumhotep* [18]) and feeding (*Nefer* [1, 2]; *Mereruka* [16]) are frequent in the tombs of the Old Kingdom. Field-hands are also shown helping their cows to give birth, positioning themselves behind the animal to assist the delivery of the calf (G 6020[4]; *Ti* [18]; *Ptahhotep* [5]; *Nyankh-Khnum and Khnumhotep* [18]). The good shepherd is occasionally seen disentangling stray sheep or calves from brambles (*Ti* [18]) or watching over browsing goats (*Nefer* [1]; Th 217[3]). As might be expected, all these animals were carefully registered under their owners' names, with some New Kingdom examples actually showing the animals being branded (Th 40[6]; 49[7]). The most pleasing scene in this repertory, however, is the exclusive property of the Old Kingdom, showing cattle led across a ford in the river: the herdsmen go ahead in a skiff and entice the stubborn herd by trailing a small calf behind them through the water. The mother plunges in

2. Aeschylus, *The Suppliant Women*, 952–3.

and the others follow, mindless of the crocodile lurking in the shallows (*Ti* [18, 19]; *Mereruka* [2]; *Kagemni* [3]; *Idut* [3]).

Other animals were less commonly shown in the tombs. Pigs, for instance, though stigmatized as enemies of the underworld god Osiris, were used as work animals and for food. They are infrequently seen in the tombs (e.g., Th 81[5]; EK 3[2]), though one curious scene shows a piglet being weaned; the field-hand places a drop of milk on his tongue and encourages the animal to lick it (*Kagemni* [3]). Other unusual animals include gazelle (*Mereruka* [7]) and hyena: the latter were perhaps used in hunting, their distinctive scent drawing the quarry's attention away from the dogs. They responded to captivity with ill grace — note the forcefeeding shown in some of the tombs (*Kagemni* [5]; *Mereruka* [16]) — and their domestication seems to have been abandoned after the Old Kingdom, as desert animals began to grow scarce.

Raising domestic fowl was yet another farmer's occupation. Chickens were apparently unknown before Thutmose III brought a few of them back from his campaigns in western Asia, but several varieties of ducks and geese were a mainstay of the Egyptian's diet from the earliest times. The raising of these animals was carried out on a large scale. Just south of the sacred lake of Amun's temple at Karnak, one can still see the covered tunnel that led from the god's poultry yard down to the water. Private establishments of a similar nature are illustrated in the tombs: one notable example (*Ti* [4]; cf. *Neferseshemptah* [2]) shows us a stockade filled with all sorts of birds and equipped with four runnels that lead to a pool in the enclosure's centre. Such farmyard activities as feeding and forcefeeding (*Ti* [3]; *Mereruka* [8]; *Kagemni* [5]) are frequently shown as well.

Fowling, fishing and other marsh industries

Bird-rearing cannot be separated from fowling in ancient Egypt: here the ways of the food-gatherer and the farmer, the breeder and the sportsman all converge. The wet, marshy areas of the Delta were teeming with wild birds that could be added to the current domesticated stock. The same conditions encouraged the Egyptians to enjoy the pleasures of the hunt, always a favoured sport among Egypt's upper classes. Sportsmen used a boomerang, but fowling on a commercial scale was done with a clapnet. The two halves of the net were spread on either side of the designated area, with the edges pegged to the ground to keep the trap open. At the strategic moment when the quarry had settled down, a signal was given by a man hiding in the reeds, either by silently pulling taut a cloth which he held behind his head (G 7530–40[4]; *Ptahhotep* [4]) or by gesturing (*Ti* [19]; Th 52[5]). At his signal, the trappers pulled with all their might on the draw-ropes attached to the pegs (*Ptahhotep* [4]; *Kagemni* [5]; *Nefer* [1]), releasing the net and causing it to spring shut. The birds were then extracted from the net, a few at a time, to be placed in boxes and carried off to the poultry yard (*Ptahhotep* [4]; *Mereruka* [2]). Birds that had been hurt by the sudden closing of the net were cared for (*Ti* [19]), while other, less desirable specimens were killed and sent off to the cookhouse (Th 52[5]). Other by-products of the hunt — baskets of eggs and such exotic birds as pelicans — are to be seen in one fine example from the New Kingdom (Th 78[8]).

Fishing was another of these marsh industries that had a vital impact on the economy. Devout Egyptians thought of fish as an impure food: the Nubian Pharaoh Piankhy, for instance, snubbed some of the provincial aristocracy by claiming that, having just partaken of fish, they were ritually defiled and could not appear before him. Nonetheless, quite a lot of fish was eaten in antiquity. Companies of professional fishermen are seen in the tombs, either operating a large net from a boat (*Ti* [19]; *Mereruka* [9]; *Nefer* [1]), or as individuals, plying small nets (*Mereruka* [5]) or angling with a hook and line (*Idut* [3]). The catch was then gutted and hung up to dry (Th 217[3]).

The marshes also yielded papyrus, used by the Egyptians for numerous items in daily life. We usually see it gathered by elderly marsh-dwellers, who prepared the reed by stripping away the husk (G 7530–40[4]) and cleaning the fibres with brushes (*Nyankh-Khnum and Khnumhotep* [8]). Related industries include mat- and rope-making (G 6020[3]; *Ptahhotep* [4]) and the building of reed boats (*Ti* [19]; *Nefer* [1]). Surprisingly, the manufacture of papyrus sheets for writing – surely the most original and renowned use that the Egyptians found for this material – is not commonly represented.

The marshes may have been pre-eminently a place for business, but in the tombs celebration reigns. The tomb owner, shown larger than life size, is seen standing in a reed skiff with his wife and children, enthusiastically spearing fish with a harpoon and bringing down flocks of birds with a boomerang (*Ti* [9]; *Mereruka* [2]). A riotous note is struck by gangs of boatmen in vessels nearby: in festive attire, their heads bound with flowered chaplets, they engage in an uproarious mock combat and tip one another into the water with their barge poles (*Akhethotep* [2]). But the most appealing thing about these scenes is the Egyptian artist's keen eye for all the strangeness and beauty of nature. Thus, in one tomb of the Fifth Dynasty, a loudly protesting hippopotamus is roped in with a barbed line, while his panic-stricken mate gives birth prematurely into the jaws of a waiting crocodile (*Idut* [3]). In another tomb, however, it is the hippopotamus who wins, by breaking the crocodile's back (*Mereruka* [1]). The artist's attention to detail is shown in exuberantly painted representations of foliage and fish, birds and butterflies (Th 52[5]; 69[7]; 78[8]). At heart, the significance of these episodes is probably religious and symbolizes the deceased's battle with chthonic forces, particularly Seth disguised as a hippopotamus. But they also embody the ancient Egyptian's joy in living and his appreciation of nature, the rendering of which makes many of these scenes true masterpieces of Egyptian art.

Households

Scenes of home life in the country are few but vivid. The houses excavated by archaeologists at El Amarna, for instance, show us ground-plans of the public and private areas, of gardens and kitchens, magazines and living-rooms variously oriented to catch the sun in winter and the shade in summer. The tombs infuse these ruins with life. In the tomb of Ineny (Th 81[4]), for instance, the tomb owner's house appears behind a gently crenellated wall, with windows to light and air the upper storey. The compound is completed at the left with a row of domed magazines and outbuildings (for details in Old Kingdom parallels, see G 6020[5]; *Nefer* [1]), while outside we find the customary formal garden around a pool (cf. Th 217[1]). A similar house from the tomb of Nebamun (Th 90[5]) shows on its roof the sloping air-shafts that ventilate the house, a system still used in modern times. The more elaborate structure shown in Neferhotep's tomb (Th 49[2]) belongs to the reigning queen: of three levels, its second-storey balcony opens on to a wide esplanade used as a reception area. The rest of this level is enclosed, though pierced by small windows, while the open area on the roof is protected by a graceful columned veranda. The painting of this scene suggests that the exterior walls were covered by slats of wood – an expensive rarity, as most houses had to rely, as today, on a painted mudbrick façade.

Egyptian households were as self-supporting as possible. Domestics were employed in the care and maintenance of the house – making beds (G 7530–40[2]), doing the laundry (Th 217[1]), tending the garden (Th 49[7]; 217[1]) and seeing to the master's transport – either his carrying chair (*Ti* [2]; *Mereruka* [16]) or his chariot (Th 49[2]; 57[5]; 69[1]). Quite often, though, servants were put to work at producing goods, either for the household's own consumption or for sale elsewhere.

Home industries: apiculture, weaving

Bee-keeping was practised throughout Egypt: men armed with smoke pots can be seen removing the honeycombs from the clay hives (Th 100[9]) and pouring the liquid honey into moulds (Th 279[7]). Of more economic importance, however, was weaving, an occupation frequently represented in the tombs. An early example shows three women twisting the flax into thread which is spun on hand-held spindles (Th 103[6]; cf BH 3[8]; 15[1]; 17[2]; and Th 279[6]) and then woven on a horizontal loom (which, however, owing to the conventions of Egyptian art, is shown upright).

Cooking and brewing

Preparation of food is a frequently shown theme in the tombs. Baking and brewing, especially, appear together, since bread was the raw material used to manufacture beer in ancient Egypt. In the discussion that follows, the scenes in the tomb of Senwosret I's vizier,

Antefoker, (Th 60[7]) will be used as the norm, with other tombs introduced for comparison.

The entire sequence begins with the crushing of the grain: two men, armed with wooden pounders, stand at a mortar and call the rhythm for their alternating strokes (cf. *Ti* [12]; Th 100[9]). After the coarse flour is sifted (cf. G 7530–40[7]; Th 100[9]), the dough is formed by moistening and then kneaded into loaves (G 6020[5]; 7530–40[7]; *Ti*[12]; *Nefer* [1]; Th 100[9]). Baking takes place either on top of a brick stove (G 7530–40[7]; Th 100[9]) or directly on the ashes (G 6020[5]; *Nefer* [1]), while another method involves the use of bread moulds: in the tomb of Antefoker, three women are forcing the dough into clay cones, the sticky mass running down the sides of the jar from which each portion is scooped. A man is next seen stirring the fire, in the midst of which the filled moulds are just barely visible (G 7530–40[7]; *Ti* [12]; Th 100[9]). An optional final step consists of glazing the fancier cakes by dipping them in honey or in hot fat (Th 100[9]).

By this stage, the cooks had to be aware of what their final product was to be, i.e., bread or beer, since bread baked for brewing had to be undercooked in order to preserve needed enzymes. This half-baked bread was broken up and placed in a vat, along with water and coarse-ground barley, and left to ferment, the result being similar to a Nubian beer called *bouza*, still made by the same methods today. The ancient Egyptians enhanced the flavour of their beer, however, by adding date juice and perhaps other substances. In Antefoker's tomb we see a man kneading a mass of dates and muttering something about their poor quality. This mass is then passed through a sieve into a tall jar: the workman, pestered by a boy who holds out his bowl for some of the sweet juice, snarls, 'Out with you, and out with her that conceived you by a hippopotamus, [you] who eat more than a king's slave who is ploughing!' This liquid had to be stirred before it was added to the large jar of fermenting barley beer (cf. G 7530–40[7]; *Ti* [12]).

Bread and beer, of course, were the twin staves of life in ancient Egypt. The basic staples of the household, they and the reiterated scenes of cooking on tomb walls were also the deceased's insurance against going hungry in the next world. Accordingly, we also see fish being gutted (*Ti* [19]; *Ptahhotep* [4]; Th 217[3]), fowl dressed (G 6020[4, 5]; *Nefer* [1]), cattle butchered (many examples: *Akhethotep* [3]; *Mereruka* [12]; *Ti* [16]; Th 60[7]), along with various other forms of cookery. Cuts of meat are boiled in a cauldron (G 6020[5]; Th 60[7]) or roasted; a fowl is stuffed (? = G 6020[5]) and held over a brazier by a spit stuck into its neck, while the cook fans the embers with his right hand (Mo'alla, tomb of Ankhtify, Col. C[3]).

Home life and leisure

Services like these exemplified the sort of idealized lifestyle that the Egyptians wished to carry with them beyond death. Along with food and drink, however, went the setting ⊢ the gracious environment and agreeable pursuits that the tomb owner might expect to enjoy throughout eternity. Moreover, the deceased would wish to be with his family, friends and retainers, all of whom are pictured around him. Servants, usually anonymous, are present to serve his needs, but sometimes a favoured house servant, or even a peasant, is referred to by name and will thus share immortality with the rest of the family. Dwarves, especially, were prized members of the tomb owner's retinue and are often seen caring for his pets (*Mereruka* [16]; *Kagemni* [6]; *Nefer* [3]). And the home circle is completed by the pets

themselves: greyhounds for hunting, monkeys and baboons (*Ti* [2, 18]; *Mereruka* [15]; *Kagemni* [6]; Th 56[3]) were favoured in the Old Kingdom and later, but other popular pets included geese (Th 55[3]) and cats (Th 52[3] = devouring fish; 217[2]).

Family solidarity was another important consideration: it was a man's descendants, after all, who maintained his cult and who themselves took comfort from the community they formed with their ancestors in the necropolis. This feeling is seen expressed in different ways. During the Old Kingdom, it is the family's immediate generations – parents, sons and daughters – who are represented with the tomb owner, usually making or receiving offerings (G 7530–40[3, 4]; *Ptahhotep* [4]). The scope has widened by the New Kingdom: siblings, cousins and still more distant relatives have joined the circle of associates to be maintained in the next world, and a new type of scene – the banquet – has been invented to accommodate them. The participants are arranged in rows, frequently holding flowers and seated before small tables laden with food. On the guests' heads are scented cones of fat (designed to melt and so anoint the merrymaker), and the floral wreaths sported by the ladies heighten the festive tone of the proceedings (BH 3[8]). Servants (usually lissom females) pass among the guests, attending to their wants (Th 15[4]; 100[6]; 181[1]). Some relatives seem to be included as much for the lustre they add to the tomb owner's pedigree as from any sense of family: the vizier Ramose, for instance, includes at his banquet (Th 55[3]) not only such notables as a royal envoy and a king's steward from Memphis, but also the renowned and later deified sage, Amenhotep, Son of Hapu (distinguished by his long flowing hair, unlike the formal wigs of the other guests). Still other examples have humorous overtones, showing (for instance) guests who are overcome by drink (Th 49[2]).

Music and dance

As works of art, the chief glory of the banquet scenes lies in their treatment of musicians. In the tomb of Nakht, three young ladies perform for the guests on a tall harp, a mandolin and a double-reed pipe. A blind harpist sits in the register above, his rolls of fat bespeaking a sedentary life (Th 52[3]; cf. 78[1]). The same ensemble is elsewhere augmented by a choir of women who clap their hands or rattle tambourines to mark the rhythm (Th 100[14]). Dancers and tumblers are also featured at these entertainments: the girls in Horemheb's tomb (Th 78[1]) are comparatively restrained, making only a few swaying motions as they play their instruments. It is in the Old Kingdom tombs, however, that contortionist dancing is seen at its finest. The artists are captured in a wide variety of styles. In the tomb of Mereruka (11), female and male dancers are arranged in two rows: the former, in short skirts and with their hair in long braids ending in pom-poms, perform a stately measure, with arms outstretched and hands touching above their heads (cf. Ti [13]); the men below dance in pairs, with sashes bound around their waists, whirling one another in intricate patterns to the clapped accompaniment of similarly garbed figures. In contrast to the usage of the New Kingdom, male dancers are frequently shown in the earlier period: they perform what seems to be a slow dance, in single file (G 7530–40[7]), but they also share the most difficult steps with women. A favourite dance, which seems even to defy gravity, involves supporting oneself on the right foot as the body is thrown back, while the left leg and two arms are thrust forward for balance (Kagemni [1]; Ankhmahor [5]). A less sophisticated measure is performed (Nefer [1]) by four women with close-cropped hair and short skirts who caper around one another, each with one arm thrown carelessly over her head.

While music and dance were often connected with formal merrymaking, a deeper level of aesthetic appreciation may perhaps be inferred from scenes in which, for instance, the wife plays the harp before her husband as they sit on their bed (Mereruka [10]). A hint of what this repertoire consisted of can be gleaned from the love poetry that has come down to us.[3] In the tombs, the model is a very ancient song (c. Eleventh Dynasty) that counsels the living to

Make merry,
But do not tire yourself with it.
Remember:
It is not given to man to take his goods with
him.
No one goes away and then comes back.

Games

Games were another favourite pastime among the leisured classes. The Egyptians were passionately fond of board games, particularly of one called Senet: the young Pharaoh Tutankhamun took no fewer than three sets of equipment for this game into his tomb with him, and the Egyptians depicted themselves enjoying it from the Old Kingdom onwards (Mereruka [18]; Th 1[1]; 296[1]; 359[2]). Another popular game, which employed a circular board, is the 'Serpent Game' (G 7102[3]): a good example, with game pieces shaped like small balls, each inscribed with a name of one of

3. See William Kelly Simpson, ed., *The Literature of Ancient Egypt*, 2nd edn (New Haven and London, 1973), pp. 296–325. A freer but more poetic rendering of some of these is found in John L. Foster, *Love Songs of the New Kingdom* (New York, 1974).

the kings of the First Dynasty, is found in the Edinburgh Royal Museum. Children's games, by contrast, tended to be athletic. Boys are seen playing at war – fencing with mock weapons and taking prisoners – and also holding races and 'tug-o'-war', along with a variety of other sports. Girls' exercises are more sedate, including one game played with mirrors, and another which involves two groups, each holding the hand of the girl in the middle and rocking back and forth (*Mereruka* [16]; *Ptahhotep* [4–5]). Such team sports seem to have been exceptional among adults (e.g., BH 15[1]; 17[2]), though foot races and rowing competitions took place in military settings.

Hunting

The field sport *par excellence* in ancient Egypt was hunting. We have already seen the tomb owner fishing and fowling in the marshes, surrounded by his family and boatloads of carousing attendants (*Ti* [19]; *Ptahhotep* [4]; *Nefer* [1]). Just as popular was the chase in the desert (*Mereruka* [4]; *Ptahhotep* [4–5]; Th 81[3]) in which the rough work was done by greyhounds: led into the field by huntsmen in colourful striped tunics, they bring to bay not only game but also lions and bulls. Hyenas, too, play an unspecified role in the hunt, perhaps (as was suggested above) acting as decoys. Later, as from the Eighteenth Dynasty, a new deadliness entered the hunt as the chariot began to be used. One excellent example (Th 56[6]) shows a swarm of animals in flight, including ostrich, hares, antelope, wild asses and foxes (one of whom lies trampled in the bush). Many sportsmen continued to prefer to hunt on foot but, from the Middle Kingdom on, the outcome was controlled by holding the hunt inside a stockade of poles and rope lashings (Th 60[6]; 100[8]). Here, as in the marsh scenes, it is the lively representation

of nature that holds our interest – a duel between a bull and a lion (*Mereruka* [4]), or copulating animals in the desert (*Ptahhotep* [4]).

Urbanism

Implicit in all of the above is the well-to-do Egyptian's view of himself as a country gentleman: even after death, as we shall see in Chapter 6, his role was defined in terms of a farming community. This is understandable, for however much of the land's wealth lay in trade, her life was tied to agriculture. But Egypt was scarcely a land without cities. Much of what is characteristic of Egyptian civilization resided, in fact, in its own peculiar style of urbanism.

By its very nature, Egyptian rural life encouraged the formation of villages: numerous settlements made it easier to control the river, to farm the adjacent land, and to assemble products for redistribution. Larger settlements, such as the nome capitals, served as centres for tax collection and other administrative needs. Throughout Egyptian history, but particularly during the Old and Middle Kingdoms, new areas were opened up for economic development by creating towns nearby. The cult centres of the gods also tended to become the nuclei of cities, as did such foundations as the 'pyramid towns' created by Pharaohs of the Old and Middle Kingdoms to administer the endowments of their mortuary cults. Although many of these places were quite small, others can truly be regarded as cities: 'Egyptian Thebes' was proverbial throughout the Greek world for its splendour; and ruins of Memphis were still so extensive in the thirteenth century A.D. as to astound the Arab traveller, Abdellatif. Very little can be seen today. The great buildings of Memphis were broken up to build the new Arab capital of Fustat, shortly after the Muslim conquest, and *sebakhin* –

peasants seeking the nitrogen-rich dirt of mudbricks to fertilize their fields — have destroyed most of the humbler dwellings. Many ancient town sites lie under the modern farmland or settlements today, so only in a few cases has the archaeologist's spade revealed something of urban life in ancient Egypt.

One of the few town sites easily accessible to the tourist is the village of Deir el-Medina. Located in a small pocket in the hills of West Thebes (see Fig. 97), it was occupied by the workmen who laboured on the royal tombs. Unlike most Egyptian villages then, it was virtually independent of the surrounding countryside. The inhabitants' needs — food, even water — were supplied by the state, and the craftsmen who lived there formed an elite group who passed their jobs on to their descendants. Space forbids discussion of the villagers' active and sometimes raucous social life, as revealed through papyri and by countless ostraca — bits of limestone or pottery used for jottings and then discarded — but we may devote a few words to the layout of this town which, for all its unusual status, is our best source for details of city life in ancient Egypt.

The community at Deir el-Medina probably owes its existence to Amenhotep I who, along with his mother Queen Ahmose Nofretari, became the patron of the workmen who lived there. His successor, Thutmose I, built an enclosure wall around the town which was then about two-thirds the size of the later settlement. The houses that gradually accumulated outside the walls, mostly to the south, were finally absorbed into the town proper during the Nineteenth Dynasty. It is this plan (with internal modifications over the next two hundred years) which is seen today. It was abandoned during the eleventh century B.C. when the danger from marauding Libyans forced the inhabitants to move behind the enclosure

wall of Ramesses III's temple at Medinet Habu.

Two unusual features set this town further apart from others. First, unlike most settlements which were built well away from their local cemeteries, this village is surrounded by the tombs of its dead, which rise up on terraces along the sides of the adjacent hills. Second, the villagers' work site was not within easy walking distance of their homes. Most of the time they were employed in the Valley of the Kings, some two kilometres distant, and reached most directly by a steep path through the hills. The workers accordingly spent the nights, not in the village, but in a camp situated on a spur that overlooks both the cultivation and the Valley of the Kings. After working for most of a ten-day 'week', the workmen were allowed to return to the village for their day of rest; and there were many holidays as well. ▷ DEIR EL-MEDINA, Chapter 19, pp. 279–81. The ruins of this camp are still visible today, and the spot, with its magnificent view, is one of the most haunting in West Thebes.

Other Egyptian town sites have been excavated, but none of them presents quite so complete a picture as Deir el-Medina. El Kab, for instance, may be visited for its imposing outer wall — over three metres thick at some points, and with ramps and stairways leading to the top. The town itself is a disappointment. The houses uncovered in the southern sector are Graeco-Roman in date, and the place is mainly notable for its double temple and for its desert chapels and tombs outside (see Chapter 20).

El Amarna is more informative. Built as the capital of the Atenist heresy under Akhenaten, it was occupied for less than a generation and thus provides a fascinating cross-section of contemporary life without the contamination of later settlements. The Egyptians were able to build here as they could nowhere else, free from the confines of a previously existing town-plan. The city's remains are found at two main sites, called the North Suburb and the Main City, which appear to have served respectively as Akhenaten's residence and his official head-quarters (see Chapter 15). Private houses are numerous, ranging from extensive villas down to slum dwellings. The very nature of the site makes the town-plan haphazard and difficult to follow, though, and many ruins are too much covered by drifting sand to yield many details for the visitor. An interesting feature that emerged from the excavation, however, is that some of the larger houses were surrounded by a cluster of smaller dwellings and functioned as manufacturing centres. Since most of the city's residents were state employees, it has been suggested that these people 'invested' surplus capital earned in royal service in ventures such as this and that they employed in these proto-factories not only their house-hold staff but also outside labourers who, for their own convenience, lived nearby.

Industries

The relations between master and man in the household industries at Amarna are writ large in the dealings of the country's great 'corporations' – the crown and the temples – with their dependants. Craftsmen plied their trade in workhouses managed by their em-ployers. They did not own their own materials or their means of production. Payment was nearly always in kind: the temples, for instance, diverted the produce of their fields and workshops to pay their employees, who in turn bartered their excess rations for other commodities. Steps in this process are perhaps illustrated in some of the private tomb chapels at Thebes. In the tomb of Userhēt, for instance, we see rows of men

delivering their quotas of cakes at the store-house door, where they are met by an overseer armed with his flail of office; while in the registers above, other men (wearing shirts this time) sit in front of the storehouse, each with his basket of cakes – perhaps their wages (Th 56[5]). A variant of this trans-action is seen in the tomb of Rekhmirē (Th 100[9]), where rations of linen and ointment are being distributed to Hittite, Syrian and Nubian women who, together with their children, have been given to the temple as slaves. Craftsmen, quite plainly, were an important element in the workforce of ancient Egypt, and in the scenes which show their activities in the private tombs we can catch a glimpse of their professional life.

Carpentry

Every carpenter who bears his adze is wearier than a field-hand. His field is his wood, his hoe is his axe. There is no end to his work, and he must labour exces-sively in [his] activity. At night-time he must [still] light [his lamp, *i.e. continue working*].

Although woodworking was one of the professions despised in the *Satire on the Trades*,[4] its craftsmen dealt in a rare and valued commodity. Wood suitable for craft-ing into objects of any size is scarce in Egypt. Occasionally in the tombs we do see a tree being cut down for woodworking (*Nefer* [2]), but this could only have satisfied a fraction of the demand. The Egyptians were thus obliged from earliest times to import wood from abroad. As long as the densely forested shores of Phoenetia lay within Egypt's sphere of influence, the Pharaohs could count on a regular supply of lumber at reasonable cost. The official fiction regarding this

4. See Simpson, ed., *The Literature of Ancient Egypt*, pp. 329–36.

arrangement is reflected in a scene from the battle reliefs of Sety I at Karnak (see below, Chapter 17, p. 229 [N.E. corner]) where the sleek princes of the Lebanon vie with one another in personally felling trees for the king of Egypt. From the account of Wenamun, an agent of the High Priest of Amun who had been sent to Byblos during the troubled closing years of Dynasty XX, we learn a different story, however, as he recounts the delays and insults he endured – even the humiliation of being shown the ledgers in which Byblite princes had recorded all the gold and silver paid by the kings of Egypt for their foreign wood![5]

Scenes of carpentry abound in the tombs of Egypt's upper classes (G 6020[1]; Ti [15]; Nefer [2]; Th 100[10]; 181[4]). Pieces of furniture – beds, chairs, doors, chests and cabinets of various sorts – are universally represented, for one's 'House of Eternity' had to be supplied with such things. Occasionally, items such as carrying chairs (G 6020[1]) and oars (Mereruka [3]) are also seen. The royal barge of King Khufu, found disassembled in a boat-pit south of the Great Pyramid at Giza and reconstructed in a museum on this site, gives some substance to scenes of boatbuilding (Ti [15]; Ptahhotep [4]) or of launching boats (Nefer [2]) found in the tombs, providing tangible proof of the craftsman's skill during the third millennium B.C.

Scenes of this sort also yield a rich harvest of details concerning the work itself. The ancient technique of splitting wood, for instance, involved lashing the beam to an upright pole and sawing it from top to bottom, the cut being kept open by inserting a weighted peg (see, for example, Ti [15]; Th 100[10]). When wood had to be bent (for instance, in making bows), the two ends of

the stick were lashed in position to a pole and the wood was cut to shape when under tension, while the reverse process was used to straighten canes: one end of the stick was fastened to the top of a short stake, and a man balanced himself on the other end (Ti [15]). The application of glue is also illustrated, with the glue-pot resting on the fire (Th 100[10]).

Some of the most elaborate examples of the carpenter's art are ritual objects, statues and shrines to be used in private and state cult. The vast majority of these have perished, though notable survivals are found among the furnishings from the tomb of King Tutankhamun, exhibited on the upper floor of the Cairo Museum. In one scene from the tomb of Ipuy (Th 217[4]) we see two large pieces under construction. On the left is a royal naos inside a columned kiosk, its canopy depicting Horus and Seth binding together the Two Lands on behalf of the deified King Amenhotep I (for whose cult the piece is intended). The finishing touches are being applied, with men swarming over the frame, hard at work with chisels and mauls. On the right we see a catafalque, also for Amenhotep I, with a bed and a richly decorated canopy. Here, too, men are busily at work – but, as the man ascending the stairs at the lower left turns his head quickly, he has his eye daubed with paint by an associate. Another workman, above, carelessly throws his maul aside, onto his colleague's foot. Two men are working on the roof, with a basket of tools between them – but at the right end, a supervisor is roughly shaking another man who has gone to sleep. Such behaviour, of course, had no place in the idealized world of the hereafter. We may be grateful that this view was sufficiently relaxed here to give us one more glimpse into the lively workers' community at Deir el-Medina.

Leatherworking

The sandalmaker is utterly wretched carrying his tubs of oil. His stores are provided with carcasses, and what he bites is hides.

Leatherworkers are sometimes associated with carpenters in the tombs, as both were involved in making military equipment such as bows and chariots. More typically, we find them engaged in what the *Satire on the Trades* regards as their usual occupation: making sandals. A fairly complete sequence of steps is seen in the tomb of Rekhmirē (Th 100[10]): proceeding right to left, we see a man stretching leather, or making it more flexible, by working it back and forth on the head of a stand (cf. G 6020[1]; *Ti* [15]). The hides are next polished by rubbing, and they are further softened by working them over the mouth of a large jar. The leather is then cut to shape: on the left, men are seen cutting, stretching and piercing the leather cord, while back in the middle, a thong is threaded through the sole of the almost completed sandal. The oversize sandals that result are frequently shown in use, and samples of this craft have been found in tombs, notably that of Tutankhamun.

Brickmaking, building and stoneworking

I shall also describe to you the bricklayer ... When he must be outside in the wind, he lays bricks without a garment. His belt is a cord for his back, a string for his buttocks. His strength has vanished through fatigue and stiffness ... [and] he eats bread with his fingers, although he washes himself but once a day.

Labourers in the building trades are pictured in the tomb of Rekhmirē (Th 100[10]). The task of laying bricks is here given to Nubian captives, an interesting parallel to the fate of the Children of Israel in the Bible (*Exodus* 1:13–14). On the left, a man is seen filling jars with water while, further right, others are hoeing the ground and filling baskets with earth. After mixing these two substances with straw to bind the mass (not shown), the mud is poured into wooden moulds and left in the sun to dry. Then, as now, most of the bricks were not fired, but were transported to the work-site as soon as the surface hardened, either in quantity with the aid of a yoke (as here) or a few at a time. Domestic architecture depended mainly on unfired bricks for the shell of a building, but any large construction would be made of stone, and its interior filled with earth as successive courses were added, or with a series of mudbrick ramps giving access. What appears to be a stone building partly obscured by such a ramp is seen on the extreme right in the tomb of Rekhmirē. Another good example is still preserved at Karnak, against the east face of the south wing of the first pylon, found here because the building remained unfinished in antiquity.

Building in stone is also illustrated in the tomb of Rekhmirē, in the two registers below the brickmaking scenes. Ships laden with stone are first seen on the bottom (right), arriving from the quarries. Masons are next seen chipping at the blocks or stretching cords across their surfaces to see whether they are truly smooth. Above, gangs of men are seen hauling huge blocks of granite with the aid of ropes and levers, while at the right sculptors shape the hard stone into statues. Since at this time the Egyptians still had only soft metals – copper and bronze – at their disposal, the required shaping of the stone was done with dolerite balls which were also used to literally pound the granite loose from the bed of the quarry: a good example of their patience is the unfinished obelisk in the granite quarries on the east bank at Aswan. Transport of granite columns, pictured on a block from the causeway to the pyramid of King Unis at Saqqara, fades into insignificance before the conveyance of Queen Hatshepsut's two great obelisks down to Thebes: the monuments are settled on the decks of two enormous barges, with groups of tugboats to guide these monsters downstream, and the profusion of masts and cables vividly evokes what must have been an astounding technological spectacle in its day (see Chapter 18, p. 258).

In addition to statuary (G 7530–40[1–2]; Ti [15]), the Egyptians excelled from earliest times in making finely crafted stone vessels. Examples of their art fill the world's museums and the perfection they achieved is all the more amazing in that the only drill available was a cumbersome instrument: consisting of a forked shaft made of hard stone, it was turned by a crank attached to its upper end, with stones lashed to the handle to provide greater stability. Even so, great strength and stamina must have been required of the operator. This process, as well as polishing vases with a stone scraper, is pictured in many tombs, both of Old and New Kingdom date (Ti [15]; Mereruka [3]; Th 100[10]; 181[4]).

Metalworking and jewellery-making

... I have seen a coppersmith at his work at the door of his furnace. His fingers were like the claws of the crocodile, and he stank more than fish excrement.

Metalworkers are among the most ubiquitous of the craftsmen represented in the tombs. They too dealt in a valuable commodity; for this reason we first see the metal being weighed, prior to distribution, doubtless so the amount could be checked against the finished product (Mereruka [3]; Th 86[3]). Most Old Kingdom examples next show the metal being melted, the temperature of the open fire being raised by men who blow into tubes fed into it. This is immediately followed by pouring the molten metal into moulds and pounding it into sheets, as required (G 7530–40[1]; Ti [15]). Occasionally, too, we see subsidiary processes, such as polishing a metal bowl that has been placed, bottom side up, on a stand (G 6020[1]). Advances in technology are reflected in later examples, as shown in the very complete sequence in the tomb of Rekhmirē (Th 100[10]): from right to left, we see the metal weighed before a scribe and men pounding, polishing and incising metal in front of an open furnace, and soldering as well. Beyond, baskets of metal — both ingots and sheets — and charcoal are being carried to the worksite, to be put to work in the furnace with its modern treadle bellows (left). The molten metal is then carried in a hod supported by two curved sticks to the mould — in this case, for a large door — and it is poured into each of the vents in turn (cf. Th 86[3]).

The jeweller pierces [stone] in stringing beads in all kinds of hard stone. When he has completed the inlaying of the eye-amulets, his strength vanishes and he is tired out ...

Jewellers, having many techniques in common with stone and metal workers, are often ranked with them in the industrial scenes in private tombs. The small perforations through beads and seals of various sorts were at first achieved by boring with a copper or flint drill, using an abrasive powder (e.g., Ti [15]). Later, the drill's speed and efficiency were increased by rotating one or more at the same time, with the aid of a bowstring (Th 100[10]; 181[4]). A distinctive feature of Old Kingdom examples – and one that still defies explanation – is that the jewellers shown working on collars and the like are generally dwarves (*Mereruka* [3]; *Nefer* [1]; *Ankhmahor* [6]). There is no contemporary evidence to suggest a reason for this usage. I think it may reflect a social prejudice that invested little people with an aptitude for the fine-detail work of the jeweller's craft.

Menial service professions

The barber shaves until the end of evening. But he must be up early, crying out, his bowl under his arm. He takes himself from street to street to seek out someone to shave. He wears out his arms to fill his belly, like bees who eat [only] according to their work.

Other trades lay outside the framework of an organized establishment, depending for their success on the practitioner's skill and the demand for his services. (Characteristically, the *Satire on the Trades* views this sort of free enterprise as a disadvantage.) The barber's milieu is shown in the tomb of Userhēt (Th 56[5]) where men wait their turn, seated under trees. Barbers must have found steadier employment in Egypt than in many other societies of the ancient world, for the Egyptians placed great emphasis on cleanliness and ritual purity: both sexes shaved their heads, making use instead of elaborate wigs, and men allowed their beards to grow only during periods of mourning.

Another marginal profession, that of the laundryman, is also occasionally seen in the tombs (Th 217[1]). The *Satire* had a low opinion of this occupation too, not only because the laundryman was exposed to danger from crocodiles at the river's edge, but because he must 'clean the clothes of a woman in menstruation' and become himself impure.

Such occupations, at least, were subject to one's own personal initiative. At the other extreme was the constant threat of forced labour, the compulsory service exacted by the crown. This system can be seen at work in the Theban tombs: in Userhēt (Th 56[5]) we see three rows of young men being inspected by scribes. Each carries in his hand a small bag to hold rations. The induction of youths into the army is illustrated in the tomb of Horemheb (Th 78[2]): at the bottom, the recruits with their sacks are brought to the door of the royal storehouse to receive their rations from the baskets of supplies stacked there. Above, scribes are recording the new men's names, and most of these are now issued bows or clubs, being grouped in rows under standard-bearers. This was not regarded as a desirable fate and, from the viewpoint of the scribal tradition, anyone enrolled in any sort of forced labour – whether on distant estates, in the army, on building projects or on quarrying expeditions – could expect danger and hardship in return for his guaranteed support.

Trade and commerce

Although foreign trade and domestic distribution of goods was largely in the hands of Egypt's major producers – the state, the temples and the high officials – the system of issuing payment in kind rather than coin left ordinary people with surpluses that they would have to trade for other necessities. The bargaining that resulted is vividly, if not too frequently, illustrated in the tombs. Following the manufacture of canes and sandals, for instance, we see these items offered for sale (*Ti* [15]). A vivid evocation of the market, with all its bustle and variety, is found in the double tomb of *Nyankh-Khnum and Khnumhotep* (6). The selling of fish and fruit predominates in this scene, while at the left we see a man mingling with the crowd and holding a baboon on a leash; an unfortunate passer-by is bitten by one of the panicked animals at the right end. Articles for sale in the remaining registers include drinking cups, fish-hooks, a variety of food and drink, and (at the bottom, right side) a bolt of linen. A later example in the tomb of Ipuy (Th 217[3]) is set at the docks. Men are seen carrying sacks of grain off the moored ships. Their contents are next emptied into baskets, and the dickering begins. Women play a prominent role in this activity, as they do today in the markets of every Egyptian village, offering bread and fruit in exchange for fresh produce. More stock-in-trade is apparently brought in at the left, while a woman supervises the stockpiling of reeds which, owing to their usefulness (for example, in making arrows), have their own market value as a raw material.

Clerical and medical professions

See, there is no office free from supervisors except the scribe's. *He* is the supervisor!

Scribes made up the managing class in ancient Egypt. The road to literacy was a hard one, for budding scribes had to memorize approximately eight hundred signs, together with the sounds and ideas (frequently, depending on the context, more than one) associated with each. Draftsmanship was another important discipline, for the hieroglyphs served a decorative as well as a practical purpose in the formal public inscriptions for which they were generally reserved. For everyday use, the signs were simplified and written with a reed brush in a flowing hand: this was the so-called 'hieratic' script which, in its later and more cursive

form (known as 'demotic'), ceased being interchangeable with the hieroglyphic from which it sprang. Young scholars were frequently reminded that the schoolboy's ears are on his back — but at the end of this rigorous training the scribe had entry into the priesthoods and the professions; even, in theory, into the highest offices of the land. ▷ CAIRO MUSEUM, ROOM 29: WRITING MATERIALS AND SCRIPTS, Chapter 10, p. 125.

The scribe's clerical skills are very much in evidence in scenes of daily life from the tombs: registering of produce and punishment of defaulters are standard vignettes. But the tombs also bear witness to the fame of Egyptian medicine throughout the Mediterranean world. In a chapel of the early Sixth Dynasty (*Ankhmahor* [2–3]) we first see (top register) an operation of unclear purpose, though the patient is being immobilized by having both his arms held. Below, the doctor operates respectively on the finger and toe of his patients. The top register on the right side is also broken, so all that can be said is that the foot (left) and back (right) are being cared for. The lower scenes are complete, however, and show the circumcision of a youth on the verge of manhood. This operation was often turned into a *rite de passage*: a stela of the First Intermediate Period at the Oriental Institute Museum in Chicago reports that the owner was circumcised along with one hundred and twenty other youths, all at the same time! None of this, however, is suggested in the two episodes shown here. On the right, we see the doctor kneeling before the patient and about to perform the circumcision with (perhaps) a flint knife. The result of the operation appears on the left: the doctor swabs the member and cautions the attendant who is grasping the patient's arms, 'Hold on to him, don't let him fall!', to which the man replies, 'I'll perform to your satisfaction.'

The foregoing survey of life and work in ancient Egypt, based on representations found in the tombs, is unavoidably incomplete: such aspects as learning and the transmission of written traditions by the scribal schools have been barely touched, although they bulk large in the surviving materials. But the picture, if not rounded, is characteristic. Idealized or stereotyped these vignettes may be, but they throb with the pulse of ancient life and evoke, at whatever distance, the ancestors of modern Egyptians.

3. The Government

Egypt, for many visitors, *is* her monuments. And these monuments, in turn, are memorials left by the people who ruled the land throughout the period of nearly 4,000 years of its ancient history. Few indeed are the antiquities that do not owe their existence to the ruling classes' ungovernable lust for fame. From pyramid to private tomb, royal rescript to humble graffito, whether they be regarded as way stations of the human spirit, signs of megalomania or simply as touristic attractions, they are the major source of our knowledge of ancient Egypt and the *raison d'être* for the abiding curiosity of later ages.

The Egyptians themselves were hard pressed to account historically for their form of government. There was, as is so often the case with ancient man, a conviction that it all went back to a divine prototype: men spoke of 'the Time of Rē', the sun god's mythical reign on earth, as a gauge of high antiquity. Gradually there evolved a tradition whereby a succession of 'gods, demigods, and spirits of the dead' were credited with establishing the pattern followed by the earliest mortal rulers. The model of divine kingship was taken for granted, as was the physical unity of Egypt itself. But, though the land between the First Cataract and the Mediterranean does form a governable unit, there was no natural reason for it to be so. Recent studies

suggest that early agriculture had a regional scope in Egypt and did not require true national planning to be effective. And if, moreover, we review the 2,600 years of Egypt's history before she succumbed to the successive world empires (starting in 525 B.C.), we discover that the land enjoyed real unity of government only for about sixty per cent of this time. The remainder — roughly seven centuries — are the so-called 'intermediate' periods, during which the country was divided into two or more principalities that co-existed, often cordially, until the overmastering power and ambition of one party succeeded in effecting a new unification. Obviously, with the 'King of Upper and Lower Egypt' being in fact master of the whole country only slightly more often than not, the idea of the sovereign as the natural ruler of all Egypt became a political fiction. But it was a useful fiction, and it lasted.

The genesis of the kingdom was also the subject of official myth-making. Tradition has it that the two halves of the Pharaonic kingdom, Upper and Lower Egypt, were pulled together by one Menes, a ruler of Upper Egypt who conquered the northern kingdom and established a new capital at Memphis, the juncture of the Two Lands. Most historians today place this event near the beginning of the First Dynasty[1] (*c.* 3100

1. The division of Pharaonic history into thirty dynasties is the work of Manetho, an Egyptian priest who wrote a history of his country in Greek, albeit based on native sources, during the third century B.C. This arrangement is sometimes arbitrary, but it is retained by modern scholars because it is convenient and seems close enough to the facts.

B.C.), identifying Menes either with Narmer or Aha, the first dynastic rulers of the country. Few qualms would be felt over this proposed sequence of events, were it not for some evidence suggesting that the unification had already taken place at some time prior to the start of the First Dynasty. If so, the process appears to have stretched over a number of generations during which various parts of the land were held in spasmodic union. Menes could thus be a composite figure – King 'So-and-so who [once] came' is one possible translation of the Egyptian *Men-iy* – and the bellicose names of the earliest rulers[2] imply an atmosphere of constant strife. The truth may never be known. What is certain is that the kings who begin to appear in contemporary records near the start of the First Dynasty are immediately recognizable as forerunners of all later Pharaohs who held their office in the Nile Valley.

In theory, the king's position was simple. Although born a mortal and retaining throughout his life all the human frailties, he was infused with godly power from the moment the hereditary kingship passed to him. By virtue of this office he was a god on earth, the living nexus between the divine and mortal spheres of activity. He alone could effectively worship the gods, standing before them as a son to his parents. Through him, moreover, was maintained the cosmic harmony that the Egyptians called Ma'at. Of the ritual scenes carved on temple walls, one of the most frequently encountered is the representation of the king offering Ma'at – shown as a tiny seated goddess, with her characteristic feather headdress – to the gods; and sometimes – to emphasize the king's role as the guarantor of Ma'at – the

hieroglyphs that make up the king's own name are substituted for the goddess's image. To the ancient Egyptians, whose idea of right order was a blessed uneventfulness in natural affairs, this was the ruler's most important function.

The king's office conferred on him certain trappings to set him apart from the common run of mankind. The most visible of these would be the panoply of royalty – crowns, sceptres and the like. The earliest kings are shown wearing a tall bulbous headpiece that is later known as the 'Crown of Upper Egypt' or White Crown (Fig. 1, a). Beginning with Narmer, the king is seen with another diadem – the Red Crown of Lower Egypt, with its distinctive coil – which was later combined with the White Crown to form 'the Two Mighty Ones' with which the royal office was bestowed (Fig. 1, b–c). An additional range of headdresses would be developed in succeeding dynasties: here we will mention only the *nemes* head-cloth, which seems to be more characteristic than the others (Fig. 1, d). In addition to the diadem, the ruler was also equipped with appropriate sceptres: the crook, which in hieroglyphic conveys the idea of 'governing', and the flail, perhaps originally an elaborate fly-whisk (see Fig. 1, e–f). On certain occasions the king also wore a bull's tail, the virile connotations of which need no explanation.

The development of the king's status can also be traced through the evolution of his titulary, the 'five great names'. His identity with Horus, falcon god of Upper Egypt, is reflected in the earliest of these, for the name is written inside a model palace façade (called a *serekh*) which the god's figure bestrides (Fig. 1, g). The impact of the unification is felt

---

2. For instance, 'Scorpion', 'Catfish' (=Narmer), 'Fighter' (=Aha), 'Stockade' (=Djer), 'Serpent' (=Djet), and 'Killer' (?) (=Den).

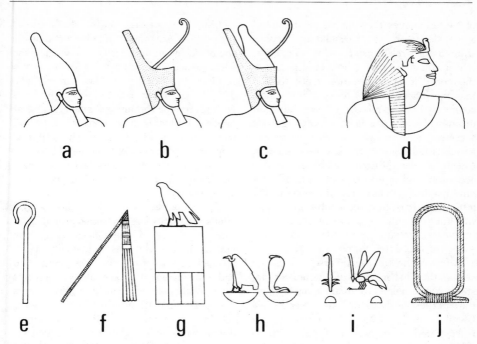

Fig. 1   Royal crowns and insignia

in another name that is preceded by the title, 'Favourite of the Two Goddesses', the vulture, Nekhbet of El Kab, and Edjo, the cobra goddess of Buto in the Delta (Fig. 1, h). Another title, 'King of Upper and Lower Egypt' (Fig. 1, i), had entered the titulary by the end of the Second Dynasty. By the Fourth it was recognized among the 'great names', though it was set apart by being enclosed within an oval name-ring that is referred to by the French term, *cartouche* (Fig. 1, j). Finally, the sun-worshipping kings of the Fifth Dynasty standardized the title, 'Son of Re', and added another name (also enclosed within a cartouche) to go along with

it. The king also acquired other divine attributes,[3] but 'Pharaoh', his most enduring title, seems originally to have described the royal household, or 'Great House'.

The ultimate expression of the king's authority was his 'appearance in glory' before his subjects. Any number of occasions could provide the excuse for one of these displays, but the most characteristic was the *Sed* festival or 'Jubilee'. During this ritual, a complex of ceremonies that could last two months or more, the king 'died' and was reborn, going through a second coronation. Some rites were celebrated twice, once for Upper and once for Lower Egypt. By the end

3. For instance, the fifth 'great name', which is variously interpreted as 'Horus of Gold' or 'Horus over the Ombite (=Seth)'.

of the ceremonies, the king had been granted a new lease on his office and had reconstituted his relationship with the gods, whose cult statues were honoured guests at the Jubilee. It is possible, though not proved, that the Jubilee had its roots in an archaic ceremony of ritual murder, whereby an aged incumbent was replaced by a more vigorous successor: in most cases, it was celebrated at an advanced point in the sovereign's reign, usually at the thirtieth anniversary of his accession, and it was repeated periodically until his death. In any case, the effect of the festival was to reaffirm the institution of kingship in Egyptian society. ▷ JUBILEE COURT, DJOSER'S STEP PYRAMID COMPLEX, SAQQARA, Chapter 13, pp. 163, 166.

A few of the Jubilee's diverse rites can be seen in the Theban tomb of Kheruef, a royal steward who helped to organize the first and third of these festivals for Amenhotep III (see Chapter 19, p. 296). The opening day is illustrated on the north end of the portico (Th 192[7–8]), as the king, accompanied by the High Priests of Memphis (whose erased figures appear above the king's), raises up the Djed Pillar and adores it in its shrine. Traditionally performed on the first day of the harvest season, this ritual conferred the blessings of stability (djed) on the land and, by extension, on its royal patron. The ceremony's further significance for kingship is emphasized by subsidiary rituals seen below: thus the mock stick-fighting alludes to the battle between supporters of Horus, the royal god of Egypt, and his opponent, Seth; and the driving of oxen and cattle 'around the walls' symbolically defines the extent of the king's possessions and refers also to the founding of Memphis by the first kings of a united Egypt. The concluding rites

of the Jubilee are seen on the south side of the portico: Amenhotep III, enthroned inside the baldachin in full regalia and wearing the short Jubilee robe, rewards his followers and receives the homage of his subjects (Th 192[3]). Leaving the palace, he next proceeds with his retinue through a jubilant throng of priests, priestesses and musicians (Th 192[4]) to the shore of a lake. There (Th 192[5]) he 'appears in glory', as on the sacred barge of the sun,[4] born anew on the dawn of a new day, as the festival comes to a rousing and appropriate end.

Only sporadically, however, did the god king's real status live up to this propaganda. The experience of one official during the Fifth Dynasty, who was accidentally struck by the king's sceptre during a ceremony and had to be reassured, 'You're all right', reflects the prevailing belief in the king's divine aura during the Old Kingdom; but things were seldom so simple thereafter. The king's divinity was less highly regarded in later years and his authority whittled down by different groups of over-mighty subjects.

One characteristic challenge came from the hereditary provincial governors who began to appear during the later Old Kingdom. Known as 'nomarchs', these magnates held virtually absolute power within their districts, co-operating with the royal house when it suited them and often quarrelling with their neighbours. A typical representative of this breed is one Ankhtify, Governor of several nomes between Edfu and Armant in Upper Egypt, who left on the walls of his tomb at Mo'alla a tantalizing glimpse into one of the obscurer epochs of the First Intermediate Period. 'I am the beginning and the end of mankind,' Ankhtify boasts, 'for my equal has not and will not come into

4. This scene is very badly damaged, and only the bottom part (particularly the prow of the boat) can be made out clearly.

being.' Certainly his was an active career, involving him not only in a war with a coalition of neighbouring nomes (including the Thebans to the north), but also in feeding adjoining districts during a period of famine. He was, for his own purposes, the king's right-hand man in southern Egypt. Less flamboyant but just as influential were the great nomarchic families whose imposing tombs (for instance, at Beni Hasan in Middle Egypt, and at Aswan) bear witness to their continued authority in the land. These people could learn to follow a strong ruler – as, indeed, they bowed before the victorious Eleventh Dynasty from Thebes and to subsequent kings of the Twelfth Dynasty – but their entrenched position rendered them dangerous. This tension finally led to the abolition of the nomes, and of most nomarchs, by Senwosret III (*c.* 1860 B.C.), but this was only a temporary solution to what was now a perennial source of conflict. ▷ BENI HASAN, Chapter 15, pp. 188–9; MO'ALLA, Chapter 20, pp. 301–2; OFFICIALS' TOMBS AT ASWAN, Chapter 21, pp. 325–9.

Another class that would eventually clash with the crown was the bureaucracy – the men who filled high state positions, and the priests. Some of these, like the magnates of the early New Kingdom who built their tombs at El Kab, already had influential local ties, but their importance swelled through the patronage of a renascent royal power. The beginning of the Eighteenth Dynasty was pre-eminently a time of consolidation. The kings, flushed with victory in Asia and undisputed as leaders of Egypt's war machine, presided over a re-organization that would shape the course of government for nearly five centuries. At the head of the civil administration were two Viziers, for Upper and Lower Egypt respectively, to whom supervision of most government offices was delegated. Egypt's far-flung colonies south of Aswan were entrusted to the Viceroy of Nubia, a new office of which more will be said later (see Chapter 4, pp. 57–8). Local government was stabilized, with royal domains throughout the country being placed in the care of royal stewards. The same solicitude was shown in administering temple property: it was not uncommon for high civil officials to hold such sinecures as, for example, 'Overseer of the Cattle of Amun', and posts in local clergies were awarded to veterans in the royal service. ▷ PRIVATE TOMBS AT THEBES, Chapter 19, pp. 279–99; PRIVATE TOMBS AT EL KAB, Chapter 20, pp. 305–8; SPEOS AT GEBEL SILSILA WEST, Chapter 20, pp. 314–15.

So long as the king maintained an energetic interest in governing the realm, he could be sure of a vast and loyal following. Royal patronage – the power to grant (and to withhold) rewards – was a potent inducement to good behaviour, and acknowledgement of the king's favour became an almost obligatory gesture in private tombs. The connection could be expressed in a number of ways. Thus the tomb owner is shown being appointed to his highest office or in the characteristic performance of his duties (Th 100[1–4]). A favourite theme was the rewarding of the deceased, a formal occasion in which the king appeared, enthroned on the dais or standing within the 'Window of Appearances', and bestowed gold collars on the beneficiary before the entire court (e.g., Th 78[2]; 188[3]). In one instance, while the king rewards his official (Th 49[3]), the man's wife is seen receiving marks of honour from the queen (Th 49[2]). Special occasions, such as royal jubilees, provided an excellent excuse for the king to single out deserving retainers. The Overseer of the Granary Khaemhēt, for example, was honoured for exceeding the expected quota for agricultural production during a jubilee year (Th 57[4, 6]); and the royal steward Kheruef tells how he and a number of colleagues were decorated, entertained at breakfast, and given places of high honour on the climactic day of Amenhotep III's first jubilee (Th 192[3]). Nor were officials averse to advertising even closer connections to the royal house: indeed, several tomb owners proudly show off their charges – princes, princesses, even future kings – seated on their knees (Th 78[3]; EK 3[3]).

While a strong official class undoubtedly helped to maintain efficient government, it brought problems too. Family feeling was strong: passing one's office on to one's son was a traditional objective and when high officials were related by blood or marriage (as they often were), the situation became even more unmanageable, for the king could not dismiss one man without offending a host of others. The crown fought back, at the end of both the Sixth and Eighteenth Dynasties, by 'adopting' powerful families who lent their support in return for the profitable connection: thus, when Amenhotep III married his queen, Tiyi, he even publicized her non-royal antecedents in an unprecedented issue of large commemorative scarabs (see Chapter 10, p. 124, Cairo Museum, Upper Floor, Room 6). But, though the king might thereby gain a supporter, he lost a crucial distance between himself and his subjects.

The priesthoods, too, were waxing powerful. As the divine sponsors of Egypt's successful imperialism in Nubia and the Near East, the gods had profited from the spoils and from ever-increasing grants of land. The most powerful corporation was that of Amun – lord of the Eighteenth Dynasty's Theban homeland and state god *par excellence* – which in time would own close to ten per cent of all cultivable land in Egypt. In addition, his High Priest disposed of the title, 'Overseer of all the priests of all the gods of Upper and Lower Egypt', a notable coup for this once obscure god and one that gave his clergy a disproportionate voice in the councils of the land. To the extent, moreover, that the priests held the intermediary roles between gods and men, the king's exclusive claim to that relationship was diminished. Whichever way he turned, it seemed, the king was hemmed in by powerful and potentially unruly subjects.

The crucial test of wills came in the middle of the fourteenth century B.C., when Amenhotep IV mounted the throne. One of the most attractive yet controversial figures in history, his is a difficult character to judge. His purpose, based essentially on a policy of 'divide and rule', seems sensible enough; but he also had a streak of genuine mysticism that would prove disastrous in the end. For better or worse, he dominated his age, shaped the course of future events, and has exerted an unquenchable appeal to the imagination of modern man.

To the earlier Eighteenth Dynasty's control over the army and the civil service, which still lay within the king's grasp, Amenhotep IV sought to add a renewed reverence for the sovereign's divinity. None of the existing great gods could help, for all of them had entrenched, power-hungry priesthoods, so the king turned to a minor figure in the pantheon, the solar disc or 'Aton', for his champion. The immediate advantage of this new cult was the intimacy it established between the sovereign and the divine: 'You are in my heart,' says the king to his new god, 'and there is no other who knows you except for your son, Nefer-kheprurē Waenrē,[5] for you have made him cognizant of your plans and your strength.'

5. This was the 'King of Upper and Lower Egypt' name, or throne name, of Amenhotep IV (see above, pp. 46–7).

The Aton had its own priesthood, to be sure, but it was firmly under the control of the king as chief officiant. More important were the unprecedented royal attributes of the Aton; for its names were written in cartouches, like the king's, and dated monuments were ascribed jointly to the earthly monarch and his divine 'co-regent'. The king was once more the nexus between man and God — if only the country could be made to accept it.

To this end, Amenhotep IV bent all the resources of royal patronage. Vital posts in the civil and military administration were filled by men who subscribed to the king's vision, and temples to the Aton were built throughout Egypt. The new religion had a number of attractive elements: an imminent, accessible symbol of godhead whose beneficence could be immediately felt in a culture that spent much of its time out of doors; a refreshing lack of ritual and mythological baggage; and a premise of equality for all men under the two 'kings' of heaven and earth. The populace was encouraged to investigate the king's religion, but the cults of Egypt's ancient gods were also maintained, as the king tried to effect his revolution by example and persuasion.

As the new religion failed to take hold, however, royal policy began to veer off into extremes. First there was the new city, thrown up in Middle Egypt on ground that 'belonged to no god and to no goddess', and named Akhetaten, 'The Horizon of the Aton': this was to be a new capital, and the king swore that he, his family and courtiers would all be buried here rather than at Memphis or Thebes. At the same time, in another slight to the traditional religion, the king repudiated his personal name, Amenhotep (meaning 'Amun is satisfied') and renamed himself Akhenaten, which probably means 'he who is effective on the Aton's behalf'. The campaign reached its height in the latter part of Akhenaten's reign, when the temples of all other deities were closed by royal command, their priesthoods disbanded and their property assigned to local Atenist headquarters. Further, the figure and names of Amun, together with the deities in his circle, were hacked away on temple walls and wherever else they were found. Akhenaten believed he could thus drive the elder gods out of existence. What his fanaticism did not allow him to realize was that his repressions were creating an opposition that would undermine the political goals of his reforms. ▷ EL AMARNA, Chapter 15, pp. 190–97; BOUNDARY STELA AT TUNA EL-GEBEL, Chapter 15, pp. 200–201.

The reaction that took place on the death of Akhenaten (c. 1334 B.C.) was predictable, as were the machinations that surrounded the boy king Tutankhamun. Representatives of official families favoured since the time of Amenhotep III fought to stave off ambitious newcomers, and when Tutankhamun died without an heir, the spoils came to encompass the throne itself. Only when the dust had settled, after the long, healing reign of Horemheb (1321–1293 B.C.), did the dynastic principle reassert itself. The Nineteenth Dynasty witnessed the glorious age of Ramesses II and Merneptah, and the no less distinguished Ramesses III held sway early in the Twentieth. With allowances made for the family feuding that disrupted the closing years of the Nineteenth Dynasty, the monarchy seemed to be as strong as ever.

The problems that had motivated Akhenaten's quixotic revolution had not, however, gone away. Attempts to balance the power of Amun with other state gods were half-hearted, and by the late Twentieth Dynasty Amun's High Priest was virtually governor of Upper Egypt. Other magnates — notably the Viceroy of Nubia and the commander of the Libyan mercenaries stationed in the north —

also had dangerously independent positions. Space forbids any attempt to disentangle the often obscure course of events in the last years of the Twentieth Dynasty. Suffice it to say that Egypt was already fragmented before the last of the Ramessides had left the scene. 'As for Pharaoh, how shall he reach this land?' inquires a contemporary of the ineffectual Ramesses XI. 'And of whom is Pharaoh superior still?' His words provide a fitting introduction to the following five centuries — a so-called Third Intermediate Period, during which Egypt was seldom governed by one hand, after which came the age of foreign domination: Persians, Ptolemies, Romans; and the end of Pharaonic civilization ▷ KARNAK, TEMPLE OF KHONSU, Chapter 17, pp. 235–6.

4. Pharaonic Egypt and its Neighbours

The very length of Pharaonic civilization lends it a deceptive air of tranquillity. The conventions of Egyptian art convey a timeless, static condition of things wherein the workings of *Ma'at*, or the cosmic ordering principle, is seen as an eternal exemption from change. Life by the Nile Valley was far from uneventful, however: the three millennia of Egyptian history are dotted with periods of internal strife; and beyond Egyptian territory, as everyone knew, lay 'the plains and hill countries, foreign lands that know not Egypt'. Nothing indicates Egypt's sense of herself so well as her handling of her three frontiers.

It was the western border that knew the earliest and most persistent foreign contacts. Moist conditions in the early savanna allowed a freer movement of peoples than today, and the earliest Neolithic culture, entering into Egypt from Libya, combined with home-grown and Asiatic influences to form the distinctive civilization of Pharaonic times. But the drying of the deserts gradually separated the Nile Valley from its neighbours. The Libyan tribes came to form separate entities, often inimical to Egypt, and the oasis dwellers — though always in touch with Egypt and usually under her control — were reduced to the status of country cousins, contributing their produce and little else.

The role of the oases in connecting the Nile Valley with Libya and southern Africa has always been a mixed blessing for Egypt. As of the late Old Kingdom we find local governors maintaining their capital at Balat,

in Dakhla; and Egyptian troops are seen hurrying along desert roads to quell disturbances in that part of the world. These roads were also vital commercial arteries, and as long as Egypt held on to this buffer zone she was safe from any sudden attack from the west. The apparent success of this policy can be gauged from the fact that the Libyan menace, while no doubt of periodic significance, seems to have degenerated quite early into something of a cliché (see Chapter 10, pp. 109–10). It must also be no accident that the Pharaohs never imposed direct control over the scattered western peoples, preferring not to interfere in tribal politics until a show of force was required. The deserts and oases were also havens for fugitives, although their remoteness could be turned to the state's advantage. In A.D. 435, for instance, the heretic bishop Nestorius was consigned to dwell in Kharga for life after being condemned by the Council of Ephesus: he was not the first of the political prisoners who have been held in the western desert down to modern times. ▷ OASES, Chapter 22, pp. 345–9.

Egypt's relations with the Middle East were more complex. Trade with the Levant can be traced back to earliest times, and in the cities on the Syrian-Palestinian coast lived the historic middlemen who secured for Egypt such products as lapis lazuli. At first, Egypt interfered only when its interests were threatened. Conflict with the nomads in the Sinai goes back at least into the Third Dynasty, when Egyptians began to exploit the rich copper and turquoise mines here;

and, as early as the Sixth Dynasty, we hear of a military expedition sent to 'Antelope Nose', identified as the Mount Carmel promontory. Overall, though, the monarchs of the Old and Middle Kingdoms preferred to influence via diplomacy and state trade. Only after a traumatic experience of foreign rule would the Egyptians turn the political configuration of the Middle East, with its many small kingdoms and settled way of life, to a more directly imperialistic end.

Fortunately, the eastern border was more easily controlled than were the many avenues in the western desert. Given the rudimentary navies of the time, the only feasible access lay across the Isthmus of Suez. In antiquity this approach was called the 'Ways of Horus' and was the main military road, running from the border at Tcharu (modern El Qantara) through the Bitter Lakes district, via El Arīsh, to Gaza. Secured by a network of fortified wells, this way could either repel or be sabotaged against an invader. Another major route into Egypt was the Wadi Tumilat further south, an ancient river channel that would be developed during the sixth century B.C., when Necho's canal linked the Red Sea with the Delta. Since this way also could be easily patrolled, an invading force would have but one option – to by-pass the Delta altogether, striking into the eastern desert for a landfall on the valley's edge. Security of this frontier was given to the district governors whose scouts patrolled the area: one such official, a nomarch of the Oryx Nome who was also Overseer of the Eastern Desert, could report that from his capital near Beni Hasan to the Ways of Horus, 'the frontier is colonized and filled with people'. Later, during the New Kingdom, this task was given over to Med-

jay tribesmen who acted as police throughout Egypt under crown jurisdiction. These arrangements were highly effective for the most part, for within her natural borders Egypt was able to develop in her own way for nearly two thousand years, with only one major eruption from abroad.

Egyptian policy in the south was yet another matter. Nubia was Egypt's only colony, a land that could be treated as properly hers. The quest for raw materials and trade routes brought the Pharaohs and southern peoples into conflict from the very earliest times: the record of military intervention goes back at least into the First Dynasty, culminating early in Dynasty IV with a campaign under Snefru that left Lower Nubia virtually depopulated. The natives' submission was required only to the extent that it gave the Egyptians a free hand in the south – freedom to exploit its mineral resources and to control trade routes with the heart of Africa. What genocide had accomplished during the Old Kingdom was achieved later by other means. During the Middle Kingdom, for instance, the border at the Second Cataract was protected by a network of forts, affording protection and tight regulation of commercial traffic to and from Nubia. Egyptian imperialism still pursued limited military objectives to obtain the most basic security and amenities from abroad. For the rest, the Egypt of the Old and Middle Kingdoms treasured her isolation, maintaining very much a 'closed door' policy towards her neighbours.

The trauma of foreign invasion changed all that. During the seventeenth century B.C., a warrior horde breached Egypt's eastern defences (probably with the help of Asiatics already settled in the Delta) and imposed

The Queen of the African country of Punt (formerly in the eighteenth dynasty temple at Deir el-Bahri in Luxor, West bank; now in the Cairo Museum)

their rule over the entire country. At about the same time, a recently arrived Nubian population stormed the Second Cataract forts and pushed the effective frontier back to Aswan. The 'Hyksos',[1] as the Asiatic overlords were called, held direct control only in Lower Egypt. In the south they were content to rule through vassal princelings who now appeared in a resurgence of local government over the centralized version. Mutual advantage dictated a Hyksos alliance with the newly formed kingdom of Nubia, moreover, so the Theban Pharaoh Kamose could well complain, towards the end of this period, that 'I sit [here], united with an Asiatic and a Nubian, [each] man possessing his portion of Egypt.'

The expulsion of the Hyksos inaugurated both the Eighteenth Dynasty and a new foreign policy. Instead of splendid isolation, the Pharaohs elected now to 'widen the borders of Egypt', to exert greater control over adjacent territories. The Nubian border was pushed far south, beyond the Fourth Cataract. In Western Asia, a buffer zone was carved out between Egypt and any of the Near Eastern kingdoms that might be tempted to repeat the Hyksos' exploit. This new Egyptian empire might best be described as an extended sphere of influence: even now, the Pharaohs preferred to operate through local princes, whose sons received their education in Egypt and who were kept in line by garrisons and threats of force. A show of military might was essential, moreover, if the Pharaoh was to be accorded the proper measure of respect by his co-equals, the 'Great Kings' of the Middle East.

Egypt's undoubted commercial power was another factor in her waxing role in the Near East. Local rulers needed the products that Egypt could command from the Nubian goldmines and her traditional trade routes with Africa. Punt, the verdant land on the Somalian coast, had been visited by Egyptians since the Old Kingdom and still supplied many exotic products for home use and for export. Egypt, for her part, needed building timber and manufactures from abroad. Once the Nile Valley had re-emerged as a viable power, it was natural for her to participate in the profitable Near East trade. ▷ PUNT RELIEFS, DEIR EL-BAHRI TEMPLE, Chapter 18, pp. 259–62.

Egyptian commercial activity in the Middle East was an old story. What was new lay in her direct involvement with international diplomacy through her Near Eastern 'empire'. These influences eventually left their mark on Egyptian society at home, introducing a heightened cosmopolitanism into life in the Nile Valley. Talented foreigners increasingly found a scope for their abilities in Egypt: some of them actually rose to high positions in the government – notably that 'Grey Eminence' of Syrian stock, Chancellor Baï, who presided over the final days of the Nineteenth Dynasty.

The palmy days of the Egyptian empire are often reflected in private tomb decoration of the period. However, these scenes are less valuable as purely historical records than for the wealth of characteristic touches with which they treat their subjects. The Egyptian artists took their models from life, but the conventions in which they worked tended to ignore the subtleties that distinguished Egypt's relationship with her Nubian subjects, Asiatic vassals, and with the Pharaoh's trading partners, the independent rulers of

---

1. A term deriving from the Egyptian *heka-khasūt* 'Rulers of foreign lands'. The racial composition of the horde is still unsolved, though excavations at Tell ed-Dabba by the Austrian Archaeological Institute should yield some answers.

the Middle East. Rather, all are treated as a single phenomenon, echoing the propagandist rhetoric by which 'the foreign chiefs come before you [=the king] in submission, their tribute on their backs'.

These triumphal processions are quite often rich in colourful details. When the police chief Nebamūn appears before Thutmose IV, he leads in groups of bound Syrian captives, while their grooms bring a tribute of captured horses and other spoils (Th 90[6]). More often though, the foreign delegations bring presents of their own free will. Cretans, clean-shaven with long, curly hair and dressed in brightly patterned kilts, bring jugs and vases, fantastically shaped and decorated (Th 86[6]). Syrians, more soberly attired in long robes, present gold, malachite and weapons — scimitars, bows and helmets (Th 86[6]) — and petty rulers prostrate themselves in the royal presence, offering their children as hostages, to remain in Egypt (Th 86[6]). Elsewhere, when the official mythology lifts slightly, we see Nubian, Asiatic and Libyan delegates standing, with arms upraised in homage, among a crowd of bowing Egyptians at Amenhotep IV's court (Th 55[6]). This is as close as the official style came to acknowledging the complex relations between Egypt and her neighbours, the kings and vassal princes of the Middle East.

The Nubian tribute scenes, although conventionalized, are somewhat closer to reality. As of the start of the Eighteenth Dynasty, affairs on Egypt's southern border had been entrusted to an official who was answerable to the king and thus held the honorific title, 'King's Son for Nubia'. This viceroy enjoyed sweeping powers: the civil government of a vast territory, from El Kab in Upper Egypt down to the Fifth Cataract in Nubia, was in his hands, and he also commanded the garrisons sent or recruited there. Some of these soldiers can be seen in the tomb of the royal scribe and commander

Tchanuny (Th 74[3]): the recruits — wearing only loincloths and divided into platoons — are drilled by officers attired in white tunics and carrying staves of office. Many of the platoons have their own standards to mark their positions in battle, and a Nubian drummer can be seen, his instrument strapped to his back, in the bottom register. Such power in private hands could be dangerous: indeed, after failing to consolidate his grip on Upper Egypt during the dying days of the Twentieth Dynasty, the Viceroy Panehsy managed to repulse the forces of the High Priests of the Thebaid and thus laid the foundation for the independent Nubian kingdom that would conquer Egypt during the eighth century B.C. (Dynasty XXV).

Before that, however, the Viceroys of Nubia had been loyal servants of the crown, and scenes in the tomb of Huy, who held office under Tutankhamun, give a representative view of their duties. Huy is first seen leaving the temple of Amun on his way south: the two state barges on the right are outfitted with gorgeous hangings to shield the travellers from the sun's rays, and one of them even has a stabling facility for the Viceroy's horses astern (Th 40[1]). Huy is next seen collecting tribute in Nubia (Th 40[2]): rows of tax-payers are seen bringing their assessment in small bags to be weighed and tallied by government scribes. At the right end, we see ships being beached, to undergo repairs before the return journey north, while supplies are assembled below. Finally, on reaching the capital, Huy presents the Nubian tribute to the king (Th 40[3–5]). In addition to the usual gold-dust and rings, and also the elaborate presentation vessels made for the royal audience (right), we see wooden and leather furniture, handsomely worked shields, and other artefacts. Exotica such as ostrich feathers, ebony wood, ivory tusks, leopard skins and native fruits can be seen in other tombs (e.g., Th 100[2]). In

Huy's tomb, these gifts are accompanied by a Nubian delegation – not the usual crowd of dancers and female servants carrying their babies in baskets on their backs (Th 78[4]), but a distinguished company of native chiefs, including a princess riding with her attendant in a chariot. By this time, Nubia was thoroughly Egyptianized, with local notables comfortably ensconced within the ruling hierarchy. Such cultural assimilation ensured the survival of Pharaonic civilization in the south long after the end of the Egyptian rule in Nubia. ▷ NUBIA TEMPLES, Chapter 22, pp. 337–44.

Patriotic effusions such as these imply a stable 'Pax Aegyptiaca' in the Mediterranean world. As with so much else in the official record, however, this is an illusion. Egypt still had to contend with forces beyond her borders which she could not control. Thus, when the Hittites destroyed the kingdom of Mitanni during the late Eighteenth Dynasty, it took nearly eighty years for the Egyptians to work out a *modus vivendi* with this new power. Contemporaries painted the struggle in glowing colours, and around the Battle of Kadesh – where the youthful Ramesses II confronted the Hittites in North Syria (*c.* 1275 B.C.) – there grew a legend widely proclaimed on public buildings in Egypt. A few details from parallel versions in the temples of Abu Simbel, Luxor and the Ramesseum convey the flavour of this propaganda. The king is first seen enthroned before the town of Kadesh: behind him is the Egyptian camp, secured with temporary defences, while below the throne two spies are being beaten for giving misleading information as to the enemy's whereabouts (*Abu Simbel*, bottom; *Ram.*, first pylon, north wing; *Luxor*, western pylon, outer face, top). The battle itself follows: the king charges into the fray in his chariot (*Abu Simbel*, top, left; *Ram.*, first pylon, south wing; *Luxor*, eastern pylon, top, right) while the opposing

forces meet on the plains surrounding the town, which itself appears to be enclosed by two branches of the Orontes River. The discomfited enemies are routed, some of them falling into the water as they make their escape (*Abu Simbel*, top, right; *Ram.*, second pylon, north wing; *Luxor*, eastern pylon, top, left). Ramesses II, the official record tells us, won a mighty victory almost single-handedly. A closer reading of the sources suggests that the battle was in fact inconclusive. It demonstrated, however, Pharaoh's ability to withstand the assault of a powerful neighbour. ▷ LUXOR TEMPLE, Chapter 17, pp. 238–9; RAMESSEUM, Chapter 18, pp. 265–7; ABU SIMBEL, Chapter 22, pp. 342–4.

More potent dangers, outside the normal channels of diplomacy, threatened all the major powers. A great movement of peoples – starting in the thirteenth century B.C., and perhaps caused by massive climatic changes in Northern Europe and the Caucasus – brought waves of desperate emigrants to the shores of Africa. Some of these 'Sea Peoples' threw their lot in with the equally needy Libyan tribes, and in the fifth year of Merneptah (*c.* 1207 B.C.) a formidably armed horde set out for Egypt. Although they were repulsed in a bloody battle, during which over 6,000 of the invaders lost their lives, the troubles did not end for another generation, until Ramesses III had confronted three invasions from Libyans and 'Sea Peoples' in less than one decade. ▷ MEDINET HABU, BATTLE SCENES, Chapter 18, pp. 268–70.

Ramesses III commemorated his victories on the façades of the fortified gates to his mortuary complex. An ironic fate awaited these buildings. Among the prisoners taken during the Second Libyan War had been soldiers who entered Egyptian service as garrison troops. These forces, swelled by fresh recruits from Libya and commanded by their native chiefs, eventually formed a powerful and independent horde on which the Pharaohs had no choice but to rely. The Twentieth Dynasty came to a chaotic end, with years of lawlessness, hard times and civil war. During the troubled years, the populace of West Thebes had to use Medinet Habu as a haven from bands of Libyan outlaws, and when Panehsy, the Viceroy of Nubia, finally confronted the local authorities (*c.* 1080 B.C.), the temple was taken by storm: the western high gate — demolished, never rebuilt, and in fragments today — is mute evidence of the attackers' fury and of the impotence of the state at this time.

The wreck of the western tower at Medinet Habu may fittingly inaugurate the lengthy Third Intermediate Period. Legitimacy yielded before armed might, and in about 945 B.C. a 'Great Chief of the Meshwesh' crowned himself the first king of the Twenty-second Dynasty. For four centuries (*c.* 1100–712 B.C.), despite years of unified rule, the land was split into rival principalities. In the end, it had to fall to the first determined conquerer from abroad. The Nubian King Piyi (or Piankhy, as he was known in Egypt) extended his suzerainty over the 'kings and princes' of the Nile Valley in the middle of the eighth century B.C. His successors ruled the united kingdoms of Egypt and Nubia from Memphis, and thereafter came successive waves of invaders — the world empires of Assyria, Persia, Macedon and, finally, Rome — under whose rule Egypt was forced to enter fully into the orbit of the Mediterranean world.

The kingdom of the Pharaohs succumbed — but its civilization lived on, enriching the cosmopolitan societies surrounding it and weaving its mystique into the collective imagination of mankind. In a curious way, moreover, it had a descendant. In Nubia, safe from interference from the north, official style remained slavishly, even aggressively, Egyptian. The kingdom of Meroe, as it became known, remained a legatee of Egyptian culture long after direct contacts between the two nations had ceased. It is one of history's sweeter ironies that it was the despised, exploited Nubians who were Egypt's foremost cultural heirs in the ancient world.

King Menkaurē protected by the goddess Hathor and
the personification of a Nome (Cairo Museum)

5. Cities of God

'They are religious beyond measure, more than any other nation.' Thus Herodotus, a shrewd observer of Egyptian customs during the fifth century B.C., sums up his impression of Egyptian religion.[1] Contemporaries must have smiled at the understatement, for the reaction of most Greeks to the farrago of native cults, the fantastic niceties of observance, is comparable to an Englishman's first encounter with the abyss of India. The transmission of this impression to the present day is due in part to the nature of the monuments: the gods' temples, in their size, solidity and large numbers, have indeed resisted the ages best. But if they are the most imposing of Pharaonic remains, they are also the most characteristic, reflecting the mentality of the people whose needs they ultimately served.

To compress the whole of the Egyptian faith into a few paragraphs would be presumptuous. To lend focus to this discussion, however, we may single out two points. Most basically, this was a religion of propitiation: the gods, masters of the universe, were worshipped with sacrificial rites so that they would perpetuate the correct order of things, a harmony the Egyptians called *Ma'at* (see Chapter 3, p. 46). The ethics that found a place in this system were always of a pragmatic rather than a dogmatic bent. The codification of holy writ (in the biblical or Quranic mould) was foreign to the ancient Egyptians' temperament: they were not a 'people of the Book'. Another determining factor was the intense regionalism of earliest Egypt: with the many local gods who endured, through the country's unification into the developed Pharaonic state, came a conservatism that fostered much of what foreigners found so incomprehensible in Egyptian religion: it was mysterious, many-faceted and often contradictory in its respect for seemingly diverse local traditions. No system could contain it all. It remained, for its duration, rooted in the folk-experience of the Egyptian people.

In time, a number of divinities transcended their local origins to become 'great gods', worshipped throughout the land alongside local deities. Such a status could be fleeting: thus Neith, city goddess of Sais in the Western Delta, never had quite the influence in later times that she apparently possessed during the Archaic Period (Dynasties I and II). Certain gods, however, acquired a fixed archetypal significance. Thus Horus, the falcon god, became the deity associated *par excellence* with kingship. The ram Khnum of Aswan, master of the potter's craft, came to be charged with the fashioning of mankind, and the sun god Rē was recognized as the source of life far beyond the borders of his home in Heliopolis. The establishment of a national capital at Memphis automatically heightened the authority of Ptah, its local god; and the sponsorship of the Theban Eleventh and Eighteenth Dynasties at two crucial periods in Egyptian history initiated the vaulting career of Amun, 'the hidden one'. Such deities, while possessing elaborate temples in their home territories, were also worshipped in shrines of local gods throughout Egypt and even had temples built for them in the remotest parts of the country. In other words, they made up the national pantheon for Pharaonic Egypt.

1. *History*, Book II, 37.1 (Loeb Classical Library).

The totality of gods reflected the forces at work in the Egyptians' universe. Since worship was an intensely regional affair, however, local pantheons emphasized home-grown deities, often allotting them major roles in the cosmic scheme of things: a case in point is the Ogdoad, or 'Group of Eight' gods from Hermopolis, who, according to local legend, presided over the creation of the world. More often, however, local deities were grouped by threes into 'triads' – the region's 'great god', his consort and their child: among the best known of these groups, for example, are the Theban Triad of Amun, Mut and Khonsu; also the triad comprising Osiris, god of the underworld, together with his wife, Isis, and Horus, their son. Other local deities were placed in the following of the main triad, and the whole group could be known collectively as an Ennead, or 'Group of Nine' – that is, three (the symbol of plurality) multiplied by itself to equal an indefinite number that encompassed, for instance, the fifteen members of the Theban Ennead.

Obviously such an arrangement had its limitations. Most local groups were too constrained by their members' place and function to have the universality and status of the truly 'great gods'. A cult spot's sanctity was not static, on the other hand, but could be increased in two ways. Deities could be introduced from other parts to enhance the local pantheon – thus, for example, Ptah of Memphis had his own temple in the precinct of Amun at Karnak. Alternatively, the local 'great god' could co-opt within himself the qualities of other divinities to express a newly revealed aspect of his personality. Amun by himself, for instance, was only the 'great god' of the Theban area; but, as Amun-Rē, he acquired the character of the sun god without losing his individuality. Indeed, his scope had been widened: the dark realm of the dead, as much

as the land of the living, eventually lay in his domain; and as greater numbers of gods came to be seen (at least at Thebes) as mere facets of the greater reality of Amun, he became an entity sufficient to nearly all the demands of his worshippers. This sort of henotheism (the absorption of many gods into one) was the closest the Egyptians ever came to a monotheism in the Judaeo-Christian sense: barring a brief period in the later reign of Akhenaten (see Chapter 3, pp. 50–51) the Egyptians never developed the idea of a single god, 'of whom there is no other'. A god might be greater than the sum of his parts, 'without his equal'; but those parts always kept their individual divinity, and the Egyptians remained happily polytheistic.

The centre of a god's domain, spiritual as well as temporal, was his temple. The size of these establishments reflected his importance, but all of them – from the smallest building up to such historic and labyrinthine piles as Amun's temple at Karnak – had essential features in common. Perhaps the simplest way of explaining an Egyptian temple is by the analogy to a mortal's residence. The forecourts, open to all comers, wherein the god's public business was transacted, lay in front. The intermediate rooms, accessible only to those in divine service and reserved for ritual purposes, paralleled the home-owner's official quarters. Inside lay the 'holy of holies', the sanctuary where the god dwelt. On yet another level of meaning, the temple was a model of the place of first creation. Outside – represented perhaps by the wavy tiers of mudbrick walls surrounding the sacred precinct – lay the waters of chaos, populated by hostile powers who had to be prevented from entering the gates: the massive pylon towers that flanked the processional way were inscribed with symbolic scenes depicting the annihilation of Egypt's enemies, so that they, and the forces they represented, would be kept from the temple. Inside the enclosure was a marsh – evoked by the hypostyle halls, with their rows of papyrus- and lotus-shaped columns – which barred the way to the centre, the spit of land projecting from the waters, on which the gods first took their stand and on which the sanctuary now rested. These elements were abbreviated in smaller buildings, expanded or multiplied in larger ones; but their presence can help to explain what otherwise seems to be a meandering and eccentric complex of features.

In theory, the king was the sole officiant within the temple. Only he could stand, as a son before his parents, in the presence of the gods, and yet act as the representative of mankind. But the sovereign, having assumed leadership of all the cults in Egypt, could not be everywhere at once. Ritual functions had to be taken over by a delegate, a local High Priest who, with his associates, acted on the ruler's behalf. The boundary between the laity and the clergy was looser in Pharaonic Egypt than it is, say, in Christendom: temple services were conducted in rotation by groups of men who, at the end of their assigned month, relinquished their office to a new deputation. Wives of local dignitaries served as chantresses in the temple choir as well as in a variety of other posts. State officials often held priestly rank or administered temple property as a sinecure conferred by the crown, and retired military men could frequently count on spending their declining years as members of the higher clergy. Most officials held at least minor orders, being known as 'pure [*wa'b*] priests' – that is, having access to areas where only the ritually pure could go. Professional clergy held a host of titles, of which 'God's servant' (conventionally translated as 'Prophet') and 'God's father' were typical.

The purpose of any bureaucracy is ultimately to perpetuate itself. A 'great god's' cult had to be lavishly endowed and his property administered by a staff proportionate to its magnitude. State deities such as Amun owned land all over Egypt: even after the turmoil of the Amarna Period and during the Ramesside Age when the Pharaohs sought to balance the power of other 'great gods', the estate of Amun sprawled far beyond its headquarters in the Thebaid, accounting for up to ten per cent of the arable land in Egypt. Although such holdings were reduced or redistributed during the successive foreign occupations of the first millennium B.C., temple estates still owned large tracts in the god's home district. The Ptolemies, and also the Romans who succeeded them, found in local priesthoods a useful medium for local administration, so it is not surprising to find enormous fiefs growing up around such *parvenu* establishments as that of Isis on Philae.

Divine ritual in this religion of propitiation centred on the offerings made to the gods as the divine masters of their earthly estates. Twice a day – each morning and evening – the High Priest would break the seal on the sanctuary door. The god's statue would then be brought forth and an elaborate 'menu' (often specified in the offering-lists carved on chapel walls) was laid before him. The statue itself was washed, anointed with fine oil and dressed in clean vestments, while temple musicians gladdened their lord's heart with song. When the god, manifest in his statue, had absorbed what he wanted of the sacrifice, the offerings 'reverted' back to the priests, who then presented them in turn to each and every deity who was worshipped here along with the principal god of the temple. In the end they were divided among the priests, who all claimed a share as part of their salaries. Since most of the daily priests served only on a part-time basis and would require just enough to pay them for the time spent away from their usual duties, this way of proceeding satisfied the demands both of ritual and of economy.

This summary account of Egyptian rites at least helps to explain the prevalence of offering scenes carved on temple walls: in these, the king presents food and drink, incense, ointment and various articles of dress to the god who promises, in return, an array of benefits — life, a long reign, 'all health and all joy for ever and ever'. Such icons emphasized the primary aim of worship, which was the appeasement of the gods by mankind's representative. Just as importantly, however, they provided a model for proper religious observance and, like the scenes of daily life in the tombs, they acted as a magical safeguard in case the temple's endowment should fail. Part of the king's function, of course, was to prevent such a terrible thing from happening; but the Egyptians, hard realists in financial matters, thought it best to take no chances.

The sanctuary was not the only arena for the god's activity. Quite often he was taken out into the more public parts of the temple: on such occasions his statue was placed inside the cabin of a portable shrine — a miniature copy of the divine river-barge — which was then mounted on carrying poles and conveyed out on the shoulders of the priests. Processions of this sort are frequently shown in the temples: see, for example, the north and south walls inside the great hypostyle hall at Karnak (Fig. 73[I]), where the priests sometimes wear falcon- and jackal-masks, acting as those ancient divine powers, the 'souls' of the primeval cities of Buto and Hieraconpolis. The many festivals celebrated each year were gala events, during which the gods appeared in public to extend their blessings on the community. It was also on these occasions that they acted as the supreme arbiters of earthly justice: important questions and appeals in litigation were then placed before

the god, who ostensibly made his bearers move forwards or backwards to signify 'yes' or 'no'. Although only a few of such oracles have survived, it seems that the gods were often called upon to intervene in mortal disputes. Thus the writer of the following letter asks a god (probably Amun) to come forth and render a verdict at once:

I was looking for you to tell you about certain affairs of mine, but you had vanished into your sanctuary and no man was admitted into it to deliver it to you. But, as I was waiting, I met Hori, the scribe of the Mansion of King Userma'atrē-Meryamun [i.e., the mortuary temple of Ramesses III at Medinet Habu], and he told me, 'I'm admitted.' I am sending him to you. Look: you must discard mysteriousness today and come out in procession so you can judge the affair of the five garments of the Mansion of King Horemheb and these two other garments of the Scribe of the Necropolis. [Details follow, and the letter concludes laconically:] Goodbye.

It is easy to be sceptical of such divine justice. Perhaps though, it enabled the authorities to deliver a fair verdict in cases where the normal channels had failed.

On other occasions the god left his temple altogether and visited other deities in their shrines. At Thebes, for instance, Amun journeyed from his temple at Karnak twice a year — once to visit the mortuary temple of the reigning king on the west bank of the Nile during the 'Feast of the Valley' (see Chapter 6, p. 75); and again, to rest in the 'Inner Chambers [Opet] of the South' at Luxor, some two kilometres from Karnak. It was at this time that Amun, the state god, visited his counterpart, the Amun who resided in Luxor Temple. Although the purpose of the 'Festival of Opet' is unknown, the flavour of the event is captured by the reliefs on the side walls of the processional colonnade at the Temple of Luxor, scenes which provide a wealth of illustrative detail on the persons and rites involved in transporting the Theban Triad to and from Luxor. ▷ LUXOR TEMPLE, Chapter 17, pp. 240–41; KARNAK, TEMPLE OF RAMESSES III, Chapter 17, pp. 227–8.

The Feast of Opet was only one of many processional feasts celebrated for gods along the length and breadth of Egypt. The continuity of such practices down to the twilight years of paganism is shown at Edfu and Dendera, two of the best-preserved temples of the Graeco-Roman period. Inscriptions in both buildings inform us that in the third month of summer[2] was celebrated the 'Feast of the Beautiful Meeting', which began with the arrival of Hathor at Edfu on the afternoon of the New Moon. After elaborate welcoming ceremonies, the statues of the two gods (Horus of Edfu and Hathor of Dendera) were placed inside the Birth House, where they spent this and every succeeding night until the festival's conclusion at the Full Moon. ▷ EDFU TEMPLE, Chapter 20, pp. 309–11.

Other solemn occasions in the sacred year can be followed in both temples. Particularly important was the 'Festival of the New Year', at which a cult statue of the deity was infused with new life when it was exposed to the rays of the rising sun on New Year's Day. Certain feasts — for example, those celebrating the resurrection of Osiris, king of the underworld — were popular all over Egypt. In addition, there were the regular monthly or seasonal observances and local feasts in honour of regional gods or in honour of some great event (for example, Ramesses III's victory over the Libyans in 1172 B.C.). During the New Kingdom at Thebes, there were about sixty yearly festivals, some of them lasting several weeks. Such gala occasions must have been keenly enjoyed by the local populace, providing relief from what

was otherwise an unceasing schedule of toil. ▷ DENDERA TEMPLE, Chapter 16, pp. 217–20; ABYDOS, Chapter 16, pp. 207–13; MEDINET HABU, CALENDAR OF FEASTS, Chapter 18, p. 273; EDFU TEMPLE, Chapter 20, pp. 309–11.

The temple in ancient Egypt was a busy place — at once the divine master's household, headquarters of his earthly domain and the focus for the worship of the community. Today those temples that have survived stand empty, echoing only to the cries of birds and the chatter of tourists. Many of them had already decayed when they lost their state subsidies with the official Christianization of the Roman Empire; and nearly all were closed during the reign of Theodosius (A.D. 379–95). The exception was Philae, the 'Island of Isis', which was allowed to remain open to the pagan inhabitants of Nubia; following their ultimate conversion, however, this last bastion of the ancient faith was closed in A.D. 553. Some temples were re-used as Christian churches: Philae itself was rededicated to St Stephen and the Virgin Mary, and painted saints' figures can still be made out at the tops of the columns in the broad hall of Thutmose III's Festival Temple at Karnak (see Chapter 17, pp. 232–4). Other temples were engulfed in the urban sprawl of Arab settlements — the clearing of Luxor Temple, for instance, had to wait until late in the nineteenth century and was not completed before the sixth decade of the twentieth. Still others (for instance, Karnak) fell slowly into ruin, impressing early travellers with their majesty in desolation. Most sacred buildings, however, were destroyed, quarried away to build the villages of medieval Egypt or (more recently) Mohammed Ali's sugar factories. Those that remain seem to be vast, uninviting places; but they can regain a semblance of life with the visitor's sense of a faith forgotten.

2. Owing to peculiarities in the Egyptian civil calendar (see Chapter 1, p. 20) this date was not tied to any one season of the solar year, but rotated with the passing centuries.

The Happy Hereafter, tomb of Sennefer (Luxor, West Bank)

6. Death and Burial

'Beautify your house in the Necropolis and enrich your place in the West.' This advice from the sage Hordedef dwells on a theme that deeply affected life in ancient Egypt. For at the end of life was death, and the ancients were well aware that 'there is no one who can return from there'. Fear of dying, however masked by euphemism, lies throughout their religious writings. In response, Egyptian mortuary beliefs emphasized the continuity of life and death: immortality in the next world could be enjoyed on terms similar to the good life which the deceased had had in this world. Proper burial after a 'good old age' was thus regarded as a fitting capstone to a successful career. The tomb, not merely the corpse's final resting place, was a vital centre, a home for the spirit of the deceased and a cult spot to his memory. Hordedef, again, expresses the Egyptian hope: 'the house of death is for life'.

In historic times, the mortuary cult was built around a complex idea of the human personality. One important force was the 'Ka', a mysterious 'cosmic double', created alongside the living person at birth and surviving after death. It is usually represented in human form, bearing its own hieroglyphic sign — two upraised arms ($\sqcup$) — upon its head. The deceased is said to join the Ka after death, but the latter appears to take his place, for it is to the Ka that mortuary offerings are always made. Another component of the Egyptian personality was the 'Ba': often depicted as a small, human-headed bird, this was the dynamic force of the tomb owner's spirit, the entity that could emerge from the tomb into the realm of the living. The dichotomy of 'body and soul' that is prevalent in the Western world finds no exact parallel in ancient Egypt. Rather, the person after death was active through various manifestations — the Ka, the Ba, the shadow, and even the corpse — each in its own distinctive sphere.

Prehistoric burials at the edges of the Nile Valley show that rudiments of such beliefs go back into remotest antiquity. The tomb itself was no more than a hole scooped out of the desert, but already the deceased was equipped with an assortment of grave goods — jars of food and drink, weapons, even treasured items of personal adornment. The unification of the Two Lands brought drastic changes, as tombs acquired increasingly elaborate sub- and superstructures. Since corpses were no longer in direct contact with the drying medium of the desert sand, they had to be preserved by artificial means and, to meet this new requirement, the art of mummification was born.

It is in the tombs of archaic Egypt that we meet the first signs of social stratification. Early royal tombs had subsidiary burials grouped around them, resting places for favoured servants of the crown. These humble burials were to develop into the massive blocks of officials' tombs that surrounded the royal pyramids during the Old Kingdom. Interment in this fashion now became a privilege, 'a boon which the king gives'. Permission to build a tomb in the royal necropolis was given by official rescript, and the crown would sometimes assume part of the cost of outfitting these 'houses of eternity': during the Sixth Dynasty, for instance, an official named Uni could boast that a sarcophagus with its lid, a libation table, the lintel for the tomb entrance and its two door-jambs all came to him from the limestone quarry at Tura by courtesy of King Pepi I. But, although the deceased proudly recorded the high points of their careers in royal service in the autobiographies they had carved in their tombs, the figure of the king himself is conspicuously absent from reliefs in private tombs of the Old Kingdom — acknowledging both the sovereign's dread aura and the power ascribed to graven images at this time.

The characteristic tomb during the Old Kingdom is today called a 'mastaba' ('bench' in Arabic), a term coined by native workmen who noticed the similarity between the squat superstructures of the tombs and the low mudbrick shelves built on the exteriors of Arab houses for use as outdoor divans. Mastabas themselves originated in the low mounds that marked prehistoric burials, and they underwent a remarkable development during the first three dynasties. Burial chambers below ground became more elaborate, with galleries for offerings and subsidiary burials, and the superstructure gradually developed into a solid, rectangular building. The cult spot, focus of the offering ritual on behalf of the tomb owner, was a niche located generally on the east face of the building and sometimes expanded by the addition of an exterior chapel. This shrine was absorbed into the body of the mastaba by the middle of the Old Kingdom, having developed into a suite of rooms decorated with scenes depicting various religious and secular themes. The purpose of these tableaux, with their representations of ritual and of the commonplaces of daily life, was partly to commemorate the tomb owner at the height of his career; but their true importance lay in their helping to maintain the deceased in the next world: scenes of farming and industries magically supplied the offering bringers who are regularly shown advancing towards the tomb owner, and they guaranteed his well-being in the same way that the ritual scenes ensured that he would be protected throughout eternity.

Mastabas might vary in size and luxury, but all had certain features in common. The most important was the 'false door', the original focus of the offering niche, now transformed into a dummy portal through which the Ba passed into the outer world. Closely connected with the false door was the *serdab*, a room closed on all sides except for viewing holes that opened into the offering hall: inside the room were placed statues of the deceased, so arranged that they might witness all the rites performed outside. Many of these wooden and stone statues now grace the world's museums, but copies have been placed in some of the tombs (e.g., *Ti*) to convey the essential impression. In some cases the tomb owner's statue is placed in the offering hall itself, so that the deceased appears to be striding forth from the shrine to receive visitors (e.g., *Mereruka*) or is seen seated, cross-legged, before the false door (e.g., G 7102). ▷ GIZA MASTABAS, Chapter 12, pp. 152–5; SAQ-QARA MASTABAS, Chapter 13, pp. 168–77.

The mastaba was already beginning to give way to other forms of burial during the Old Kingdom, as officials began to take advantage of the hilly desert terrain that adjoins the Nile Valley throughout Egypt. The transition is most easily observed at Thebes, where officials' tombs in the earlier Eleventh Dynasty were arranged in rows within an artificial ridge cut through the low desert. These burials (called by their Arabic name, *saff*, 'row') were in fact extensions of the royal tomb, being comparable to rooms in a palace wherein the king occupied the most elaborate suite. Later in the Dynasty, when the sovereign's own funerary arrangements had become grander, officials were allowed to excavate their own tombs out of the Theban hills nearby. The next millennium saw the development of a characteristic type of burial that, with all due allowances for exceptions and extensions in plan, consisted of four major parts: (1) an outer courtyard; (2) a portico, or broad front hall, usually decorated with scenes that reflected the tomb owner's career, scenes of daily life, etc.; (3) a long hall beyond this, orientated towards either a statue niche or a shrine, and decorated with funerary scenes; and (4) a burial chamber. The latter was frequently entered from the rear of the long hall, but occasionally also from the front room (Th 55) or from the tomb's outer courtyard (Th 96). ▷ WEST THEBES, PRIVATE TOMBS, Chapter 19, pp. 279–99.

Many of these features can still be appreciated despite the ruinous state of the Theban necropolis. The brightly painted burial chambers of Sennedjem (Th 1) and Sennefer (Th 96) are deservedly on every tourist's itinerary: the ceiling of Sennefer's room is especially noteworthy, with its grape-laden vines that create the beguiling impression of an arbour. Some of the tomb chapels themselves are no less distinguished, and in addition to the carved or painted scenes on the walls, there are often lifelike statues of the deceased and his family (Th 49[10]; 57[9]; 69[8]; 296[4]). The visitor should also spare at least a glance for the ceilings, as these are often splendidly painted with a variety of geometric and floral motifs. Earthly prototypes for these 'houses of eternity' are sometimes evoked in paint, as in the stunningly realistic beam that runs down the centre ceiling in Tetaky's chapel (Th 15).

No less care was lavished on the exteriors of the tombs, for here the deceased's status and family connections were displayed for all the world to see. Exposure of such features to the open air has ruined most of them, but the interested reader can form an impression by taking a few pains. The tomb chapels at Deir el-Medina are easily visited, and a few of the small mudbrick pyramids that surmounted them have been reconstructed in modern times. Some of the larger examples of this feature lie in the Ramesside cemetery at Dra-abu'l-Nagga: the tombs of Nebwenenef (Th 157), Bekenkhons (Th 35) and Tchanefer (Th 158) are particularly well endowed with large, mudbrick pyramids that overlook spacious courtyards and an expansive view of the Nile Valley beyond. More individual and perhaps more rewarding is the cluster of Eighteenth-Dynasty tombs at the north end of Sheikh Abd'el-Quma, near the tomb of the Chief Steward, Senenmut. Above his mostly damaged tomb (Th 71) a niche carved out of the rock still contains a large block-statue of the deceased: as usual with pieces of this type, Senenmut is portrayed squatting, a robe entirely enveloping his limbs; on his lap is his pupil, Nefrurē, daughter of Queen Hatshepsut, with her head visible above her teacher's knees. Senenmut's gaze is fixed on some point of the eastern horizon — perhaps on the Luxor Temple, whose god (as we shall see) had close ties with the realm of the dead. This spot is not often seen by visitors, but anyone who makes the climb will be rewarded by the quiet intensity of image and setting.

Equally impressive in a more obvious way is a neighbouring tomb that belonged to one Raya, a chief prophet in the mortuary temple of Thutmose III (Th 72). Here, for once, the outer face of the tomb is mostly preserved, and we see a central ramp ascending on to an upper terrace. The similarity to the plan of Queen Hatshepsut's temple in the bay of Deir el-Bahri to the north is striking and, almost certainly, deliberate. The tomb's entrance is set into the back wall of the terrace, where the visitor may also see the remains of two elaborately moulded 'false doors' in mud plaster set into the side walls. These few remains, preserved by chance and remoteness from the ways of man, are all that is left of the once splendid façade of the Theban necropolis during the great days of the New Kingdom.

The later tombs at Thebes have also left substantial traces above ground. Built during the seventh and sixth centuries B.C. by local magnates, they possess immense, elaborate substructures, true 'mortuary palaces' that deserve a visit. Gateways to such tombs, marked by vast mudbrick pylons such as those of the steward Montuemhēt (Th 34), still dominate the bay of Deir el-Bahri. For all their visibility, though, the tombs themselves are below ground, reached by steep staircases cut into the rock (Th 279) and opening, beyond a covered reception area, into an open 'sun court' that, in the case of Montuemhēt, was nobly proportioned, and decorated with hieroglyphic symbols and statues of the deceased. The sides of the sun court give access to a number of small chapels belonging to the tomb owner's associates, with the deceased's own mausoleum at the far end of the court. Only one of these great tombs of the Twenty-sixth Dynasty (Th 414) is open to visitors: excavated and restored by the Austrian Archaeological Institute, its decoration is not well preserved, but it amply conveys the grandeur of one of these 'mortuary palaces'. Such tombs were the last manifestation of Theban glory before the balance of power shifted irretrievably to the north. Later rulers added to the Theban temples, sometimes with a lavish hand, but not one major tomb was built in the Theban necropolis after the close of the sixth century B.C.

Few sights are more melancholy than this pillaged city of the dead. The ancients themselves were haunted by the spectre of such decay: 'the nobles and spirits too, they built tomb chapels,' muses the Harper's Song, 'but ... their walls are dismantled and their cult stations are no more, as if they had never been.' The deceased's grave goods might be stolen, his cult cease, the very stones of his tomb taken away for another's benefit. Even before this, the tomb chapel might be violated by the deceased's enemies, who would hack out his name and figure in order to impair his chances for survival in the next world. And yet, despite dangers which threatened with dispersal not only the tomb but the deceased's very corpse, the Egyptians continued to bury their dead in the traditional manner. Perhaps, given their view of the beyond as a continuation of life as they knew it, no other fate seemed possible. Recourse was had to magic, to spells engraved on tomb walls and the sides of coffins, or painted on papyrus 'Books of the Dead', to preserve the deceased's burial and guide him on his journey to the next world. Part of the tomb's magical apparatus, as we have seen, were the reliefs and paintings that decorated its walls — the scenes of daily life and ritual vignettes that were substituted for the offering cult when it lapsed. Thanks to this memorializing impulse, we are able to eavesdrop on the last vital episode in the tomb owner's career, the day of his burial.

In the tombs of the Old Kingdom near Memphis, the first episode of the funeral takes place at the deceased's door. We see the corpse borne from the house in its coffin, while a crowd of relatives bewail him with dramatic gestures: both men and women tumble down in a faint, to be helped up by their neighbours (*Ankhmahor* [4]; similarly *Mereruka* [14]); meanwhile other mourners tear their hair in ecstasies of grief (G 7102[2]). Besides the pallbearers, the funeral procession is made up of a lector priest who is in charge of the ritual; the master embalmer, who will supervise preparation of the mummy; and one or two female mourners who impersonate Isis and Nephthys in mourning for the dead Osiris.

The cortège now proceeds to the river, where the boats are pushed from their moorings by swimmers. Following an offering ritual at the landing-stage on the west bank of the river, some sequences proceed directly to the tomb (e.g., *Mereruka* [14]). Of necessity, however, the procession had to make at least two stops before its arrival in the necropolis itself. The first of these was the 'purification tent', where the corpse was ritually cleansed with natron to prepare it for mummification. The building seems to have been divided into two compartments (G 7101[1]) with separate entrances (G 7102[2]), and it was located either on a canal or near an abundant source of water. From here, the cortège made its way to the embalming house. By fortunate chance, both the elevation and ground-plan of this building are preserved, in the tombs of Idu (G 7102[2]) and Qar (G 7101[1]) respectively. The interior of the building is reached by going down a passage through the enclosure wall into an open court, thence down another passage into the house itself. The plan is deliberately arranged so that the destination of any doorway was invisible to persons standing outside, implying that the embalmers' rites were shrouded in secrecy at this time. A group of female mummers is seen outside the embalming house in Qar's tomb: their contribution, presumably, would

have been made before the body was carried inside.

Mummification took approximately seventy days. During that time, the corpse was emptied of all corruptible material and packed in natron to dry. The heart and, sometimes, the kidneys were left inside the body cavity while, of the other organs, the liver, lungs, stomach and intestines were preserved separately and placed inside the so-called 'canopic jars' to await burial with the body.[1] The corpse, once completely dried, was removed from the natron, washed, oiled and wrapped in linen bandages. Mummies of wealthier persons were outfitted with a funerary mask that portrayed an idealized image of the tomb owner's features.[2]

At the end of the prescribed seventy days, the finished mummy was handed over to the relatives. The funeral could now begin in earnest, as we see the cortège leaving the embalming house, the coffin being drawn on a sledge by oxen (G 7102[1–2 top]). The final rites are generally dealt with quite briefly in tombs of the Old Kingdom, but sporadically certain features emerge that will assume greater importance later. Thus, in a tomb of the Fifth Dynasty (*Idut* [4]), we see for the first time the *teknu* – a priest who mimes the part of the deceased and is dragged on a sledge to the tomb door: he is shown here as an oblong, oval shape, his form quite hidden under the wrapping placed over him.

The journey across the river, 'to the west', was greatly stressed, no doubt because it symbolized the deceased's entry among the

---

1. The jars were given the name 'canopics' by early Egyptologists, who wrongly connected the modelled heads of the four sons of Horus on the lids with the clay images of the god of Canopus in the Delta. Some canopics are uniformly modelled with human heads, but others distinguish Imsety (human) from Hapy (baboon), Kebeh-senuef (jackal) and Duamutef (falcon). Canopic jars were less used during the late period, when the preserved viscera were packed inside the body cavity.

2. In the Graeco-Roman Period, these masks could be replaced by a lifelike portrait of the deceased which was placed over the face of the mummy – the so-called 'Faiyūm portraits' (see Chapter 10, p. 125).

blessed dead. Sometimes we are shown a whole flotilla of vessels, each bearing a statue of the deceased (*Mereruka* [14]) – 'this', we are assured, 'is on behalf of the Ka of Mery [= Mereruka's nickname]'. A more extended symbol of the same thing (*Idut* [4]) shows the cortège arriving in the town of Sais: above the waiting ships and the procession bearing the deceased's coffin (now lost) we see rows of vault-roofed Lower Egyptian shrines, with their lotus-bloom standards. The absorption of this Delta ritual into the funerary sequence for all of Egypt illustrates the open, eclectic spirit of Egyptian religion: not every funeral would make the pilgrimage to Sais, but the representing of this and other exotic rituals in the tomb would magically confer their protection on the deceased.

The funeral rites themselves seem actually to have been quite simple. At the door of the tomb, butchers slaughtered and dressed the sacrificial cattle. A repast was now laid, under the supervision of the lector priest, with female dancers and clappers enhancing the festive ambience (*Mereruka* [14]). The offering ritual ended, the mourners took their leave. The deceased had joined the community of his ancestors.

Mortuary rites during the Old Kingdom suggest that the deceased's hereafter had none of the complexity associated with the fate of the king. The dead man's survival in the next world depended, rather, on his descendants' concern for his cult. The same programme thus continued, with many additions and few modifications, into the Middle Kingdom, so that in the Twelfth-Dynasty tomb of Antefoker (Th 60[3]) the funeral procession unfolds along familiar lines. In the upper register we see the coffin brought by its priestly attendants to the west bank. It is next dragged from the landing stage on a sledge, while mourning women herald the deceased's arrival in the necropolis. After the embalming (not shown), we see a later stage of the procession in the middle register: the sledge with the mummy is drawn by a team of oxen assisted by the tomb owner's 'nine friends'. In front, also on sledges, we see the *teknu* – recognizably human now, squatting inside his wrapping – and the canopic chest, containing the four jars with the mummified entrails of the deceased. The procession to the entrance of the burial ground occupies the lowest register, where the cortège is met by four dancing figures who wear tall cylindrical hats of wicker-work: these are the *muwu*-dancers who welcome the deceased to the cemetery and prepare him for the funeral rites to follow.

The ceremonies at the tomb are not shown in Antefoker's tomb, but appear in several tombs of the early Eighteenth Dynasty. In the chapel of Rekhmirē, for instance, no fewer than eleven registers on a very high wall are needed to show sixty-eight rituals (Th 100[11]), nothing less than a collage of ceremonies – some of them current, others not – which are assembled here to confer magical protection on the deceased. A full description would be pointless, as many of these scenes are either ill understood or emphasize themes that are developed in other episodes. A few of the more important may be singled out, even though some of them were no longer celebrated at this time.[3]

One of the most noticeable episodes is the 'ritual in the garden' (registers 3–4, right end): here, the corpses of eight bulls are seen arranged around a rectangular pool and a formal garden opens out at the right, with two women making an offering before four basins of water (cf. Th 15[2];

---

3. In the following discussion, the scenes in Rekhmirē's tomb will be taken as the norm, with other tombs brought in as parallels.

81[10]). Through this sacred enclosure the tomb owner passed on his way to the necropolis. Its verdant appearance, with copious streams of water, emphasizes the deceased's needs in the cemetery, where moisture is scarce. Otherwise, the slaughtered cattle and rows of shrines suggest that there were certain powers that must be appeased before the deceased could enter the realm of the dead. Other stages of the funeral procession are seen below (registers 7–11), with rows of servants bearing the deceased's funerary equipment and miscellaneous offerings. In register 9 (left) we see the tomb owner seated on a jar, while two other men pour streams of water over him: this will be seen in later tombs as the purification of the deceased's statue (Th 107[1]) or his mummy. In yet another sequence, obelisks are set up, the earth is hacked, and shrines are purified (register 5, centre), while the *teknu* lies on a chair in the feigned sleep of death (cf. Th 96[1]). Perhaps these rites before the tomb anticipate the tomb owner's resurrection, along with the rising sun.

Egyptian conservatism in religious matters kept such vignettes in the repertory of private tomb decoration long after the ceremonies themselves had changed. At the same time, new currents were making themselves felt. The appearance of the gods in Rekhmirē's tomb – of Osiris, lord of the underworld; Anubis, jackal-headed patron of embalmers; and the goddess of the western cemetery – is itself significant, for it continues a fairly recent expansion of a private person's right to address the gods directly (cf. Th 15[5]). The adaptation of the king's mortuary cult for the common man – a process that had been going on since the end of the Pyramid Age – is increasingly reflected in private tombs, particularly starting with the New Kingdom. The mummy of the deceased is now prepared by Anubis himself (Th 1[4]; 96[3]) and he is judged in the presence of Osiris: his heart, seat of the emotions and the intellect, is weighed against a feather that represents the principle of Ma'at, the order of the universe and timeless measure of rectitude. If the sins piled on the deceased's heart outweigh the precepts of Ma'at, he is thrown to the 'Devourer', a demon whose appearance combines the worst features of a crocodile and a hippopotamus. If, however, the test does not go against him, he emerges 'triumphant' against any accusation of wrongdoing and may enter paradise. (Among many examples, see Th 1[4]; 69[5]; 78[6]; 296[1, 3].)

The acceptance of Osiris as lord of the dead widened the ethical focus of Egyptian religion and had a profound effect on private expressions of piety. Especially in the Middle Kingdom, people from all walks of life outfitted not only a tomb in their locality, but also a cenotaph, or dummy tomb, at Abydos. Here, in the district of Osiris, a small chapel built around a stela commemorating the tomb owner and his family served to place him under the god's protection and guarantee him eternal life. Abydos became a renowned place of pilgrimage, especially during the annual mysteries that celebrated the god's triumph over the forces of evil represented by the followers of Seth.[4] As of

---

4. According to a legend that is most completely preserved in Graeco-Roman sources, Osiris was murdered by his brother Seth, who dismembered the body and scattered the parts throughout the world. They were collected by Osiris' sister, Isis, and buried at Abydos, though not before Osiris miraculously reconstituted himself and engendered a son on Isis. The child, Horus, was raised to manhood by his mother and eventually defeated the forces of Seth. The contendings of these two beings, both in the field and at the tribunal of the Lord of All, as well as the compromise achieved between them, were both popular literary themes in ancient times and they concretely illustrate the Egyptian idea of Ma'at as the balance between two opposing forces.

the Middle Kingdom, this pilgrimage (like the journey to Sais in the Old Kingdom) was frequently shown in the tombs, with the coffin proceeding on board ship to Abydos and returning thence to be buried (Th 57[8]; 60[2]; 69[6]; 78[5]; 81[10]; 100[11]; 279[1–2]). ▷ ABYDOS, Chapter 16, pp. 207–13.

A more realistic view of the funeral rites begins to appear in the tombs of the mid-Eighteenth Dynasty at Thebes. Again the sequence begins with the crossing of the Nile: the coffin, enclosed in a catafalque, is generally preceded by one or more boats filled with the burial party, but the principal difference from earlier examples is found in the professional mourners – wailing women with dishevelled hair and streaming eyes who swarm over the ships and strike theatrical postures of grief (Th 49[4]; 181[2–3]). Modern descendants of this breed may still be found today, setting up their ululating cry whenever a member of the community dies.

On reaching the western side, the funerary procession is formed, a characteristic example being found in the tomb of the vizier Ramose (Th 55[4]). In the top register we see the principal members of the burial party. Two catafalques are shown, one for the coffin and the other for the canopic chest. The place of honour at the rear of the procession is taken by the four High Priests of Amun – the dead man, after all, had been one of the prime ministers for the entire land – and other high officials pull the sledges on which the catafalques rest. In front of them is the familiar figure of the *teknu*, who is trundled along by a mixed team of men and oxen while a priest sprinkles drops of milk

before the beasts to 'purify the way'.[5] The lector priest marches in front of the procession, his papyrus in his hands, ready to pronounce the ritual, followed by his lay acolytes, their arms raised in adoration. Below, in the second register, we see other persons in the cortège – the members of the deceased's family at the left end and the offering bearers who transport the burial equipment to the tomb. A gaggle of wailing women comes next, and the procession reaches the door of the tomb with a mixed assortment of priests, relatives and offering bearers (cf. Th 49[4]; 181[2]).

The focus of Ramose's funeral procession is the Western Goddess, who stands behind the tomb to welcome the deceased into the necropolis. The tomb itself is a tall round-topped building, with a band of small circular shapes forming a frieze below the roof.[6] Offerings are laid out before the entrance, sometimes in small open kiosks with grape vines trailing from their trellised roofs (Th 181[3]). Later, under the Ramessides (Dynasties XIX–XX), the tomb is shown as rectangular in shape, preceded by a portal and a columned porch. Surmounting the building is a small pyramid (see above, p. 69) which is often flanked by effigies of Anubis, while a paean to the deceased's virtues is carved on to the stela set up outside (Th 296[3]).

The final ceremonies at the tomb revolved around a ritual known as the 'opening of the mouth', whereby the mummy was made into a sentient being, capable of using its eyes, ears, nose and mouth. A fairly full (and thus repetitive) account of this ceremony is found in the tomb of Rekhmirē (Th 100[15]), with abbreviated versions in other tombs (e.g., Th

---

5. This group is more frequently shown pulling the deceased's own sledge (see Th 181[2]).

6. These are clay funerary cones, baked hard and set into the mud-plaster facing of the tomb's front court as a decorative feature. Though these objects have no aesthetic appeal out of context, they are often of interest in that the blunt end of the cone is stamped with the deceased's name and titles, thus enabling one to identify the owners of tombs whose interiors have been destroyed.

69[6]). Since a large part of this rite consisted of touching the mummy's mouth with various instruments, notably an adze – thus, perhaps, 'putting the finishing touches' on the deceased in his new form? – these objects, along with various shrines and canopic jars, are sometimes shown assembled for the tomb owner's benefit and his eternal use (Th 57[1]). More often, they are seen in the hands of priests officiating before the tomb (Th 56[2]). In the more detailed funerary scenes (Th 181[3]) the lector priest is seen reading a spell while another priest holds the adze in readiness and a colleague pours water over the mummy or a statue of the deceased (cf. Th 55[2]; 57[8]; 96[6]; 107[2]). Another, rather cruel ritual involved amputating the foreleg of a living calf (Th 296[3]) and presenting it to the mummy. Since the hieroglyph of the foreleg signifies 'strength' or some similar idea, it may be that this ritual transferred the vital force of a still-living being to the deceased.

At the close of the funeral rites the deceased was believed to have passed from his previous mode of existence into the state of the blessed dead. Thus would he continue to exist, both in the necropolis and in the nether world, sustained by the offerings of his mortuary cult or (if need be) by the magical substitutes displayed on the walls of the tomb. But this was not the deceased's only link with the land of the living. The ties between the living and the dead were also maintained through yearly festivals such as the Feast of Sokar, when this inert god of the dead passed through the necropolis.

▷ MEDINET HABU, FESTIVAL COURT, Chapter 18, p. 271.

Another, more popular occasion of this sort was the 'Beautiful Feast of the Valley' through which the community of the living reaffirmed its ties to the ancestors in the necropolis. The festival began when Amun, state god of Thebes, left his temple to cross over to the mortuary temple of the reigning king on the west bank: the populace of Thebes followed in the wake of the procession and, on reaching the other side of the river, scattered to visit their relatives in the cemetery. Soon the necropolis was filled with the unaccustomed sound of revelry, as a ritual meal was laid before statues of the deceased and the living banqueted in honour of the dead. Later, when the state ritual at the temple had come to an end, the god's servants were sent to bear his greetings to the revered dead. Troupes of lay priests, singers, dancers and priestesses devoted to Hathor, Mistress of the West, now made their way through the necropolis and sanctified the tombs as they passed (Th 96[1]). As a concrete sign of divine favour, the family now presented the deceased with the Bouquet of Amun: especially blessed under the great god's aegis, this token symbolically extended to its recipient the wish for a long (or, in this context, eternal) life.[7] In the tombs, the deceased is characteristically shown presenting bouquets to his ancestors and receiving them himself from his closest relatives (Th 56[2–3]; 74[1]; 96[7, 8]).[8]

Whatever the tomb owner's bonds to the world of the living, his place was still in the

---

7. In Egyptian the words 'bouquet' and 'life' sounded much the same and were spelt in almost the same way (roughly, *ankh*).

8. A modern survival of this and other visits to the dead in antiquity has been seen in the custom practised today at the 'smaller feast', after the month of Ramadan, when the Muslim community celebrates the end of the fast by visiting the cemetery, decorating the tombs with palm branches and distributing baskets of food to the poor in the name of the deceased.

tomb and the netherworld. Mythological scenes that reflect the fate of the deceased after death begin to appear in the Eighteenth Dynasty, showing him at work in the 'Field of Reeds', a vast estate where he was expected to labour as a peasant – albeit in the most favourable conditions. Although high officials and even kings did not disdain to show themselves thus employed (Th 1[5]; 57[8]; cf. Medinet Habu Temple of Ramesses III, Room 26, North Wall), they characteristically preferred to have servants work for them. Thus developed the little wooden figures called *shabtis* (or *shawabtis*) who acted as substitutes for the master. As time went by, prosperous Egyptians kept masses of these figurines in their tombs, one for each day of the year, as well as overseers, as in any well-run household. The figures were now also made of stone or ceramic and were called *ushabtis* because they 'answered' (*ushab*) for the deceased when he was called for work in the fields of paradise. Along with the servant statues placed in tombs of the Old and Middle Kingdom, they are the mainstay of many Egyptian collections in the world's museums today.

Other scenes show the strange beings that the tomb owner might meet in the realm beyond death – the serpent Apophis, enemy of the sun god, Rē, as he passes through the caverns of the night, shown providentially cut to pieces by a friendly cat (Th 1[1]; 359[4]); or the tree goddess, dispensing water to the tomb owner in his dry abode in the West (Th 1[ceiling]; 49[6]; 96[4]); or the Bull of Heaven, with the Seven Celestial Cows and the sacred oars that delimit the four corners of the sky, whose protection is secured by the tomb owner on his way across the heavens (*Tutankhamun*, West wall). At Thebes especially, the tomb owner pays particular reverence to the goddess Hathor who, as the Mistress of the Western Mountain, is seen issuing from the mountainside in the form of a cow (Th 296[3]).[9]

The presence of these vignettes in private tombs only re-emphasizes the extent to which the royal hereafter had been appropriated for general use. For, as expressed in the Pyramid Texts, 'the king belongs to the sky', and the ruler's triumph over death was seen in terms of the sun's victory over the forces of darkness. In the royal tombs (see Chapter 7) the dead king was associated with the sun's journey through the underworld and its glorious rebirth at dawn. Now, private individuals could also take part in this voyage. During the Ramesside period, scenes from the Book of Gates came to enjoy great popularity in the tombs and, in particular, the deceased is often shown worshipping the guardians of the twelve gates that divide the hours of the night (Th 359[1]).

Not only mortal men, however, came to rest in the cemeteries of Egypt. The great god Osiris himself was said to be buried at Abydos, and other cult spots evoked their own memories of the days when the gods ruled on earth. In West Thebes, for instance, was found the tomb of the Ogdoad, the eight creator gods of the religious system of Hermopolis, in Middle Egypt. These beings had been adopted by the Thebans, who 'buried' them at Medinet Habu, on the site of the small temple later incorporated into Ramesses III's mortuary complex. At their head was the local god, Amun, who was himself beginning to acquire the manysidedness of a truly cosmic god. Amun was everywhere – pre-eminently, of course, in his temple at Karnak; but another form of

---

9. This is part of the goddess's traditional iconography: compare similar scenes and features of the Hathor chapels from Thebes (Cairo Museum, Chapter 10, p. 112; Deir el-Bahri, Chapter 18, p. 262); and Dendera, Chapter 16 (pp. 213–21).

Amun dwelt in the Temple of Luxor, and still other manifestations of his godhead resided at various spots on the west bank. As early as the Nineteenth Dynasty, the Amun of Luxor would visit the small temple at Medinet Habu, there to undergo a complex series of changes in which he was successively his own grandfather, father and son. Amun's involvement with the cycle of death and resurrection eventually conferred on him a full range of Osiride characteristics, making him in truth a god of the living and the dead. ▷ MEDINET HABU, SMALL TEMPLE, Chapter 18, pp. 273–4; KARNAK, TEMPLE OF OPET, Chapter 17, p. 236.

Still other parts of the necropolis were reserved for the sacred animals. Egyptians thought it natural that a god should possess a 'living image' on earth — that the divine presence should enter the body of a chosen animal during its lifetime and pass, at its death, into another member of the species. Foreigners regarded this practice as bizarre, even in that idolatrous age, but it was an eccentricity that continued to attract the curious to Egyptian cults. The most famous of the Egyptian sacred animals was the Apis, a bull identified as the living *Ba* of Ptah, Lord of Memphis. Gradually, by a familiar process, he developed ties to Osiris and other deities and, as 'Osorapis', he was finally identified during the Ptolemaic period with 'Serapis', a composite deity whose cult was designed to appeal both to Egyptians and to the Greeks who were settling along the Nile in ever-increasing numbers. The Apis Bull retained his identity throughout all this, however, and despite the erection of a grandiose 'Serapeum' at Alexandria, his sanctuary at Memphis held the respect of the ancient world. The vast catacombs wherein the bulls were buried, as well as other animal cemeteries elsewhere in Egypt, still command the visitor's awe. ▷ SERAPEUM AT SAQQARA, Chapter 13, p. 176; TUNA EL-GEBEL, BABOON AND IBIS GALLERIES, Chapter 15, p. 203.

The cemeteries of ancient Egypt were true necropoleis, 'cities of the dead'. Gods and demigods, kings and mortals, all who constituted Egypt's links with her past were venerated here, and this attitude explains much about the permanence sought for these 'houses of eternity'. Christianity and, later, Islam reversed this emphasis: men who trusted in a salvation beyond this world no longer needed the paraphernalia of earthly life in their tombs. But folkways die hard, and both in the earliest Christian cemeteries and in modern Islamic practice we see, however irrationally, the imprint of the tomb cities of Pharaonic Egypt. ▷ TUNA EL-GEBEL, PRIVATE TOMBS, Chapter 15, pp. 202–3; KHARGA OASIS, CHRISTIAN CEMETERY AT BAGAWAT, Chapter 22, p. 346.

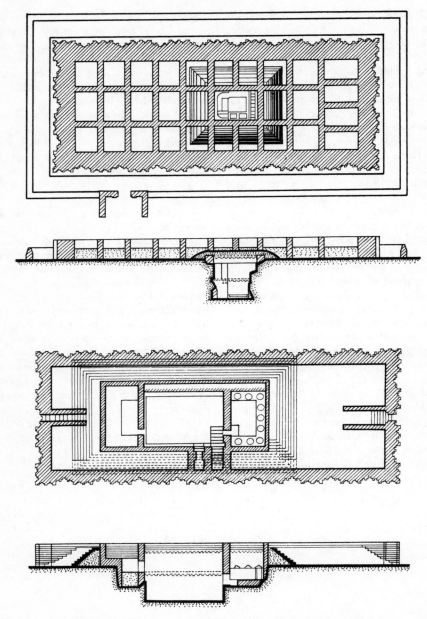

Fig. 2   First Dynasty mastabas (plans and cross-sections): with central mound (*top*); and with stepped central mound (*bottom*)

7. Mansions of Eternity

No monuments are so identified with the mystique of Egypt as the graves of the Pharaohs. From the fabled immensity of the pyramids — above all, the Giza group — to the mysterious corridors of the tombs in the Valley of the Kings, these hypogea have exerted an irresistible fascination for tourists of all periods. Nor is their vogue a modern one. Scribes of the Eighteenth Dynasty left graffiti to attest their admiration of the pyramids at Saqqara and Meidūm, and during the reign of Ramesses II the great tombs in the northern cemetery were refurbished by his son Khaemwēse, the High Priest of Memphis. The Greeks, avid consumers of Egyptian exotica, also marvelled at the royal tombs: modern visitors to the Nile Valley will no doubt recognize something of their local guide's 'tall tales' in Herodotus' account of the Great Pyramid.[1] As stupendous feats of engineering or as supposed repositories of mystic lore, these monuments are the pre-eminent tourist attractions of Egypt.

The prototypes of the great tombs were rather modest buildings of mudbrick, of which the earliest examples (from Dynasties I and II) were found at Abydos and at Saqqara. Known today as *mastabas* (see Chapter 6, p. 68) they consisted of subterranean burial-chambers surmounted by a mound of rubble, the whole then being enclosed within an elaborately niched façade

(see Fig. 2 top). The external appearance of the mastaba is believed to correspond to the ruler's earthly palace, just as the inner mound harkens back to the primitive cairn placed over the pit tombs of prehistoric times. It was this last feature that was probably to develop, first into a solid stepped structure of mudbrick encased within the body of the mastaba, and eventually into the early stepped pyramid that dominated the king's funerary complex (see Figs. 2 bottom; 3).

King Djoser's pyramid at Saqqara, the earliest structure of this type, was originally conceived as a mastaba (Fig. 3, A). Following two successive modifications in the plan, (Fig. 3, B and C), however, the building was re-designed as a pyramid having initially four, then finally six steps (Fig. 3, D and E). The pyramid's original height came to about sixty metres, with base measurements of 121 metres (east to west) by 109 metres (north to south). The burial chambers, as in earlier tombs, were sunk in the bedrock on which the pyramid rested (Fig. 3, F). Various subsidiary buildings, all enclosed within a wall having the familiar 'palace façade' niching of earlier mastabas, made up the remainder of the complex. Along with these innovations in conception and design, King Djoser's monument was the earliest in which stone was employed as the medium for large-scale construction. Beginners' caution

OVERLEAF The step pyramid of King Djoser (Saqqara)

1. *History*, II, 124—6.

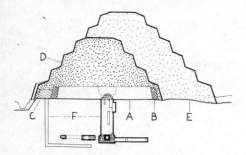

Fig. 3 Evolution of Djoser's tomb from a
mastaba to a stepped pyramid

Fig. 4 The pyramid at Meidūm, section
looking west

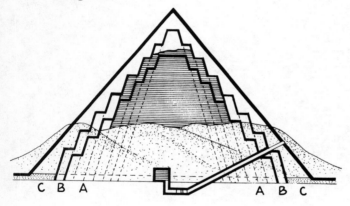

is evident throughout the complex, but it marks the first appearance of what became a traditional dichotomy between mudbrick used in perishable domestic architecture, and the 'good workmanship of eternity' in stone.

The transformation of this early stepped structure into a true geometric pyramid occurred near the beginning of the Fourth Dynasty at Meidūm: the outer courses of this monument have for the most part collapsed, but archaeologists have determined that the originally planned steps (Fig. 4, A and B) were deliberately filled with a smooth limestone casing (C). Another development was the placement of the tomb's entrance above ground level, in the body of the pyramid — apparently a device to foil would-be grave robbers. No mere practical refinement, however, can explain the basic change in design, the source for which is perhaps best sought in the symbolic purpose of the pyramid itself. In Egyptian hieroglyphs, the sign associated with the idea of a stairway was ⌂ : this is also the profile of a stepped pyramid. In the earliest funerary literature we hear of the king's ascent to heaven by means of a stairway formed by the rays of the sun.[2] The association of these symbols is perhaps fortuitous, but the basic pyramidal shape — evocative of the spreading rays of the sun — was also connected with the *benben*, a stone fetish kept in the sanctuary of the sun god Rē at Heliopolis. The evolution of the king's tomb into a true pyramid, then, could be seen as an architectural development that expresses the continuity of religious beliefs in harmony with later mythological concepts.

The apogee of the 'Pyramid Age' was reached with the well-known Giza group (mid-Fourth Dynasty), wherein the builder's art reached a perfection not equalled in later ages. With few exceptions, however, pyramids continued to be built as royal tombs for longer than a millennium, down to the start of the New Kingdom. Construction standards became shoddier with the passing years and most later pyramids seem like shapeless piles of rubble today, though their internal arrangements, with elaborate precautions against robbery, evince considerable ingenuity. Outside, the fully developed complex was equipped with a mortuary temple (usually set against the pyramid's eastern side) and with a smaller, subsidiary pyramid south of the king's monument, which perhaps housed the dead ruler's mummified entrails or represented a separate dwelling for his Ka or his other manifestations. A covered causeway connected this complex (which was surrounded by smaller pyramids of the royal family and by tombs of more distant relatives and high officials) to the edge of the cultivation, where a 'valley temple' allowed formal access to the precinct — especially during the season of high Nile, when goods and personnel must have been discharged at these buildings' quays. Starting

with the Fifth Dynasty and continuing into the Sixth, the walls of the burial chambers inside the pyramid were inscribed with 'Pyramid Texts', a collection of spells (some of them very old even then) intended to provide for the king's resurrection and eternal glory. These, however, were virtually the sole decoration within the royal tombs, which preserved a classic simplicity until the New Kingdom.

It is with the start of the Eighteenth Dynasty at Thebes that the decisive break with tradition occurs. These rulers, abandoning the pyramids of their predecessors, opted instead for hidden tombs in the Theban hills: Thutmose I's builder speaks of excavating his master's tomb, 'no man seeing and no man hearing'; and the earliest tombs, by the remoteness of their location and difficulty of access, do seem to defy the grave robber's efforts. The secret, of course, could not be kept for long: entrusting the work to the men of the village of Deir el-Medina (see Chapter 2, p. 36) was bound to make both the location and internal arrangement of any tomb more or less a matter of public knowledge. The concentration of royal burials in the area now known as the Valley of the Kings did create a sacred precinct apart from private cemeteries at Thebes, however, and it was here that the rulers of the New Kingdom — from the Eighteenth to the Twentieth Dynasties — made their tombs for the next five centuries.

The topography of the royal valley was well suited to the type of tomb that now became standard for Egyptian rulers. Some earlier features are still retained in the tomb plans of the Eighteenth Dynasty — notably in the placement of the burial chamber at an angle to the entrance corridors (generally turning towards the left), an arrangement

---

2. See R. O. Faulkner, *The Ancient Egyptian Pyramid Texts* (Oxford, 1969), p. 183 (Utterance 508, § 1108), 196 (Utterance 523, § 1231).

that perhaps reflects mythic geography of the next world. As from the mid-Nineteenth Dynasty, however, a simpler plan was universally adopted, consisting of a succession of corridors leading in a straight line to the burial chamber. These developments are accompanied by an increasing ripeness in decorative style and a proliferation of the religious 'books' that represented, often in bewildering detail, the stages of the king's resurrection.

'To the sky, to the sky!' This is the dead king's way, to which all creation complies (willingly or by force) in the Pyramid Texts. Salvation here lies in being integrated with the rhythms of nature – to rise and set with the sun or the circumpolar stars – and this theme is continued in the mortuary compositions of the New Kingdom. In the earliest of these 'books', called *What is in the Netherworld*, there are twelve divisions corresponding to the hours of the night, through which the barque of the sun (represented in his 'aged' aspect as a ram-headed deity) progresses towards the dawn (Fig. 5): the array of mythological beings he encounters on the way assists him until he is reborn in the shape of a beetle – the Egyptian symbol for the state of 'becoming' – in the morning. Early copies of this composition appear on the walls of the burial chamber in the tombs of Thutmose III and Amenhotep II, the vignettes being rendered in a simple, even severe, style reminiscent of a papyrus manuscript, from which they were undoubtedly drawn.

Other mortuary texts find their way into the royal tombs by the end of the Eighteenth Dynasty. Similar in theme and even format to the *Book of What is in the Netherworld*, they nonetheless shape and combine mythological material in ways that are only implied in earlier compositions. In the *Book of Gates*, for instance, the fifth stage of the sun's journey takes place in the judgement hall of Osiris

(Fig. 6), where a follower of the hostile god Seth (in the form of that taboo animal, the pig) is belaboured by a monkey, canonically one of the 'worshippers of Rē' at his rising owing to the fearful clamour these animals raise at dawn. Each of the night's twelve hours is marked by a portal with its guardian serpent, and in the concluding episode Nūn, god of the watery abyss, is seen rising up with the barque of the sun held triumphantly in his arms (Fig. 7).

Still other compositions depart altogether from the genre's traditional 'divisions', while retaining its thematic core. The action of the *Book of Caverns*, to give one example, is played on two levels. On top we see the journey of the sun, who is gradually transformed from his aged ram's figure into the sacred beetle of the reborn disc. Note the oval envelopes or 'coffins' which enclose a number of the sun god's followers while they wait for new life. The opposite side of this progress – figuratively and literally – is pictured in the lower registers of the sequence, where the enemies of Rē are marshalled and finally annihilated at dawn (Fig. 8). The complementary 'Books' of the Day and the Night, on the other hand, view the cycle in terms of the sky goddess, Nūt: her figure, personifying the vault of heaven, stretches across the top of the entire scene, as she swallows the sun in the evening (Fig. 9) in order to give birth to it at dawn (Fig. 10). The vast repertoire of mythical beings in all these 'Books' seemingly defies analysis. *In situ*, however – with astronomical vignettes on the ceilings, to allow the deceased to tell the time and plot his way through the night sky – these compositions must be seen as providing the tomb owner with the information he would need if his celestial destiny were to be fulfilled.

The king's apotheosis was reinforced by the ceremonies held in his mortuary temple: here the funeral rites took place, and also the

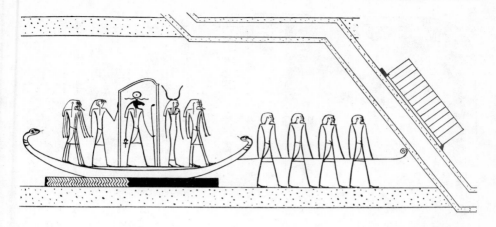

Fig. 5   The Night-Barque of the Sun, from *The Book of What is in the Underworld* (from A. Piankoff, *The Tomb of Ramesses VI*, Fig. 77, Pantheon Books, New York, 1954)

Fig. 6   The Judgement Hall of Osiris, from *The Book of Gates* (A. Piankoff, op. cit., Fig. 45)

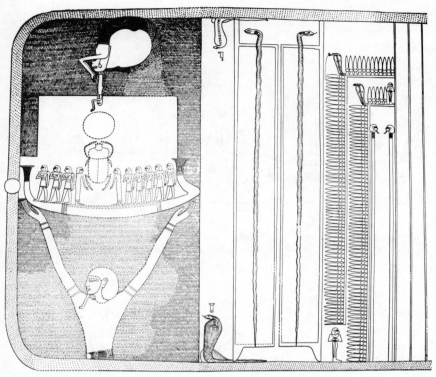

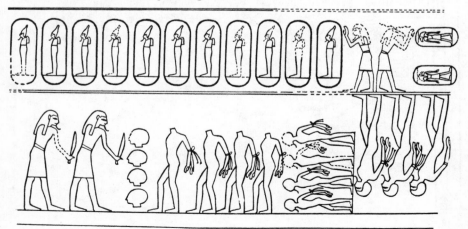

Fig. 7   Sunrise, from *The Book of Gates* (A. Piankoff, op. cit., Fig. 73)

Fig. 8   The 'Coffins' of the Unborn Gods (*top*), and the Enemies of the Sun (*bottom*), from *The Book of Caverns* (A. Piankoff, op. cit., Fig. 11)

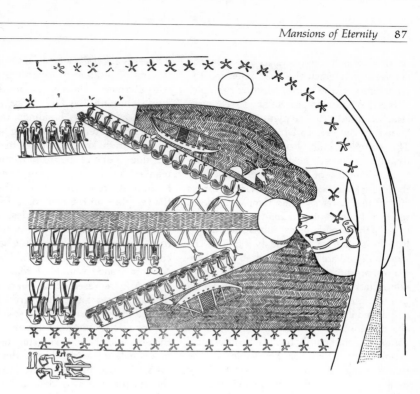

Fig. 9   The Sky-Goddess Nūt swallows the Evening Sun, from *The Book of Day* (A. Piankoff, op. cit., Fig. 133)

Fig. 10   The Rebirth of the Sun, from *The Book of Day* (A. Piankoff, op. cit., Fig. 130)

continuing cult designed to maintain the connection between the dead ruler and the community of the living. Mortuary temples in the Old Kingdom, as we have seen, were attached directly to the pyramid, but little is known of the uses to which they were put. The complex built around King Djoser's pyramid consisted mostly of dummy structures, simulacra of buildings employed by the living king, here rendered in stone for his eternal use. Later pyramid temples all seem to have been equipped for the worship of royal statues (perhaps as 'substitute bodies', like the statues of individuals found in the *serdabs* of private tombs); and all had sanctuaries, presumably with false doors through which the dead king could re-enter the world of men. Since the private mortuary cult is largely a democratization of a system originally designed for the king, the latter's tomb complex would hardly have lacked the ritual defences provided for his subjects. The ruined condition of most older funerary temples, along with the overall lack of inscriptions, makes a more precise analysis difficult, though hypothetical reconstructions of their cultic purposes have been suggested from time to time.

The New Kingdom, once again, witnessed a break with tradition. Since the topography of the royal valley discouraged extensive constructions above ground, mortuary temples were now erected far from the tombs, at the border between the Theban hills and the cultivation. Thanks to the preservation of a number of these structures, with their reliefs and inscriptions, we know something about the way in which they functioned. All the Theban mortuary temples lay within the 'Estate of Amun', a god who already by the Middle Kingdom was absorbing characteristics of other deities, including gods of the dead. Deceased rulers, as the gods of their mortuary temples, were identified with the form of Amun worshipped there: the deified

Ramesses III, for instance, was regarded as 'Amun-Rē residing in [the temple] "United with Eternity"'. Emerging from the netherworld through the false door (which remained, as in earlier buildings, the focus of the mortuary temple), the king would take his place in the main sanctuary to receive the cult due to one of the many forms of Amun manifest in the territory of Thebes. More traditional rites were held in other parts of the temple — in the sun court, for instance, where the king's celestial destiny (as developed in the religious 'books' found in the royal tombs) was celebrated. Chapels dedicated to Hathor, mistress of the Western Mountain, and to Anubis, lord of embalmers, were also represented, as were the king's deified ancestors and other 'great gods' who figured in the afterlife of the sovereign.

Nor was the mortal ruler, the vehicle for the principle of divine kingship, neglected. A model palace was attached to the temple for his spirit's use, and in a suite of rooms near the sanctuary he was identified with Osiris, ruler of the underworld. In this he differed from the common man who achieved the status of an 'Osiris' only after his life had passed the scrutiny of the nether gods. The king, on the other hand, exercised the prerogatives of a blessed soul without question: his 'justification before the Great God' was never in doubt because at death he *became* Osiris, while his successor took his place on the 'Horus-throne of the living'. Nothing illustrates the eclecticism of Egyptian religion so well as the composite personality of the king, with its varied human and divine aspects. The mortuary temple, standing at the point where the two spheres met, tried to do justice to both.

The civil war at the end of the Twentieth Dynasty brought an end to the proud sequence of tombs and temples in West Thebes. Given the quasi-independent posture of the south, where ruling High Priests of Amun occasionally claimed royal status, the royal tombs of the reigning house were pointedly moved elsewhere – to Tanis, for instance, where a number of royal burials from the Twenty-first and Twenty-second Dynasties were found (see below, Appendix, pp. 354–5). Most Egyptian rulers of the late period were probably buried in the Delta, where adverse conditions for archaeology no doubt explain the paucity of material evidence for royal tombs. Even the great monuments of the Ptolemaic age in Alexandria – the *Sema* in which the remains of Alexander the Great rested, the imposing mausoleum of the Ptolemies, and the separate tomb which Cleopatra VII had built for herself and Mark Antony – survive only in the descriptions made by ancient writers: the buildings themselves have vanished.

But the ancient tombs were not forgotten. Reports from investigations of alleged tomb robberies during the late Twentieth Dynasty show that many tombs, both royal and private, were being pillaged during these economically blighted times. The royal tombs at Memphis had doubtless been violated as much as a thousand years earlier. At Thebes, the ruling priesthood ultimately confronted the issue by removing the royal mummies from their ravaged tombs: the corpses were rewrapped, placed in what was left of their coffins and secretly disposed in two 'caches' (one above Deir el-Bahri, the other in the tomb of Amenhotep II), where they remained for nearly three millennia until their discovery in the late nineteenth century. A few tombs miraculously escaped despoliation and were forgotten – most notably the burial of Tutankhamun, which was discovered amidst great international excitement in 1922. The other tombs, stripped of their contents, lay open to the casual visitor. Graffiti on their walls (mostly in Greek and Latin) record the admiration, bemusement, or often simply the presence of tourists during late antiquity: even an illiterate serving-man – 'Tekhos (?), called Dionysis' – could leave his name in the tomb of Ramesses VI, with the pathetic note, 'My mistress wrote [this].' During the Middle Ages, the shaft tombs suffered, at worst, a temporary occupation by squatters. At Giza, however, the pyramids lost their subsidiary buildings and much of their outer casing to the building of modern Cairo. The face of the Great Sphinx (according to a tradition preserved by Arab writers) was mutilated by religious fanatics in the fourteenth century A.D. It is the rediscovery of Egypt in the last two centuries, with the influx of interested tourists and scholars, that has done most to arrest the deterioration of the royal tombs and to restore them to the legacy of mankind.

Statue head of Graeco-Roman 'Pharaoh' (Yale University, Peabody Museum)

8. Graeco-Roman Twilight

When Alexander the Great entered Egypt in the autumn of 332 B.C., he came ostensibly as the latest in a long train of conquerors. For the previous four centuries, Egyptians had endured foreign rule by Nubians, Assyrians and Persians with spasmodic assertions of independence. The Macedonians were welcomed as deliverers from the hated Persian yoke, but nationalist sentiments still stirred in a country recaptured by Persia barely a decade before. Few would have suspected, especially when Alexander died suddenly in 323 B.C., how permanent the new state of affairs would be. For the next millennium, first under the dynasty founded by the Macedonian general Ptolemy and then — after 30 B.C. — under imperial Rome, Egypt's destiny was inseparable from that of the rest of the Mediterranean world.

The later history of Egypt is to a great extent the history of its foreign residents. Greeks and Macedonians — due to the overpopulation of their homelands — swarmed into the Middle East; in Egypt, as elsewhere, they were welcomed with land and privileges. A grant of property, called a cleruchy, was made to any foreign mercenary who settled in Egypt, so long as he held himself liable for military service. Such grants were frequently passed on from one generation to the next, creating a class of small landholders loyal to the crown and set apart from the great mass of native peasants. These Greek settlers formed their own local organizations, were governed by their own laws, and had legal matters adjudicated in different courts from those used by the Egyptian populace. These provisions, enacted early in the Ptolemaic period, were broadly retained by the Romans, who further enhanced the position of the Hellenized elite by institutionalizing its social organization. Magistrates selected from the ranks of this upper crust undertook religious, educational and local economic duties under the supervision of the home governors. Such offices — initially honorary or purely administrative in character — would eventually assume a sinister importance as the Hellenized bourgeoisie increasingly had to shoulder the burdens of the establishment to which they belonged.

The jewel of the Greek East and the hub of Egypt was Alexandria. Founded by the conqueror on a shrewd assessment of the site's commercial possibilities, the city surpassed all expectations, remaining the capital of Egypt for the next thousand years and achieving an economic and intellectual eminence matched only by Rome and eventually by Constantinople in the ancient world. Its Library and 'Museum' — the latter a research institute devoted to various branches of scientific and literary study — came to be virtually synonymous with the concept of higher learning and fostered a tradition of scholarship that persisted, even under adverse conditions, into the fifth century of the Christian era. The Ptolemies' administration was centred in Alexandria, and many of the most important servants of the crown — ministers, ambassadors and the like — came from the ranks of its citizens. The cosmopolitan populace, while dominated by Greeks, included Egyptians and other Orientals, among them the largest and most influential Jewish community outside Palestine. Even today, Alexandria seems to be a Mediterranean, rather than an Egyptian, city. Its special character was emphasized in antiquity by an organization of its citizens along the lines of the classic Greek city-state, although (owing to the unruly behaviour of its 'numberless people') the political machinery that went with it was suppressed a great deal of the time.

Life under the Romans (who also governed Egypt from Alexandria) was much less brilliant. The city's commercial vitality, though, could not be extinguished, outrunning even the prosperity which its location and fine harbours had brought it under the Ptolemaic kings. Exports of produce and of manufactures — glass- and metalwares, textiles and pottery, along with specifically local products such as faience, perfumes and papyri — flowed through the city. And it was Egyptian grain, shipped from Alexandria, that supported the cash-crop economies of Greece and Rome during late antiquity. The city was also well placed to act as the middleman for the rich eastern trade with India and southern Africa that came in from the Red Sea. ▷ ALEXANDRIA AND ENVIRONS, Chapter 11, pp. 133–43; ANCIENT HERMOPOLIS (ASHMUNEIN), Chapter 15, pp. 199–200.

Culturally, then, the East was now firmly inside the Greek orbit. But true Hellenism, with its accent on individual rights and achievements, was doomed to a hot-house existence in the successor states that followed Alexander. This was nowhere truer than in Egypt which the Ptolemies governed as their personal estate. All land, with a few stated exceptions, belonged to the crown. Products such as oil and papyrus were government monopolies, and most residents of Egypt paid a poll tax, over and above the normal levies that swelled the royal exchequer. The results might have been benefi-

cial had the Ptolemies viewed the country's welfare as their own. Instead, the wealth of Egypt was dissipated in the wars resulting from Ptolemaic ambitions in the Mediterranean, commerce was disrupted, and the land itself neglected.

The Roman takeover of Egypt in 30 B.C. restored the country's economic stability, but made no fundamental changes in its subject status. The Egyptian grain that fed Italy was too vital, and Egypt itself too easily defensible, for the emperors to risk any trouble from that quarter. Now, more than ever, Egypt was the personal preserve of the sovereign: members of the Roman Senate were forbidden to set foot in Egypt without the emperor's permission, and the imperial prefect — lest he be tempted to aim for the purple by himself — was appointed from the relatively humble ranks of Rome's Equestrian order. The initial impact of Roman rule seemed positive enough. Augustus set his army to clearing out the irrigation system which the last Ptolemies had neglected, and Tiberius rebuked a prefect who had sent taxes in excess of the stated amount with the words, 'You should shear my sheep, not flay them.' But the system itself was vicious. Designed to squeeze out the greatest possible profit for the Treasury, it emerged in all of its repressiveness during the later Empire, when the government's demands ran parallel with the progressive impoverishment of the taxpayers. Local gentry were held responsible for a variety of administrative and financial burdens, and their assumption of the magistracies that went with them was enforced by increasingly savage penalties. To such a state had Egypt fallen during the last centuries of her ancient history.

The exploitative character of foreign rule was no doubt felt most keenly by the native Egyptians who formed the bulk of the population. True, they were ruled according to their traditional laws and customs, but otherwise they enjoyed few benefits from either the Ptolemaic or the Roman government. Belonging mostly to the peasant or artisan class, they were subject not only to the common taxes, but also to *corvée* labour on government projects, from which Greek settlers were exempt. Of course, there is no reason to believe that the peasants' lot was that much better under the Pharaohs; but never before had native Egyptians experienced such sweeping discrimination from a master class. Unlike the Greek immigrants, Egyptians did not have any larger forms of political or social organization that were recognized before the law. High government offices were filled mostly by men of Greek ancestry, and an Egyptian would have to acquire a second language – Greek – as well as some of the cultural attitudes that went with it before he could hope for even the lowliest post in the administration. Egyptians, in effect, suffered dispossession within their own country; and in this respect the period of Graeco-Roman rule differed from all previous foreign occupations of the Nile Valley. Rebellions occasionally erupted in Upper Egypt, but nationalist feeling could not prevail against professional armies. The pattern was destined to repeat itself for over two millennia, and it is only within this last century that native Egyptians have regained full mastery over their land.

The cultural imperialism of the Graeco-Roman age is clearly expressed in the religious policies of the Ptolemies and of Rome. It is not that native religion was persecuted – we shall see that it received state patronage – but rather that the most prestigious cults were those that appealed to the Hellenized elite. Prominent among these were the cults devoted to deified rulers of the past and, later, to the genius of the living emperor; but the most significant was the worship of Serapis. The genesis of this god is obscure, but most authorities are agreed that he was

brought to Alexandria from Asia Minor under the first two Ptolemies. He appears characteristically as an old man with flowing hair and beard; a bushel, symbolic of plenty, rests upon his head, and at his side crouches Cerberus, the dread hound that guarded the entrance to the Classical Greek underworld. Just about the same blend of vegetative and chthonic symbols is found in the god Osor-Hapi, the Apis Bull of Memphis, who contributed his name and his Egyptian identity to the Alexandrian Serapis and profited greatly thereby. The purpose of this syncretism, however, seems to have been to create for the new Greek settlers a local god with whom they could sympathize rather than one who would bridge the gap between Greeks and natives. The Alexandrian Serapis cult remained essentially a non-Egyptian affair: its rituals, buildings and community of worshippers were always predominantly Greek, and although Serapis came to be virtually identified with Alexandrian religion, he had little currency in the rest of Egypt. ▷ MEMPHIS, RUINS OF SERAPEUM, Chapter 13, pp. 161–3; SAQQARA, CATACOMBS OF THE APIS, Chapter 13, p. 176; ALEXANDRIA, RUINS OF SERAPEUM, Chapter 11, pp. 136–7.

The Egyptian temples, paradoxically, did very well under Graeco-Roman rule. The Ptolemies, and the Roman emperors after them, inherited the trappings of the traditional Egyptian divine kingship and also the Pharaohs' role as the sponsor of all the gods. As kings of Egypt in the native mould, they could control the last great representatives of Egyptian civilization, the local priesthoods, and thus turn all their prestige to the government's benefit. The Western 'Pharaohs' responded with a judicious measure of generosity and regulation. Priests were exempt from personal taxes, though the number of persons allowed on each temple's staff was to be strictly controlled under the Romans. Temple properties constituted a separate category, called 'sacred land', and were administered for them by the state. Temple workshops were exempted from state monopolies, at least to the extent that they were permitted to make certain items (for example, fine linen) for their own use. And, with traditional benevolence, the 'Pharaohs' built lavishly for their gods: the great temples of Dendera, Esna, Edfu, Kom Ombo and Philae, as well as innumerable smaller buildings, are the more obvious relics of their devotion. Equally valuable, though, was the consolidation of many older shrines at this time, without which such monuments as the Temple of Amun at Karnak would be in far worse condition today. Such conspicuous piety demonstrated – however distantly – the government's interest in its Egyptian subjects. Foreign visitors, too, found these buildings to be imposing show-places of the exotic and the occult. Egyptian religion by now had little else to offer: the old self-sufficient view of the world had been blasted away for ever, and though the cult of the mother-goddess Isis retained its popularity throughout the Mediterranean world, Egyptian ritualists at home cloaked their spiritual emptiness in elaborate displays of ritual legerdemain and obscurantist manipulations of the moribund hieroglyphic script. ▷ DENDERA, Chapter 16, pp. 213–21; MEDAMŪD, Chapter 16, p. 223; ESNA, Chapter 20, pp. 301–4; EDFU, Chapter 20, pp. 309–13; KOM OMBO, Chapter 20, pp. 316–18; PHILAE, Chapter 21, pp. 334–5.

Classical paganism, as long as it lasted, could nurture what was left of Pharaonic culture. Without official sponsorship, however, the old Egyptian faith had not the vitality to stand alone. What had begun in A.D. 313, when the Edict of Milan granted formal toleration to the Christians, swept to a triumphant finish in 383, when the pagan temples were closed by order of the Emperor Theodosius. All that remained was to clear away the last vestiges of these outworn faiths. In 391, in response to a recent outbreak of rioting between pagans and Christians, Theodosius decreed that the temple of Serapis, the very symbol of paganism in Alexandria, should be levelled to the ground. Its defenders, recognizing the hopelessness of their cause, abandoned it to its fate, and the Christians – led by the imperial prefect and the Patriarch Theophilus, together with a force of armed men – marched in procession to depose the false god. As the historian Theodoret tells the story, there was a moment of awed silence in the sanctuary when the great statue stood revealed; then Theophilus ordered one of the soldiers to strike it with his axe. A gasp of fright accompanied the first blow; another, and Serapis' head rolled on the ground, while a colony of startled mice poured out of the wormeaten fabric of the idol. Scenes such as this, played out along the length of the Nile Valley, extinguished the last flickering embers of a civilization that had commanded the respect of the civilized world. It had run its course. Now it was only of antiquarian interest.

9. Pharaonic Heritage

Egypt's most enduring gift to the West has been the mystique of her own antiquity. Already, in ancient times, her nearest neighbours acknowledged her as the font of all learning and technology, and the Greeks, whatever their opinion of local customs, regarded Egypt as the mother of medicine, philosophy and the arts. The demonstrable antiquity of Egypt's gods intrigued those who sought a common origin for the pagan religions, and on its own terms the oracle of 'Jupiter–Ammon' at Siwa held its own among the religious centres of the Mediterranean. Religion, in fact, was the chief of Egypt's intangible exports in the ancient world. Especially in late Antiquity, as faith in the Olympian gods waned, Egyptian cults vied successfully with other Eastern religions for the attention of Western man. Isis, 'the Mother of God', enjoyed a tremendous vogue all over Europe, and connoisseurs of religious experience turned to Egyptian mysteries when home-grown beliefs had paled. Even the triumph of Christianity could not dispel this aura of 'mystic Egypt': going underground, through the farrago of late Medieval magic, it has continued to lend its credentials to the 'Tarot of the Egyptians' and other occultist lore.

Some Egyptian contributions were, of course, more substantial. The civil calendar of twelve months and 365 days was successfully modified, first into the Julian and then into the Gregorian calendar that is used today. The division of the day into twenty-four hours, similarly, was first developed in Egypt, passing thence into Greek astronomy and finally into common usage in the Western world. Most Western writers, though, were content to be tourists in Egypt, noting curiosities, but often accepting far-fetched explanations in place of the facts that a more thorough immersion in Egyptian society might have unearthed. Given the methods and viewpoint of the times, it is rather pointless to complain: ancient Egyptian civilization, as embodied in the priestly corporations and the peasants who tilled the soil, was no match for the brilliant Hellenized life of the major cities. Still, the prejudices and flaws of the Greek and Latin authors who dealt with Egypt must be taken into account: their works contain masses of accurate and detailed information, much of it recorded at first hand; but they can be seriously misleading if they are not set beside native Egyptian records.

Until fairly recently, however, the Classical sources were virtually all that Western scholars had to work with. The Christianizing of Egypt destroyed the ancient religion, the only institution that remained in touch with native traditions. The ancient written language died also, leaving the fantastical half-truths of Classical writers in almost sole possession of the field. The Arab conquest only completed the isolation of the Nile Valley from the Western world. With the Mediterranean divided into hostile Saracen and Christian camps, Egypt was virtually *terra incognita* for over a millennium.

The rediscovery of Egypt came during the nineteenth century. For over three centuries previously, it is true, Western travellers had

been making their way into the country and bringing back reports of what they saw. But the full emergence of Egypt into the consciousness of the West came about through a series of providential accidents. In 1798, Napoleon embarked on his Nile campaign. Although it came to an inglorious end several years later, this expedition had two lasting effects. First, the scholars whom Napoleon had brought with his army and who spent their time questioning, sketching and taking notes on everything they saw, be it ancient or modern, often under alarming conditions, ended by producing the groundbreaking *Description de l'Égypte*. This detailed, richly illustrated report on Egypt's contemporary civilization and its monuments aroused the public's interest in things Egyptian. Curiosity might have ebbed, however, but for a chance discovery that supplied the key to the hieroglyphs. In 1799, while looking near Rosetta for stone to strengthen their coastal fortifications against the English, a French detachment came upon a broken stone slab inscribed with ancient characters: hieroglyphic on top, demotic — the cursive writing of the Late Period — in the middle, and Greek on the bottom. Later researches would yield other bilingual texts, but this one was the first, offering the best chance yet for the decipherment of Egyptian language. The importance of this find was seen at once — why else did the English, when they forced the French to evacuate Egypt in 1801, include in their terms a demand for the surrender of the Rosetta Stone? It rests in the British Museum to this day, but it was a Frenchman, again, who succeeded in solving the mystery. By meticulously comparing the Greek with the hieroglyphic and demotic versions of the text, Jean François Champollion was able not only to affirm the correct reading of the names 'Ptolemy' and 'Cleopatra' in Egyptian, but to establish the essentially phonetic nature of the script. By 1822, Champollion was able to read before the Académie Française a paper containing the basic principles of his decipherment. This pioneering work had to overcome the doubts of scholars still influenced by the alleged allegorical significance of Egyptian writing but, by the middle of the century, Champollion's system was overwhelmingly recognized as correct. At last the ancient Egyptians could speak to Western man in their own tongue. The decipherment of the ancient Persian, Babylonian and Assyrian languages that came at about the same time further conspired to put the ancient Near East firmly back on the map, and scholars were able to ride a crest of popular enthusiasm that their own discoveries did much to generate.

In an indirect way, Napoleon's expedition also helped to make Egypt more accessible to foreign visitors. By 1806, the ruling Mameluke class, discredited by its inability to withstand the French, had been exterminated by a Balkan adventurer named Mohammed Ali. Having secured Turkish recognition of himself as Pasha of Egypt, Mohammed Ali embarked on an all-out policy of modernization: agriculture was improved and Western industries introduced. Young Egyptians were now sent abroad to acquire technological skills; but Mohammed Ali, impatient of delay, also encouraged qualified Europeans to live and work in Egypt, and his welcome embraced those scholars who were bent on reading Egypt's ancient history from the walls of her monuments. In 1828–9, Champollion and his Italian colleague, Ippolito Rossellini, journeyed through the Nile Valley, copying inscriptions as they went. A

'Cleopatra's Needle' on the Thames Embankment, London

better-organized and munificently funded expedition came (1842–5) when Karl Richard Lepsius led a team of draftsmen and architects through Egypt and the Sudan on a commission from the Royal Prussian government. These scholarly forays prepared the way for the continuing fieldwork that has been carried out since the late nineteenth century by government-sponsored institutes, by privately constituted bodies such as the Egypt Exploration Fund (later, Society) of Great Britain, and by museums and universities, of which the Epigraphic Survey of the University of Chicago's Oriental Institute (U.S.A.) is an example.

Hard on the scholars' heels came the collectors — men whose aim was the acquisition and removal of antiquities. By and large, this was a new departure in Egypt. The Romans, to be sure, had carried off imposing curiosities — obelisks and large statuary — to decorate their capitals and imperial residences,[1] but Egypt seems to have been spared the kind of systematic looting that deprived Greece of so many of her art treasures. Centuries of neglect and vandalism have taken their toll. During Champollion's visit, newly discovered tombs at Saqqara were being broken up so that their painted reliefs might grace the walls of wealthy householders in Cairo. Ancient buildings were the quarries for the new: many a Medieval town was built out of the debris of Pharaonic cities and, even in the nineteenth century, Mohammed Ali did not scruple at getting material for his new sugar factories by razing whole temples at Armant and

Elephantine. But this, in ages less historically minded than our own, was hardly unusual: the Pharaohs themselves had 'reused' their predecessors' monuments in this way. Such sporadic despoliation was accelerated, though, as museum officials and private entrepreneurs tried to satisfy the demand for antiquities that a revival of interest in ancient Egypt had done so much to stimulate.

Early collectors conducted their operations on a scale that excites mingled astonishment and alarm. During the first thirty years of the nineteenth century, men like Bernardino Drovetti and Henry Salt — respectively the French and British Consuls-General — behaved like pirate chieftains, sending their agents all over Egypt in search of papyri and *objets d'art* which would eventually be sold to museums in London, Turin, Paris and Berlin. Later, as conditions began to settle down under Mohammed Ali's successors, restrictions were placed on the more outrageous forms of lawlessness. An Antiquities Service was established in 1858 to supervise the clearing and consolidation of the monuments, and a national museum to house the objects found in the field. Trade in antiquities was thus restricted, although in fact there were a host of ways, legal and otherwise, whereby pieces of 'museum quality' might be acquired.[2] Dispersal of Egyptian treasures into foreign museums did have a positive side, for it awakened the public to a fuller appreciation of the richness and diversity of Egyptian art, and thus created an atmosphere that was conducive to research. Contemporary apologists also argued that the objects

---

1. The mudbrick emplacement for the scaffolding used to lower an obelisk in the court between the seventh and eighth pylons at Karnak (see below, Chapter 17, p. 235) can still be seen *in situ*; the obelisk probably went to Constantinople.

2. No one with a bit of larceny in his soul will find it easy to resist the exploits of Sir E. A. Wallis Budge, who visited Egypt in 1886–8, 1896 and 1902 as an agent for the British Museum and published an account of his activities in the autobiographical *By Nile and Tigris* (London: John Murray, 1920).

were better off in foreign museums, rather than in Egypt where the chances of careless destruction were great. What this rationalization produced, however, was a vicious circle, as the demand for Egyptian art fostered the very treasure-hunting mentality that placed the monuments in such danger. The problem is still with us today. Visitors to Egypt will see, in the ravaged antiquities that still stand, all too many reminders of human indifference and greed.

The century and a half since Champollion's decipherment have seen changes, both in Egyptology and in the conditions under which it is practised. Gone are the freewheeling days of exploration — of unsupervised 'digs' and of the gifted dilettante, floating down the Nile on his houseboat; the specialist has replaced the gentleman-at-large. The tide of nationalism, similarly, has swept away European control of the Antiquities Service, which since 1952 has been staffed exclusively by Egyptians. To some, there is a sense of lost romance: certainly, nothing within the last fifty years has matched the excitement that greeted the discovery of Tutankhamun's tomb in 1922. What is generally forgotten is that this excavation was a model for its time, marking a new era of professionalism in field archaeology; and that the aftermath, however unpleasant, established Egypt's sovereign right over her own antiquities. The last quarter-century has witnessed an encouraging pattern of international co-operation, as the nations of the world have worked with Egypt, and with each other, to save the Nubian monuments from the waters blocked by the Aswan High Dam. The temples of Abu Simbel and Philae, among others, have been preserved, and many other sites have been excavated and studied. Within the discipline itself, there has been a change in emphasis: the collector has given way to the compiler and now, in this century, to the analyst. Vast collections, of both objects and papyri, are stored in museums and universities around the world, waiting to be studied. The by-ways of the Nile Valley are still to be explored with an archaeologist's eye, and major sites must be excavated and recorded properly. In a sense, the discovery of Egypt is just beginning.

PART TWO

10. Cairo and Environs

Cairo, capital of modern Egypt, is the port of entry for most visitors to the country. Located between the east bank of the river and the high limestone cliffs of Mokkattam, it is pre-eminently a Muslim site: the Arab conqueror 'Amr set up his camp at Fustat, north-west of the Roman fortress of Babylon (see below), and the central city of El-Qahira — today the area of the bustling Khan el-Khalili bazaar — was only established in A.D. 973. The wealth of Islamic monuments in Cairo falls outside the scope of this guide, which will confine itself to the few remains of the Roman and Pharaonic ages before proceeding to that great treasure-house of antiquities, the Cairo Museum.

'OLD CAIRO'

Remains of the Roman predecessor of Cairo are found in the southern part of town: ask the taxi-driver to take you to *Masr el-antikka* or (better) *Mari-Girgis*, and you will be deposited in the street of that name. A few metres north of the Greek Orthodox Monastery of St George, a sloping walk takes one below the level of the street and into the old quarter, with its ancient Christian churches. Of particular importance is *Abu Serge*, with the traditionally revered resting-place of the Holy Family in the basement sanctuary: the church itself is dedicated to two Roman soldiers, Sergius and Dacus, who suffered martyrdom. Other points of interest in this quarter are the Church of *St Barbara* and the

Ben Ezra Synagogue, and the traveller should have no difficulty in finding his way to these sites along the well-marked streets.

Back outside, on Mari Girgis Street, turn south towards the two ruined towers that flank the entrance to the Coptic Museum (see Fig. 11): these are remains of the Byzantine fortress of Babylon, the ruined walls of which extend around much of the old quarter. The ancient keep, just south of these towers, is now under the church called *El-Muallaka* or 'hanging church', which was the seat of the Coptic patriarch from the eleventh to the fourteenth centuries and is itself one of the most beautiful of the churches in Old Cairo. The Roman remains can be explored by way of the garden of the Coptic Museum, where a modern staircase leads down into the fort. Owing to the rising ground water, this area is partially flooded, but visitors should be able to make their way along planking laid down for their convenience to the old water gate (Fig. 11, A), from which the last Byzantine governor made his escape during the Arab invasion.

COPTIC MUSEUM

Open daily 9 a.m. to 4 p.m. (winter), 9 a.m. to 1 p.m. (summer), with opening time an hour later on Sundays.

Room 1 (see Fig. 11) contains sculptures of mixed pagan and Christian motifs. Note carved plaques representing David and Bath-

View of modern Cairo

sheba, and Hercules and the lion (south wall); Aphrodite on the half-shell, a bearded bust of a Nile god, and sea-horses with fish (east wall), and nymphs mounted on fish (north wall).

Room 2 has similar objects but different motifs, mostly floral designs. The sixth-century fresco showing the apostles (north wall) is notable.

Room 3: Objects in this room were found at the monastery at Bawit, near Deirut in Upper

Egypt: note the painted niche (east wall, centre) showing Christ in glory over figures of Mary and the apostles.

Rooms 4–7 are filled with fragments of the important monastery of Apa Jeremias at Saqqara (south of the causeway of Unis: see Chapter 13). Many of these are architectural elements sculpted with geometric and floral designs, often intertwined around the central figure of the cross. Evidence of anti-Christian zeal can be seen in the mutilated figures of the apostles in the niches displayed in Room

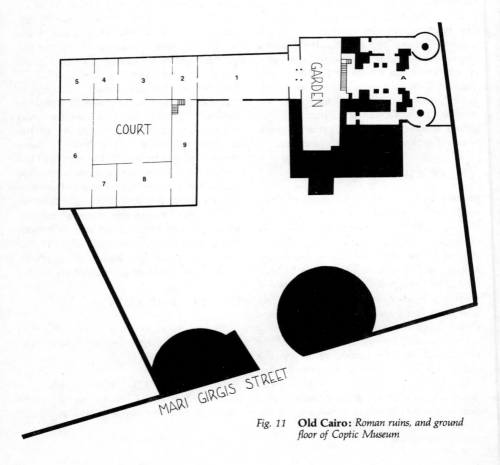

Fig. 11 **Old Cairo:** *Roman ruins, and ground floor of Coptic Museum*

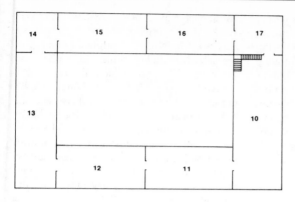

Fig. 12   Upper Floor of Coptic Museum

6, north wall. The episcopal throne found at the monastery is exhibited at the west end of the same room.

Room 8: Some remarkable figured pieces are seen amidst the usual decorative friezes: note the lions chasing a gazelle (west wall, north half) and the stone grilles carved in the shape of a gazelle (centre, north) and an elephant (centre, south). A more conventionally pious note is struck with the contrasting figures of Virgin and child, and of the three children and the angel in the fiery furnace (west wall, south half).

Room 9 is mainly devoted to frescoes: note Adam and Eve (west wall), the geometric and floral designs and the figures of the saints (north and south walls). Paintings from the cycle of St Samuel, son of St Stephen, are shown on the east wall: we see the saint riding side-saddle on horseback, following a larger armed figure, similarly astride.

At the east end of this room a staircase leads to the upper floor (see Fig. 12), into

Room 10: Coptic manuscripts — papyri and ostraca, as well as plain and illuminated codices — are displayed in the cases of this room.

Rooms 11 and 12 contain an exhibit of Coptic textiles, including some well-preserved altar cloths and vestments.

Room 13: Two cases at the west end of this room are filled with small objects — worry-beads, decorative buttons, carved combs of wood and bone, and small icons in cases. Larger icons are displayed about the room: note a fine representation of Saints Peter and Paul in a mother-of-pearl frame (north wall, west), a vivid martyrdom of St Zachary (south wall, east) and (at the south-east corner) two saints with pigs' heads — a curious survival of the compound animal/human divinities of Pharaonic Egypt.

Room 14: Carved wood panelling is displayed on the walls. In the cases there are more small objects — combs, spoons, crosses, clamps and other decorative figures.

Room 15: Metal objects — weapons, lamps and candelabra, pitchers, flasks, censers, and some gold jewellery — are exhibited in the cases.

Room 16 contains objects of devotion: note the large crucifixes (centre, north) and the great gilded book covers (east wall).

Garden: This pleasant spot, opening south of Room 1 on the ground floor, is overhung with balconies shrouded with interesting examples of *mushrabiya* — the elaborately carved wooden lattice-work of the Islamic period. Older fragments are arranged on the portico and in the garden proper — plaques (note the Lamb of God in the portico, east wall), column capitals, stone lions and, curiously, a baboon gargoyle. The Roman fortress is entered at the south end (see above, p. 103).

HELIOPOLIS

Practically nothing remains of this once great city, the 'On' of the Bible, dedicated to the sun god Rē and to Atum, the primeval creator. A suburb, 'Pithom' or Estate of Atum, was built for Pharaoh by the Children of Israel (*Exodus* 1:11), but only the solitary obelisk of Senwosret I is left standing today in the northern Cairo suburb of Mattariya: the location is inconvenient, and few visitors will seek it out.

PETRIFIED FORESTS

Evidence of the lush prehistoric vegetation around Cairo is found in the desert, east of the city. From Mokkattam one may proceed by car (four-wheel drive recommended) east, into the Wadi Lablab to the smaller petrified forest. A larger forest lies east of Maadi, the elegant south suburb of Cairo, at the end of a track up the Wadi el-Tih. Access to these areas is subject to the discretion of the military authorities, and the traveller should secure both a knowledgeable guide and the necessary permits before setting out.

THE EGYPTIAN MUSEUM, CAIRO

The Egyptian national museum for Pharaonic antiquities was created by Said Pasha in 1857, at the urging of the Egyptologist Auguste Mariette. The original building, in the suburb of Bulaq, could not contain the growing collection, which in 1890 was moved to a palace in Giza, and finally to the present building at the northern end of Tahrir Square, constructed by the architect Marcel Dourgnon in 1897–1902. The museum's contents are constantly being shifted or rearranged, but the major pieces may be expected to remain in their places for some time to come. This itinerary reflects conditions in the spring of 1982.

Hours: daily 9 a.m. to 4 p.m. (closed Fridays 11.30 a.m. to 1.30 p.m.).

Garden: Entering the Museum's grounds through the gates at the south end, one comes first upon a broad esplanade, in front of the building. Note the pool, filled with papyrus and lotuses — both rarely found today in modern Egypt — in the centre. Some of the larger pieces in the museum's collection are grouped around the esplanade. Note, in particular, the limestone chapel of a Prince Shoshenq (Third Intermediate Period) at the east end, along with the triad of Ramesses II with Ptah and Sekhmet; the black granite baboon, identified with the god Khonsu, dedicated by Psusennes I (central circle, opposite north-west corner); and the limestone stela of Snefru from Dahshur (museum façade, west of entrance). The marble monument to Mariette, with its bronze statue, is at the west end of the garden.

So vast are the Cairo Museum's collections that an attempt to 'do' it in one day will exhaust the visitor without doing justice to the treasures found there. Three itineraries are accordingly proposed, embracing the ground (I) and upper floors (II, III), allowing a comprehensive stroll through the galleries on three or more visits. Visitors with little time to spend in the Cairo Museum should proceed at once to Itinary II (below, p. 118) which gives an overview of the more spectacular pieces, with special emphasis on objects from Tutankhamun's tomb.

Itinerary I will be devoted to the statuary and other large objects on the ground floor (see Fig. 13). With the exception of the foyer (Rooms 43, 48) and the atrium (see below, pp. 113–15), materials are organized throughout these rooms in roughly chronological order.

Room 48: The foyer is dominated by large statues of Ramesses II placed in three corners of the room: note the divine standards held by the pair which flanks the main entrance. A giant statue (Late Period) of the deified sage

Fig. 13   Cairo Museum, ground floor

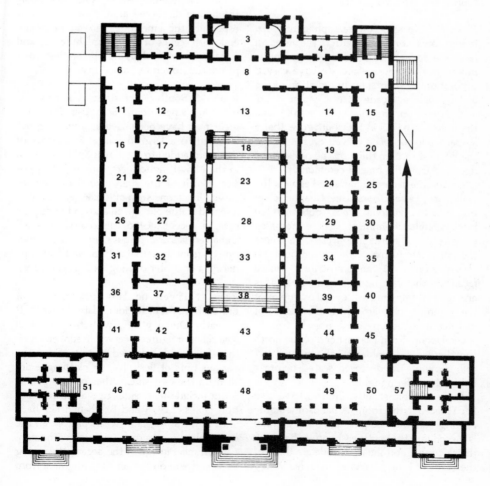

Amenhotep, son of Hapu, stands in the north-east corner. Note also the alabaster panel of the official Ra-wer and the head of King Userkaf (Dynasty V) in the south-west corner. Recent acquisitions by the Museum are periodically displayed in the centre of this room, and also in its northern annex, Room 43. On the west side, in the thickness of the door leading into Room 47, note the two colossal Osiride figures of Senwosret I in limestone, from Karnak (north) and Abydos (south).

Room 47: Old Kingdom sarcophagi are seen in two rows, north and south of the aisle. All have the appearance of massive rectangular boxes, but the more elaborate have carved decoration on their sides in imitation of the archaic palace façade (see Chapter 7, p. 79). Note, on the first (No. 6007) and the last (No. 6170) in the south row, that a leopard skin has been carved on the top of the lid, as if thrown there by the priest as he departed from the funeral ceremonies.

Behind the sarcophagi, ranged against the walls, are 'False Doors' (see Chapter 6, p. 68). Of the various types, note (1) the black granite monument of the nomarch User (No. 632, north side, west end), where the transverse planks of the closed door are clearly shown; (2) an uninscribed 'palace façade' further east, notable for its clean lines and red painting; and (3) several examples of the common type in which the 'door' of matting is rolled up at the portal's top. In several examples at the east end of the north row there is an 'entablature' above the door-roll, showing the deceased seated before a fully laden offering table.

Some notable small sculptures have also been placed in this room. A handsome statue of King Teti (mottled pink and black granite) is tucked into the south-east corner. Between the sarcophagi on the north side are three of the triads of King Menkaurē from his Valley Temple at Giza, each one showing the king flanked by the goddess Hathor (at his right side) and by another figures who represents one of the nomes of Egypt.

Room 46: Beyond the entrance, which is flanked by a matched pair of granite statues of King Senwosret I, the centre of the room is dominated by the seated figure of King Djoser from the *serdab* of his Step Pyramid at Saqqara (see below, Chapter 13, p. 166). Fragments from Old Kingdom tombs are displayed along the walls: note especially the limestone slabs at the south end, with scenes of agriculture, butchery and a harbour with shipping, belonging to a provincial governor named Ipy.

Room 51: South of the stairway is an enormous lion's head found at Abusir: this fragment may have been used as a water-spout attached to a large building. Fragments of the beard added to the Great Sphinx at Giza in the New Kingdom are shown just opposite. North of the stairs, we find a boldly carved limestone stela of one Aperefnetcher, a seated statue of a queen and, in the display case, a recent (1976) discovery of small alabaster vessels, plaques, linen and other objects from the burial of Princess Khamerer-nebty, a daughter of King Isesi (Dynasty V).

Room 41: Limestone slabs from the tomb of one Neferma'at at Meidūm (late Dynasty III or early Dynasty IV), with their unusual treatment of figures – carved in sunken relief, then filled with coloured paste to show the various tints of flesh, hair or clothing – are seen on the east side. Other objects in this room include (east side) two alabaster libation tables (119 A and B), shaped like beds with lion frames; and (west) part of a false door belonging to one Iyneferef, with finely painted relief image of the deceased wearing a leopard skin on the jambs; a fragment from the tomb of Kaemrehu (Saqqara, Dynasty V) showing scenes of agriculture, metalworking and scribes with defaulters; the life-size wooden statue of Tepemankh (Dynasty V); and, near the entrance to Room 36, the false door of Meryrēnefer with its statue of the tomb owner (Dynasty VI, from Edfu).

Room 42: Some of the finest statuary of the Old Kingdom is found here. The famous diorite image of Khafrē (Dynasty IV), protected by the falcon god, Horus, occupies the place of honour in the centre of the room. On its left is the life-size wooden statue of Ka-aper, known as the *Sheikh el-Beled*, 'Chief of the Town', because of the similarity which the workmen who excavated it found between it and a local dignitary. A squatting statue of a scribe, in painted limestone, is on the right. The sides of the room are filled out with statuary and other objects. One of the few extant monuments from the reign of Khufu (apart from the Great Pyramid) is in the south-west corner, a stela found in the diorite quarries in the western desert of Nubia, more than 1,000 kilometres up the Nile from Cairo: this monument was set up by the workmen on the expedition inside a hastily built shrine (shown in photograph) and though the piece itself is quite roughly done, it is interesting as an *ex voto* coming from such a remote corner of Egypt's world at this early date.

Among the objects on the north side of the room are the wooden false door of Iyka (centre) and the painted limestone group of Nyankhrē with his wife and two boys. On leaving, note the two pairs of granite columns which come from the mortuary temples of Sahurē and Unis respectively.

Room 36: The north and south walls on the east side are occupied by limestone slabs, carved in low relief of exquisite quality, from the funerary temple of Sahurē at Abusir. On the south fragment we see the tribute in animals from Libya and also a procession of deities that represent natural forces: note the zig-zag water pattern on the figure of the 'Great Green' sea, or the grains of wheat (in paint, somewhat faded) on that of the harvest god. On the north wall the young king is suckled by the goddess Nekhbet as the ram-headed Khnum watches. Between these fragments, on the east wall, are the inscribed slabs known as the 'Coptos Decrees', enactments dating from various points in the Old Kingdom which exempted the estates of the god Min from the exactions of the Pharaoh's civil service.

An assortment of statues is displayed along the aisle in front of the east and west walls. Among these objects note the vandalized fragment of a granite doorjamb from Hieraconpolis north of the window: dating to the reign of Khasekhemwy, last king of the Second Dynasty, this is the earliest extant evidence that such hard stone was employed in monumental architecture during the archaic period in Egypt. Nearby there is a display of sculpted prisoners' heads in rows, a favourite decoration used in temples of the Old Kingdom and later (cf. the high gate and palace façade in the temple of Ramesses III at Medinet Habu, Chapter 18, pp. 267–8, 272–3).

Room 31: Another fragment from the mortuary temple of Sahurē (Dynasty V) is found on the south wall, east side, depicting a victory over the Libyans. Seshat, goddess of writing, is seated on top (right), recording the numbers of prisoners (left), who are seen facing left and raising their arms in supplication, and of the animals – oxen, asses, goats and rams – carried off as booty (middle register). The king was shown on the left, in the act of striking a Libyan chieftain dead. This part is missing here, but we do see the horrified reaction of the Libyan's wife and two boys on the right (bottom register) as they watch the slaughter, accompanied by the god and goddess of the Libyan desert. Dramatic as this relief is, it boasts an even more curious history, having been copied virtually unchanged – down to the victims' names – for Pepi II (Dynasty VI) and Taharqa (Dynasty XXV).

Moving up the east wall, Case B has an interesting collection of 'reserve heads' – sculptures that were included in the tomb furniture in case the tomb owner's own head should go astray – and also a plaster death-mask, one of the earliest examples of the funerary mask that will become so common in later ages. The west side is dominated by the exquisitely carved wooden panels of Hesirē (Dynasty III) on which the tomb owner is shown in various poses and costumes. Of historical rather than aesthetic interest is the stone slab on the south half of the west wall, inscribed with the 'autobiography' of Uni, a high official who flourished in the great days of the Sixth Dynasty and whose life-story provides much of what we know about this period; and (north side of the room) stelae from the Wadi Maghara, being records of the Egyptians' exploitation of the Sinai for copper and turquoise from the early Old Kingdom into the Ramesside Period. Conflicts with native tribes are reflected on the stelae of Niuserrē (west wall, north side), Snefru (north wall, east side) and Sahurē (east wall, north side) where we see the king triumphing over a fallen enemy.

Room 32: Of all the masterpieces grouped in this crowded room, pride of place must go to the perfectly preserved double statue of Rahotep and his wife Nefret which occupies the centre of the room: the sensitive use of colour highlights the serenity expressed on the couple's features. On the south side of the room, two large statues of the priest of Ptah Ranefer, with their contrasting hair-

styles and serious expressions, face one another from the east and west corners. The famous panel of painted 'Meidūm geese' occupies the centre of the south wall. Note, on the west end, a limestone relief from Saqqara depicting an orchestra at a banquet: the musicians, all of them male, accompany a troupe of female dancers and clappers with two flutes – double- and single-pipe – and a harp, to the conspicuous enjoyment of their audience. Another fine relief (west wall, north half) shows boatmen jousting on skiffs painted a bright green, the water beneath being dotted with flowers and lily pads.

The most interesting piece on the north side of the room (east half) is the statue of the dwarf Seneb with his wife: Seneb's relatively small size has been cleverly minimized, as it is in the false door just behind, with its several vignettes of Seneb seated. Note, in the north-west corner, two copper statues – the larger of them exceeding life size – which have been restored here as a group. The original relationship of the pair is uncertain (the smaller was found, stuffed inside the larger one and dumped into a pit at Hieraconpolis), but if they were originally displayed together, they would represent King Pepi I either with his Ka or with his son and eventual syccessor, Mernerē (Dynasty VI).

Room 26: We now enter the first of several rooms devoted to monuments of the Middle Kingdom. Begin at the south-east corner with the imposing painted limestone statue of King Nebhepetrē from his temple at Deir el-Bahri (see Chapter 18, pp. 256–8). All along the east wall are fragments from various temples, including (south wall) a small false door from the mortuary temple of Amenemhēt I, and (centre) sections of the enclosure wall of Senwosret I's pyramid at Lisht: note especially the elaborately carved panel with a falcon god astride the palace façade; and in front of this the block statue of the Chancellor Hotep, which is one of the earliest of its kind.

Moving to the west side of the room, we encounter the large sarcophagus of the vizier Dagi (cf. Chapter 19, p. 293), its interior decorated with the 'Coffin Texts' and with representations of the objects Dagi would need in the next world. The entrance to Room 21 is flanked by two statues of Senwosret II's queen, Nefret: note the eye sockets, with their inlays (now lost), a feature more often found in wooden statues.

Room 21: Of special interest is the single limestone pillar on the west side, which must have come from a building similar to the 'White Chapel' that is now re-erected at Karnak (see Chapter 17, pp. 236–7): on its sides we see Senwosret I embraced by Ptah (south), Amun (east), Atum (north) and Horus (west). South of the window, there is an intriguing family shrine of the late Old Kingdom from Saqqara, consisting of an offering table before a series of small false doors, all in limestone. Further north, we find a black granite naos of Senwosret I: the figure of Amun, erased by the Atenists in the late Eighteenth Dynasty, has been crudely restored here. Two statues of Senwosret III, with his habitual scowl, flank the entrance to Room 22 (east wall), while the display cases contain a selection of painted stelae.

Room 22: A mélange of elements from private and royal burials combine to give this room its majestic aspect. The tomb chamber of Harhotep acts as the centrepiece, its walls vividly painted with the usual objects displayed for the deceased's posthumous satisfaction, and the stone sarcophagus is outfitted with a cornice, as if it were itself a 'mansion of eternity'. Around the exterior of this room are exhibited ten seated statues of Senwosret I – note the side panels of the thrones, where the unification of the Two

Lands is performed either by Nile gods or by Horus and Seth – and opposite, against the north and south walls of the room, are large Osiride figures of the king wearing the red crown (north) and white crown (south). All of these statues formed part of Senwosret I's mortuary temple at Lisht and they convey an idea, both of the style of these buildings (of which no contemporary examples remain standing), and of the continuity of some features into later eras (cf. the second courts of the Ramesseum and of the temple of Ramesses III at Medinet Habu, Chapter 18, pp. 265, 271).

At the south-west corner, note the fragmentary stela that showed a king with his dogs at his feet. This piece, too, has a curious history, for it belonged to King Antef II (Dynasty XI) whose ruined pyramid was examined during the tomb-robbery trials in the reign of Ramesses IX (Dynasty XX, *c.* 1110 B.C.). The stela was still in place, the inspectors found, and 'the figure of the king stands upon this stela, with his dog, named Behek, between his feet'. The hound so named, however, is actually in front of his master (top right) and is only one of five who are shown here, along with an attendant. Obviously the inspectors were in a hurry!

Among the objects on the north side of the room, Case A is especially interesting for the upper part of a queen's Ba-figure (No. 6319), with its human head and bird's wings.

Room 16: The outstanding pieces in this room are the large black granite sphinxes from Tanis and Bubastis. Long believed to be monuments of the foreign 'Hyksos' kings of Egypt (Dynasty XV), they are now recognized as the work of one of the last kings of the Twelfth Dynasty, probably Amenemhēt III. All were usurped for Ramesses II (with Merneptah's names added) when these statues were moved from their original locations to decorate the new royal residences in the Delta. Another imposing piece, also of late Middle Kingdom date, is the black granite dyad (east side) of Nile gods with flowing beards and sombre expressions, who bear offering tables laden with the sustenance that the Nile brings. Against the west wall, under the window, note the curious limestone shrine with its two statues of King Neferhotep I (Dynasty XIII).

Room 11: This is the first of several rooms in which objects from the New Kingdom are displayed. Of particular interest are a number of pieces from the time of the female Pharaoh, Hatshepsut: a white limestone sphinx of hers appears on the west side (south half), and she is also shown as a young king, drinking milk from the udder of the Hathor cow in the marsh (headless limestone group, west side, north half). A statue of Hatshepsut's favourite, Senenmut, kneeling with a Hathor emblem, is seen south of the entry into Room 12, on the east side (No. 592). Thutmose III, the queen's nephew, is represented best by the famous statue in schist (north-east corner), where he appears in the White Crown; but he is also shown on the west side of the room — kneeling with the Hathoric emblem, and standing with an elaborate offering table in his arms (bottom only). The statue head of another powerful lady, Queen Tiyi (Amenhotep III's consort), occupies the centre of the room at the north end.

Room 12: The focus of this room is the painted shrine from Deir el-Bahri at the east end (see Chapter 18, p. 256). The painted reliefs inside show Thutmose III with his wife and daughter offering to the goddess, and the statue found inside the shrine is placed directly in front of it: the Hathor cow is red with black spots, and Amenhotep II appears between her legs, being suckled by his 'mother' (cf. Room 11).

The rest of the room offers a good selection of Eighteenth Dynasty statuary. Beginning at the north-west corner, note the large serpent statue in black granite, from Athribis in the Delta (*temp.* Amenhotep III); and the figure of Amenhotep II wearing the White Crown and accompanied by another serpent deity, Meretseger. A statue of the god Khonsu with the youthful features of Tutankhamun stands at the centre of the north wall, flanked by several figures of the sage Amenhotep, son of Hapu, against the pillars. Equally impressive is the cool loveliness of the Egyptian queen whose head in limestone, wearing a double diadem, appears in the north-east corner. On the opposite wall (centre) there is a curious statue of the Memphite earth god, Ta-tenen, sporting plumes set in an archaic wig and wearing a Libyan kilt. Further west are a black granite block statue of Senenmut and his pupil, Princess Nefrurē (cf. Chapter 6, p. 69), and a standing statue of 'King' Hatshepsut in red granite. Before leaving the room, note the painted wall-panels from El Amarna (late Eighteenth Dynasty) displayed high on the west wall.

Rooms 6 and 7 form the western half of the main hall on the north side of the museum. Large statues and sphinxes belonging, among others, to Hatshepsut occupy the central aisle. Note also the lioness-headed Sekhmet statues in Room 6, and the great quartzite stelae against the north wall, commemorating the restoration of the old religion after the Amarna heresy period by Tutankhamun (usurped later by Horemheb: No. 560), and the Asiatic campaigning of Amenhotep II (No. 6301). On the walls are many fragmentary tomb reliefs, especially from the ravaged New Kingdom necropolis at Saqqara: note particularly one (in Room 7, north side, middle) showing two men — ushers, perhaps — who are followed by several ranks of worthies, their arms up-raised, and are greeted by a crowd of young dancing girls and women, banging on tambourines, at the left side.

Room 8: This section of the hall continues in the manner of the two previous rooms with Ramesside colossal statues (south side, east and west), and sphinxes of Ramesses II and of the obscure Seventeenth Dynasty king, Sankhenrē Mentuhotep 'VI' A few objects from the Amarna collection in Room 3 are also kept here, including the model of a private house from the Heretic Capital (south) and the wooden sarcophagus of the mysterious king who was re-buried in the tomb of Queen Tiyi in the King's Valley at Thebes during the reign of Tutankhamun. Egyptologists are generally of the opinion that this was the final resting-place of Smenkhkarē, Akhenaten's successor; and it is suggested that the coffin originally belonged to Kiya, a minor wife of Akhenaten and (perhaps) the mother of Smenkhkarē and Tutankhamun.

Room 3: On entering, the visitor's eye is first caught by the large statues of Akhenaten (from Karnak) placed against the walls of the room. All of them emphasize his angular features and androgynous physique, but one (south-east corner) has the added singularity of being quite naked, with no genitalia indicated: among many explanations for this anomaly, I incline to the view that Akhenaten here shows himself as the primeval creator god in whom all the world's contrasting potentialities reside. Smaller pieces include a quartzite head of Neferiti, unfinished, its incompleteness stressed by the ridges left to accommodate the crown, which was to have been made of another material. A selection of jewellery, pottery, tiles, seals and cuneiform tablets found at the site, are displayed about the room: note especially

the exhibition of 'palace ware' pottery in the east recess. Among the many statues, votive pieces and relief fragments exhibited elsewhere, note especially the canopic chest of Akhenaten itself (reconstructed from the fragments found in the royal tomb at Amarna) and also the alabaster canopic jars — clearly female in inspiration — that were buried with the final occupant of Queen Tiyi's tomb. Painted pavements from Amarna, mounted high on the walls, complete the displays in this room.

The Atrium contains a collection of pieces that, principally owing to their size, are not exhibited in the rooms allotted to contemporary objects. In the following discussion, pieces will be dealt with in sequence moving from south to north.

At the top of the stairs (Room 38), in the corridors east and west of Room 43, do not miss the wooden funerary boats of Senwosret III: found at his pyramid complex at Dahshur, they were probably buried there for the king's everlasting convenience once they had ferried him across the river for the last time. On the stairs, note the cartouche-shaped sarcophagus of the divine votaress Nitocris, daughter of Psamtik I (west side, No. 640) and the reconstructed sarcophagus of Ay, with its protecting goddesses at the corners (cf. Tutankhamun's sarcophagus in his tomb: see Chapter 18, p. 250) on the east side (No. 624). At the base of the stairs are (east) two red granite statues of Amenemhēt I, and (west) a statue of Khaneferrē Sobekhotep IV in red granite, and a black granite figure of the official Mentuhotep.

The southern third of the atrium floor (Room 33) is filled with sarcophagi and other bulky pieces. Especially imposing is the red granite sarcophagus (south row, centre) and lid (centre, east) of Psusennes I: originally made for Merneptah some two centuries previously, it was taken over for Psusennes' use and is notable for the elaborateness of its carved decoration, including the figure of the king on the lid's exterior, its head protected by the goddess of the north wind, while a relief figure of the sky goddess Nūt spreads itself over the body of the deceased inside. To the east of the lid is a remarkable black granite 'table' (No. 621) in the shape of a bed, with lions' head bosses and animal legs, on which a recumbent Osiris is brought to life by Isis and other deities. In the next row to the north, we see the black granite capstones from the pyramids of Amenemhēt I (Dahshur) and Khendjer (South Saqqara). The red quartzite sarcophagi of Thutmose I and Hatshepsut from the Valley of the Kings at Thebes stand at the west side of the hall in this section.

The centre of the atrium (Room 28) is occupied by a large fragment of painted plaster pavement from El Amarna. Statues and sarcophagi are placed against the side walls: on the west side are Thutmose II in limestone (south); Senwosret I, usurped by Ramesses II, from Tanis (middle); and another Twelfth Dynasty statue taken over by Ramesses II, while on the east are three others also usurped from their original owners.

North of the Amarna pavement, in Room 23, we find large architectural fragments. First are two huge lintels in limestone from Medamūd, the one on the west side belonging to Senwosret III, the other being a poor copy by Sekhemrē-Khutowy (Dynasty XIII): the kings appear, enthroned, inside the Jubilee kiosk. North of this is a limestone chapel from Dendera (see Chapter 16, p. 213), on the back wall of which King Nebhepetrē smites the entwined plant emblems of Upper and Lower Egypt, while the symbolic 'Uni-fication of the Two Lands' proceeds in the sub-scene below. Other fragments of this building, showing Nebhepetrē with his ancestors, are kept on the east side of the room. The monument, which was erected prior to the Eleventh Dynasty's victory over the northern kingdom, is frankly propagandist in spirit, and it is thus interesting that another 'saviour' of Egypt, Pharaoh Merneptah, found it worthwhile to inscribe the outer doorjambs of the already 1,000-year-old building, as if to stress the similarity of his and Nebhepetrē's achievements.

The atrium's *pièce de résistance*, as it were, takes up most of the north stairway (Room 18), being the truly colossal (and much restored) statue of Amenhotep III and Queen Tiyi found at Medinet Habu. The royal couple, enthroned with three of their daughters at their sides, possess an air of affability, even smugness, that leaves no beholder in doubt of their conviction that 'bigger' in this case meant 'better'. In front of this piece, and dwarfed in comparison, note the granite offering table from Senwosret I's pyramid chapel at Lisht. Flanking the Eighteenth-Dynasty colossus are two shrines in red granite, dedicated by Ramesses II to the sun god, both from Tanis: the side walls are decorated with reliefs of the king making offerings to various manifestations of the sun god, and inside, against the back wall, are three statues: Atum and Khepri (= the rising sun) beside a third figure, possibly Amun.[1]

More statues in red granite appear at the top of the stairs: a dyad of Ramesses II and Ptah-Tatenen from Memphis (west) and a triad of Ramesses II with Isis and Hathor (east side). On the north landing (Room 13) finally, we find two more monuments of the Middle Kingdom from Medamūd, portals of Senwosret III (west) and Sekhemrē-Khutowy

---

1. Amun is not referred to on the sides, however, so it may be the king, wearing Amun's feathered crown, who is represented.

(east), decorated with scenes of the king being led by his attendant deities through the gate, etc. The quality of the later monument is somewhat better than the lintel we have seen previously (above, p. 114) but — with the figures' stubby legs and the crude (if lively) portraiture — it is still inferior to the Twelfth Dynasty original. On the east side, among several stelae placed here, note the so-called 'Israel Stela' of Merneptah (No. 599): this inscription, here carved on the back of an earlier memorial of Amenhotep III, is a hymn of victory, eulogizing Merneptah's triumph over a combined invasion of Libyans and 'Sea Peoples': in its peroration the words 'Israel is laid waste: its seed is not' constitute the earliest mention of the Israelites in Egyptian records.

Room 9 is furnished in the same way as the western part of the hall: stelae and relief fragments are on the walls, large pieces occupy the centre. Note, in front of the two red granite palm columns that flank the entrance to Room 4, a fragment of a private tomb from Saqqara that was inscribed during the reign of Ramesses II with a condensed list of kings. Further east, on the south wall near the border between Rooms 9 and 10, is a limestone group from Abydos in which Horemheb appears with Osiris, Isis and Horus. A similar group, uninscribed, is on the north side of the room.

Room 4 contains a collection of Graeco-Roman coins and medals.

Room 10 is dominated by the large black granite statue of the god Hauron in the form of a falcon, protecting the infant Ramesses II: note the king's sidelock of hair, a sign of

extreme youth, and the characteristic posture of his hands.[2] At the south-west corner is a colossal statue of Tutankhamun, usurped for Horemheb and found in the latter's mortuary temple in West Thebes: a duplicate of this piece is in the museum of the Oriental Institute, Chicago.

Room 15: The cases in the centre of the room contain statuettes of the Eighteenth and Nineteenth Dynasties. Among the wealth of important objects, note (in Case B) a remarkable statuette of Ramesses II prostrate, making an offering, while on the base are incised leaves from the Ished-tree,[3] each one inscribed with the king's name. Stone slabs and large statues are arranged along the walls of the room: note especially (north-east corner) the painted tomb relief of the royal scribe Siēse, who is seen being purified by a priest. The diorite statue of the god Amun-Rē seen against the west wall, south of the doorway into Room 14, is also very fine; and note as well elaborate figured windows in stone, from the palace of Ramesses III at Medinet Habu, displayed above (see Chapter 18, pp. 272–3).

Room 14 is a treasury of sculpture from the later New Kingdom. Facing out, just inside the entrance, is a heavily restored group showing Ramesses III crowned by Horus and Seth. Note also the group showing Ramesses VI, with his attendant lion, subduing a Libyan prisoner (743). Other important objects in the north-east corner include the crystalline limestone statue of Sety I, with its (now missing) inlaid eyes, necklace, belt ornament and bracelets; and the grey granite trough, with reliefs of the *rekhyt* (=subject people) birds carved on its sides, and supported

---

2. The child's figure is also a rebus for the king's name: the sun's disc has the value *Ra*, the child himself *mes*, and the emblem in his left hand *su*, thus *Ra-mes-su*, 'Ramesses'.

3. A mythological tree on the leaves of which the gods wrote the names and years of reigns of Egypt's kings.

by modelled figures of Syrian and Negro captives.

A shrine from Abu Simbel occupies the centre of the north wall: inside a naos, the sacred beetle, symbol of the rising sun, and the moon god (here manifest as a baboon) are acclaimed by four other baboons.[4]

Turning to the south half, we see on the west wall the tomb lintel of Ramesses III's Master of Horse Pahemnetcher, who appears in the act of leading horses and saluting his master's cartouches. The sinister figure of the crouching Seth animal, protecting the Ramesside king between its legs, occupies the south-west corner, while on the south wall are seen a number of private monuments, including the limestone block statues of one Khay, who holds a naos containing a figure of Osiris (west) and of Rē-Harakhti (east). Finally, in the south-east corner, note the painted limestone relief in which a bellicose Ramesses II threatens Nubian and Asiatic captives with his hatchet.

Room 20 contains an assortment of pieces from the later New Kingdom and the Third Intermediate Period. Elements from the palace of Ramesses III at Medinet Habu are mounted on the west wall, and statues of the later period are exhibited at the centre of the room: especially notable is the Nubian figure, with his shaved head, pendulous breasts and large belly.

Room 25: Of the larger pieces in this room, note the coffin lid of King Harsiēse (a rival of the Libyan Twenty-second Dynasty, from Thebes), with the lid modelled to represent a falcon instead of the customary king's figure. Important members of the clerical administration of Thebes appear in Cases D and E: in the latter, the divine votaress Ankhnesneferibrē, daughter of Psamtik II (Dynasty XXVI), is shown wearing the horned disc and plumes of a goddess, perhaps in connection with a ritual wherein she assumed the deity's role. Behind her stands Psamtik, chief jeweller, wearing a shirt under his strapless gown and holding a naos in front of him.

Room 24 displays a good number of the masterpieces of Late Period sculpture. A rather unpromising beginning is made with the Memphite tomb reliefs exhibited in the entrance passage: the figures are nicely carved with some realistic touches, but they lack the solidity of the Old Kingdom originals on which they are based and the composition of the scenes is too often cluttered. Once inside, however, one is faced by the statues of Isis, wearing the horned disc headdress (No. 856); of Osiris, enthroned (No. 855); and of the Hathor cow, goddess of the Western Mountain of Thebes, who protects one of her devotees, a man named Psamtik. Behind these statues is the reconstructed remnant of a giant naos from Saft el-Henneh in the eastern Delta, dedicated by Nectanebo II (Dynasty XXX) to the god Sopdu, 'Lord of the East' and defender of Egypt during Asiatic invasions. The scenes on the side walls of the shrine represent the statues and portable shrines of Sopdu in his various forms (usually hawk-headed), and of the other divinities worshipped in this part of Egypt.

Other important pieces are displayed on the sides of the room. Near the centre of the north wall, for instance, is the black granite head of Taharqa (No. 1185); note also, in the north-west corner, the statue of the priest Pedamenōpe as a squatting scribe (in red granite). On the south wall, near the centre of the room, is the great schist statue of the hippopotamus goddess Taweret, behind which note the cartouche-shaped basin in

---

4. Baboons were considered sacred to the rising sun, probably because they howl at dawn.

black granite. The black granite bust of the Fourth Prophet of Amun and Mayor of Thebes, Montuemhēt (No. 935),[5] east of centre, is one of the triumphs of ancient portraiture: the man's advanced age and his intelligence are delineated with a subtlety that makes all but superfluous the receding hairline shown as well.

A number of historically important stelae are kept in this room as well, among them the black granite 'Satrap Stela', dedicated on behalf of the young Alexander II by the first Ptolemy before he formally claimed kingship in Egypt (north-east corner); the decree in which the High Priest of Amun, Yewelot, son of Osorkon I, provided for the property of one of his sons (north-west corner); and the 'Adoption Stela' of Nitrocris, wherein it is related how this daughter of Psamtik I was acknowledged as the heiress of the office of divine votaress at Thebes by the last Nubian princess who held the title (south-east corner).

Room 30 is devoted to monuments of the Nubian (Twenty-fifth) Dynasty. The divine votaress Shepenwepet II, daughter of the conqueror Piankhy, is represented by a statue of schist (once gilded) displayed in a case to the east of the entrance. Pride of place, however, goes to her aunt and predecessor, Amenirdis I, whose graceful alabaster statue stands in the centre of the room. In this room, also, are found the great dedicatory stelae that are our main source of information concerning the Nubian kings. The stela of King Piankhy (or Piyi, as it was pronounced in his own language) is on the east side, near the window, while on the west side of the room are the inscriptions of Tantamani (No. 938), the last king of the Twenty-fifth Dynasty to rule in Egypt, and a later Nubian 'Pharaoh', Harsiotef (No. 941).

Room 35: A mixed collection of pieces from the Late Period is displayed here. A naos dedicated to the god Thoth by Nectanebo II is exhibited on the east side, near the window, while nearby is a curiously eclectic royal figure – bearded, in Greek fashion, but wearing the kingly headcloth and double crown – that represents the Roman Emperor Caracalla. On the west wall (north side), note the remains of the red granite stela of the Persian King Darius, relating his re-opening of the canal of Pharaoh Necho through the Delta to the Gulf of Suez (see Chapter 1, pp. 21–2).

Room 34 contains works of the Graeco-Roman Period in Egypt. A Roman orator stands at the centre, near the entrance, while at the north-east corner is the 'trilingual' Decree of Canopus, inscribed in hieroglyphic and Greek (front), and in demotic (left side): discovered about half a century later than the Rosetta Stone, this text records a series of honours voted by the Egyptian priests on behalf of Ptolemy III and his queen, Berenice. Stelae from the 'Bucheum', the burial vaults of the sacred bulls from Armant, are found in the centre of the room, ranging in date from Nectanebo I (Dynasty XXX) to the Roman Era, and dealing with the 'reigns' of successive Buchis bulls. Paintings from the late tombs at Tuna el-Gebel (see Chapter 15, pp. 202–3) are exhibited on the west wall, above the cases: note the scenes from the Oedipus legend on the north side. A large number of Hellenistic and Roman sculptures, both full statues and heads, are displayed throughout the rest of the room.

Room 40 contains a display of objects from post-Pharaonic Nubia. Typical specimens of relief – derivative, yet almost comically swollen in style – appear on the east side of

5. Owner of Theban Tomb No. 34 in the Asasif (see Chapter 6, p. 70).

the room, along with display cases full of bronze ritual utensils and objects of daily use. Offering tables, inscribed with the cursive 'Meroitic' script, are to be seen on the south side of the west wall, next to a display of sculpture (centre) — including native versions of the human-headed Ba bird. The most imposing piece in the room, however, is a limestone relief (west wall, north half) showing the god Serapis, bearded and in armour, accompanied by a goddess (Graeco-Roman Period).

Room 45: Grave goods from the late Nubian tumuli of Ballana and Qustul are exhibited here. Pottery vessels are displayed against the east wall, while in the centre are bronze bowls, censers and candelabra (Cases 5 and 6) and a fine wooden chest, inlaid with ivory (Case 7). Silver vessels, censers and statuettes are displayed in the cases found on the west side of the room.

Room 44 displays more of the artefacts in bronze and precious metal from Ballana and Qustul, including cases of jewellery and exhibits of contemporary weapons. The most effective display is of the fittings for the war-horses, which are exhibited on full-size models.

Room 50 is predominantly given over to sarcophagi of the Late Period, with Hellenistic statuary displayed on the south end. In the centre, note the large sarcophagus of the General Pedisamtowy, who is mentioned (as 'Potasimto') in a Greek inscription at Abu Simbel describing his return at the head of an army after campaigning further south for Psamtik II in 590 B.C.

Room 49 is once again devoted to late sarcophagi: the coffins are exhibited between the columns of the hall and in the centre, while their lids are placed against the walls.

South of the entrance to this room, note the large statue of Alexander II in Egyptian dress, but with a Greek hair-style quite apparent under his royal headcloth. Among all the sarcophagi, note especially the coffin of Djedhor, the dancing dwarf of the Serapeum, whose naked life-size figure is shown on the lid (north-west corner). The wooden sarcophagus of Petosiris, with its inlaid eyes and hieroglyphs, from Tuna el-Gebel (Chapter 15, p. 202), is at the west end. Two red quartzite statues of Ptah from Memphis (*temp.* Ramesses II) that flank the western exit bring us back, momentarily, to the New Kingdom, and into the foyer of the museum.

The Upper Floor is less easily followed than the lower, and the exhibits are more numerous and diffuse. Accordingly, there will be two itineraries on this level, one of them for the objects from the tomb of Tutankhamun and similarly spectacular pieces, and the other devoted to the articles of daily use grouped in the inner rooms on this floor.

Itinerary II, comprising the Tutankhamun collection, jewellery, the burial of Hetepheres and the treasures from Tanis, will proceed down the east and north outer corridors (Rooms 45 to 15, and 10 to 6, with detours into the rooms at the north end of the Museum: see Fig. 14).

Room 45: On entering, the visitor is greeted by the two life-size ebony statues that stood guard over the entrance to the tomb's burial chamber. The king's ostrich-feather fan is exhibited in the south-west corner of the room. The rest of the west wall is furnished with boxes and chests from the tomb, and also with displays of small coffins containing mementoes of the king and his family. Most prominently exhibited is the great portable image of Anubis on carrying poles, found in the 'Treasury' of the tomb.

Room 40: On the west wall (south end), note two gilded serpent statues with their shrines, deities who evidently played a part in the king's afterlife. The remainder of the room is filled with elaborately ornamented chests: note the king's gameboards at the south-east corner. In the cases against the east wall, note the hunting equipment – boomerangs, staves, and one of the king's bucklers.

Room 35: Ornamental boxes of ivory and precious wood fill the southern half of this room: note especially the famous 'painted box' (centre east), with its vibrant – and probably fictitious – scenes of Tutankhamun in battle. On the west wall are cases of royal *shawabtis* (see Chapter 6, p. 76) and other amulets – model hoes, baskets, etc. – that were to give the king all that

Fig. 14   Cairo Museum, upper floor

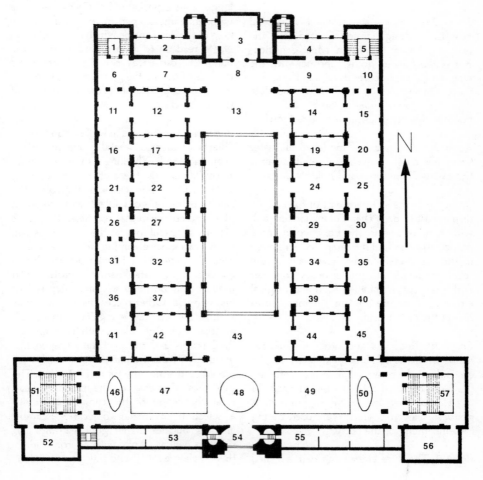

he needed in the Fields of the Blessed. More of Tutankhamun's hunting equipment is displayed against the east wall, including staves, arrows, a tapestry-work quiver and an inlaid wooden bow case.

Room 30: Shown in this room is a display of ebony statues, plain and gilded, of the king and various deities: it is believed that these figures had a magical role to play in assisting the king on his journey through the underworld.

Room 25: Various thrones and stools, all beautifully designed and crafted, are the main exhibits in this room. Most conspicuous is the famous golden throne, with the king and queen represented on the backpiece. On the west wall are more *shawabtis*, some of them gilded (south side), and boomerangs, used in hunting birds (north).

Room 20: A display of modelled alabaster vases fills most of the room, while against the east wall are canes and holders for fans.

Room 15: In the southern part of the hall are displayed the beds that Tutankhamun took with him for use in the next world: note particularly the folding camp-bed exhibited in the south-east corner. The walls of the room are lined with model boats, together with cases for mummified food and magical emblems to ensure the tomb owner's comfort in the next world.

Room 10: Bouquets and other organic remains from the tomb are exhibited on the east side of the room, while in the centre are the large beds, with the modelled heads of the Hathor cow and of the hippopotamus goddess, Taweret, which were used during the embalming of the body.

Room 9: The third embalming bed, adorned with heads of the lioness Sekhmet, is in the centre of the room (east end), along with the gilded frame for a canopy or sunshade. Note also (west) the alabaster canopic chest, with its outer shrine of gilded wood, and the lids, each one carved to the shape of the king's head, covering the four cavities that received the embalmed viscera of Tutankhamun. On the south wall, east of the cases that contain textiles from the tomb, we see a wooden bust, covered with stucco, carved to a remarkably realistic likeness of the young king. Note especially the 'Osiris bed' – a wooden frame shaped in the profile of the king of the dead, inside which a layer of earth was spread on to a linen base. Prior to the burial, the earth was 'sown' with grain and moistened so that the grain would germinate in the tomb, providing a concrete symbol of the resurrection.

Room 4 contains the jewellery and other objects of precious metal found in Tutankhamun's tomb. The king's solid-gold inner sarcophagus is at the east end. Proceeding westward, we find cases that display 'the small coffins of gold inlaid with coloured glass and cornelian that contained the king's viscera: a careful look at the cartouches will show traces of reworking, for these pieces seem to have been taken from the burial equipment of Tutankhamun's brother and predecessor, Smenkhkarē, and adapted for his own use. Other pieces displayed in this section are the king's regalia – the crook and flail of royalty – along with the mummy's gold braces and the pectorals, shaped like vultures with outstretched wings, which were placed on the mummy for its protection. The gold mask that covered the mummy's head is at the centre of the room, along with a selection of smaller objects – scarabs, amulets, buckles in red gold, earrings and rings, as well as a knife with an iron blade – then a relative rarity, and thus one of Tutankhamun's prized possessions. In the western half of the room are cases containing more pectorals and earrings (centre), a disarmingly simple headband in beaten gold (north) and gold finger-rings, finger- and toe-sheaths from the mummy, and sandals (south). The second of the three inner coffins that house the mummy, made of wood covered with gold leaf and other precious inlays, is at the west end.

Rooms 7 and 8 are filled by the four great shrines, of gilded wood with incised decoration, that enclosed the king's sarcophagus in the burial chamber. The walls of these shrines are inscribed, inside and out, with spells from *The Book of the Dead* and other mortuary compositions, and also with figures of the various deities to be encountered in the Underworld. These religious texts and representations took the place of similar materials that would normally appear on the walls of a royal tomb, but which had to be omitted in the hastily prepared burial of Tutankhamun.

Room 13: Chariots found in the tomb of Tutankhamun are found at the north side of the room, as it opens into Room 8. Further inside are objects from the tomb of Yuya and Tchuya, one of the few burials in the Valley of the Kings to have escaped plundering in antiquity. The deceased were the parents of Queen Tiyi, thus parents-in-law to Amenhotep III, and though not of royal blood they were buried in the royal valley with many 'heirlooms' donated by members of the family. The couple's coffins are exhibited on the east side of the room, and their chariots in the centre. Other grave goods are exhibited in the western part of the room: note especially (Case S) the two chairs donated by Princess Sitamun, a daughter of Amenhotep III, the smaller of which was apparently used when she was a child. The larger chair is notable not only for its elegance, but for having survived the Empress Eugénie of France, who sat on it when she visited the newly discovered tomb in 1905.

Room 3 contains a display of Pharaonic jewellery, the cases being numbered and arranged in roughly chronological order. Beginning in the west recess, note the threaded stone and bead necklaces of the First Dynasty (north-west corner). The golden head of a copper falcon (Dynasty VI) is in a case at the west end of the north recess, while the circlets and collars of the Middle Kingdom princesses are found at the opposite end. Do not miss, in the middle of the north recess, Queen Ahhotep's gold figured necklace. Note the heavy serpent earrings in red gold displayed on the north side of the case in the centre of the room, and also the treasure buried with a child of Queen Twosret (Nos. 4192–99) in the north-east quarter. The famed 'Treasure of Tod', a collection of silver Asiatic vessels found buried in the Middle Kingdom temple at that site (see Chapter 20, p. 301), is found at the north end of the east recess; but a more elaborate display of gold and silver vessels and of heavy metal jewellery is found at the centre of the room.

Room 2: The outer room of this suite contains objects from the Fourth Dynasty burial of Queen Hetep-heres, consort of Snefru and mother of Khufu, the builder of the Great Pyramid at Giza. The tomb was found in 1925 in the cemetery east of Khufu's pyramid. The evidence indicated that it was a reburial, apparently following the violation of Hetep-heres' original tomb at Dahshur. When the sealed sarcophagus was opened, however, it proved to be empty — a fact that has prompted speculation that Hetep-heres' effects were moved to the greater security of the Giza area amidst a massive conspiracy to keep the mummy's disappearance from her son. Be that as it may, it is owing to the painstaking work of both excavators and conservationists that the Cairo Museum now has the splendid exhibit on hand. The queen's canopy, bed and chair are at the west end of the room, while the canopic box and coffin of alabaster are against the south wall. In the centre of the room is a box of gilded and inlaid wood (found in pieces on top of the coffin and entirely reconstructed). Toilet articles, including small golden razors, are exhibited at the north side, while a selection of alabaster and pottery vessels from the tomb has been placed at the north-east corner.

The inner rooms of this suite house the principal objects from the burials of the kings of the Twenty-first and Twenty-second Dynasties at Tanis. Against the south wall of the first room, note the silver hawk-headed coffin and canopic coffinettes of Shoshenq II, whose wooden outer coffin is set against the west wall (north end). Vessels, jewellery and masks of gold, silver and copper fill the rest of this room. In the second room is the black granite sarcophagus, silver coffin, and the gold mask and sheathing from the mummy of Psusennes I. *Shawabtis* from the royal burials are displayed on the walls.

Itinerary III actually comprises two circuits that will cover the remaining galleries on the upper floor. The first begins in Room 43 (portico above the atrium, on the south side of the Museum), moving generally in a clockwise direction through the inner rooms, and back to the point of departure. The second will start on the landing of the south-east stairwell (Room 50) and proceed counter-clockwise through the Museum's southern hall, stopping at the exhibits on the south side, until it returns to the starting point. By following these optional itineraries the visitor may view the objects in an intelligible order and save unnecessary duplication as well (see Fig. 14).

Room 43 is devoted to objects of daily use from the Archaic Period (Dynasties I and II). In the cases on the east side (Q and R), note the stone bowls and serving trays, their graceful shapes and thin walls demonstrating the skill attained in working stone by the end of the Second Dynasty. Further west are rows of cases containing spindle whorls, some of them inlaid (A); wooden adzes, and articles of cloth, string and rope (E); wooden sickles (F); spears, canes, copper piercers and gaming pieces (G); and arrows (H).

Corridor 42: A limestone panel, inlaid with blue faience tiles, from Djoser's Step Pyramid at Saqqara is found on the south wall. Further north are cases with articles from other tombs built in the area around Memphis, all from the early Old Kingdom.

Room 42 is devoted to objects of the Archaic Period. Among the exhibits of stone vessels and inscribed jar-sealings on the north side of the room, note the tomb stelae of the Seth Peribsen (east wall, north), of Queen Merit-Neith (north wall, east), and the Horus Djer (west). The *pièce de résistance*, the famous schist palette of King Narmer triumphing over a Northern enemy (from Hieraconpolis), is at the west end of the room: even if it falls short of proving the identity of Narmer with the legendary King Menes, this monument is still the earliest to document the unification of the northern and southern kingdoms. Note also the seated statue of King Khasekhemwy (late Dynasty II) and the statue in black granite of an official who bears, inscribed on his shoulder, the names of the first three kings of the Second Dynasty. The cases on the south side have exhibits of copper vessels, slate palettes (both plain and decorated), statuary, and vessels in stone and pottery. Case F at the south-east corner contains an interesting assortment of objects, including a glass model lion and a tiny ivory label from Nagada that perhaps bears a contemporary reference to the legendary unifier of Egypt, King Menes. Also on the east side of the room, note the game boards, gaming pieces, and also fragments of the annals of Egypt's earliest kings – stone stelae, set up in the temples during the later Old Kingdom and preserved only in tantalizing fragments today.

Room 37: Among the varnished or brightly painted wooden chests and coffins stored here (First Intermediate Period to Dynasty XVIII), note at the west end of the room the funerary equipment of General Mesehty (from Assiūt). The deceased's head rest, collars, staffs, mirror and sandals are displayed on top of his wooden coffin. The models of Nubian and Egyptian troops exhibited nearby attest to the strategic military importance of Assiūt during the First Intermediate Period.

Corridor 32 has a display of remains from royal burials at Dahshur, including the large Ka statue of King Auyebrē-Hor of the Thirteenth Dynasty; his funerary mask, and various objects – incised gold strips, canopics, canes and stone vessels – of a Middle Kingdom princess.

Room 32 contains models, simulacra of real people and things used in the tombs. Boats are exhibited on the south end of the room. Note also the stone models of trussed geese in a case near the south-east corner. Head-rests of wood and stone are found at the west end, and on the north side is a collection of servant statuettes, either single figures or groups. Alabaster tags and tiny offering tables, as well as copper miniature

dishes, tables and utensils are found in cases at the east end.

Corridor 27: on the east side is material from the burial of Princess Nefruptah, a daughter of Amenemhēt III, from Hawara, including jewellery and silver jars. Flanking the entrance to Room 27 are objects of the so-called 'pan grave' people, whose burials began to appear on the desert edges in Upper Egypt during the Second Intermediate Period and who may be the ancestors of the Medjay tribesmen who were the state police during the New Kingdom.

Room 27 contains models taken from scenes of daily life, notably those from the tomb of Meketrē (Dynasty XI) from Thebes. Of special interest are models of granaries; men fishing from reed boats; a weaver's hut; a carpentry shop; a garden kiosk, with its mandatory pool of water; and the assessment scene, with cattle being driven before a porch on which scribes are seated and at work. Cases along the walls are filled with funerary equipment, including (north wall) clay 'soul houses' and offering tables, alabaster containers for trussed geese, and model daggers and sandals.

Room 22 is devoted to mortuary equipment of the New Kingdom, starting with the two wooden statues of Isis that flank the entrance. Inside, the objects displayed are small and generally amuletic in nature. *Shawabtis,* some with model coffins, are exhibited at the south-east corner. Painted boxes and shrines occupy the tops of the cases along the south wall, with statuettes (Ba figures, Isis and Nephthys, Anubis, etc.), scarabs, statuettes and other amulets exhibited below. A display of painted stelae, made of stuccoed wood, appears at the west end, along with head-rests of various materials (south of door); more *shawabtis* and pectorals, of cloth and cartonage, appear on the north side. Note, in the profusion of small objects exhibited on the north wall, the funerary statuettes, some in the form of Osiris, others with the lineaments of the hawk-headed Sokar, one of the protectors of the necropolis. Amulets include the *Udjat-eye* (the 'whole' eye of Horus, which ensures corporeal integrity), boomerangs for the deceased's use in the next world, and many more. Note the cartonage masks, pectorals, sandals and foot sheaths used on mummies (east end).

Corridor 17: The objects exhibited here come from the Saqqara cemetery of the Aramaic colony in Memphis during the Late Period. Most characteristic are the clay coffins, with the faces of their owners modelled on their lids.

Room 17 exhibits the burial equipment of two notables of the Eighteenth and Nineteenth Dynasties. Sennedjem (Theban Tomb No. 1) was a civil servant who lived, probably during the long reign of Ramesses II, at Deir el-Medina. In addition to the wooden coffins of the deceased and his wife, still mounted on the wooden sledges on which they were dragged to the tomb, there are chairs and stools, *shawabtis*, and elaborately painted boxes and jars. Note especially the plumb-bob and other instruments of Sennedjem's profession (centre, south case). The doorleaf to the burial chamber, on which the deceased is shown playing draughts, completes a funerary ensemble that reveals the style to which a member of the middle class could aspire during the New Kingdom. On the west side of the room is the furniture of Maherpra, a youth of negroid stock who was a boyhood companion of Amenhotep II and was buried in an undecorated tomb in the Valley of the Kings. In addition to his outer and inner coffins, Maherpra was given two

additional inner coffins, the purpose of which has not been explained. He was also given an elegantly painted copy of the *Book of the Dead* (his dark skin realistically portrayed in the painted vignettes), and other conventional burial equipment, including alabaster canopic jars (still swathed in their outer coverings), jars of food, jewellery, arrows inside a leather quiver, and a gaming box with the board on its lid (cases centre and west).

The Western Corridor of the Museum (= Rooms 41, 36, 31, 26, 21, 16 and 11) is devoted to an assortment of wooden coffins and canopic chests, illustrating their development across the ages. Although some of the coffins are covered with mythological scenes and texts, many are quite simply decorated, with a pair of painted or inlaid eyes on the side opposite the owner's head to give him a 'window on the world'. A number of mummies, still fully wrapped, complete the funerary ensemble in several parts of the gallery. The wooden coffin-lid of Ramesses II stands in the centre of the hall (west wall), while at the north end are simple coffins of woven reeds, as well as some curious 'openwork' models that permit the mummy to be seen from the outside.

Room 6: Among the collection of scarabs exhibited here (along with necklaces and pectorals of faience 'mummy beads'), note the cylinder seals, faience stamp rings, large 'heart scarabs' inscribed with a spell to prevent the deceased's heart from testifying against him in the Underworld, and the royal scarabs, particularly the large commemorative issues of Amenhotep III, on which such events as the king's marriage to Tiyi were announced. Return from here to

Room 12: Many of the objects exhibited in this room, from the burials of the kings and high priests of the New Kingdom, should be already familiar from their better-preserved parallels in the Tutankhamun collection. Among the pieces exhibited on the north wall, note the wigs (Case L), preserved victuals, and the painted cloth palls (northeast corner); and above all, the chariot frame of Thutmose IV, with scenes of the king rampant against his enemies carved on the sides (east end). Tomb equipment of the High Priests and their families (along with some royal *shawabtis*) occupy the north wall, while remnants from the burials of Amenhotep II, Thutmose IV, Thutmose III and Horemheb are located to the east and on the south side of the room. From the eastern doorway, cross the central gallery of the Museum to

Room 14: Mummies of the Graeco-Roman Period are displayed on the north wall, while to the south are contemporary mummy masks and 'Faiyūm Portraits', painted panels with the features of the deceased placed over the face of the mummy.

Corridor 19 exhibits the magical statue of 'Djed-Hor the Saviour', its surface almost entirely covered with hieroglyphic spells, and with a trough cut into the base so that his petitioners might collect the liquid offering poured over the image's head and use the remnant, now sanctified by this contact, as medicine. Compare the similarly used plaque of 'Horus on the Crocodiles', with its basin, just to the south.

Room 19 offers a wide array of statuettes of the Egyptian gods. On the south side, proceeding west to east, are Osiris (Cases K, L, M); Isis, sometimes with Horus the Child, and also with her sister, Nephthys (N, O); and Horus, sometimes shown as Horus the Child (P, Q). On the north side of the room (going east to west) are Bastet (A); Amun, both wearing his tall plumes and as a ram,

and Nefertem, with the characteristic lotus on his head (B); various deities, especially the hippopotamus Taweret (C); Sekhmet the lioness, the Hathor cow, and Ptah (D); Ihy, portrayed as a bandy-legged child, Thoth, both as an ibis and a baboon, and more Sekhmets (E); more statues of Thoth, and Neith, with the Red Crown (F); various deities, especially Bes, the presiding spirit at childbirth (G); Anubis and Bes, along with amuletic sistra sacred to Hathor (H); and various sacred animals, including ichneumons, serpents, crocodiles and fish (I).

Room 24 is devoted to a display of Egyptian draftsmanship. Papyri (all *Books of the Dead*) are exhibited on the north and south walls, while in the cases below are ostraca with trial drawings and specimens of writing. Model plaques and heads in the round — sculptors' trial pieces — are shown at the east end of the room, and more of the same on the west side, along with several unfinished examples to show the method of work.

Room 29 houses an exhibition of Egyptian writing and writing materials. Here one can see the development of the cursive script, from flowing hieroglyphic to more ligatured hands (called 'hieratic'), and down to the late 'demotic' writing. The 'Coptic' writing employed into the Christian era consisted of the Greek alphabet, amplified by certain hieratic signs that were used for sounds not found in the Greek language (e.g., *sh*). Papyri, again, are mounted on the walls — religious texts on the south side, and business documents in hieratic and demotic on the north. Other media of writing are displayed in the central case: on the south side (west to east) are bones, reeds, linen, solidified mud, stone flakes and pottery; writing boards, leaves from Coptic codices, and Aramaic and Greek papyri are shown on the north side (east to west). A case at the east end contains a display of scribal palettes, pens, inkwells, pigment grinders, blank papyrus, and scrapers, used to smooth the often rough surface of papyrus.

From *Corridor 34*, containing a display of textiles as well as a pair of palm-fibre fans, proceed into

Room 34, where an interesting collection of objects used in daily life is assembled. Cosmetic accessories are found on the west side, consisting of mirrors (north of doorway) and ornate bowls that contained oils and perfumes (centre). On the south side, we begin with the case of recreational objects – dolls, balls, gaming boards and pieces, including dice (I). Next are weapons: wooden canes, spear points and daggers of bronze and copper (J); bows, arrows and arrowheads (K); axes, boomerangs, maceheads and shieldholders (L). An enormous wooden sledge placed between these cases is a reminder of the huge scale of Egyptian building operations. A collection of weights and measures, including the Egyptian unit of length, the cubit rod, is found in the next case (M), followed by builders' tools: stone and wood clamps to hold blocks together, plumb-lines, wooden mauls, stone pounders, and metal chisels (N). The cosmetic arts return on the east side with a display of decorative unguent spoons (centre). On the north side of the room, there is a collection of door- and window-frames, door bolts, axes, adzes and picks (A). In the next case, grinding stones are exhibited on top, with lamps, tweezers and brushes shown below (B). Harpoon heads, knives and needles are displayed next, followed by implements used in Egyptian agriculture: hand and ox-driven ploughs on top, together with hobbles for animals, picks and cord sieves (C, D). An assemblage of musical instruments complements the representations seen in

tomb paintings (E), and the exhibit concludes with more toilet articles: phials, boxes, combs and fan handles (F).

Passing along *Corridor 39*, where more textiles and examples of the sandal maker's craft are shown, enter

Room 39, which houses a collection of vessels and figurines in various wares. Terracotta pieces are displayed at the west end of the room, with bronze vessels, ornaments and statues in the corresponding portion of the eastern section. There is also a collection of wooden tags and panels (east, south half), glazed ware (south, middle), and glass (south, west half, and centre, middle).

Room 44 is mostly devoted to the decorations that graced the palace interiors in ancient Egypt. Glazed tiles, with designs of geometric shapes, floral patterns, hieroglyphs and figures, from Piramesse (Qantir) in the Delta and from the palace at Medinet Habu, are found in the east half of the room (north and south). Fragmentary pavements – notably, the brightly coloured ox-head motif from the palace of Amenhotep III in West Thebes – are exhibited high on the north wall. Note also the miniature house models, architectural elements, and also two granite clamps, used to hold blocks of masonry in position (north-east corner). Bronze decorative elements, wooden doors, metal fittings and chains are found on the north side (west). An odd assortment of pottery is found in the south half of the room, along with votive plaques deposited in the foundations of new buildings.

Exit on the east side, through Room 45, to

Room 50, where the main exhibit is the ornate leather funerary pall of Princess Istemkheb (Dynasty XXI). Note also the water clock of Amenhotep III – an alabaster urn that told the hours as it emptied – near the south stairway. From here proceed along the north side of Room 49 to

Room 48: Between the cupola and the inner hall, on the north side, note the remarkable limestone sarcophagi of the Princesses Kawiyet and Ashayet (Dynasty XI), with their bold, but oddly graceful reliefs carved on the sides. In this vicinity, look for the *vitrine d'honneur*, wherein some of the finest small pieces in the Museum are gathered. Note particularly the black steatite head of Queen Tiyi, with its resolute expression (No. 4257); the gilded censer (top); the tiny statuette of Khufu (No. 4244); and the glazed hippopotami and three dancing dwarves in ivory (south side of the case).

From Room 48, continue in a counter-clockwise direction around the Museum's south-west corner. The cases arranged along the wall are filled with wooden inner coffins: note especially those which exhibit the feathered 'rishi' pattern, the body being enfolded in protecting wings. Many of the coffins displayed here come from the caches of royal and priestly burials that preserved the integrity of these artefacts down to modern times.

Readers interested in prehistory and the earliest periods of human activity in the Nile Valley should visit the two rooms tucked into the south wall of the Museum. An exhibition of artefacts – pottery, harpoon heads and knives of flint and obsidian, and specimens of matting – is placed in the foyer between them.

Room 53: On the stairs, note the remains of pre-Dynastic paintings on mud-plaster from Hieroconpolis (north) and the bottom of a large stone figure of the god Min of Coptos (south). The outer room of the suite is filled with pottery of the early periods, but also with slate palettes (east and west ends), jewellery (north-east corner), toilet articles and flint knives, some with incised handles decorated with gold (west quarter of the room).

The inner room contains animal mummies (some of them sacred animals) and their equipment, as well as a few plant specimens.

Room 54: Stone pounders and axes are exhibited on the stairs. Inside are flint tools and weapons, with a collection of mortars and pestles in stone against the east wall. From here proceed along the south side of

Room 49, which is devoted mostly to foundation deposits – models and plaques that were buried under new temples to protect the building from harm and eternally memorialize the builder. Model baskets of faience and limestone, tiny bronze adzes and other tools, alabaster bricks, plaques and model sacrificial offerings are concentrated on the eastern half of this corridor. Beyond, mostly in the middle, are faience jars and flasks, ornaments and inlay figures, vessels of glass and bronze, and also bronze inlay figures of Pharaohs and Nile gods – objects of modest elegance, with which this visit to the Egyptian Museum comes to an end.

Fowling and fishing scene from the tomb of Nakht

11. The Delta

Ancient records indicate that a good number of important cities, both ports and cult centres, flourished in the Delta during ancient times. Stone and brick monuments do not fare well in the moist climate, however, and many Delta sites are unrewarding to all but the most dedicated visitor. Few travellers, in fact, see more of Lower Egypt than the two cities of Cairo and Alexandria, a situation compounded in recent years by travel restrictions on foreigners. All main roads are open again, but it would be wise to inquire before setting out to any of the remoter spots mentioned in these pages.

The Delta

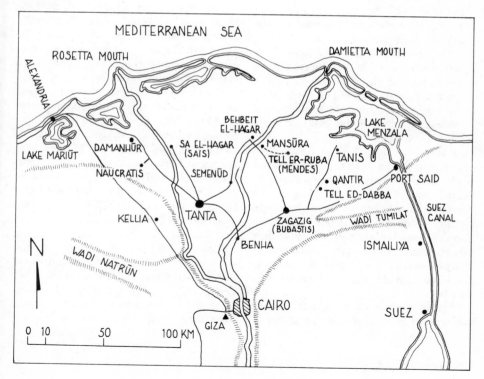

THE EAST DELTA

The length of the excursion (one way) is 167 kilometres (km.). Leaving Cairo on the road through the cultivation to Alexandria, go 49 km. north to Benha, then take the right-hand turning for *Zagazig* (87 km.): in the south-east corner of the town is the mound of Tell Basta (ancient Bubastis), home of the cat-goddess Bastet and capital of the eighteenth nome of Lower Egypt. Herodotus, who visited the place, reckoned that the annual feast in the goddess's honour was the greatest in all of Egypt. As many as 700,000 pilgrims gathered there from all parts of Egypt, and his report of the festal procession finds many an echo in scenes from the tombs:

> When the people are on their way to Bubastis, they go by river, men and women together, a great number of each in every boat. Some of the women make noise with rattles, others play flutes all the way, while the rest of the women, and the men, sing and clap their hands ... But when they have reached Bubastis, they make a festival with great sacrifices, and more wine is drunk at this feast than in the whole year beside.[1]

Excavations conducted since 1887 have yielded rich dividends to museums, but not much can be seen today. Of the main temple, located south of the main road, one can see fragments of a columned court, blocks of a portal decorated with jubilee scenes by Osorkon II, and of a hypostyle hall, leading to a sanctuary built under Nectanebo II. Many blocks from earlier periods, re-used in the present temple, are found strewn over the site.

Moving north of the main road, we find two rows of pillars that mark the site of an Old Kingdom structure (Sixth Dynasty, time of Pepi I) beyond which were the catacombs where the cats sacred to Bastet were buried.

Leaving Zagazig by the north-east road, proceed through Abu Kebir (113 km.) to Fakūs (124 km.), and there turn off the main road towards *Qantir*. On the way you will pass *Khatana* (128 km.), and near-by *Tell ed-Dabba*, the site of the Hyksos capital, Avaris: excavations now in progress have uncovered important information about these still obscure conquerors, but the site has nothing for the ordinary visitor. Beyond, at *Qantir*, was Piramesse, 'The Estate of Ramesses', Delta capital of the Nineteenth and early Twentieth Dynasties: not much remains *in situ*, though tiles and similar decoration from here are displayed in the Cairo Museum (see Chapter 10, p. 126). Because the local branch of the Nile began to dry up, the site was abandoned during the Twentieth Dynasty and many of its more portable monuments moved to *Tanis*, which is the final destination of this journey.

Eighteen km. beyond Qantir (51 km.), take a left turn, then go another 4 km. further (155 km.). From here, it is another 16 km., through increasingly desolate countryside, to the village of *Sa el-Hagar* (167 km.). The enormous mound that marks the site of Tanis is east of the road: capital of the 24th nome of Lower Egypt, ancient *Djāne* (= *Zoan* of the Bible [*Numbers* 13:22]) had its golden age relatively late in Egyptian history. From that time, however, its strategic position and harbour on Lake Menzala made it the first commercial port, until the Greek settlement at Naucratis (mod. El Nibeira, in the West Delta) and, later, the rise of Alexandria reduced it to a backwater. Enough survives from Tanis' great days, however, to make

---

1. Herodotus, *History*, II, 60.

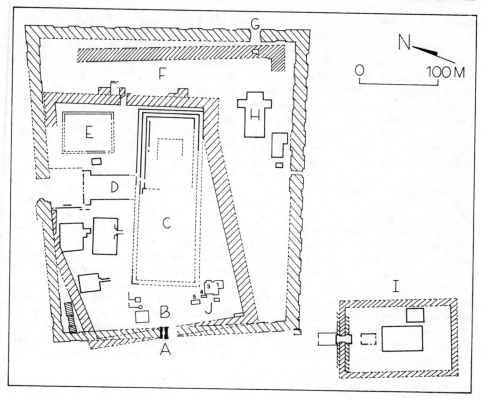

Fig. 15   **Tanis**

this site one of the most imposing in the Delta.

The great temple was located inside a double enclosure wall that today, owing to the huge mounds of rubble, is only seen sporadically. Enter on the west side, through the gate of Shoshenq III (Fig. 15, A), flanked by colossal statuary. Beyond is the avenue leading to the main temple (B), consisting of a colonnade with (originally) over fifteen obelisks from the time of Ramesses II. The collapse of these monoliths (some of which have been transported elsewhere) adds to the jumble of fallen masonry and statues that formed the remainder of the building (C).

Many of these blocks are superbly carved, and though few architectural remains are left *in situ*, the massiveness of the complex is all the more striking in its eerie, featureless setting.

To the north, but still within the inner enclosure wall, is the adjoining temple of the Thirtieth Dynasty (D) as well as several smaller buildings. The sacred lake (E) is at the north-east corner. Outside the east gate, note the ruins of a granite temple (F) with Old Kingdom palmiform columns re-used by Ramesses II and Osorkon II. South of this, facing a limestone gate built into the outer wall by Ptolemy I (G), are ruins of a temple dedicated to Horus, patron of Egypt's eastern border-town of Tcharu (H). Outside the wall, to the south-west, is a temple dedicated to Mut and Khonsu (I), wherein also the Canaanite goddess Astarte was worshipped.

Before leaving the inner enclosure, inquire if it is possible to visit the royal tombs of the Twenty-first and Twenty-second Dynasties (Fig. 15, J, Nos. 1, 3–5). Consisting only of underground chambers of stone with no superstructure, they yielded a rich trove of burial equipment now on display in the Cairo Museum (Chapter 10, p. 123).

T.1 belongs to Osorkon II, and consists of four limestone rooms before a burial chamber of granite. The third chamber was later converted into a tomb for Takelot II who was laid to rest in a Middle Kingdom coffin appropriated for the occasion. The decoration on the walls is devoted to episodes from the Osirian and solar mythological cycles (see Chapter 7, p. 84).

T.3 was built for Psusennes I but contained no fewer than four burials, three of them kings: Psusennes was buried by his successor, Amenemope, who built his own (undecorated) sarcophagus chamber in the same tomb. The burial of Shoshenq 'II', a co-regent of Osorkon I who never enjoyed an independent reign, was placed in the vestibule about a century later: the grave goods, including Psusennes' massive sarcophagus (appropriated from Merneptah, of the Nineteenth Dynasty), are all in the Cairo Museum (Chapter 10, p. 123).

T.4 was left unfinished by Amenemope, but his yellow quartzite sarcophagus, with its granite lid made from a re-used block of the Old Kingdom, can still be admired.

T.5 belongs to Shoshenq III and contains two sarcophagi, the larger of which (made out of an architrave dating to the Thirteenth Dynasty) may fairly reflect the political division and relative poverty of the country at this time.

THE CENTRAL DELTA

Sites in the central Delta (see Map, p. 129) may be reached from Zagazig, albeit on secondary roads. About 45 km. north of Zagazig is Mansūra: cross the Damietta branch of the Nile about 5 km. further north, to arrive at *Behbeit el-Hagar*, where the tumbled remains of a once-splendid temple are to be seen: built of massive pink- and grey-granite blocks, this temple to Isis was begun during the Thirtieth Dynasty and finished under Ptolemy II. The ruins are extensive, and the entire temple could conceivably be rebuilt. Until then, however, it will be difficult to obtain much of a sense of the building's former appearance.

A secondary road leading south-east from Mansūra proceeds some 25 km. to the village of Sembellawīn, from which a track leads another 15 km. to Tell er-Ruba, site of ancient *Mendes*. Portions of the Twenty-sixth Dynasty temple enclosure are still intact, but the ruins as a whole will make little sense to any but the archaeologist.

THE WEST DELTA

The road to Alexandria through the cultivation (223 km.) takes the traveller past a number of ancient sites, all in a poor state of preservation. Leave Cairo, as in the previous itinerary, by way of the Shubra district, arriving at the town of Benha after 49 km. North-east of town, note the great mound of *Tell Atrib*, the Athribis of the ancients, of which only some of the main streets and (to the west) the ruins of the temple to Horus-Khentikhety can be made out.

Cross the Damietta branch of the Nile and proceed to Tanta (93 km.), where the road is divided into two main branches, the eastern of which proceeds north-east to Mehalla el-Kūbra, then a few kilometres east to Semenūd (ancient Sebennytus) and thence north again, along the Damietta branch, to Behbeit el-Hagar (see above, p. 132). A side road between the two main branches goes north, through the town of Basyūn, before reaching *Sa el-Hagar*, the ancient Sais (28 km.). Virtually nothing is left of this ancient and important site.

The western branch of the main road leaves Tanta in the direction of Alexandria. A side road branches off to the west (47 km. from Tanta), after another 3 km. reaching the village of El Nibeira, site of the Greek commercial centre of *Naucratis* where — again — there is little to be seen. Resuming the main road, proceed north-west once more, through the town of Damanhūr and finally into the city of Alexandria.

An alternative road from Cairo to Alexandria runs through the desert (225 km.): turn off the Pyramids road just below the Giza plateau, before reaching the Mena House Hotel. Although slightly longer than the road through the cultivation, this way is easier to negotiate and also allows the visitor an opportunity to stop at the *Wadi Natrūn*. A former oasis, the area enjoyed a moist climate in antiquity that is much reduced today, with only a few monastery gardens to relieve the general dryness that has spread over the wadi depression.

Of the approximately fifty monasteries that flourished in the Wadi Natrūn early in the Christian era, only four remain active. The most southerly of these, the monastery of St Makarios, lies 89 km. north of Giza, some 5 km. due west in the desert along a serviceable track. The most dynamic of the extant foundations, it has also been heavily rebuilt and affords only a few glimpses of the old buildings amidst the modern improvements.

The Wadi Natrūn rest-house (103 km. from Giza) is the point of departure for a visit to the other three monasteries. Two of these, Deir Amba Bishoi and Deir es-Suriani

('Monastery of the Syrians'), lie quite close to each other and allow visitors access to their churches and some of the monks' common rooms, as well as into their *kasr's* or keeps — high towers, closed off from the other buildings by means of drawbridges, into which the monks would retreat when under attack from marauding Berbers. The fourth monastery, Deir Amba Baramos, lies to the north. The monks here are governed by a more severe rule than in the other establishments, and there are no distinguishing points of interest that may warrant a great effort to be admitted.

More characteristic of Egyptian monasticism are the communities of anchorites — monks who lived in cells apart from one another, gathering only to celebrate the divine office. A detour from the desert road will lead to one of these, at *Kellia*, which was discovered and excavated during the 1960s. Leave the main road 154 km. north of Giza, proceeding 20 km. north-west in the direction of Abu el-Matamīr; next turn south along the Nubariya Canal, following the track for 17 km. before crossing the canal and arriving (after 3 km.) at the site known locally as Kusur el-Rubeyyat. The hermitages of Kellia extend for roughly 20 km. in the vicinity. The remains, dating from the fourth to the ninth centuries A.D., are insignificant in themselves, but cumulatively they convey a powerful and austere impression.

ALEXANDRIA

Ancient Alexandria has vanished, engulfed in the modern town. The Christians converted many of the ancient monuments into churches and destroyed others; but the major decline was under the Arabs, who left many old buildings to decay, used quantities of others as quarries and, when the canopic branch of the Nile silted up during the twelfth century, allowed the city to remain

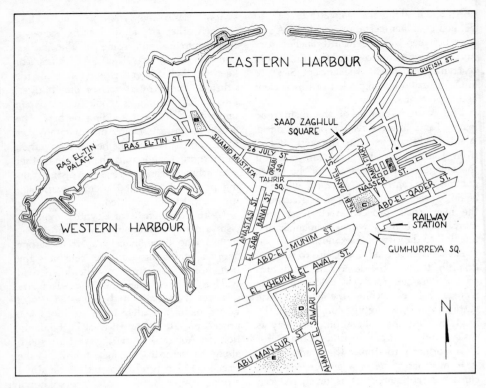

EASTERN HARBOUR

EL GUEISH ST.

SAAD ZAGHLUL
SQUARE

RAS EL-TIN ST.

SHAMID MUSTAFA

26 JULY ST.

ORABI SQ.

RAS EL-TIN
PALACE

TAHRIR
SQ.

NEBI DANIEL ST.

NASSER

ST.

ABD-EL-QADER ST.

WESTERN HARBOUR

ANASTASI ST.

EL SABA BANAT ST.

ABD-EL-MUNIM ST.

RAILWAY
STATION

GUMHURREYA SQ.

EL KHEDIVE EL AWAL ST.

ABU MANSUR ST.

AHMOUD EL SAWARI ST.

N

Alexandria

without a navigable connection with the rest of Egypt. The site was a wretched backwater in 1798 when Napoleon landed, and only under the sponsorship of Mohammed Ali and his successors did the city recover some of its old vitality. Alexandria today has an emphatically European air quite unlike any other Egyptian city. The ancient remains are scattered, however, and in general are not well preserved.

The most celebrated of the local sights in antiquity was the *Pharos* or lighthouse of Alexandria (see Map, A). Built on an island in the eastern harbour, it was connected to the city by a long dyke, the 'Heptastadion' (long sanded up; it is a

natural peninsula today). Originally some 120 metres high, the lighthouse was constructed in three stages — a circular section built on an octagon, which rested on a square base. At the top was apparatus for heliography during the day and for reflecting a fire at night, with the possible addition of another device — a mysterious 'mirror' that could detect ships far out to sea. Neglected by the Arabs, the building finally succumbed to two disastrous earthquakes, and the spot is marked today by the squat mass of the fort built by Sultan Qaitbay in 1480. Most of the complex, which is still used by the military authorities, is off limits to tourists, and the two very mediocre museums housed in the building (devoted to marine biology and naval history) are scarcely worth the visitor's time.

On leaving Fort Qaitbay, proceed towards the western harbour and the Ras el-Tin palace. The palace itself lies in a military area and is off limits, but a short distance to the north-east, on Midan Ibrahim Pasha, is the small *Anfushi Cemetery* (B on the Map, p. 134, and see Fig. 16). The tombs (dating to the third and second centuries B.C.) each consist of a sunken court, giving on to individual mortuary suites that accommodated one or more burials. The best preserved rooms have their walls painted to imitate marble or alabaster panelling.

On entering the right-hand tomb group (see Fig. 16, I–II) we encounter painted mythological scenes on the walls of the stairway: facing the entrance (a) we see the deceased led into the presence of Osiris and Isis by Anubis; another picture at the bottom of the stairs (b) shows Horus presenting the tomb owner to Osiris and Anubis in the Underworld. In the more elaborate of the two suites inside we see, at the end of the elaborately painted outer hall, two crouching sphinxes at either side of the entrance to the burial chamber, with the solar disc carved on the cornice above the door (c).

In the left-hand tomb-group, the vestibule of the tomb opposite the entrance is provided with benches, either for the use of mourners or to receive the grave goods deposited in the tomb (d). A large sarcophagus of rose-coloured Aswan granite dominates the burial chamber (e). In the other suite, to the left of the court, we find a number of subsidiary burials introduced during the Roman period (f).

In the centre of town, at the north end of Midan el-Gumhureya (see Map, p. 134, C) there is a municipal park on the site of *Kom el-Dik*. Inside is a small Roman amphitheatre, built during the second century A.D. and remodelled in later centuries to serve as an assembly hall for religious associations. The building today has thirteen rows of seats

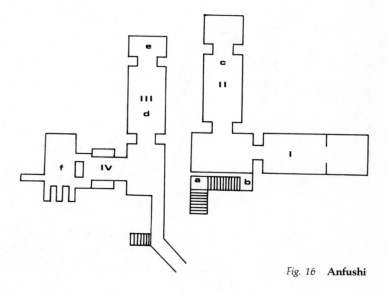

Fig. 16   **Anfushi**

(accommodating about 800 persons) made out of white and grey marble. The many-hued stone columns at the top helped to support the structure's domed roof (now collapsed). North of the theatre, in another sector of the park, are the remains of an immense Roman bath built out of mud-brick: only partly excavated at present, it is to be restored in the same manner as the amphitheatre.

The *ruins of the Serapeum* (see D on the Map, p. 134, and see Fig. 17) are located in

Fig. 17   Serapeum area ('Pompey's Pillar')

one of the more Oriental parts of town: the site is bounded on the north by a large Muslim cemetery. This, the hill of Rhakote, was the oldest part of Alexandria, so it is not surprising that the site has yielded a number of Pharaonic monuments amidst the Classical ruins. The most imposing of the remains is a giant column of granite (Fig. 17, A) set up in honour of the Emperor Diocletian after he had quelled a rebellion here in 297 A.D. A statue of the emperor probably stood on its capital, but during the Middle Ages visitors from the West assumed that a globe containing the head of Caesar's rival Pompey had been exhibited from here, and it has been known ever since as 'Pompey's Pillar'. At the edge of the terrace south of the column are two red granite sphinxes (probably Ptolemaic) flanking a headless black granite sphinx of the late Eighteenth Dynasty (B). Statues of Ramesses II and Psamtik I stand nearby. The temple proper lay west of the column. Virtually nothing remains, but visitors are taken into subterranean galleries (D), some of which were burial vaults for sacred jackals, beneath the temple of Anubis. Still other galleries (C) have shelves set into the walls — the only standing reminder of a foundation that had made Alexandria the intellectual capital of the Graeco-Roman world. The great Library, located in another part of the city, had probably been destroyed during the turmoil that accompanied the fall of the house of Ptolemy. This smaller library remained, adjoining the Serapeum, until its collections of pagan literature were dispersed by the Christian zealots who took control of Alexandria in the fifth century A.D. Ruins of similar galleries can be seen in the desolate area that lies south of the visitors' tunnels, pitiful remnants of the imposing buildings that once stood on this site. In the south-east corner of the enclosure, now turned into a park, note the colossal limestone statue of Isis Pharia (E), a deity associated with the Alexandrian lighthouse, which was recovered from the sea off Fort Qaitbay.

Not far from the Serapeum area are the *Kom es-Shogafa catacombs* (E on the Map, p. 134, and see Fig. 18). This complex is much later than the Anfushi cemetery, dating to approximately the first half of the second century A.D. Unlike the Anfushi group, moreover, this is a mass tomb of the type used in antiquity by burial corporations whose members paid dues to give one another decent funerals. Originally, perhaps, the tomb belonged to a wealthy member of the Alexandrian bourgeoisie, but in its final form it boasts a warren of passages and burial chambers on several levels, not all of which are accessible to the average visitor.

We enter the catacomb by means of a spiral stairway that terminates in a landing (Fig. 18, A): the dead were lowered by ropes down the well in the centre and passed through the large openings at the bottom.

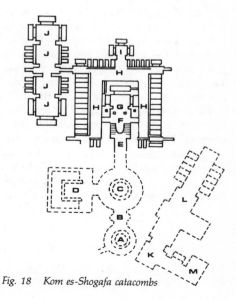

Fig. 18   Kom es-Shogafa catacombs

Infirm members of the cortège could rest on benches set within a niche at either side of the vestibule (B): note the half-shell carved into the vaulted upper halves of each niche. Beyond is another landing (C), built around a second well: the rotunda has a domed ceiling supported by eight pillars, and casts of five marble heads found at the bottom of the shaft are displayed at various points.[2] A doorway on the left side (from the vestibule) passes into a large pillared room (D) with great stone couches set into its three sides: this was the *triclinium*, the banquet-hall where members of the funerary party met in memory of the dead. Guests reclined on the couches (which were piled with mattresses for the occasion) and dined off a wooden table in the centre of the room.

A stairway (E) now leads down into the lower storey, to the so-called 'central tomb', which was in fact an elegant façade for the rather simple burials that took place here. The porch (F) is supported by two papyrus columns with elaborate floral capitals – full-scale examples will be seen in the great temples of Upper Egypt. On the side walls are niches containing statues of a woman (left) and a man (right) – perhaps the original owners of the tomb, if these images have more than a purely representative value. Two serpents, bearded and wearing the double crown, are carved on to the walls at either side of the entrance to the inner room: in their coils they hold the pine cone of Dionysos and the serpent staff of Hermes, thereby associating themselves with the protection these gods confer on the dead. A similar intent probably lies behind the gorgons' heads carved on the shields above them, perhaps with the purpose of repelling evil influences from the tomb.

Passing through the portal (surmounted by its winged disc and frieze of cobras), we enter the mock burial chamber (G).[3] Carved images of Anubis (right) and Seth-Typhon (left), both in the armour of a Roman soldier, flank the entrance. Sarcophagi, decorated with festoons of grape leaves, gorgons' heads and ox skulls, are set into the remaining three walls: the lids do not lift off, but the cavity can be reached from the passage at the back, so perhaps the bodies were placed in them during the funeral ceremonies. The walls at the back of each of these niches are carved with Egyptianizing funerary scenes. In the central niche we see on the back wall the mummy, lying on a lion-headed couch, protected by Horus, Anubis and Thoth, with three canopic jars under the couch; a priest is seen officiating before the deceased (male and female respectively) on the side walls. The two side-niches, with small variations, are similarly decorated, showing the king before the Apis Bull on a pedestal and a winged goddess. Finally, the galleries around the outside of the chamber (H), with a principal niche (I) and a subsidiary – later? – suite (J), are lined with shelves cut into the rock, to contain the bodies or cinerary urns of the deceased.

Another group of tombs is situated on the upper level and can be entered through a breach in the wall of the rotunda (C). Beyond the well room (K) is a charming painted tomb (L), with scenes painted on the white stuccoed walls: at the back, Isis and Nephthys protect the mummy of Osiris in the presence of two horned figures. The

---

2. The originals are in the Graeco-Roman Museum (see below, pp. 140–41).

3. Owing to the proximity of the Mahmudiya Canal, which connects Alexandria to the Nile, the floor is covered with water; but planking has been laid down for the visitor's convenience.

scenes on the side walls are faded, but the pilasters preserve their colour, showing the human-headed Ba-bird (inner face) and also a falcon god – no doubt one of the four sons of Horus – standing on a lotus with a flower in his hand (outer face). The large hall beyond (M) is fancifully called the 'Hall of Caracalla' because the great quantity of bones, both of men and of horses, found on the floor recalls the story of a famous massacre of Christians under that emperor. The walls of this and other adjoining chambers are pierced with the usual shelves designed to hold the bodies of the dead.

ALEXANDRIA MUSEUM

The Graeco-Roman Museum (see Fig. 19), in which many objects found in and around Alexandria are exhibited, is found just off Nasser Street of Kom el-Dik (F on the Map, p. 134). It is open daily from 9 a.m. to 4 p.m.,

except on Friday, when it closes between 12 noon and 2 p.m. (in summer) or between 11.15 a.m. and 1.30 p.m. (in winter).

The Vestibule: Two headless sphinxes, dated to the reign of Apries, occupy dominant positions. Proceed to the left into

Room 6: The largest object exhibited here at present is the great diorite statue of the Apis Bull found near 'Pompey's Pillar': set up during the reign of the Emperor Hadrian (A.D. 117–38), the idol was buried with a number of others during the Christian sack of the Serapeum in 391. A collection of Roman masks and funerary stelae are displayed along the walls of this room.

Room 7: Pharaonic antiquities are exhibited in this and adjoining chambers. Note, in the centre of the room, the large red granite statue of Ramesses II with one of his

Fig. 19 **Alexandria,** *Graeco-Roman Museum*

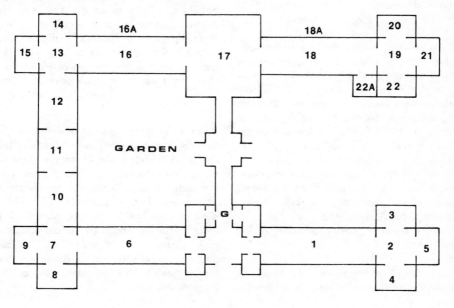

daughters by his side. The two headless sphinxes flanking this piece were originally carved under Amenemhēt IV of the Twelfth Dynasty, but the inscriptions were re-carved for Ramesses II. In the niches flanking the doorway from Room 6 we find two basalt statues of Isis. Note also the black granite priest, holding a naos containing a figure of the triumphant Horus (Roman Period) to the left of the entrance to Room 9. All the above pieces were found at Abukir, 24 km. east of Alexandria. Of the smaller antiquities displayed about the room, the most striking is the small Hathor column capital, with the goddess's head carved on each of its four sides, from a small shrine once located in Alexandria.

Room 8: Mummies and sarcophagi, gilded and painted, form the bulk of this room's exhibits: note the contrast between the Pharaonic mummies, with their elaborately painted cartonage masks and sheathings, and the later mummies, with their patterned layers of bandages and life-like portraits of the deceased set over their faces.

Room 9: The objects in this room were taken from the temple of the crocodile god Pnepheros at Theadelphia (Batn Herit) in the Faiyūm. On the left side is a wooden door which (according to a Greek inscription on the right) was dedicated by an Alexandrian citizen in 137 B.C. On the left side of the room is the portable shrine on which the living god was borne during processional feasts: a crocodile mummy is now displayed on the stretcher. Frescoes from the temple are exhibited on the west wall. Among smaller objects, note the statue in black basalt of the lion goddess Sekhmet against the east wall.

Room 10: A mélange of late Pharaonic objects is displayed in this room. Painted wooden coffin lids are arranged along the north and east walls, and the display-cases contain a variety of amulets, statuettes, vases and coloured glass. Among the large objects, note the colossal red granite head of Ptolemy IV from Abukir in the centre of the room, and the fine black granite statue of a vizier, wearing the formal dress of the Eighteenth Dynasty, in the south-east corner. A fine torso of Medusa, with traces of her headdress of serpents still remaining on her shoulders, is found in Case F (north-east quarter of the room).

Room 11: Assorted pieces of a mixed Egyptian and Hellenistic style are shown in this room, which also boasts a mosaic pavement at its centre. On the south wall we see a number of so-called 'Agathodaimon stelae' – small plaques bearing images of these divine serpents and their worshippers. Large sculptured fragments from the Egyptianizing temple at Athribis in the central Delta occupy much of the north wall: the human-headed god Tutu, wearing a curious crown worked with the heads of sacred animals and birds (right), faces Horus of Athribis (left), with a broken inscription in Greek between them. Statues of deities and of officials are also displayed in various quarters of the room.

Room 12 is given over to statuary of the Graeco-Roman Period: note especially the fine head of Julius Caesar to the right of the entrance (No. 3243) and, in the centre of the room, a large statue of the Emperor Marcus Aurelius. Against the east wall we see a famous bust of Serapis, with flowing locks and beard and with the characteristic grain measure on his head. Near the east doorway, in the centre of the room, note the bronze head with glass inlaid eyes of the Emperor Hadrian.

Room 13: More Graeco-Roman sculpture. The limestone head of a queen facing the entrance, with its royal serpent head-dress, is believed to represent the features of Cleopatra VII (No. 21992). A colossal statue of one of the Roman emperors stands in the middle of the room: the head (of Septimius Severus) was added later. The display-cases exhibit a variety of small objects found in excavations around Alexandria: note the painted stucco fragments from ancient buildings (Case B) and the model altars in limestone (Case C). Statues of orators and poets stand in the niches at the corners of the room.

Room 14: Miscellaneous statuary. On the floor is a mosaic pavement that originally showed the head of Medusa: her coiffure of serpents can be made out at the sides, but the central part of the mosaic is destroyed. Model architectural elements — for instance, miniature temple façades and small columns — are exhibited on the walls.

Room 15: Tomb paintings: note especially (in the centre of the room) a not-too-idealized scene of country life, showing a water-wheel turned by two oxen: the painting, in subdued greens and browns, is impressionist in style, avoiding the fussiness of other essays in this genre. Other paintings (including an elaborate candelabrum on the south wall) and painted architectural fragments line the sides of the room.

Room 16: A wealth of Graeco-Roman statues is displayed in this hall. On entering, note the colossal marble forearm, its hand gripping a ball (centre, north half); and the giant eagle, dating to the Ptolemaic Period, found on the Aegean island of Thasos (centre, middle). Opposite the ballplayer's arm, on the west wall, is a headless personification of the Nile — naked on his rocky throne, with his left arm resting on a hippopotamus and holding a cornucopia: the two nude children under the inscription on the throne represent the river's height during the Inundation. Nearby (No. 17838) is a haunting bust of Demeter Selene, her slightly uncanny expression heightened by the two horn-tips projecting from her forehead. A curious stela in high relief, found in the south-east corner, represents the god Cronos — a composite figure, half human and half goat, with a lion's head, four wings and a nimbus around its head, holding in its hands two keys, two snakes and a thunderbolt, and having a torch resting against its right shoulder. Of special quality also is the sarcophagus lid against the east wall just north of the entrance to Room 16A, on which, sculpted in the round, reclines an old man, his pose and expression both eloquent of great weariness in repose.

Room 16A: Small objects are displayed in cases arranged around the room, with larger pieces of sculpture between them. Note especially (Case 4: east wall, north half) the bust of Alexander the Great (top) and a sculptured toad — probably an accessory to a fountain in a private home. A funerary stela in the Greek style (east wall, centre) shows a lady with her serving woman. In the south half of the room, note the black granite head of a young god (?), with his thick locks of hair, parted lips and anxious expression (Case 2, middle, left); and the heads of Serapis (Case 1, middle), with their serenely thoughtful features.

Room 17: The central position is taken by a huge headless statue of an enthroned Roman emperor, carved out of porphyry — the largest sculpture yet found in Alexandria. A mosaic on the floor (centre) shows a family gathering in the country: the members of the party sit inside a kiosk, while in the garden outside cherub-like huntsmen pursue birds and animals (including a crocodile and a hippopotamus at the top right corner). Other mosaic fragments are mounted on the walls, and around the room are displayed stone sarcophagi, both of the box and 'bathtub' types. One fine example, against the north half of the west wall, is carved with scenes from Greek mythology: on the façade, note the sleeping Ariadne, with the god of sleep behind her head and with Dionysos and his followers on the right side (left); and the drunken Heracles being helped homewards (right). Among the other statues displayed in the room, the Hercules standing to the right of the entrance to Room 18 is especially fine.

Room 18: Just inside the entrance is a small case containing several spectacular examples of Alexandrian coloured glass. More mosaic fragments are on the floor, and a large wooden statue of Serapis is in the centre of the room. The cases against the walls yield an interesting cross-section of objects of daily use — vases, lamps, moulds, statuettes and other bric-à-brac. Note the children's toys in Case J (west wall, north), and the ceremonial amphora having around its neck an artificial wreath of green leaves and golden berries (east wall, south corner).

Room 18A: More small objects, similar to those in Room 18. Especially fine, though, are the terracotta statuettes: these 'Tanagra' figurines, named after their city of origin in Northern Greece, are noted for their polychrome painting against a white background. The Alexandrian collection, spanning from the third century B.C. to the first century A.D., is especially informative about ladies' fashions in the ancient world, but there are also some highly individualized pieces — notably, the lamp showing a winged Eros embracing Psyche, or the crouching Negro (Case R), and images of tradesmen (Case E).

Room 19: Stone and pottery jars are exhibited along the walls: the clay pots are plain or moulded, glazed or painted. Cinerary urns are displayed at the corners of the room. Note too the iridescence of the decomposing glass phials in Case F (centre, south).

Room 20: More funerary urns, with examples (centre, east half) of mortuary wreaths — either with gold berries (cf. Room 18) or gilded plaster flowers.

Room 21: Still more funerary urns, together with a few skulls added for effect. The most interesting of the room's contents, however, is found on the south wall, consisting of a collection of stamped jar handles: these impressions — one of the earliest examples of commercial labelling — identify the potter and his place of origin.

Room 22: An assortment of fragments from Canopus — architectural elements and mosaics — is displayed along the walls. Note the curious mosaic floor, with its inlay of rough coloured pebbles set into cement.

Room 22A: This room is the 'treasury' of the museum: plaques of silver and gold and of painted pottery, inscribed in Greek and Egyptian on behalf of Ptolemy III, formed part of the foundation deposits for buildings in the Serapeum complex (east wall, south; south wall, east). Ptolemaic, Roman and Byzantine coins of gold and silver are found further along the south wall, while gold-leaf ornaments, gold jewellery and bowls, and cameos are displayed on the north side. In the centre of the room, note the hollow silver torso of Aphrodite and the richly detailed silver cup, with its riot of grape vines worked along the exterior.

The Garden of the museum is tightly packed with antiquities, the overflow from the galleries. The administrative offices are on the south side of the passage. In the south-east corner are two reconstructed tombs – one of them (first century B.C.) having three funerary couches under a niche carved in the half-shell motif; the other (third century B.C.) has a single pillowed couch in stone. Note in the south-west section (just north of the stairs) a small but finely carved statue of Amasis and a woolly ram in marble next to it.

The north garden is even more densely packed: note the statues of Ramesses II with one of his daughters and of Mark Antony (in green granite) as Osiris. At the west end is the shrine of the crocodile god Pnepheros (cf. Room 9): two crouching lion statues precede the first of three portals, at the end of which is the painted shrine where the crocodile mummy lay. A Greek inscription on the pylon informs us that the donor, one Agathodemos, was an Alexandrian citizen.

Room 'G': Another prominent Alexandrian called Isidore dedicated the limestone gate that flanks the eastern doorway, and also the marble foot (north half), both commemorating divine intervention in healing his broken leg. Nearby (from the same temple) are 'canopic' jar figures of Osiris in the form under which he was worshipped at Canopus (Abukir): one wears a conical hat, the other a disc with plumes. We now pass once again through the vestibule of the museum and into

Room 1: The contents of this and the adjoining rooms date to the early centuries of the present era and are mostly Christian in inspiration. Exceptions to this rule must be made, however, for the two stone plaques showing Leda and the swan, and also for the delightful pair of young women leaning with their backs against a cornucopia (all east wall). The Christian votive inscriptions and stelae, together with the ubiquitous 'pilgrim's flasks', exhibited along the rest of the east and west walls strike a number of recurring themes, especially where St Menas, patron of the Mariūt area near Alexandria, is concerned: legend has it that the martyr's shrine was founded there when the camel bearing his corpse stopped there and refused to go any further; and this incident provided the germ for St Menas' characteristic stance between two camels on many of these pieces. Note, in the centre of the room, the giant basket column capital, hollowed out for re-use as a baptismal font. A congealed hoard of coins, a woollen cushion and an interesting assortment of ivory artefacts (some of them carved with pagan themes) are found in the central cases of the north half of the room; and a Christian mummy – tightly bandaged and with a cross painted on its neck – can be seen at the south end.

Room 2 is filled with Coptic architectural fragments and stelae.

Room 3: Facing the entrance is a large alabaster statue of the Good Shepherd, found at Mersa Matruh. Along the walls are painted fragments of stucco from monasteries at Kom Abu Girgeh – St Menas with his camels (east, north half), a winged angel (east, south half), mandalas (south, west half) and assorted saints (north). Note also the pottery coffins, shaped like large slippers, with an opening left at the top of one end: the outer surface of the larger coffin is painted with a bandage pattern.

Room 4 is dominated by the display of Coptic textiles on the walls. A storage jar from the Wadi Natrūn, elaborately painted with birds, fish and assorted fruits, with a figure of Christ (?) in the medallion, is located at the centre of the room.

Room 5: More Coptic textiles. In the central display case there is a curious pottery model, representing either the Labyrinth of Minos or a water-cooling system.

ENVIRONS OF ALEXANDRIA

Practically nothing remains at the ancient site of Canopus, 24 km. east of Alexandria at *Abukir.* The western road out of the city passes between the sea and Lake Mariūt (see the Map, p. 129) to reach *Abusir,* the ancient Taposiris Magna (48 km. from Alexandria, south of the road). The main point of interest here is the lighthouse, a model of the Alexandrian Pharos that is one-tenth the size of its prototype. The building has been reconstructed, and a wooden staircase leads up to the summit. West of the tower is the limestone temple enclosure: the two pylon towers, though uninscribed, strike an Egyptianizing note, but the interior underwent many changes at the hands of its Christian inhabitants, so only the foundations of the church and adjoining structures remain today. The area to the south, between the temple and the lighthouse, is filled with ruined houses overlooking the desolate fringes of Lake Mariūt.

The road from Alexandria continues, through the war memorials at El Alamein (103 km.) to Mersa Matruh (291 km.), a resort town. The road to Siwa branches off some 15 km. further west, while the main thoroughfare meets the Libyan border at 225 km. from Mersa Matruh. A visit to the Oasis of Siwa is worthwhile for anyone with the time, interest and resources for the attempt (see Chapter 22), but it may be impossible for political reasons: check with a travel agent or the local authorities.

The Great Sphinx, in the mortuary complex of Khafrē (Giza)

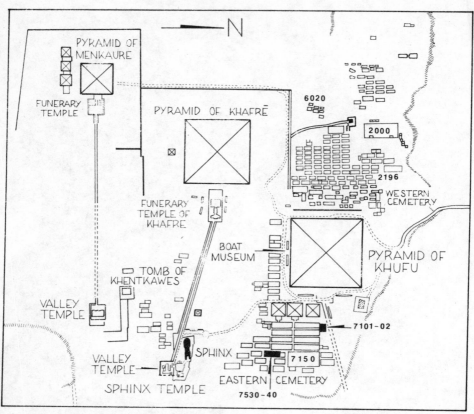

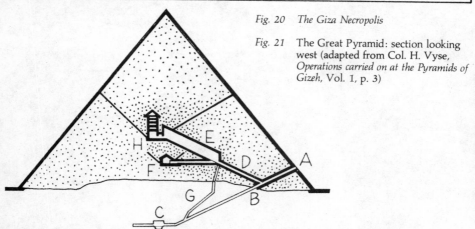

Fig. 20   The Giza Necropolis

Fig. 21   The Great Pyramid: section looking
west (adapted from Col. H. Vyse,
*Operations carried on at the Pyramids of
Gizeh*, Vol. 1, p. 3)

12. Giza to Abusir

The monuments discussed in this chapter lie in the northern extension of the Memphite cemetery. Congested conditions at Saqqara, just opposite the capital, had already prompted kings of the later Third Dynasty to shift their tombs further north (Zawiyet el-Aryan), setting a precedent for the far-flung burials of the Fourth Dynasty (Giza, Abu Rawash) and those of the Fifth Dynasty, situated somewhat closer to Memphis at Abusir (see Map, p. 181).

GIZA

The great tombs of the Fourth Dynasty rise up on the plateau of Giza (Fig. 20), a short distance south-west of Cairo. Built at the height of the Fourth Dynasty, their immensity is strikingly revealed when they are first seen, at a distance of several kilometres, from the road which the French Empress Eugénie inaugurated in 1896 during opening ceremonies for the Suez Canal.

The main road ascends to the top of the plateau just north of the *Great Pyramid*, which is generally the first to be visited (Fig. 20). The largest of the Giza group, it is preserved to 137 of its original 146 metres in height, with a base measurement of 230.38 (originally 232.77): the reduction in its dimensions is due mostly to the removal of the outer casing of limestone from the Tura quarries across the river, of which a few blocks are still preserved *in situ* at the base

of the pyramid. This imposing monument, which even in its denuded state accounts for 2,352,000 cubic metres of stone, was built by Khufu (called Cheops by the Greeks) – an achievement that gave him ever after an unflatteringly tyrannical reputation, even in the native traditions of his country.[1]

The presently used entrance to the pyramid is the tunnel cut into the building's core, according to Arab legend, by Caliph Ma'amūn in the ninth century A.D. Located a short distance below the building's original entry (Fig. 21, A), it soon connects with the descending gallery (B) leading 112 m. down, into the bedrock of the plateau, to a small room that was the original burial-chamber of the pyramid (C). The lower reaches of this passage are usually kept locked, however, so the visitor has no choice but to enter the ascending corridor (D) that opens on to the so-called Grand Gallery (E). A horizontal passage from the bottom of this hall leads into the so-called 'Queen's Chamber' (F), a small room with a pointed roof and a niche in the east wall that was perhaps meant to hold a statue of the king. The 'Queen's Chamber' was left unfinished when the pyramid was closed, suggesting that it too was designed as a burial chamber before a more ambitious plan was put into effect. Note, too, the opening (G) that leads down into the original descending gallery (B) and which perhaps served as an escape route for the workmen charged with blocking the bottom of

1. See the passage in Herodotus cited above (Chapter 7, p. 79); also the tale from Papyrus Westcar translated in William Kelly Simpson, *The Literature of Ancient Egypt* (New York: Yale University Press, 1973), pp. 15–30.

the ascending corridor (D) after the king's funeral.

The Grand Gallery (E) is a continuation of the ascending corridor, but conceived on a far grander scale: 8.5 m. in height and 47 m. long, it is roofed with a corbel vault of unprecedented dimensions and is miraculously engineered to avoid the accumulation of pressure on any single point of the structure. The visitor passes through a low passage at the top of the Grand Gallery into a small room, sheathed in red granite, with four slots that contained the granite portcullises which were lowered after the funeral to obstruct the way to the burial chamber. This room, built entirely of red granite, is known as the 'King's Chamber' and is devoid of decoration or any furnishing other than a lidless sarcophagus in black granite. The weight of the masonry above the ceiling — which itself weighs about 400 tons — is relieved by five compartments above, the uppermost having a pointed roof (H). Ventilation of the burial chamber is provided by two air shafts that proceed from the north and south walls to the surface of the pyramid.

The mortuary temple on the east side of the pyramid is preserved only in the basalt pavement still found there. The causeway down to the cultivation has virtually disappeared, and the remains of the valley temple have been engulfed by the village below. East of the pyramid and across the road are three queens' pyramids, of which the southernmost was graced by the addition of a chapel in the late period and was regarded as the shrine of 'Isis, Mistress of the Pyramid'. The Great Pyramid is surrounded by five boat pits that housed vessels used during the funeral of the king. The pit on the south-west side is still unexcavated, but the south-eastern pit yielded a completely dismantled river barge that was perhaps used during Khufu's funeral. The vessel has been reconstructed and now rests in a building set up on the site of the discovery.

The *Pyramid of Khafrē* (Chephren in Greek), a short distance south-west of the Great Pyramid, is almost as large as its neighbour (136.5 m. high, with a base measurement of 210.5 m. each side), and is preserved virtually to its full height due to the preservation of the limestone casing at the building's apex. The lowest course of the pyramid's outer 'skin', however, is composed of red granite blocks (preserved best at the west end of the south side), the hard stone's solidity helping to minimize the risk of slippage in the outer casing.

The internal arrangement of Khafrē's pyramid is simple when compared with the inner chambers of the Great Pyramid. The principal entrance (Fig. 22, A) opens into a descending corridor that proceeds horizontally on reaching bedrock to the burial chamber (B). Inside the chamber which, except for the limestone gabled roof, is entirely cut out of the rock is a rectangular granite sarcophagus set for most of its height into the floor. Nearby is the broken lid, found in this condition by the Italian explorer Giovanni Belzoni when he opened the pyramid in 1818. A peculiarity of this monument is its possession of a second entrance (Fig. 22, C) hewn into the pavement below the main entrance. The descending corridor plunges sharply into the bedrock, then becomes horizontal for a short distance before turning up again to join the corridor that leads into the burial chamber. A room is cut into the west side of the lower passage (D), and it has been suggested that the lower gallery was begun on the assumption that the pyramid itself would be located some distance further north. Both ends of the lower gallery are still blocked with stones and are inaccessible to visitors.

Khafrē's mortuary temple is separated from the east side of the pyramid by

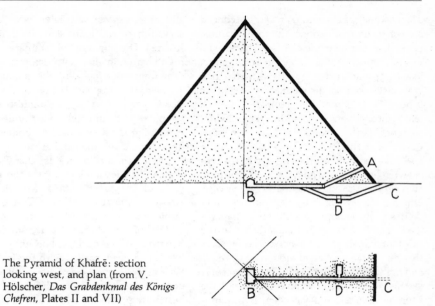

Fig. 22   The Pyramid of Khafrē: section looking west, and plan (from V. Hölscher, *Das Grabdenkmal des Königs Chefren*, Plates II and VII)

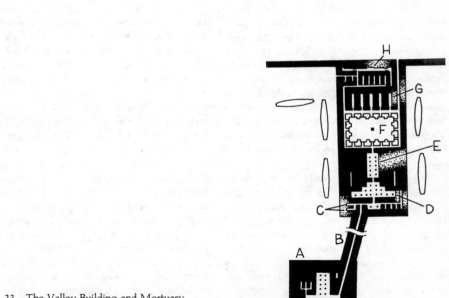

Fig. 23   The Valley Building and Mortuary Temple of Khafrē (Hölscher, op. cit., Plate III)

a limestone pavement. Although reduced almost to its foundations, the main features of its plan can be made out (see Fig. 23). Its lowest course was sheathed in red granite, like the pyramid itself, and the hard stone was also used as panelling for chambers inside the building. The temple's entrance leads into a narrow corridor (Fig. 23, C) running north-to-south: it has been suggested that the two chambers at the south end were reserved for the worship of the two crowns of Egypt, while the four northern chapels were shrines, for the king's viscera, which were protected by the four presiding deities of the canopic jars. A central passage leads into two columned halls (D, E), at the sides of which are two narrow enclosures that may have contained models of the day- and night-barques of the sun. The open court at the centre of the temple (F) must have been an impressive place when it was preserved: the unroofed area was surrounded by a cloister supported by red granite piers, while from recesses in all but the corner piers projected seated statues of the king, each nearly four metres high. Behind the open court were five chapels (G), each with a niche in the back wall to hold a statue of the king. The five smaller chambers behind these chapels were probably magazines attached to them, while in the corridor at the very back of the temple (H) was the false door, the final and most crucial focus of the mortuary cult.

The causeway (Fig. 23, B) runs down the side of the plateau to the valley temple (A) which, unlike most other buildings of this sort, is substantially preserved. Built of local limestone with a facing, external and internal, of red granite, it conveys a sense of mass out of proportion with its relatively small dimensions. It was here that the purification and embalming rites were performed before the king's funeral, the building later being used to house the statues

and other regalia associated with the preservation of the limbs and royal status of Khafrē. The amount of statuary actually found here — in all, twenty-six pieces, whole or in fragments, including the famous diorite statue of the king with the falcon god Horus (see Chapter 10, p. 109) — suggests that the temple served ultimately as a glorified *serdab*, containing multiple substitute bodies for the deceased's use if the need arose.

Just to the north, beside Khafrē's causeway and valley building, rises the gigantic mass of the *Great Sphinx*. Known to the Arabs as Abu Hōl, 'Father of Terror', it was fashioned out of a limestone outcropping left by the builders of the Great Pyramid, having the shape of a crouching lion with a human head. The head, carved with the features of Khafrē, was once provided with a royal uraeus-serpent on its forehead and with a beard (fragments of which are in the Cairo Museum; see Chapter 10, p. 108), and the whole perhaps represents the king manifest as the sun god, here acting as the sentinel of his pyramid. Between the creature's legs is a small altar and a votive stela left by King Thutmose IV of the Eighteenth Dynasty, describing how the Sphinx appeared to him in a dream to foretell his accession to the throne, and how the king in gratitude cleared away the sand that had engulfed the Sphinx's body. The temple in front of the Sphinx, built at about the same time as Khafrē's valley temple and with the same materials, is far less well preserved. The New Kingdom temple of the Sphinx, on the rise north-east of the colossus, is in similarly poor condition.

The *Pyramid of Menkaurē* (Mycerinus in Greek) stands in the south-west corner of the plateau. By far the smallest of the Giza group (about 66 m. high, 108 m. in length on each side), it appears to have been left unfinished at his death, for the lower sixteen courses are sheathed in red granite blocks, some of which had not been given their final smooth

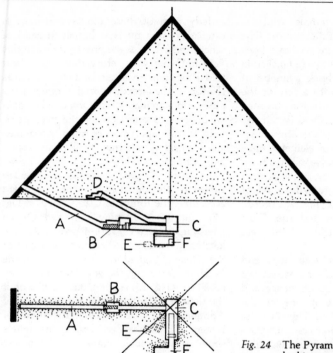

Fig. 24 The Pyramid of Menkaurē: section looking east, and plan (Vyse, op. cit., Vol. II, pp. 72 and 80)

dressing when work on the pyramid was stopped. The entrance, as usual, is on the north face of the building, with the familiar descending corridor (Fig. 24, A) leading into a short passage that opens into an antechamber: the carved stone panels on the walls of this chamber (B) are among the few purely decorative features inside the Giza pyramids. A horizontal corridor leads from here into a long, rectangular room (C) oriented from east to west. This chamber underwent a number of changes before reaching its final form. Originally it was the burial chamber of the first plan of the pyramid, reached by a descending corridor located above the present gallery (D). When the pyramid was enlarged, the floor of this room (C) was lowered, so the outlet from

the earlier passage may now be seen near the ceiling. Still later, the room was enlarged westward, serving as a vestibule to the two chambers that were now added. The first, off the north-west corner (E) has a total of six niches, the distribution of which is so reminiscent of the entrance suite in Khafrē's mortuary temple (see above, p. 150, at C) that it seems certain that the canopic jars and personal regalia of Menkaurē rested here. In the second room (F) – the burial chamber proper – was found a splendid basalt sarcophagus with carved panel decoration which, unfortunately, was lost in a shipwreck on its way to England.

The three queens' pyramids south of Menkaurē's monument were never finished. Signs of hasty and incomplete execution also abound in the mortuary temple, which is built against the pyramid's east side. The inner and outer walls were to have been faced with black granite, but were finished in painted plaster over crude brick: a number of examples of this, along with a few of the granite blocks already *in situ*, can be seen inside the building. The temple is actually better preserved than Khafrē's and the plan is similar, though a number of elements have been rearranged or (in inessential features) suppressed. The valley temple at the bottom of the causeway is too ruined to be of interest, but a number of fine sculptures, ornaments of the Boston and the Cairo Museums (see Chapter 10, p. 108) were discovered there.

North of the Menkaurē causeway and opposite the Great Pyramid, we may notice a curious tomb whose size, prominence and composite structure make it one of the landmarks of the area (see Fig. 20). Its owner, a lady named *Khenthawes*, was probably a daughter of Menkaurē and was also the queen of Userkaf, founder of the Fifth Dynasty. It consists of a rectangular hillock cut from the surrounding rock, on which a mastaba-like structure was built out of limestone blocks. The chapel, with remains of a granite false door inside, is found at the south-east corner of the lower level. A descending corridor at the rear of the chapel leads to the burial chambers. This complex of magazines and cult rooms is apparently unique in Old Kingdom architecture, but some visitors might find the descent hazardous and it is not recommended.

The private cemeteries of Giza are laid out around the pyramids that dominate the site. The earliest burials were located east and west of the Great Pyramid, with later cemeteries situated near the other two, but the orderly plan of these blocks of tombs is often disrupted by later burials, usually of officials who held some priestly office in this Fourth Dynasty cemetery during the later Old Kingdom. From an eminence (such as the top of the Great Pyramid, if one has the pluck and stamina to climb it[2]) one can gain an impressive overview of the necropolis, with its rows upon rows of tombs, organized along a grid system that is still plain despite later intrusive buildings.

Most of the private tombs at Giza are closed to the public. Of those which are accessible, the tombs of Qar (G 7101 = Fig. 27), Idu (G 7102 = Fig. 28) and Queen Mersyankh III (G 7530–40 = Fig. 29) are located in the Eastern Cemetery, just east of the Great Pyramid (see Fig. 20). In the Western Cemetery, the small tomb of Iasen (G 2196 = Fig. 25) is open, but the visitor, if the time permits, might ask the Inspector of Antiquities at Giza to open the tomb of Iymery (G 6020 = Fig. 26), as its reliefs show many notable vignettes of life and work during the Old Kingdom. Otherwise, one may wander through the Giza cemeteries, although one of the local guardians may insist on accompanying you. In the Western Cemetery, an indelible reference-point is the enormous stone mastaba located on the northern side (G 2000): although undecorated, it appears to have been built for a person of high rank during the reign of Khufu or Khafrē, and in size it is rivalled only by the mastaba of Prince Ankh-khaf (G 7150) in the Eastern Cemetery. Also noteworthy is the large, porticoed tomb of Seshemnefer IV, situated just off the south-east corner of the Great Pyramid, which has been restored to show off the noble façade of a favoured official during the early Sixth Dynasty.

2. This is actually forbidden by the Egyptian authorities, for the ascent is exhausting and the descent hazardous.

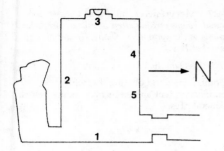

Fig. 25 **Iasen** *Tenant of the Great House*

(G 2196)   Dynasty V or VI

1 Presentation of offerings before deceased and family.
2 Deceased with offering list, and scenes of cooking, offering bringers, butchers, dancers and musicians.
3 Niche with statue.
4 Agricultural scenes.
5 Deceased fowling in canoe.

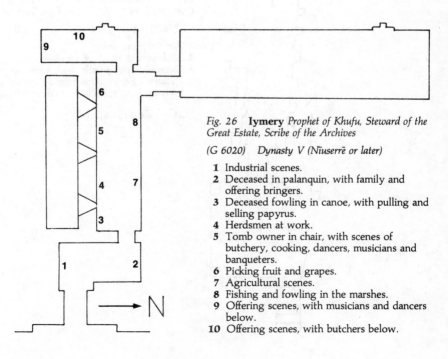

Fig. 26 **Iymery** *Prophet of Khufu, Steward of the Great Estate, Scribe of the Archives*

(G 6020)   Dynasty V (Niuserrē or later)

1 Industrial scenes.
2 Deceased in palanquin, with family and offering bringers.
3 Deceased fowling in canoe, with pulling and selling papyrus.
4 Herdsmen at work.
5 Tomb owner in chair, with scenes of butchery, cooking, dancers, musicians and banqueters.
6 Picking fruit and grapes.
7 Agricultural scenes.
8 Fishing and fowling in the marshes.
9 Offering scenes, with musicians and dancers below.
10 Offering scenes, with butchers below.

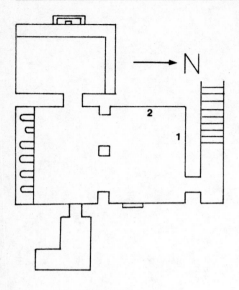

Fig. 27 **Meryrēnefer** *called* **Qar** *Overseer of Pyramid Towns of Khufu and Menkaurē, Inspector of priests in the pyramid of Khafrē, Tenant of pyramid of Pepi I*

(G 7102)   Dynasty VI

1 Tomb owner and offering list, with purification tent and embalming house below.
2 Funeral rites.

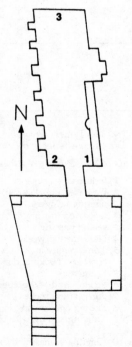

Fig. 28 **Idu*** *Tenant of pyramid of Pepi I, Overseer of priests of Khufu and Khafrē pyramids*

(G 7102)   Dynasty VI

1 Funeral processions.
2 Mourners at house of deceased.
3 Deceased in palanquin, with scenes of children's games, dancers and musicians, brewers, bakers, cooks and offering bringers.

* *Father or son of Qar (G 7101).*

Fig. 29 **Mersyankh (III)** *King's daughter**
Queen of Khafrē

(G 7530–40) *Late Dynasty IV*

1 Industrial scenes.
2 Industrial scenes (*continued*), servants at work,
  and 3 niches with 6 scribe statues of priests.
3 Mother of deceased.
4 Fowling, mat making and agriculture before
  father of deceased.
5 Rendering accounts.
6 Agriculture.
7 Musicians and singers at banquet, with
  cooking and serving food, and wine cellar.

* *Granddaughter of Khufu, daughter of King's son Kawab.*

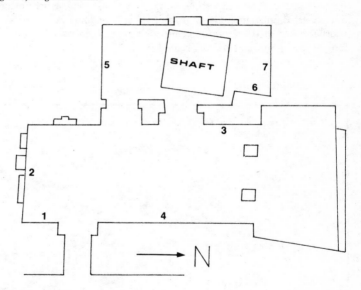

ABU RAWASH AND ZAWIYET EL-ARYAN

The Pyramids of Giza form a northern extension of the Memphite necropolis, which includes other far-flung sites in the vicinity. Some 7.5 km. north, at ABU RAWASH (see Map, p. 181), are remains of a huge mudbrick pyramid (owner unknown) and, 2 km. beyond in the desert, the ruined pyramid of Djedefrē, the immediate successor of Khufu.

Five km. south of Giza is ZAWIYET EL-ARYAN (at present a military zone, forbidden to the public) where a gigantic trench cut into the rock leads down 110 m. to the floor of the burial chamber, 25 m. below the surface: this unfinished monument is attributed to an ephemeral king of the Fourth Dynasty. The badly damaged 'layer pyramid', about 1.5 km. further south, probably belonged to Khaba, a ruler of the late Third Dynasty.

ABUSIR

The Fifth Dynasty cemetery of Abusir lies about 12 km. south of Zawiyet el-Aryan (see Map, p. 181): to reach it, turn south on the road through the cultivation just in front of the Giza plateau, proceeding as if to Saqqara, and turn off at the village of Abusir, where a track leads to the desert's edge. Only four of the fourteen pyramids built on this site can be clearly made out today and, like all such monuments after the Fourth Dynasty, they are so poorly made – mere cores of small stones encased in Tura limestone – that they have settled into mounds of rubble. The southernmost of the group (Fig. 30, A) belonged to *Neferefrē* and is badly ruined. Next,

(B), is the unfinished monument of *Neferirkarē* which, had it been completed, would have been slightly larger than Menkaurē's pyramid at Giza. Both the valley temple and the ramp leading to it were appropriated for *Niuserrē's pyramid* (C), the axis of the causeway being altered to align with it.

The area north of the mortuary temple is filled with mastabas, including (D) the elaborate tomb of Ptahshepses, a high official and relative of King Niuserrē. Now excavated by the Czech expedition of the Charles University, Prague, the tomb retains much of its superstructure and is thus an excellent example of an elaborate, fully developed mastaba.

Fig. 30   Abusir Cemetery

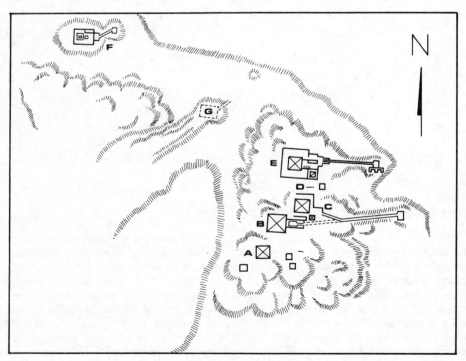

The chapel (see Fig. 31) is entered at the north-east corner of the building and proceeds through two more rooms to an offering hall with three niches, each originally containing statues of the deceased, set into the back wall (4). The reliefs are ordinary and not well preserved: freight boats are found at (1) and industrial activities — scenes of wood- and metal-working, with sculptors — at (3). The tomb was evidently a tourist attraction even in ancient times, for at (2) there is a graffito, written in the cursive hieratic script, that commemorates the visit of two scribes during the fiftieth year of King Ramesses II (c. 1229 B.C.). The second portico is also of interest, for it preserves two columns with lotus capitals, the earliest examples known.

Turning left (= south), we pass through a portico decorated with scenes showing the transport of the tomb owner and /or his statue (5), and enter a broad open court. The passage around it was originally supported by twenty square pillars, many of them still in place. A door at the north-west end of the court (6) leads into a suite of rooms from which one gains access, down a passage, to the burial chambers, in which the sarcophagi of Ptahshepses and his wife may still be seen. Doors on the south and south-west sides of the central court lead to offering rooms equipped with niches, but the south-west entrance also gives access to a more curious feature: at the south-west corner of the tomb is a double room, the curving walls and

Fig. 31 **Abusir** *Tomb of Ptahshepses*

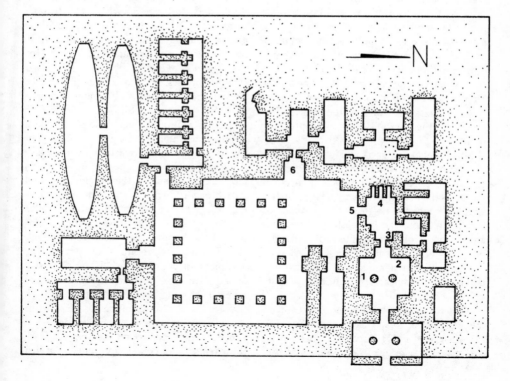

oblong shape of which show them to have been meant to receive full-size boats — whether simulacra of the day- and night-barques of the sun, or the actual barges used in the tomb owner's funeral, it is hard to say. Certainly they are unusual in private tombs (cf. the mastaba of Kagemni at Saqqara, Chapter 13, p. 173) and their presence here may owe something to the deceased's exalted rank and his relation by marriage to the royal family.

The *Pyramid of Sahurē* that lies beyond (Fig. 30, E) has settled badly, but enough of the mortuary temple remains to show that it conforms to the Fourth Dynasty plan. Reliefs from the sides of the open court are now preserved in the Cairo Museum (Chapter 10, pp. 109–10). Beyond lie the usual statue niches and rear sanctuary. Both Sahurē's complex and that of Niuserrē possess subsidiary pyramids, a normal feature of royal tombs beginning with the Fifth Dynasty. A curious feature of Sahurē's valley temple is its two ramps, perhaps reflecting conditions during the Inundation season differing from the rest of the year. The portico of the valley temple was supported by graceful palm columns, examples of which are also displayed in the Cairo Museum (Chapter 10, p. 109).

Sun temples of Userkaf (Fig. 30, G) and Niuserrē (F) lie north of the Abusir cemetery, at Abu Ghurob. Of the two, Niuserrē's temple is the better preserved, being situated about a kilometre north of the pyramid of Sahurē. The site can be reached (somewhat arduously on foot) from Abusir, or across the desert by horse or camel from Giza. Since it is marginally in a military area, however, check on the advisability of having permits before setting out.

Niuserrē's sun temple, one of several in the Memphite area, was dedicated to Rē, the solar god of Heliopolis. It had as its central feature a huge obelisk, called a *benben*, modelled after the ancient fetish kept at Heliopolis itself: this image apparently combined the symbolism of the primeval hill with that of the wide-spreading rays of the sun. Like all buildings at the cultivation's edge, the sun temple was equipped with a valley building (Fig. 32, A) from which a causeway led up to the main enclosure. All these features are badly damaged today: the painted reliefs which once covered the temple walls were excavated in fragments, most of them now in German museums or in Cairo. The great obelisk, piously restored under Ramesses II, is now fallen. Yet about this mangled ruin there remains a sense of sheer mass that makes it still one of the most imposing monuments in Egypt.

The remains of the causeway (B) lead into a vestibule (C) opening on to the various parts of the complex. Disregarding the right-hand turning, which leads to the magazines (D), one may move forward into a large courtyard, dominated, in its centre, by the remains of an altar (E). Victims for the sacrifice were prepared in the two slaughterhouses (F and F') at the north end of the complex, and remnants of the drainage system can still be examined. The corridor south of the vestibule leads into a long passage running along the south end of the court (G), and which was originally decorated with scenes illustrating the king's jubilee. At the end of this corridor we find two broad rooms. The first, designated as the 'Chapel' (H), contained further jubilee reliefs as well as scenes depicting the foundation of the temple, the official cattle count, etc. The second room is known as the 'Chamber of the Seasons' (I) and is justly famed for its once dazzling array of painted reliefs illustrating the varieties of nature — 'all that the solar disc encompasses'. From this ruined chamber we pass, finally, into the corridors that lead around the obelisk (J). All these features, of course, are ruined; but just

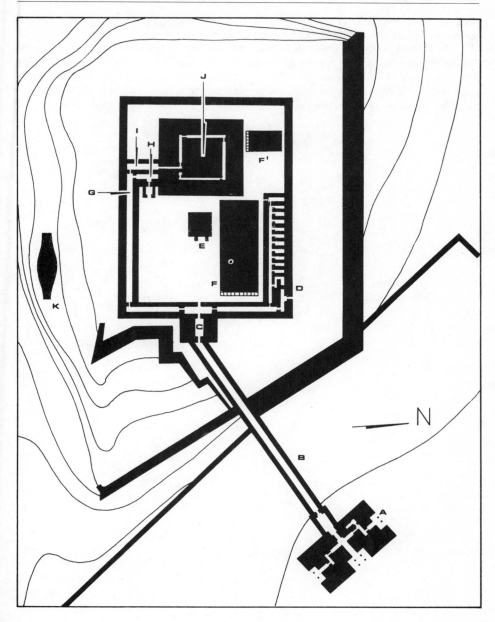

Fig 32   **Abu Ghurob** *Sun Temple of Niuserrē*

south of the temple, built on the desert floor, are remains of an immense brick-built model of the solar barque (K), the vessel that drew the sun through the caverns of the night and across the daytime sky. The presence of these solar features suggests that the temple was modelled, to some extent, on the main shrine of Rē in Heliopolis. But the position of the complex in the pyramid field at Abusir, and the contents of the reliefs, may indicate that it served a function similar to that of Djoser's 'Jubilee Court' at Saqqara (see below, Chapter 13, pp. 163, 166), with special emphasis on the king's relationship with the sun god.

13. Memphis and Saqqara

The ancient capital of Memphis was situated on the west bank of the river, some 24 km. south of Cairo. The ruins were sufficiently extensive in the twelfth century A.D. to excite the wonderment of Arab travellers, but relatively little survives today. To reach the site, take the main road to Upper Egypt south from the town of Giza to the village of Bedrashein (c. 24 km.), then turn west. Alternatively, follow for about the same distance the road that runs south, through the cultivation at the edge of the desert, turning west on to the same connecting road which leads, through fields and groves of palm trees, to the enclosure where the main tourist attractions are displayed.

The ruins cover such a wide area, most of it engulfed by fields in cultivation, that the majority of visitors will only see the few monuments collected near the south end of the site. The most impressive piece (Fig. 33, A) is a gigantic limestone statue of Ramesses II: one of a pair, the present fragment is over ten metres high, despite the loss of its legs, and is housed in a building constructed around it. Its companion was moved to Cairo in 1955 and now stands in the square opposite the railway station (fittingly, at Ramesses Square). Other fragments of statuary are grouped around the museum, with the fallen statue of Ramesses II behind the building, lying within a grove of palm trees, being particularly picturesque (B). The garden to the east is built around a graceful limestone sphinx of the New Kingdom (C). Visitors who have the time and inclination may push on beyond this modern enclosure

to examine what is left of the palace of Ramesses II's successor, Merneptah (D).

The tourist enclosure lies at the south end of the great enclosure of Ptah, patron deity of Memphis. The god's temple was surrounded with additional sanctuaries, and visitors are often taken to see the embalming house of the Apis (E). The last rites of the sacred bull were celebrated here, before the mummy was taken to the great burial galleries at Saqqara (see below, pp. 168, 176),

Fig. 33   Ruins of Memphis

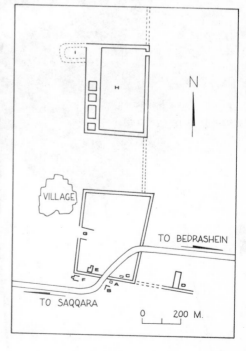

and visitors may admire the alabaster embalming bed, over five metres long, three
metres wide and one metre high, which dates
to the Twenty-sixth Dynasty. Other small
buildings, including a sanctuary of Ramesses
II (F), are clustered near the south-west
corner of Ptah's enclosure, and the western
hypostyle hall of the temple itself is found,
half-submerged by ground water, some 200
metres to the north (G). The trek further
north, to the remains of both the Roman
encampment (H) and the mudbrick palace
platform of King Apries (I) is recommended
only to the most venturesome.

The principal necropolis for ancient Memphis was Saqqara, a high bluff from which the
tombs of the First Dynasty and (more conspicuously) the great step pyramid of Djoser
tower over the countryside. From Memphis,
follow the road to Giza a short way to
the north, then turn west, purchasing your
entrance ticket to the site at the base of the
plateau, opposite the valley building of King
Unis (see Fig. 34).

Most visitors will begin with the *Step
Pyramid of Djoser*. The first monumental
construction built entirely out of stone, the
complex was surrounded by a niched limestone rampart, over 10 m. high and stretching 544 m. from north to south, 277 m. from
east to west. Spaced along the wall are
fourteen carved portals, of which only the
southernmost on the east side functions as a
true doorway (see Fig. 34, A). This use of
'dummy' architectural features is typical for
the complex as a whole, and visitors may
best examine the wall near the entrance,
where it has been reconstructed.

Imhotep, the architect of Djoser, was
regarded as one of the sages of ancient
Egypt and was later deified. It is easy to see
why. Despite the unprecedented problems of
building so extensively in stone, the complex represents a bold challenge to the
imagination and has resisted the centuries
remarkably well. The experimental nature of
the project is apparent once inside the colonnade (B): Imhotep's engineers were accustomed to working in mudbrick, and their
distrust of the new medium is reflected in the
small size of the blocks used throughout the
complex. The development of a suitably
monumental 'language' would take time, so
elements used in lighter constructions are
often reproduced in stone: the niched façade
of the complex is one example; but it is also
seen in the simulated log-roofing of the
entrance passage and in the two false stone
doorleaves that rest against the side walls of
the vestibule (mostly reconstructed). The
ribbed columns that support the roof of the
colonnade, similarly, were not trusted to
stand freely of their own accord, so they are
engaged to the sides of the passage by low
tongue-walls. The number of recesses thus
formed corresponds closely to the number
of the nomes, and it is suggested that each
contained a statue of the king as ruler of
Upper or Lower Egypt, appropriately arranged on the north and south sides of the
passage.

Immediately north of the colonnade is a
complex of buildings connected with the
King's Jubilee (see Chapter 3, pp. 47–8):
from the west end of the colonnade, turn
north, then east again, past a building known
as 'Temple T' (C) – which, from its design,
may have been a model of the king's palace –
into the south end of the Jubilee Court (D).
The sides of the court are lined with dummy
buildings, those on the east having the
narrow elevation and curved roof of the
shrines of Lower Egypt (🏛), while most of
those on the west side are modelled after the
canonical shrines of Upper Egypt (🏛): a
ziz-zagging corridor, with simulated door-

Wooden statue – popularly known as the Sheikh el-Beled – found in a tomb at Saqqara (Cairo Museum)

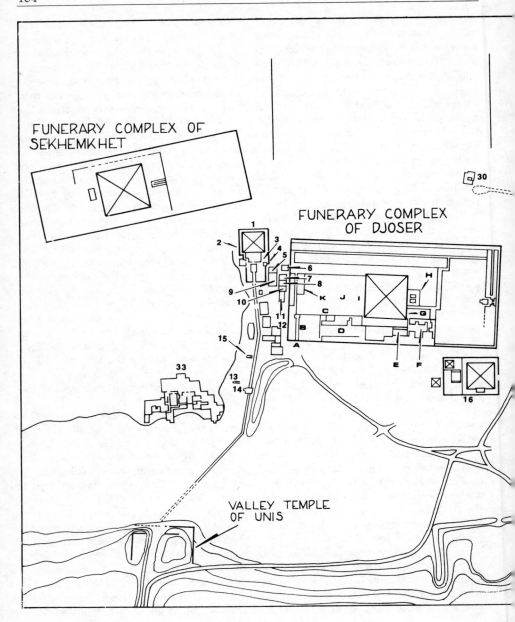

Fig. 34 **North Saqqara**

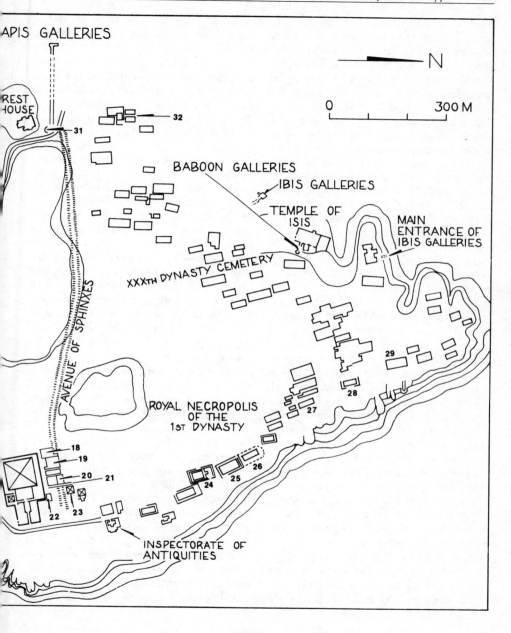

APIS GALLERIES

REST HOUSE

32

N

0   300 M

BABOON GALLERIES

IBIS GALLERIES

TEMPLE OF ISIS

MAIN ENTRANCE OF IBIS GALLERIES

31

XXXTH DYNASTY CEMETERY

AVENUE OF SPHINXES

ROYAL NECROPOLIS OF THE 1ST DYNASTY

29

28

27

26

25

24

23

22

21

20

19

18

INSPECTORATE OF ANTIQUITIES

leaves at the entrances, leads to the doorway of each chapel, and the shrines are further separated by a model of a wooden fence in stone. The two southernmost of these buildings are also provided with a stairway on the left side, leading up to a statue niche that doubtless once held an image of the king. The other chapels on the west side have simpler façades (⊓) and may have represented robing rooms used by the king during the ceremonies. The entire group of buildings evokes, of course, the gathering of Egypt's gods to witness the rebirth of the king at the Jubilee. At the south end of the court is the double dais, whereon the kings of Upper and Lower Egypt were consecutively enthroned. The masonry between the court and the colonnade also contains passages that may be connected with some ritual event in the Jubilee.

North of the Jubilee Court are two mysterious structures, the 'House of the South' (E) and 'House of the North' (F), so called because they are believed to represent the archaic shrines of Upper and Lower Egypt at Hieraconpolis and Buto. Each building is preceded by a court, in the east wall of which is a recess with engaged columns having lily (south) and papyrus (north) capitals – these flowers being the heraldic emblems of the two parts of the country. A doorway in the south wall of each 'house' leads, via a bending passage, into a cruciform sanctuary provided with statue niches. The ceilings are, once again, carved to a simulate log roofing, and on the walls of the passage in the 'House of the South' are visitors' graffiti in ink, written during the New Kingdom.[1]

Against the north side of the pyramid at the eastern corner is the *serdab* (G) from which the king's statue gazed out upon the world through two holes drilled in the building's face: the present occupant is a copy of the original statue, now in the Cairo Museum (Chapter 10, p. 108). The mortuary temple (H), badly ruined, is unlike later examples in its internal arrangement, in its location (on the north rather than the east side of the pyramid), and in the position of the tomb's entrance corridor through the centre of the building. The curtain walls at its entrance, designed to screen the interior from profane eyes, are still substantially preserved.

The interior of the pyramid, being dangerously unsound, is not open to visitors: one of the blue tile doorways from its lower galleries has been removed and is now in the Cairo Museum (see Chapter 10, p. 122). Traces of the pyramid's several stages (see above, p. 82) can be seen on the east side. On the south side of the pyramid, a gallery cut during the Late Period leads to the top of the shaft, at the bottom of which the granite roof of the burial chamber can be seen. It too is normally closed, but may be visited by special arrangement.

The expanse of the south court is dominated by a low altar (I), built near the south face of the pyramid, and by two curious B-shaped structures (J) – these last perhaps marking the limits of a course that the king had to run during the Jubilee in order to demonstrate his vitality. In the south-west corner of the compound is the so-called 'South Tomb' (K), apparently a prototype of later subsidiary pyramids (see above, p. 83). Atop the east wall of the building's sanctuary is an elegant frieze of stone cobras. Although the interior of the South Tomb (like the 'Saite' entrance to the pyramid) is formally closed, visitors can occasionally be admitted by special arrangement. The burial chamber (made of granite, like that within

---

1. It is these texts that ensure the identity of the builder of the Step Pyramid with the 'Djoser' of the king lists. In the pyramid complex he uses only his Horus Name, Netcherikhet = 'Godly of Body' (see Chapter 3, pp 46–7).

the pyramid) is inaccessible, but the surrounding galleries are inlaid with blue tiles — imitating wall hangings — and have false doors, similarly decorated, with relief figures of the king carved in their recesses. Visiting these galleries is an unforgettable experience, the more so since comparable chambers inside the Step Pyramid may not be seen.

From the top of Djoser's south tomb, a path runs through a group of private mastabas to the *Pyramid of Unis* (see Fig. 34, *1*). The structure itself, in typical Fifth Dynasty style, is unremarkable, but several features command attention. First are the two chambers inside the pyramid, the walls of which are inscribed with the earliest extant 'Pyramid Texts' and (in the sarcophagus room) with elaborate painted decoration simulating coloured wall hangings. Outside, note the shaft running south from the pyramid's north-east corner, leading down into a warren of rock-cut galleries connected with the demolished tomb of Hotepsekhemwy (Fig. 34, *3*), first ruler of the Second Dynasty. The restoration inscription of Khaemwēse, son of Ramesses II and High Priest of Ptah in Memphis, survives in part and is carved on to the south face of the pyramid.

Unis' mortuary temple is largely destroyed and was invaded by later structures (see below, pp. 168—71), but the granite false door can still be made out against the east face of the pyramid. Further east, beyond the pavement of the building, are large boat pits carved out of the rock and encased in limestone blocks. The corridor of Unis' causeway is preserved for over 700 m. of the way down to the valley temple. Among the fragments of reliefs from its walls are scenes of the transportation of granite columns from the Aswan quarries; hunting and metal-working scenes, like those found in private tombs; market scenes; a battle between

archers, and ships full of prisoners imploring the king's mercy; and a haunting depiction of people starving during a famine. Remains of Unis' valley building may be glimpsed from the road, across from the kiosk where tickets to the Saqqara necropolis are bought.

The Unis causeway may also be reached by walking south, a short distance from the entrance to Djoser's complex. On reaching the causeway, turn left (= east), encountering at the south side a number of tombs that were buried when the causeway was built (see Fig. 34). From east to west, these are the tombs of Nyankh-Khnum and Khnumhotep (*14* = Fig. 38) and Nefer (*13* = Fig. 37). Unis' boat pits are south of the causeway as it turns towards the pyramid. As the esplanade of Unis' ruined mortuary temple is approached, the king's subsidiary pyramid is seen at the south corner. The contemporary tombs of the Fifth Dynasty stand in rows to the north. The southern group, closest to the temple, belonged to Unis' two queens, Khenut (*5*) and Nebet (*9*); behind these buildings, to the north, is another row of mastabas comprising the tombs of the vizier Iynefret (*7*), Unis-ankh (*8*),[2] Princess Idut (*10* = Fig. 35), and the vizier Mehu (*11* = Fig. 36). A later mastaba (*6*), probably dating to the Sixth Dynasty, is located to the west of this group, built against the enclosure wall of Djoser's complex: belonging to one Haishutef, it is an interesting example of a mudbrick mastaba possessing a carved stone chapel set inside. Continuing along the north edge of the mortuary temple, the visitor will come across the immense tomb shaft of the Saite general, Amun-Tefnakht (*4*); another shaft, at the pyramid's north-east corner, leading to the subterranean burial of King Hotepsekhemwy of the Second Dynasty (*3*). Finally, south of the pyramid, there is another deep shaft (*2*), outfitted with a cast-iron spiral

---

2. The chapel of this mastaba has mostly been removed and is on display in the Field Museum, Chicago.

staircase. At the bottom are found three tombs of the Persian Period, belonging to the chief physician Psamtik (centre), the admiral Djenhebu (west) and Psamtik's son, Pediēse (east). These tombs are marked by great simplicity of decor – note the tastefully incised hieroglyphic spells on the walls of Pediēse's chamber and the stars speckling the vaulted ceiling – that belies their technical sophistication: particularly striking are the huge sarcophagi that seem to dwarf the small rooms in which they are placed.

Three other royal tombs in North Saqqara are less frequented by visitors. South-west of the Unis complex is the unfinished *Step Pyramid of the Horus Sekhemkhet*, a successor of Djoser (see Fig. 34): the lower courses of the enclosure wall, the pyramid's descending corridor (cut in the rock and surmounted by several courses of masonry), and the prodigiously deep shaft of the south tomb are the main points of interest here. The *Pyramid of Userkaf* (16) lies east of Djoser's enclosure wall: in poor condition, like most Fifth Dynasty pyramids, it is exceptional in having its mortuary temple situated on the tomb's south side, perhaps because the ground to the east was too uneven for such a building. More typical is the *Pyramid of Teti* (17), north-east of the Step Pyramid complex: the burial chambers, which may be visited, are inscribed with Pyramid Texts, and there is an especially well-preserved south pyramid adjoining the mortuary temple.

Some of the finest private tombs at Saqqara lie north of Teti's Pyramid: moving east from the north-west corner of the pyramid are the mastabas of Mereruka (Fig. 34, 18; Fig. 39) and Kagemni (19 = Fig. 40). Then, after passing by two ruined tombs, we turn right (= north) and proceed down the famous 'Street of Tombs' (21) belonging to Neferseshemrē, Ankhmahor (20 = Fig. 43)

and Neferseshemptah (Fig. 41). In this burial complex of the Sixth Dynasty, the grouping of tombs is noticeably freer than in the rigidly controlled cemeteries of the Fourth Dynasty at Giza.

The road along the edge of the plateau, north of the local inspectorate of antiquities, leads to the tombs of the First Dynasty rulers. Little remains of these once-imposing monuments, but those interested in doing so may examine the tombs of Qa'a (Fig. 34, 24), Djet (25), Merneith (26), Djer (27), Aha (28) and Den (29). Some of the painted brick niching of Qa'a's tomb is preserved under a low shed, and the visitor may also examine what is left of the remarkable low bench surrounding Den's tomb, with its modelled clay bulls' heads fitted with natural bulls' horns – a hecatomb for eternity, surrounding the king's final resting place. Retracing our steps to the pyramid of Teti, we proceed along the road north of Userkaf's and Djoser's pyramids. West of the latter we find the superb Fifth Dynasty tomb of Akhethotep and his son, Ptahhotep (Fig. 34, 30; Fig. 42): one of the very finest tombs in the cemetery, it may be visited on the way to or from the present rest house.

From the rest house, go down the northern slope, reaching a curious semicircle of Greek statues (Fig. 34, 31). This is the beginning of an avenue that runs from east to west, between the temple complex of the living Apis (now lost) and the catacombs where the dead bulls were buried. The entombment of the sacred bulls on this spot dates back at least into the Eighteenth Dynasty, but the sections of the Serapeum that can be seen today are all much later. The philosopher's 'circle', for instance, was set up by Ptolemy I as a wayside shrine: the best preserved are, from left to right, Plato (standing), Heraclitus

TOMBS AROUND THE PYRAMID OF UNIS

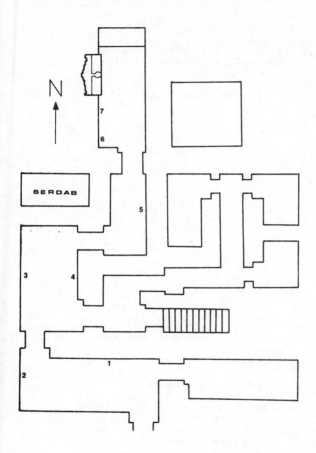

Fig. 35   **Idut** *Daughter of Unis (?)**

Dynasty V

1 Men fishing with net.
2 Scribes and defaulters.
3 Agriculture (top), with hippopotamus hunt, fishing and fording cattle below.
4 Funeral scenes.
5, 6, 7 Personified estates and offering bringers, with butchers below.

* Originally belonged to a man named Ihy, usurped for Idut's use.

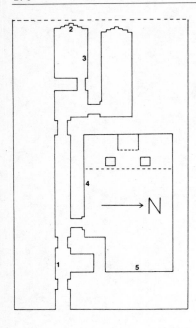

Fig. 36 **Mehu** *Vizier*

Early Sixth Dynasty

1 Trapping birds.
2 Stela, with offering scenes at sides.
3 Offering bearers.
4 Meryrēankh* seated before offering table, with offering bearers below.
5 Men felling ox, etc.

* *Usurped this room from original owner.*

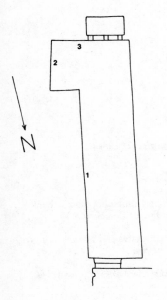

Fig. 37 **Nefer** *Inspector of artisans, inspector of singers*

Dynasty V

1 5 registers: (i) goats browsing; plucking papyrus, building reed boat, defaulters and scribes; (ii) men fishing, marsh, cattle tending; (iii) netting fish, baking, putting birds in boxes, fowling with clapnet; (iv) winepress, treading grapes, jewellers, dancers, storehouse; (v) agriculture, boatmen jousting in marsh, sailing vessels.
2 4 registers: (i) goats browsing; (ii) launching ships; (iii) carpentry, felling trees; (iv) tending cattle.
3 Offering scene before deceased, with musicians, dwarves with pets, etc.

Fig. 38 **Nyankh-Khnum** *and* **Khnumhotep**
*Royal hairdressers**

Dynasty V

1 Funeral processions.
2 Tomb owners in marsh.
3 Tomb owners oversee butchery, carpentry and boatbuilding.
4 Baking and brewing.
5 Birds netted and caged; gardening; deceased crossing to West.
6 Market scenes; deceased crossing to West.
7 Funeral procession; boats crossing to West.
8 Tomb owners inspect fishing, fowling, marsh industries.
9 Oil ships, desert hunt, fruit harvest and viticulture.
10 Tomb owners in litter borne by asses (side walls).
11 Tomb owners, with offering bringers and animals.
12–13 Agriculture.
14 Industrial scenes, with personified estates below.
15 Tomb owners at table, with musicians and dancers below.
16 Tomb owners embracing.
17 Fishing and fowling in marsh.
18 Tending to and fording cattle.
19 Tomb owners with offering-list ritual and offering bearers.
20 False doors of deceased.

* *Jointly decorated tomb.*

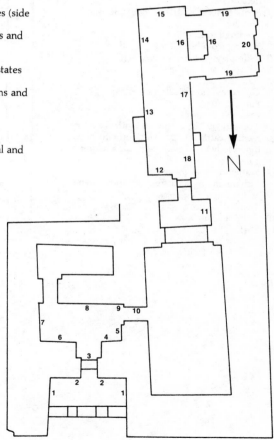

TOMBS AROUND THE PYRAMID
OF TETI

Fig. 39 **Mereruka*** *Vizier, Overseer of the Town, Inspector of Prophets in the pyramid of Teti*

Dynasty VI

1. Hippopotamus hunt.
2. Gardening (top), with fowling and fording cattle below.
3. Carpentry and making stone vessels.
4. Hunt in desert (top), with industrial scenes below.
5. Fishing, preparing fish, caging birds.
6. Village headmen report, with scribes and defaulters.
7. Scribes present cattle accounts, lead in gazelles.
8. Feeding birds.
9. Fishing from boat.
10. Wife playing harp for husband.
11. Clappers and dancers.
12. Butchers.
13. Granaries and viticulture scenes.
14. Funeral rites.
15. Pets and dwarves.
16. Tomb owner in palanquin, with scenes of feeding cattle and gazelles, force-feeding hyenas, dwarves with pets, and children's games.
17. Statue of tomb owner.
18. Fishing and agriculture, with tomb owner and wife playing *senet*.
19. Tomb of Wife.
20. Tomb of Son.
21. Shaft.

* *Wife was King's Daughter of Teti.*

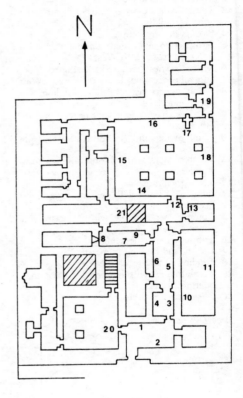

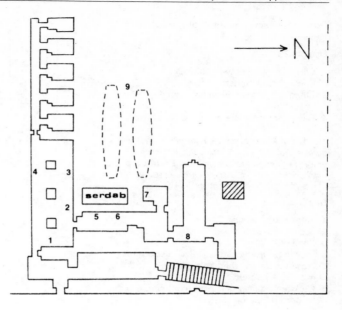

Fig. 40 **Kagemni** *Vizier, Inspector of Prophets, Overseer of the pyramid town of Teti*

Dynasty VI

1 Dancers and acrobats.
2 Fishing and fowling, with hippopotamus hunt.
3 Tending animals.
4 Scribes and defaulters.
5 Fowling with net, fattening hyenas, feeding ducks and geese in aviary, including force-feeding geese.
6 Deceased in palanquin, with servants preparing oil and tending pets.
7 Agricultural scenes.
8 Butchers and offering bringers.
9 Boat pits (on roof).

Fig. 41 **Neferseshemptah** *Steward of Teti Pyramid*

Dynasty VI

1 Offering bringers with animals.
2 Fowl yard, with netting fowl.
3 Offering bringers (including caged hedgehog).
4 False door, with statues and bust of deceased.

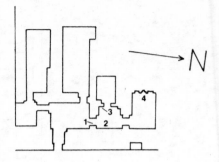

Fig. 42 **Akhethotep** *Inspector of Prophets for pyramids of Isesi and Menkauhor, Inspector of priests for pyramid of Niuserrē and* **Ptahhotep** *Overseer of pyramid town of Djedkarē [Isesi], Overseer of the Two Treasuries**

Late Dynasty V

1 Agricultural scenes.
2 Scenes in marshes.
3 Butchers.
4 Fowling, fording cattle, collecting papyrus, etc., in marshes; children's games; viticulture; hunt in the desert.
5 Children's games and hunt (continued), and herdsmen tending cattle.

* Double tomb: Akhethotep's chapel is on main axis, with that of his son, Ptahhotep, on south side.

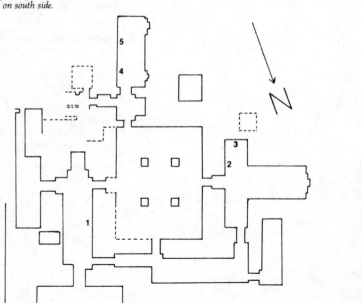

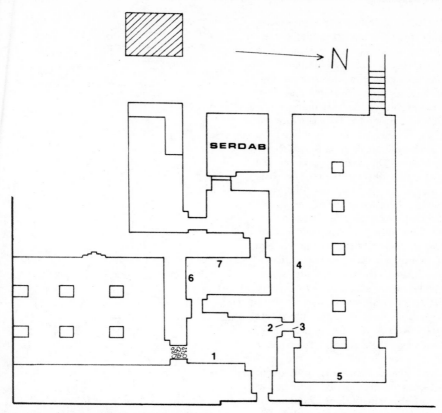

Fig. 43   **Ankhmahor** *Vizier, First under the King,*
Overseer of the Great House

Dynasty VI

1 Agricultural scenes.
2–3 Surgical operations.
4 Funeral procession.
5 Women dancing.
6 Jewellers, metalworkers and sculptors.
7 Netting fowl.

(seated), Thales (standing), Protagoras (seated), Homer (seated), Hesiod (seated), Demetrius of Phalerum (standing, and leaning on a bust of Serapis), and Pindar (seated).

The entrance into the subterranean galleries is located some 300 metres west, where a long staircase suddenly plunges into the earth. Once inside the first hall, turn left (see Fig. 44), by-passing the sarcophagus lid of the Apis buried under Amasis, which lies in the passage. The main gallery of the catacomb runs at right-angles to the first hall, giving access to the twenty-eight side-chambers in which were buried the sacred bulls who lived from the mid-Twenty-sixth Dynasty down into the Ptolemaic Period. These rooms are not small — the average height is about 9.5 metres — but their dimensions are dwarfed by the monster sarcophagi, carved out of single blocks of red or black granite, or of limestone, that fill them. Of those still in place, note the interments made under Amasis (A), the Persian 'Pharaoh' Cambyses (B),[3] and under Khebebesh, the last ruler of Egypt before the brief Persian re-conquest and the subsequent Graeco-Roman domination (C, with lid at D). The most elaborate of these sarcophagi is found at the far end of the main gallery (E).

The visitor may next explore the monuments of north Saqqara by proceeding some 300 m. north of the Greek statues to the tomb of Ti (Fig. 34, 32; Fig. 45). One of the largest mastabas in the necropolis, it is well preserved and carefully reconstructed, giving a good impression of such a tomb's appearance during the Old Kingdom.

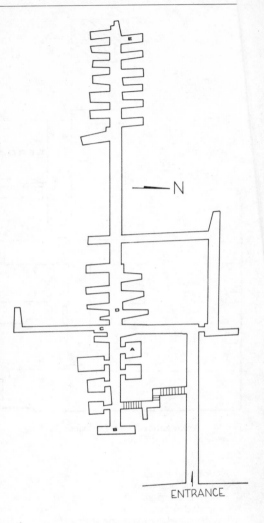

Fig. 44   Apis Galleries of the Serapeum

---

3. Herodotus' account of Cambyses' impious stabbing of the Apis and of its secret burial by the priests (III.29) is thus shown to be hostile propaganda.

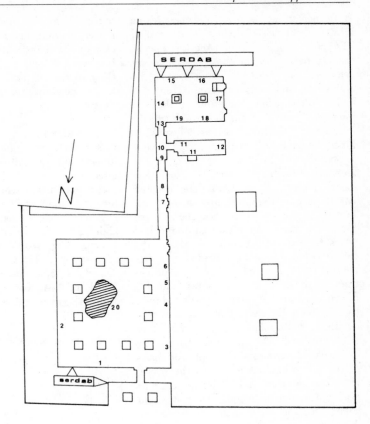

Fig. 45 **Ti** *Overseer of the pyramids of Niuserrē and Neferirkarē, overseer of sun temples of Sahurē, Neferirkarē and Niuserrē*

Dynasty V

1 Overpowering and butchering ox.
2 Deceased in palanquin receives reports; servants with funerary furniture and pets.
3 Feeding geese and cranes.
4 Fowl yard.
5 Deceased receiving reports.
6 Deceased watching boats, animals and fowl.
7 False door of wife.
8 Offering bringers
9 Boating and hunting in marsh.
10 Sledge dragged by men, with butchery scenes below.
11 Offering bringers.

12 Cooking, brewing, pottery making.
13 Musicians and dancers.
14 Agriculture.
15 Boatbuilding, industries, market scenes.
16 Tomb owner (with musicians and butchers, below) inspects viticulture, tending birds and cattle, scribes with defaulters.
17 False doors, with offering bearers.

Serdab *Statue chamber, with cast of tomb owner's statue visible through spy holes (original in Cairo Museum).*

18 Tomb owner, with dwarf and pet; tending and fording cattle.
19 Hippopotamus hunt, with marsh industries (fishing, gathering papyrus, etc.).
20 Shaft.

A further group of animal cemeteries is located about half a kilometre north-east of Ti's tomb, grouped around the low hills at the northern edge of the Third Dynasty cemetery (see Fig. 34). Travellers of the eighteenth and early nineteenth centuries had reported seeing 'the tombs of the bird mummies' here, but the site was virtually ignored until the British archaeologist W. B. Emery began his excavation in 1965. Emery hoped to find the tomb of Imhotep, the architect of the Step Pyramid who had been deified in antiquity and was later equated with Asclepius, the Greek god of medicine. Instead of the Asclepion, however, Emery found the burial complexes of the sacred ibises, falcons and baboons, and also of the sacred cows who were regarded as incarnations of Isis, the mother of the Apis. In front of the main catacombs was found a sacred enclosure, substantially built during the Thirtieth Dynasty, that contained the 'Mother of the Apis' temple and other chapels as well. The catacombs behind are extensive, sometimes running into the shafts of the Old Kingdom tombs to the south. From the evidence yielded by the excavation, which came to an end in 1976, it would appear that the site was in continuous use during the Late Period until the closing of the temples by Theodosius in A.D. 383, and that a Coptic monastery was built on the ruins some time later.

The animal cemeteries of North Saqqara are not yet open to the public, though visitors may form a general impression of the exterior remains. Also off limits, though promising for the future, is the cemetery of the New Kingdom that lies south of the Unis causeway, beyond the ruins of the monastery of Apa Jeremias (Fig. 34, 33). The excavations of Great Britain's Egypt Exploration Society began in 1975 with the discovery of the long-sought tomb of the General, later King, Horemheb; and preli-

minary soundings indicate that many important monuments lie buried nearby. Since clearance and restoration have just begun, however, it will be many years before these sites will add yet another chapter to the seemingly inexhaustible cemetery of Saqqara.

The southern reaches of the Memphite necropolis are far off the tourist's usual itinerary. Visitors with less than a specialist's interest will lose little by not seeing most of these monuments which have the characteristic features of Fifth and Sixth Dynasty pyramids already seen. At the north end, about 2 km. south of the monastery of Apa Jeremias (Fig. 46, A) and nearly opposite Saqqara village (B), is the pyramid of Pepi I (C), whose name, *Men-nefer*, '[Pepi is] Established and Beautiful', came to apply to the capital's southern suburb and, in time, to the

Fig. 46 **South Saqqara**

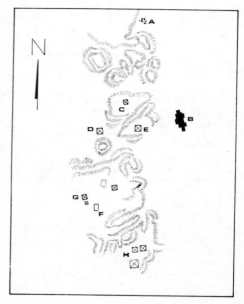

whole of Memphis itself. Not far to the south are the pyramids of Mernerē (D) and of Isesi (E), the latter having its mortuary temple exceptionally well preserved. At the south end of the necropolis is the funerary monument of Pepi II (G), substantial fragments of whose mortuary temple have been restored *in situ*. More unusual is the royal tomb that adjoins it, the burial place of Menkaurē's successor, Shepseskaf, who abandoned the pyramidal form in favour of a curious oblong building in the shape of a sarcophagus (F). Called *Mastabat el-Faraūn*, 'Pharaoh's Bench', it is constructed of enormous blocks of local limestone, sheathed, at one time, with the finer limestone of the Tura quarries. The burial chambers, built entirely of granite blocks, have vaulted ceilings, but are otherwise similar in layout to those of the late Fourth and of the Fifth Dynasties. Beyond Shepseskaf's monument lie pyramids dating to the late Middle Kingdom (H).

Visitors wishing to go to South Saqqara may rent horses or camels at the rest house near the Apis galleries. Otherwise, a view of these monuments may be had from the top of Djoser's enclosure wall, above the South Tomb.

14. The Southern Pyramid Fields and the Faiyūm

The cemeteries south of Memphis range even farther from the capital than the northern sites discussed in Chapter 12. Some of this, to be sure, can be explained on political grounds: the location of the Twelfth Dynasty's capital near Lisht, for example, and that dynasty's interest in the Faiyūm no doubt account for the choice of these sites for royal tombs. It is somewhat more difficult, however, to understand the reasons for the selection of Meidūm — some fifty kilometres south of Memphis — near the start of the Fourth Dynasty.

The *Dahshur* cemetery (Fig. 47), which begins about 2 km. south of the *Mastabat el-Fararūn*, remains in the possession of the military authorities and is thus completely off limits — a pity, for it is dominated by two of the earliest 'true' pyramids, both belonging to Snefru, founder of the Fourth Dynasty. The northern, so-called 'red' pyramid (Fig. 47, B) is generally reckoned as the earlier of the two: a possible indication of the builders' caution is that the angle of inclination, instead of the 52° customary in later pyramids, is only 43° 36'. The burial chamber is choked by sand and inaccessible. Its southern neighbour, called the 'Bent Pyramid' (C), is unique also in possessing two entrances, in the north and west faces respectively, each leading to a burial chamber with a high corbelled roof. A small

Pyramid fields from Abu Rawash to the Faiyūm

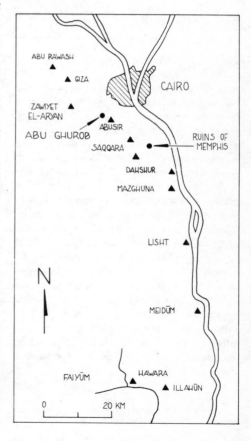

Pyramid and causeway of King Huni at Meidūm

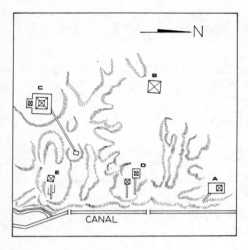

Fig. 47   *The Dahshur Necropolis*

subsidiary pyramid is located opposite the building's south face; and on the east side of both pyramids is a small chapel, dominated by limestone stelae carved with the name and image of the king – a design for the mortuary temple characteristic of the earliest royal tombs rather than for those of the high Pyramid Age.[1] The whole complex is enclosed by a retaining wall, and a causeway leads down to the rectangular valley temple. The change in the pyramid's angle of inclination (which goes sharply from 54° 31' to 43° 21') may be due to the need to complete the pyramid in haste on the king's death: the upper courses do seem to be laid with less care than those below. A recent suggestion that the change in angle was influenced by the near-contemporary collapse of the pyramid at Meidūm, while ingeniously argued,[2] has not persuaded many authorities.

The royal cemetery of Dahshur is completed by three pyramids of the Middle Kingdom – the stone structure of Amenemhēt II (D) standing between the mudbrick pyramids of Senwosret III (A) and Amenemhēt III (E). They represent the northern extension of a necropolis built around the Twelfth Dynasty capital near *Lisht*, some 25 km. south (see Map, p. 181). The pyramids of Amenemhēt I and Senwosret I can be seen from the main road (i.e., the road from Cairo to Upper Egypt: see Chapter 13, p. 161), but they are scarcely to be distinguished from the rolling desert that surrounds them. Travellers with insufficient time to examine the remains *in situ* will find several impressive elements from both mortuary complexes in the Cairo Museum (see Chapter 10, pp. 110–11).

Continuing another 22 km. south on the main road from Cairo, the traveller will see the massive *Meidūm pyramid* rising up on a bluff at the edge of the desert: to reach it, turn west on to the paved road south of the pyramid. The trouble taken to visit this remote spot will be repaid, not only on account of the monument's immense size, but also owing to its importance as the earliest 'true' pyramid (see Chapter 7, pp. 80–82, and Fig. 4). Visitors during the Eighteenth Dynasty left graffiti that attribute this structure also to King Snefru, but it is believed that he only completed it for his predecessor, Huni. To reach the entrance, 18.5 m. above ground level on the north face, one must climb a ladder set against the side of the pyramid and step off the top rung into the descending corridor: this is easier than it sounds. At the bottom of the descending corridor a short passage leads into a shaft, at the top of which is the

1. Snefru's stela is now exhibited in the garden of the Cairo Museum, while similar monuments from earlier dynasties are found upstairs in Room 42 (Chapter 10, pp. 106, 122–3).

2. Kurt Mendelsohn, *The Riddle of the Pyramids* (London: Thames and Hudson, 1974); see below, p. 183.

impressive burial chamber, its corbelled roof projecting above the bedrock into the masonry of the pyramid. Outside, there is a small and well-preserved mortuary temple of the archaic type situated on the east side, on the terrace behind which are two stelae that, had they been inscribed, would have named the owner of the monument. The irregular shape of the pyramid today (it is sometimes known as the 'false' pyramid) is due to the collapse of the masonry that was inserted between the steps of the original structure to form the geometric pyramid – a disaster that it seems most reasonable to place during the late New Kingdom, at the earliest (but see above, p. 182).

The far reaches of the pyramid field are found at the south-east edge of the Faiyūm: from the Meidūm pyramid, follow the road south-west until it joins the main road coming from El Wasta (west bank of the Nile). First to be sighted (about 22 km.), south of the main road, is the *Illahūn* pyramid of Senwosret II. Built out of mudbrick around a limestone core, the pyramid itself is in ruinous condition, but the visitor who has the interest and resources to travel the desert track leading to the site will be able to examine the king's pyramid city, situated next to the valley temple. Established to maintain the endowment for the king's mortuary cult, the town is laid out in regular blocks of workers' barracks, with the larger officials' houses advantageously situated to enjoy 'the cool breath of the north wind'. Although other such pyramid cities are known for the Old and Middle Kingdoms, Illahūn is the only extant example: compare the workers' village in West Thebes, at Deir el-Medina (Chapter 19, pp. 279–81).

Continuing west on the main road from El Wasta, the visitor reaches the edge of the Faiyūm after another 12 km. Instead of following the main road south, to Medinet el-Faiyūm, turn north and follow the track along the canal to the pyramid complex of Amenemhēt III at *Hawara*. Well preserved down to the Graeco-Roman era, this was one of the great tourist attractions of ancient Egypt. The mortuary temple, with its numerous chapels for the nome gods of Egypt, was so extensive and complex that it was known to the ancients as the 'Labyrinth' (Strabo, *Geographica*, Book XVII, I, 37). So complete is the destruction, however, that it is only with an effort of imagination that these buildings can be visualized against the pyramid's south face today. The pyramid itself, built of mudbrick, has lost its limestone casing, and the interior – designed with considerable ingenuity to foil grave-robbers – is inaccessible.

THE FAIYŪM

Although the visitor may proceed from Hawara into Medinet el-Faiyūm, the more customary approach is from the north: the road leading on to the Giza plateau, skirting the north edge of the cemeteries, turns south through the desert. The Faiyūm, though much reduced from its ancient dimensions (see Chapter 1, p. 19), is still one of the garden spots of Egypt. The first site to be reached, however, has fallen beyond the edge of the present cultivation: this is *Kom Ushīm*, the ancient Karanis where – at 79 km. from Cairo – the visitor may refresh himself at the rest house and inspect the local museum before proceeding out to the site. Amidst the welter of ruined houses, the principal attractions are the camp (near the rest house) and the two temples, of which the main temple of the crocodile gods Pnepheros and Petesuchos is the more interesting: this undecorated limestone building is laid out on conventional Egyptian lines, with the quay, oriented north-east, at the head of a canal (now vanished) leading down the processional way into the temple.

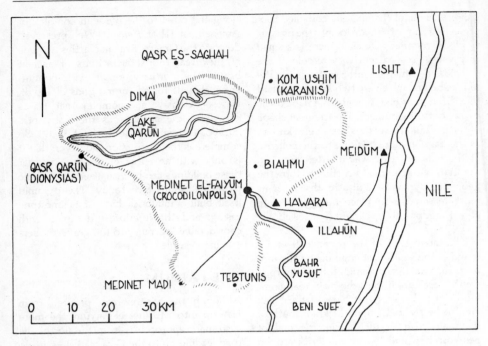

The Faiyūm

Note, inside the sanctuary, the hidden chamber below the altar, perhaps used by the priests in delivering oracles.

Another 5 km. south brings the traveller to the shores of Lake Qarūn, the remnant of the famed Lake Moeris. Before this, however, it may be desired to strike off to the west, north of Lake Qarūn, along the track that begins just opposite the rest house at Kom Ushīm. At a distance of some 25 km. at the foot of the prominent Gebel Katrani, is a small, uninscribed temple, known locally as *Qasr es-Saghah*: scholars are divided in dating this building, which at any rate can be assigned to no period later than the Middle Kingdom. Another 8 km. south, towards the lake, is the Graeco-Roman town of Soknopaiou Nesos (today called *Dimai*):

the site is well preserved because of its remoteness, with a broad processional way ending at a large ruined temple of the Ptolemaic period. Both these sites may be visited by those interested in probing the deserted outer reaches of the Faiyūm, but a vehicle with four-wheel drive is recommended for those proceeding overland from Kom Ushīm. The journey may also be made by crossing the lake at Shakshūk, but in this case all arrangements (including donkeys for the trek to the ruins) must be made in advance, as there are *no* facilities on the north shore of Lake Qarūn.

The main road south to Medinet el-Faiyūm is 5 km. from Kom Ushīm. On the way, stop at the village of *Biahmu* where, by the railway embankment, are two great limestone pedestals, over 6 m. high, that once held gigantic statues of Amenemhēt III. From Medinet el-Faiyūm itself, go a short distance to the north-west on a secondary road to *Kiman Fares* for the more substantial ruins of ancient Crocodilonpolis-Arsinoe (called Shedyet by the Egyptians): the ruins extend over four square kilometres, including remains of a Middle Kingdom temple, expanded by Ramesses II, and the ruined Ptolemaic temple at the north end of the site. Shedyet, as its Greek name indicates, was the home of the crocodile god, Sobek, and was a place of pilgrimage, and even tourism. In 112 B.C., for instance, an official in the Faiyūm received a letter informing him that

Lucius Memmius, a Roman senator ... is sailing up from Alexandria to the Arsinoite nome to see the sights. Let him be received with special magnificence, and take care that ... (among other things), the titbits for Petesuchos [= Sobek] and the crocodiles, the conveniences for viewing the Labyrinth, and the offerings and sacrifices be provided; in general, take the greatest pains in everything to see that the visitor is satisfied ...

The visitor today may also see remains of the pool where the sacred crocodiles lived. Although the town itself must go back at least into the Middle Kingdom, most of the visible ruins are Graeco-Roman in date: in particular, the baths (with their two sections, for men and women respectively) are a substantial survival.

From Medinet el-Faiyūm most of the region's other sites may be visited along secondary roads. To the north-east, some 40 kilometres from Medinet el-Faiyūm, is the site of *Kôm el-Hammâm* (ancient Philadelphia): many of the late mummy portraits in museums around the world come from its necropolis, and the site is of some note to papyrologists as being the 'model town' set up by Apollonius, minister to Ptolemy II Philadelphus, and well known thanks to the recovery of the correspondence of his steward, Zeno. Another road, south-west of Medinet el-Faiyūm, leads to the village of Abu Gandir, which is the nearest approach to the important site of *Medinet Madi*: its chief monument is a small temple, built during the later Twelfth Dynasty by Amenemhēt III and his son, Amenemhēt IV, dedicated to Sobek, Horus and the harvest goddess Ernutet, which can be reached across the intervening two kilometres of desert on foot or by a suitable car. One of the few religious edifices of the Middle Kingdom still extant, it is well preserved and is enclosed at both ends by additional constructions of Ptolemaic and Roman date, thus happily reflecting the joint achievements of the Twelfth and Ptolemaic dynasties in developing the Faiyūm. Still another itinerary leads to the western edge of the depression, to *Qasr Qarūn* (ancient Dionysias). In ancient times the start of a caravan route to the Bahriya Oasis, the town site is enhanced by the remains of two temples of the Late Period: the larger one has two storeys and has been reconstructed by the Egyptian Department of Antiquities, while the smaller temple is later (of Roman date) and built of brick, with columns of the Ionic order inside. Visitors to the site may also see remains of the municipal baths and of a Roman fortress (dated to Diocletian) which retains both its inner and outer features to a considerable degree.

From Medinet el-Faiyūm, the main road departs to the south-east, rejoining the highway to Upper Egypt at Beni Suef (about 42 km.). From here it is another 120 km. to the city of Minya (see Map. p. 10), where hotels and other touristic facilities are available to help the traveller visit the monuments of Middle Egypt.

15. Middle Egypt

Middle Egypt is the productive heartland of the country: the valley is at its widest from the Faiyūm down to Mellawi, and visitors who travel through the opulent countryside by car will see many reminders of a rhythm of life — roads built on embankments high above the fields, villages perched on the mounds of still more ancient settlements — that has vanished since the yearly inundation ceased. The ambience is leisurely, provincial if you like — and so it was in antiquity. With one brief exception, the kings did not maintain a formal residence in Middle Egypt, so the country was administered by local magnates whose monuments will be the principal subjects of this chapter.

The first major site to be found near Minya is *Beni Hasan*, which can be reached by driving south from the city (*c*. 20 km.) to the village of Abu Korkas. Turn east in the middle of town, towards the river bank, and cross the Nile by means of the local ferry. Donkeys will be available on the east bank for the trek up the hill to the tombs, and/or south to the rock-cut chapel of Queen Hatshepsut (the Classical 'Speos Artemidos', known today as *Stabl Antar*). Allow two hours for a visit to the tombs, with at least two hours more for the round trip to Speos Artemidos.

If time permits a visit to both sites, it is better to proceed to the speos first, as the long donkey ride (*c*. 3 km. each way) is most pleasant in the cool of the morning. The track follows the river bank, then turns east, through a picturesque village, into the desert beyond. The wadi in which the speos is located was inhabited by Christian anchorites during the first millennium A.D., but earlier traces of humanity abound — in particular, an unfinished chapel (on the right, shortly before reaching the speos of Hatshepsut) decorated in the time of Alexander II.

The shrine of Queen Hatshepsut is dedicated to Pakhet, 'She who scratches', a lion-goddess of the district. Located on the south side of the wadi, it is unfinished: the Hathor-headed capitals to the columns on the façade have barely been roughed out. Above the entrance is a long, eulogistic text wherein Hatshepsut recalls the disorder within Egypt under the Hyksos yoke and extols the beneficence of her own rule. The front hall inside the chapel (see Fig. 48, A) is decorated with painted scenes showing Hatshepsut in the presence of the gods: the names in the cartouches are those of Sety I, however, who otherwise did little to bring the speos to completion. The inner room (mostly unfinished) is dominated by a statue of the

Fig. 48   The 'Speos Artemidos' of Hatshepsut

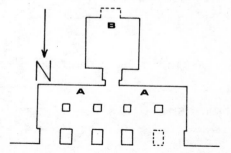

Akhenaten, heretic pharaoh of El Amarna (Cairo Museum)

goddess, carved out of the rock, in a niche placed high up on the back wall (B).

The way back to Beni Hasan goes through the ruins of a village just south of the site: local guides will tell you that it was a nest of pirates, cleared out by order of Mohammed Ali, but the town seems already to have been deserted when Napoleon's men visited the site in 1799. The donkeys will be left at the guardian's house, at the south end of the cemetery, the last stage of the ascent being made on foot.

The thirty-nine tombs on the upper level of the bluff at Beni Hasan (see Fig. 49) belong to the nomarchs of the nomarchs of the Oryx Nome, dating to the First Intermediate Period and Middle Kingdom (Dynasties XI–

XII). Since the decoration of the tombs proceeds along rather similar lines in most cases, it is enough to visit the few tombs that are open in order to get a representative impression of the site. Attentive visitors will note a number of themes — wrestling sequences, scenes of siege and battle, and of the warrior nomarch collecting taxes from his subjects — that are eloquent reflections of the uncertain living conditions that prevailed during the later First Intermediate Period. The necropolis's location on the east bank also results in some peculiarities in plan: note, for instance, that the false door is generally located on the west wall, canonically the zone of the dead in ancient Egypt (see Chapter 6, p. 67).

Fig. 49 **Beni Hasan**

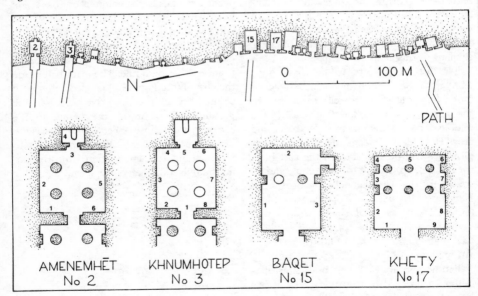

(BH 17) **Khety** *Dynasty XI*

1 Scenes of fowling, papyrus harvest, etc., in the marsh.
2 (Registers i–ii) Hunt in desert; (iii) barbers, linen makers; (iv) spinning and weaving;

women's games and dancing; (v) clappers and dancers before statue of tomb owner dragged on sledge; (vi) painting statues, carpentry, men playing at draughts.
3 (i) Hunt in desert, continued; (ii) musicians; (iii) deceased and wife.

4 (i–ii) Offering bringers; (iii) metal workers; (iv–v) bringing gazelle and other animals; (vi–vii) bringing captured birds to deceased.
5 (i–v) Wrestlers: the movements can be followed because the combatants' bodies are painted in contrasting shades; (vi–viii) battle scene, including fortress under siege at middle left, and piles of slain at (viii) right.
6 Scenes of vintage and wine making; sports and acrobatics.
7 Deceased under sunshade with his retinue, including dwarves and a club-footed man.
8 (i–ii) Dancers and cattle in procession before deceased's statue; (iii–v /right) offering bringers and butchers; (iii–v /left) agricultural scenes; (vi) ploughing.
9 (i–iii) Scenes of country life; (iv–v) boats in funeral rites; (vi–viii /right) butchers and offering bringers; (viii /left) false door.

(BH 15)   Baqet III   *Dynasty XI*

1 (i) Hunt in desert; (ii) barbers, linen makers – note overseers interfering in quarrel here – and painters; (iii) women spinning and weaving, performing acrobatics, playing ball, dancing; (iv) scribes counting cattle, defaulters; (v) musicians, goldsmiths, painters, sculptors; (vi) men fishing with large net, boatmen jousting, plucking papyrus, capturing birds.
2 (i–vi) Wrestlers; (vii–ix) battle scene, as in BH 17: note, at (vii) right, man being blinded (?) by captor.
3 (i) Deceased's statue pulled on sledge, with offering bringers; (ii–iii) scribes counting cattle, punishment of defaulters; (iv–v) industries and marsh scenes, including sports at (iv–v) right, and playing draughts at (vi) right.

(BH 3)   Khnumhotep*   *Early Dynasty XII*

1 Above door: (i) *Muwu*-dancers, men dragging shrine (see Chapter 6, p. 72) with statue of deceased; (ii) men with tomb equipment.
2 (i–iii) Agricultural scenes; (iv) journey to and from Abydos; (v) gardening scenes, including a *vineyard, and an orchard with fig trees.
3 (i–iii) Hunt in desert before deceased at right, including *Asiatics bringing gazelles at (iii) right; (iv–vi) snaring and bringing birds, bringing and tending cattle, scribes with defaulters.
4 *Deceased fowling in reed skiff.

5 Above door: *Deceased snaring birds, including hoopoe.
6 *Deceased spearing fish in marsh.
7 Deceased and wife seated before laden offering tables and offering lists, with *offering bringers and *butchers.
8 (i) Fullers and carpenters; (ii) potters; felling trees, boat building; (iii) journey to Abydos; (iv) preparing food, *women weaving; (v) sculptors and other industries.

*This is easily the most distinctive tomb at Beni Hasan: architecturally it is identical to the adjoining chapel, BH 2, in that both have impressive exterior façades and are divided inside into three naves, each with a lightly vaulted roof; and both have small statue rooms at the back (only the bottom half of the deceased's statue being preserved here). Khnumhotep's 'autobiography', running along the base of the walls (which have been painted to simulate granite panelling), is a mine of information concerning the nascent Twelfth Dynasty's relations with their powerful vassals, the nomarchs. The wall paintings, too, are unmatched for their vibrancy and delicate colouring. Unfortunately, most of the surfaces badly need cleaning: only a few famous vignettes (noted with *) have been treated so far and stand out clearly from the surrounding fog.*

(BH 2)   Amenemhēt*   *Early Dynasty XII*

1 (i) Leather workers; (ii) makers of bows and arrows, stoneworkers, carpenters; (iii) metal workers; (iv) potters; (v) cultivating flax and making linen; (vi–vii) agricultural scenes.
2 (i) Hunt in desert; (ii) dancers and acrobats before statue of deceased on sledge; (iii–vi) men making various deliveries of birds and animals, including granary and scribes with defaulters, all before deceased, with his dogs and military escort.
3 (i–iii) Wrestlers; (iv) attack on fort, etc.; (v) journey to Abydos.
4 Offering bringers, offering list before deceased.
5 Offering bringers, offering list before deceased and his wife.
6 (i) Vintage scenes; (ii) brewing; (iii) fishing; (iv) storerooms with food and other products; (v) musicians at left, false door in middle, fording cattle and baking at right.

The deceased was Khnumhotep's predecessor. Although the plans of their tombs are similar, the decoration in Amenemhēt's chapel harks back to the themes of the earlier period. Note the elaborate painted decoration on the ceiling, and the remains of a statue group in the back room (probably the deceased with his wife and mother).

EL AMARNA

Akhenaten's capital, El Amarna, is some 45 km. south of Beni Hasan. To reach it, proceed to Kafr-Khuzâm, 10 km. south of Mellawi (= the second village) where a small hand-painted sign on the east side of the road indicates the way to the riverbank: here the traveller may avail himself of a motor launch (if the party is large enough and arrangements have been made in advance) or a sailboat to cross the Nile to El Till, on the east bank. Once there, it is best to refuse donkeys (unless one has all day and sightseeing desiderata are modest) in favour of one of the several tractors that haul wagons full of visitors across the wastes of Akhetaten. The city originally extended over more than fifteen kilometres on the plain, bordered by hills in which the tombs are found (see Fig. 50). Since the ruins are scattered, and some of them have been covered by wind-blown sand since their excavation earlier this century, we will concentrate on two important areas in the city before visiting the private tombs.

Fig. 50 **El Amarna** *overall plan*

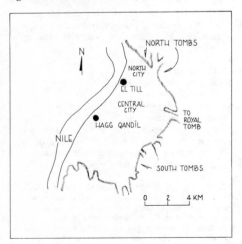

Local guides encourage visitors to see the north city, which is fairly close to the north-east edge of El Till. This seems to have been where Akhenaten and most of his courtiers resided, and among the welter of royal and private buildings found here, one will probably visit the so-called 'Hall of Foreign Tribute' and the 'North Palace'. These once imposing buildings are reduced practically to their foundations: an idea of their original beauty can be evoked from paintings preserved in the Cairo Museum (Chapter 10, p. 114 = Room 28) and elsewhere, as one wanders through the broad halls and colonnades of this short-lived royal city.

Perhaps more satisfying is a visit to the official, or 'central', city: to reach it, go south through the village of El Till and follow the track along the cultivation's edge that corresponds to Akhetaten's main street. When two mudbrick pylons appear in the middle of the road, you have reached the city's administrative centre, for these are the remains of a narrow 'bridge' (Fig. 51, A) that connected the 'King's House' on the east with the official palace on the western side. The latter (D), a vast and complex building, could not be completely excavated and many of its features are obscure. The buildings on the east side of the road are more comprehensible. Immediately south of the bridge, for instance, is a temple (C), the mudbrick pylons of which are remarkably well preserved. Inside, we proceed through two courts into the sanctuary area, which is mostly destroyed. From here, we can enter the 'King's House' (B), a complex of magazines and retiring rooms that gave on to a court, on the north side, where the rewarding of state officials took place. The 'Window of Appearances', universally represented in the tombs, was located here, though the remains are hard to make out today.

Other buildings of Akhetaten's official quarter — the foreign office, records archives

(E), as well as the military and police head-quarters (F), are located behind the 'King's House', to the east. To the north are offices and storerooms (G) pertaining to the great temple of the Aton, which itself lies on the north edge of the central city (H). Although conceived on a grand scale, this building is difficult for visitors to grasp, for most of the

precinct was filled with open-air altars (I, J) suited to the worship of this solar god, while enclosed cult chambers (K), unlike those in most Egyptian temples, were few. A large altar (L) – the so-called 'Hall of Foreign Tribute' – bestrides the enclosure wall near its north-east end. Owing to the savage thoroughness of the destruction,

Fig. 51 **El Amarna** *the Central City*

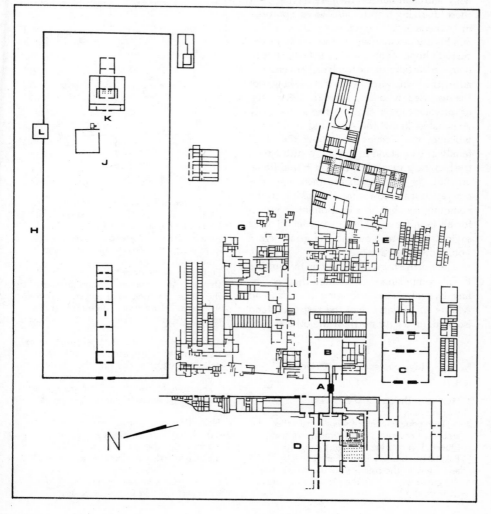

most visitors will carry away only an impression of the sheer vastness of the temple Akhenaten built for his god.

Next to be visited are the tombs of favoured officials on the outskirts of the city (Fig. 50). The scenes that decorate their walls have an abiding charm – for the elongated, oddly graceful forms, the liveliness of the subject matter, and the not infrequent tenderness and humour of their rendering. But these charming features also serve a purpose in Akhenaten's 'programme'. Since Osiris and his divine circle were proscribed, the deceased's hope of salvation lay in being able to come to the door of the tomb daily in order to adore the living Aton. Thus it is the king, not the deceased, who dominates the decoration of private tombs at El Amarna, for only Akhenaten 'knew' the Aton and could truly worship him. Scenes that show the royal family at ease stand in marked contrast with the hieratic pose of the Pharaoh in traditional art. But, for all their charm, these episodes convey, not the lowering of the king to the common man, but his elevation into a model for all Egyptians: Akhenaten, in effect, was saying, 'Hitherto, you had the gods before you. Now you have me.'

The northern group of tombs is opposite El Till, comprising six decorated chapels. The first two of these, belonging to *Huya* and *Meryrē II*, are later than the rest and stand isolated, on a spur north of the others.

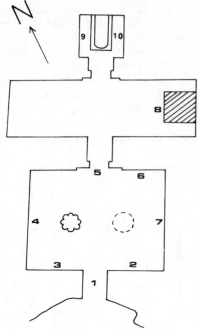

Fig. 52 **Huya** *Steward of Queen Tiyi**

(EA 1)

1 Hymns to the Sun, and deceased worshipping.
2–3 Two complementary scenes that reflect the ambience of Huya's employment, showing Queen Tiyi and her youngest daughter, Baketaten, dining with Akhenaten, Nefertiti and a few of the couple's six daughters: note the gusto with which the participants enjoy their meal.

4 On a state occasion in the twelfth year of Akhenaten's reign, the king and queen are borne in a carrying chair to the Hall of Foreign Tribute, there to receive homage from their vassals (shown below and at the right side).
5 Lintel above the door to the inner room, showing Akhenaten and his queen saluted by their daughters (left), and Queen Tiyi with Baketaten before Amenhotep III (right), reflecting Huya's service to both branches of the royal family.
6 Top: Huya is decorated by Akhenaten from the Window of Appearances; bottom: a delightful vignette showing the interior of a sculptor's shop.
7 Akhenaten, followed by his entourage, leads his mother to a 'sunshade' temple he has built for her.
8 Shaft (this room not decorated).
9–10 Shrine, with offerings and funerary equipment shown on side walls and unfinished statue of deceased at rear wall.

* *Huya took office on the death or retirement of Kheruef, for whose tomb (Th 192) see Chapter 19, p. 296.*

Fig. 53 **Meryrē II** *Superintendent of the Household of Nefertiti*

(EA 2)

1 On thicknesses, deceased adores the rising sun.
2 Queen pours a drink through a strainer into king's cup.
3 King and queen in Window of Appearances reward deceased.
4 Akhenaten and Nefertiti enthroned in Hall of Foreign Tribute receive homage of the 'chiefs of foreign lands'. This, of course, is the pendant to the scene in Huya's tomb, and the festive nature of the occasion is conveyed not only by the foreigners in their native dress, bringing exotic gifts, but by scenes of wrestling and other sports (right side).
5 A damaged scene, mostly executed in black paint, that showed the deceased being rewarded by Smenkhkarē, Akhenaten's successor, with his consort, Akhenaten's eldest daughter, Meritaten. (The rest of the tomb is not finished.)

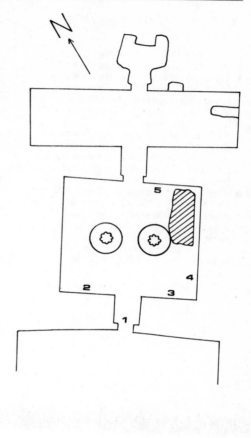

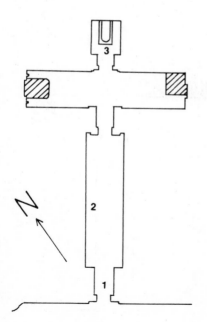

Fig. 54 **Ahmose** *Fan Bearer on the King's Right Hand*

(EA 3)

1 Hymns to the Sun.
2 The two registers on this wall were never completed, giving the visitor an opportunity to see different stages in the preparation of the finished relief. On top, the king and queen in their chariot (in ink) proceed, with their armed guard, to the temple of the Aton. Below, the royal family is seated inside the palace, while a small orchestra performs music in one of the side rooms (behind).
3 Statue of the deceased.

Fig. 55 **Meryrē I** *High Priest of the Aton*

(EA 4)

1 Large carved floral standards.
2 Deceased with wife worships the rising sun.
3 The deceased is borne on the shoulders of his friends to the Window of Appearances, where he is rewarded by the king.
4 The king and queen go by chariot to the temple of the Aton.
5 Akhenaten and Nefertiti, with two of their daughters, present a laden offering table to the Aton: note the unique representation of the rainbow, rendered in multicoloured bands below the disc.
6 Top: Meryrē accompanies the royal family on a visit to the Aton Temple; bottom: the deceased is appointed to office: on the right, note the harbour of Akhetaten, and the state cattle barns above; the palace, with its extensive gardens, is on the left. (The remainder of the tomb is unfinished.)

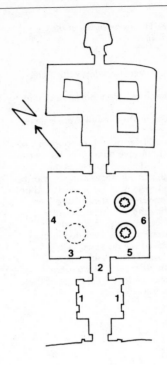

Fig. 56 **Pentu** *Royal Physician*

(EA 5)

1 The king, queen and one daughter before the temple of the Aton.
2 Deceased appointed to office.

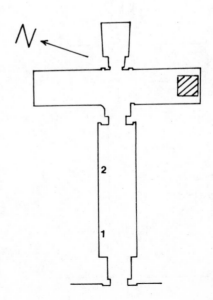

Fig. 57 **Panehsy*** *Chief Servitor of the Aton in Akhetaten*

(EA 6)

1 Outer lintel: the royal family adores the solar disc.
2 Top: the king and queen (wearing elaborate crowns) adore the Aton; bottom: the royal family, including the king's sister (future wife of King Horemheb) Mutnedjemet, accompanied by her two dwarf attendants.
3 Deceased rewarded with collars by king and queen.
4 The royal family in chariots, with their honour guard.
5 Stairway leading to unfinished burial chamber.
6 Deceased before Akhenaten (wearing Red Crown) and queen.
7 The king and queen celebrate ritual at temple of the Aton.
8 Coptic baptistery.
9 Deceased as an elderly, obese man, with daughter, adoring the sun.
10 Entrance to second burial chamber.
11 Shrine, with vandalized statue of deceased at back wall, with funerary offerings depicted on right.

* The decorated façade is preserved here, as it is not in most other tombs at Amarna; but the interior was modified by the Copts.

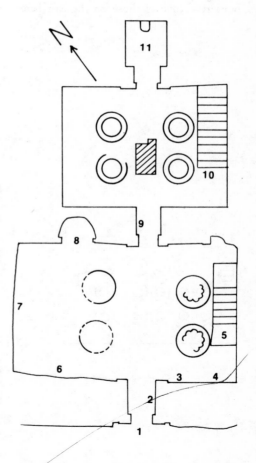

Both the tomb of Akhenaten (located 12 km. up the so-called Royal Wadi; inaccessible to motor vehicles) and the southern group of private tombs, opposite the village of Hagg Qandil, are now inaccessible to the public. Wind-blown sand has blocked the entrances of some private tombs in recent years, and nearly all decoration found in the royal tomb has since been destroyed. On the off-chance that permission to visit the southern group is obtained, however, a few of the most accessible are described here.

Akhenaten defined the limits of his city by setting up fourteen boundary stelae at its outskirts. None of those on the east bank is easily reached, however, though the northernmost stela on the west bank will be visited in connection with the Late Period cemetery at Tuna el-Gebel (see below, p. 200).

The modern district capital is Mellawi, far from desolate Akhetaten, and a few kilometres' distance from the ancient local centre of Hermopolis (El Ashmunein). A museum devoted to finds made in Middle Egypt is located on the south side of the main street that goes west through the town. It is not a major collection, but should be visited if there is also enough time to examine the ruins at Ashmunein and at Tuna el-Gebel.

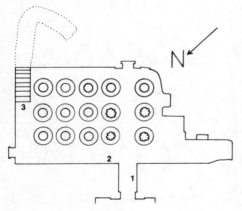

Fig. 58 **Ay** God's Father, Fan Bearer at the King's Right Hand*

(EA 25)

1 Ay and his wife kneeling, adoring rising sun, with hymn to the Aton above.
2 The deceased and his wife (upper parts cut away, in the Cairo Museum) are rewarded by the royal family: note the festive atmosphere, including dancing figures below. At the right, the tomb owner is shown leaving the palace.
3 Shaft (unfinished).

* Ay occupied an anomalous but powerful position at Akhenaten's court. He may have been Nefertiti's father (his wife, called Tiyi, was the Queen's wet-nurse), and Ay himself seems to have been a member of old Queen Tiyi's family. He acted as counsellor to Akhenaten and Tutankhamun, and briefly assumed the throne on the latter's death (see Chapter 18, p. 250). The layout of his Amarna tomb is imposing enough, but — surprisingly — it is one of the roughest of all the unfinished tombs at this site.

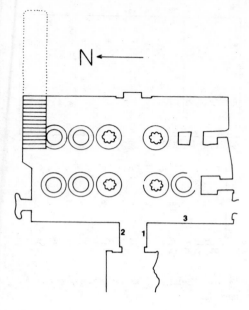

Fig. 59 **Maya** *Fan Bearer at the King's Right Hand*

(EA 14)

1 Deceased worships the rising sun.
2 Royal family (including Mutnedjemet with her two dwarves) worships the sun.
3 Fragmentary scene (investiture? Cf. EA 4[6], bottom), with palace gardens, harbour.

Fig. 60 **Tutu*** *Chamberlain*

(EA 8)

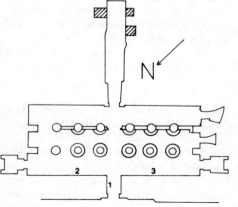

1 King adoring the Aton: note that parts of the relief were carved in such inferior stone that they were replaced with stone patches that have since fallen out.
2 The king, enthroned, greets the deceased at the door of the palace.
3 The deceased is rewarded by the king and is shown congratulated by his friends on leaving the palace: note the details in the palace behind the king, e.g., the men sweeping the floor under the Window of Appearances.

*** *As minister of protocol at Akhenaten's court, Tutu had numerous connections with the diplomatic corps, and his name frequently appears in the cuneiform correspondence, written on clay tablets, found at El Amarna. His tomb, one of the most elaborate from an architectural standpoint, is unfinished.*

MELLAWI MUSEUM

Hours: 9 a.m. to 1 p.m. Closed on Wednesdays.

Room 1: On the north wall, note the tomb paintings from Tuna el-Gebel and the limestone statue head from Hermopolis (A); also the colossal disc from a statue of Thoth (B) and remains of cartonage from ibis mummies (C). A royal head of the Late Period is exhibited in the north-east corner (D). The two sides of the room are lined with ibis statuettes (E), ibis coffins of various materials (F), ibis and hawk mummies (G) and eggs (H). At the south end is a large statue of Thoth as an ibis, with a figure of Ma'at (I). Note, on leaving, a statue dated to the Graeco-Roman Period (J).

Room 2: The objects are exhibited in four rows. On the east, phials and combs (A), the canopic jars of one Ankh-Hor (B), and the wooden coffins of one Imhotep (C), followed by four stone sarcophagi of the Graeco-Roman Period (D), and the mummy of a young woman against the south wall (E). In the centre of this wall is perhaps the finest piece of the museum, the painted limestone group statue of Pepi-Ankh-Hor with his wife (F), and in the middle of the room are Graeco-Roman funerary masks (G), amulets (H), and jewellery (I). On the west side are statuettes and fragments (J), Graeco-Roman faience *shawabtis* (K) and several splendidly painted wooden coffins of the Middle Kingdom, including a child's coffin (L): note, on one of these, how the hieroglyphs that represent beings who might harm the tomb owner – e.g., serpents – are symbolically mutilated by being incompletely carved. Against the south wall (M) is another Graeco-Roman coffin, belonging to a young woman.

Room 3: At the north end, note the bronze reliefs (A), a tomb painting of the goddess Isis

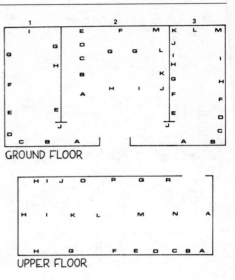

GROUND FLOOR

UPPER FLOOR

Fig. 61 **Mellawi:** *Museum, ground floor and upper floor*

(B) and the statue head of a Pharaoh (C). Beyond are various statuettes from the Graeco-Roman Period: a priest (D), Horus the Child (E), Osiris (F), Isis (G), Thoth as a baboon (H) and other sacred animals (I). Next, on the east side, are baboon coffins of wood, dedicated by Ramesses II and re-used later (J). Against the south walls are baboon mummies, one in a shrine (K, L), and a hideous statue of a dog in orange plaster (M).

Room 4: A staircase in the north-west corner of Room 3 leads to the upper level, a large room containing a variety of objects. Against the west and north walls are glass and faience vessels (A), with pottery vessels beyond (B), including an engaging specimen modelled with the features of the god Bes. Next are terracotta figures (C), flint and copper knives, stone weights and mauls, a mortar and pestle (D); stone offering tables and shrines (E); baskets, a bronze horn, and a fragmentary cubit rod from the time of Amenhotep III (F). Note the stone model windows from the Graeco-Roman cemetery at Tuna el-Gebel (G), followed by the cases filled with pottery vessels (H) and lamps (I). Stone fragments are exhibited against the south wall, including a window, offering tables, model buildings, and a relief, perhaps from one of the tombs at El Amarna (J). Greek inscriptions on stone occupy the central aisle (K), along with linen cloths with ink dockets in Egyptian (L), papyri and seals (M), and fragments of carved and inlaid wood (N). Back on the south wall are wooden coffin lids and masks from the Graeco-Roman Period (O); coins (P); textiles, rope and musical instruments (Q); and a collection of pottery and small stone censers (R).

ASHMUNEIN

To reach the site of ancient Hermopolis, follow the main artery west through Mellawi, next turning north for a distance, then west

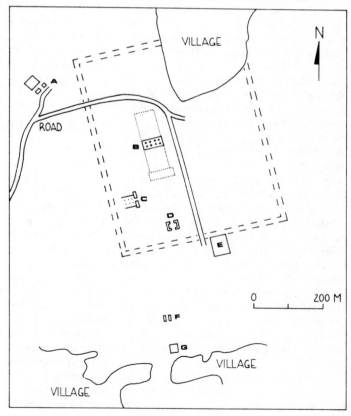

Fig. 62 **Ancient Hermopolis** (Ashmunein)

once more. The approach to the ruins is heralded by glimpses of the once-massive mudbrick walls from across the fields. Turning north on to an access road, eventually we come to the old archaeological mission house, in front of which are two enormous statues, dating to the reign of Amenhotep III, of the god Thoth as a baboon (see Fig. 62, A). Although still not fully reconstructed, these figures are nonetheless impressive for their sheer size (about 4.5 m. high without their bases) and for the elegance of their carving.

Another subsidiary road leads through the ruined temples that are the site's main attractions. The area is large and overgrown with grass, but those who wish to make the most of their visit will traverse the grounds on foot, starting at the north (i.e., back) end of the Temple of Thoth (see Fig. 62, B). This building in its present state was rebuilt by Nectanebo I and received numerous additions at the hands of the Graeco-Roman rulers of Egypt. Regrettably, it is now flooded: the water table has overtaken the ancient ground level, so only a general idea of its dimensions may be gained today. West of the temple's processional way (C) is the small limestone temple of Amun, begun under Merneptah and finished by Sety II: the pylon and hypostyle hall are substantially preserved, but the back of the building is reduced to ground level. Further south (D) are remains of a gateway dating to the later Middle Kingdom: the façade and passage still survive, but are entirely surrounded by water. Other remains, both Pharaonic and later, abound in this area, for the temple enclosure was surrounded by the streets of the city in late antiquity; but these survivals are badly ruined and difficult to make out.

Outside the enclosure of the Thoth Temple is the site's outstanding monument — the Christian basilica, built out of re-used blocks from a Ptolemaic temple to the royal cult (Fig. 62, E). Graceful standing columns recall the church's former splendour, and those with the time and patience to do so may observe many interesting details in the ground plan. Greek inscriptions on the architraves lying on the ground inform us that 'the cavalry militia serving in the Hermopolite nome [dedicated] the statues, the temple and the other buildings within the sanctuary, and the stoa' to the deified Kings Ptolemy II and III with their wives, 'for their benevolence towards them'.

The remainder of the site is largely fragmented and overgrown, offering but a few tantalizing glimpses of its former state. At the south end — which is further than most visitors get — two seated 'colossi' of Ramesses II (F) stand before the pathetic remains of another temple, while nearby — at the edge of the village — is a fragmentary temple dating to the reign of Nero (G).

TUNA EL-GEBEL

The necropolis of Ashmunein during late antiquity was located 11 km. from the city: the main road leads west, across the Bahr Yusuf (see Chapter 1, p. 19), and turns south along the edge of the desert. Before reaching the late cemetery, the visitor will see the *northern boundary stela of Akhenaten* to his right, on the face of a low cliff (see Fig. 63). The place is easily reached on foot, revealing on the right a large tablet with the obligatory relief of the king and queen offering to the Aton on top, while the text below records Akhenaten's oath not to alter the city's limits nor to be buried in any place other than Amarna. Two headless statues of the king and queen stand to the left, each one supporting a tall offering table inscribed, at the sides, with figures of the couple's three eldest daughters.

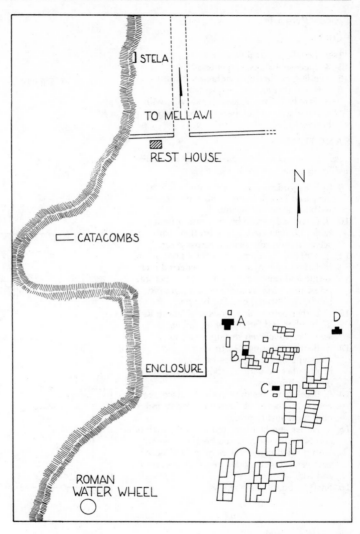

Fig. 63 **Tuna el-Gebel**

Fig. 64 **Petosiris**

PORTICO

1–2 Jewellers, metal workers.
3–4 Incense makers, carpenters.
5 Tending cattle (top), vintage (bottom).
6 Farming scenes.
7–8 Family before deceased and wife, with sub-registers of butchers (7) and offering bringers (8).

SANCTUARY

(N.B.: The east and west halves are dedicated to the father and brother of the tomb owner respectively.)

9 (i) Tree goddess with father and mother; (ii) deceased before father; (sub-scene) cattle with herdsmen in swamp.
10 (i) Deceased before brother with offering table; (ii) deceased before brother; (sub-scene) men fording cattle across river.
11 (i) Offering bringers; (ii) funeral procession, including offerings, coffin on wheeled bier, shrine and canopic jars on sleds, all before priest purifying mummy before pyramid tomb; (sub-scene) offering bringers.
12 (i) Father before nine 'gods who adore Rē'; (ii) brother and family before father; (sub-scene) cattle driven through swamp.
13 (i) Brother adoring, led to Osiris, and worshipping four groups of deities; (ii) brother before various gods; (sub-scene) offering bringers.
14 (i) Brother adores nine gods; (ii) deceased before brother; (sub-scene) crocodile and hippopotamus fighting.
15 (i) Father and brother before Osiris, with Isis and Nephthys; (ii) sacred beetle crowned with horned diadem rises on palace façade between winged goddesses, followed by Ba and Isis.
16 Shaft to burial chambers.

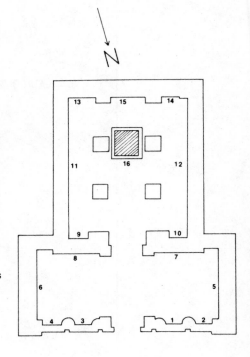

A short distance beyond lies the rest house of Tuna el-Gebel, with the necropolis lying just to the south. Consisting of numerous chapels and other monuments arranged in streets, this is a true 'city of the dead', although some buildings have features that merely imitate those of contemporary buildings: note, for example, the latticed stone 'windows' surmounted by a frieze of cobras. Only a portion of the site has been excavated, so the dunes of drifted sand that lie to the south may fairly be expected to reveal a great deal more.

The first of the tombs to be encountered is also the most splendid: this is the *tomb of Petosiris* (Fig. 63, A), a high priest of Thoth who probably lived in the fourth century B.C. and whose inlaid wooden coffin is exhibited in the Cairo Museum (see Chapter 10, p. 118). The tomb itself resembles a small temple, with its pillared portico and the large altar in the Greek style that dominates the court in front. The reliefs inside the tomb blend Egyptian motifs — some of them not attested since the Old Kingdom — with a style heavily influenced by the conventions of Greek art: it is not elegant work, but has great vivacity and retains most of its original colour (Fig. 64).

The visitor's wanderings through the sand-swept, deserted streets of the necropolis will reveal many varieties of taste and style: some tombs, for instance, are painted with mock stone panelling, a feature found more often in tombs at Alexandria. A number of these tombs lie open, and the guardian has the key to others. The *tomb of Isadora* (Fig. 63, B), dating to the early second century A.D., is distinguished by its sparse decor — two Greek texts in memory of the young girl buried here — and by the large sculpted half-shell over the funerary couch at the rear of the chapel; but all possible elegance is dissipated by the tasteless display of Isadora

herself in a case set inside the first chamber. The *Oedipus tomb* (C) was decorated with scenes illustrating the Greek Theban cycle: the originals have been removed to the Cairo Museum (Chapter 10, p. 117), but copies of these and other paintings are exhibited on the walls. Of some interest, although regrettably closed to the public, is yet another painted tomb of the Late Period (D), which contains a highly unusual representation of the deceased's shadow, seen as a black, skeletal figure (see above, Chapter 6, p. 67).

South-west of the tombs is an ancient waterworks with a shaft 34 metres deep, designed to supply the area with water during the Roman era. Returning to the north, the visitor will pass the remains of a stone balustrade which, it is believed, defined the enclosure wherein the sacred ibises were raised. The underground galleries where Thoth's 'living images' were buried lie beyond, south-west of the rest house. A small baboon gallery is found at the bottom of the stairs, to the left. The ibis burials in the south and west catacombs are much more extensive: a number of stone ibis sarcophagi are kept in the main passage, and the large rock-cut side-chambers are packed with pots containing bird burials. The guide will be able to show the way to the tomb of a local High Priest of the late Pharaonic period who was buried in one of the annexes to the ibis catacombs.

MELLAWI TO SOHAG

Local cemeteries of the early Pharaonic age were located on the east bank, across the river from Mellawi. Directly opposite the capital is *El Bersha*, where the nomarchs of the Middle Kingdom were buried. Most of the tombs are in a lamentable state of preservation, featuring the motifs commonly found at this time, but of particular interest is the *tomb of Thut-hotep II* (*temp.* Senwosret II–Senwosret III): the plan (Fig. 65) recalls those of the later tombs at Beni Hasan, and on the left-hand wall of the principal chamber (A) there is a unique scene, depicting the transporting of a colossal statue of the tomb owner towards the portal of his mortuary temple. Inquire at Mellawi Museum or at the local inspectorate before making this excursion.

A number of important provincial cemeteries are found between Mellawi and Sohag. The absence of any detailed description in this guide results from practical considerations, for under present conditions very few travellers will visit these sites. The Old Kingdom necropolis of the nome is located a few kilometres south of El Bersha, at *Sheikh Saïd*, on the east bank. Back on the west side, the road leads 24.5 km. south from Mellawi to Kussiya, from which it is another 8 km. west to the cemetery of *Meir* (Dynasties VI–XII). Important tombs of the First Intermediate Period and Middle Kingdom are found in the necropoleis to the west of the city of *Assiût* (79 km. south of Mellawi). Co-operation of the local antiquities officials is desirable in any proposed visit to these sites, and even more complex arrangements may be necessary for the Assiût cemetery, which lies in a military area.

The road to the *Kharga and Dakhla Oases* is entered some 8 km. north of Assiût (73 km. south of Mellawi: see Chapter 22).

Sohag, the next large city, lies 93 km. south of Assiût. A road leading to the north-west from town ends at the edge of the desert (*c.* 12 km.) near the 'White Monastery' – so called because it is built out of limestone blocks quarried from the pagan temples in the ruined city of Athribis nearby. The building's external appearance, with its neat masonry, sloping walls and ornamental cornice, at first sight suggests a Pharaonic

Fig. 65 **El Bersha** *tomb of Thut-hotep II*

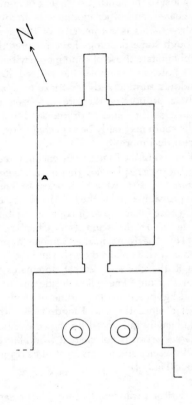

monument re-used in the Christian era. However, it was constructed during the fourth century A.D. by St Shenûte and served as a monastic stronghold from which Shenûte imposed his will throughout the area on Christian and pagan alike. Consisting of an enormous basilica, with the sanctuary at the east end, flanked by a long courtyard at the south side, it has been much altered since its construction, but the original plan is still clear and the whole is a fascinating document of the early Christian era in Egypt. A similar building is found about 5 km. to the north: known as the 'Red Monastery' because of the fired bricks used in its construction, it is smaller than its neighbour and is partially engulfed by the adjoining village, so it is seen to best advantage from the desert, to the north-west.

OVERLEAF Painted reliefs of exquisite quality in the temple of Sety I

16.   *Abydos to Luxor*

As at El Ma'abda, some 27 km. north of Assiūt, the desert hills that have hugged the east bank of the Nile now fall away, allowing some scope to the valley on both sides of the river. The road from Sohag continues south as before on the west bank, however, although there is a newly paved track running along the east bank as well. The great bend, where the river flows from east to west, begins a few kilometres south of Nag Hammadi, continuing (about 55 km.) until the city of Qena is reached. One may continue south from Nag Hammadi on the west bank, through the desert, or cross the river at Nag Hammadi for a more scenic but slightly lengthier trip on the east bank.

ABYDOS

At Balliana (36 km. south of Sohag) turn west, towards the desert, for the necropolis at Abydos. This was the cemetery *par excellence*, the home of Osiris, 'Chief of the Westerners'; and Egyptians from all walks of life aspired to be buried here. Failing that, they built cenotaphs – dummy tombs – or chapels for themselves on the holy ground. The necropolis was thus continuously in use from the earliest times down to the fall of paganism, but only a fraction of these crowded memorials survives today.

Of the royal monuments constructed here from the First Dynasty on, the *Temple of Sety I* (Fig. 66, A) is the largest and most imposing

Fig. 66 **Abydos** *Cemeteries and temples*

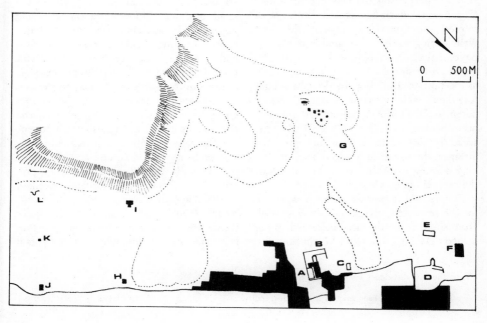

remnant. Built of fine white limestone, it contains some of the most delicate reliefs found in Egypt, many of them retaining their colours in virtually pristine condition. To reach these, the visitor first passes through the temple's two courtyards, both now in ruins: note, however, the ablution tanks, built to help the priests maintain their standards of ritual purity, in the first court. A doorway at the south-west corner of the second court leads to what is left of the temple's administrative complex: at the centre of this area is a small audience hall, complete with a limestone throne dais, while in the back are mudbrick magazines (see Fig. 67, X).

Sety I's temple 'was in the process of completion when he entered heaven'.[1] The first two courts, along with the portico, were built substantially by his successor, Ramesses II, who to the south of the central portal is shown worshipping the local 'triad' of Osiris, Isis and Sety I. Ramesses was also responsible for decorating the first hypostyle hall (Fig. 67, A) which has as its main point of interest the seven doorways in the west wall, leading to the same number of chapels beyond the second hypostyle hall (B). The seven processional ways should have begun at the portico itself, but the doorways built for them were filled in when Ramesses completed the portico. The contrast between his rather hasty workmanship and that sponsored by his father is striking: note, for instance, the sequence of reliefs showing the king offering to Osiris on the north wall of the second hypostyle hall.

The second hypostyle forms a vestibule for the seven chapels set into its west wall. From south to north, these belonged to the deified Sety I (C), Ptah (D), Rē-Harakhti (E), Amun-Rē (F), Osiris (G), Isis (H), and Horus (I). The scenes carved on the west wall show these gods issuing from their respective sanctuaries to confer various benefits on the king, while below these are niches for the statues of the related divinities that are shown (nicely carved and painted) on their walls.

The seven chapels are each roofed with a false vault. Six of them have false doors built against the western end walls to serve as the shrine's cult focus: the chapel of Osiris (G) has instead another doorway that passes into a suite of rooms dedicated to that god, of which more below. In all the chapels the decoration reflects ritual episodes that took place on the few annual occasions when the gods' statues were brought in their sacred barques from another room in the temple and installed inside the chapels. In six of the seven (the shrine of Sety I excluded), the selection of scenes is so similar that one description can apply to all. The first sequence[2] (north wall, east end) shows the king opening the doors of the shrine, raising his hands in adoration before the statue, and offering incense. Next (north wall, west end), he offers sacrifice before the divine barque, sometimes followed by another offering before the statue (top); then he cleanses the god with a towel, performs the 'laying-on of hands', anoints the statue's forehead and clothes it with fresh garments (bottom). Another offering ritual follows (south wall, east end): incense is burned and the statue purified with water (top), and the king presents gifts of new clothing and jewellery in the shape of elaborate collars (bottom). Finally (south wall, west end) the god's statue receives certain insignia and its crown is steadied by the king, who then presents it

---

1. From the long dedicatory inscription on the portico.

2. On the wall: the actual sequence of the rites is disputed.

Fig. 67 **Sety I** *Temple*

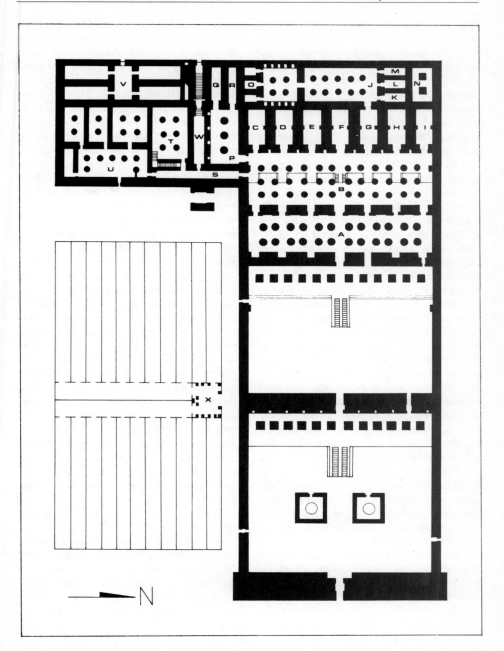

with the crook and flail – symbols of the royal power – and with jars of ointment (bottom). The final sacrifice before the barque is then followed by the ceremonial scattering of sand out of a shallow dish.[3] The king is shown departing (in most of the chapels) on the south side of the east wall, obliterating his footprints in the sand with a long whisk, thus ensuring the inviolability of the sanctuary until the next service takes place.

The reliefs in King Sety's chapel (Fig. 67, C) are different, stressing rather the recognition of his sovereignty by all the gods. First (north wall, east end, top) he is led into the temple by a delegation of gods who next perform the ceremonial 'unification of the Two Lands': the king is enthroned between the goddesses Edjo and Nekhbet, while Horus and Thoth lash together the heraldic plants of Upper and Lower Egypt supporting the throne (bottom). At the west end of the north and south wall we see the usual veneration of the divine barque (top), but the more important ritual is the presentation of a list of offerings to the king by Thoth and by Iunmutef, a priest-like figure dressed in a leopard skin and wearing a braided side-lock of hair, who acts as the king's advocate before the gods. Finally (south wall, east side) the king is led forth from the temple, as the Iunmutef secures the assent of the assembled gods (top), and is borne in triumph in a palanquin carried by the souls of the Lower Egyptian town of Pe (hawk-headed gods) and the Upper Egyptian Nekhen (jackal-headed), preceded by the Iunmutef and by the standards of the gods of the Two Lands (bottom).

The opening that takes the place of a false door at the back of the Osiris chapel (G) leads into a suite consecrated to that god. The walls of the first chamber (J) are covered with representations of the king offering to Osiris and other members of his circle, from which the visitor may derive a good impression both of the variety of Egyptian gods and of the apparatus of worship. The three chapels at the north end are dedicated to Horus (K), Sety I (L) and Isis (M): in the two outer rooms, the king offers to the gods on the side walls, receiving benefits from them at the back, while in King Sety's shrine the king is presented with regalia and cult objects throughout. The preservation of the original colours is especially vivid in these chapels and in the larger room in front of them. The visitor should also be aware of a secret room (although it is inaccessible) behind the three chapels, probably used as a crypt wherein the most valuable of the temple treasures were stored (N).

The preservation of the inner chambers of the Osiris suite is very poor. It is here, however, that the sacred mysteries of Osiris's resurrection were probably celebrated, as indicated by a fragmentary relief on the west wall of the central chapel at the south end (O): here we see Osiris recumbent on a bed, attended by the king and other deities, while Isis (in the form of a kite) hovers over Osiris's body. This relief (unfortunately not well preserved) is the climactic moment during which the revived Osiris begets his son Horus on Isis before passing into the Underworld – a sequence we will encounter more fully developed in the temples of the Late Period (see below, pp. 218–19).

Back in the second hypostyle hall, the visitor next proceeds to the south end, to a chapel in which Sokar and Nefertem, Osiris's northern counterparts, were honoured. Both gods were mortuary deities of the Memphite area – Sokar representing the potency for life in the earth, and Nefertem (in the form of a lotus bloom that closes at night and re-

3. Sometimes omitted or transferred to the previous episode.

opens in the morning) associated with the solar cycle of death and rebirth. Both were eventually assimilated into Osiris' greater personality, but they have a small suite to themselves in Sety's temple. The principal feature of the outer hall (P) is the presence of four statue niches, to hold images of related deities, in the south wall. The two chapels, of Nefertem (Q) and Ptah-Sokar (R), contain various reliefs showing the king offering before these and other divinities: note the hawk-headed form of Sokar, and the lotus blossom that crowns the head of Nefertem in his human and leonine aspects.

Early Egyptologists were most fascinated with the 'Gallery of Lists' (S) in which King Sety – accompanied by his eldest son, the future Ramesses II – offers before a list of his predecessors. This list now appears to be a selective and edited version of the fuller king lists preserved in contemporary archives, and it seems that the cult of the royal ancestors was performed here, as in the similarly circumscribed area of Thutmose III's temple in Karnak (see Chapter 17, pp. 233–4). Otherwise, the purpose of this southern extension of the temple appears to have been utilitarian: the barques of the resident gods, for instance, were kept in a room off the central hall (T), and to the south were butchers' quarters (U) and magazines (V). A transverse hall and a stairway (W) lead out to the cemeteries behind the temple. This section was decorated by Ramesses II, who is shown here in rituals that stress his mastery over unchecked, inimical nature – fowling (south), and subduing a wild bull, in the company of his eldest son (north).

The ground immediately behind Sety's temple is occupied by the so-called *Osireion* – in reality, an elaborate cenotaph which Sety built for himself, but which was completed about seventy years later by his grandson, Merneptah (see Fig. 66, B). Its design imitates, no doubt intentionally, the

earlier New Kingdom tombs found in the Valley of the Kings at Thebes (see below, Chapter 18, pp. 247–56). First there is a long passage (Fig. 68, A), painted with offering scenes and with extracts from the Book of Gates (see Chapter 7, p. 84). The monument's axis bends sharply at the end of the passage, going into two transverse halls (B and C) inscribed with astronomical and mythological scenes, and also with selections from the Book of the Dead. From here we proceed into the focal point of the building – an enormous hall (30.5 × 20 m.) built out of red granite, which served as the dummy burial chamber (D). The sarcophagus and canopic chest were placed on an 'island' in the centre of the room, surrounding which was a canal filled with water at all times of the year. The roof of this, along with the neighbouring chambers, has collapsed and the entire lower level is now filled with ground water, obscuring its main features. A

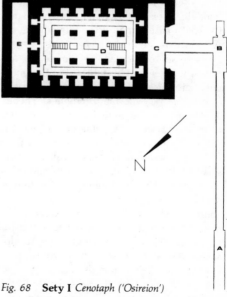

Fig. 68 **Sety I** *Cenotaph ('Osireion')*

modern staircase, which brings one down into the central hall, enables the visitor to see as much as is possible of its overgrown interior. The final transverse hall (E) preserves remains of the vaulted roof and also finely carved astronomical reliefs, including a splendid representation of the sky goddess Nūt supported by Shu, god of the air.

The *Temple of Ramesses II*, located about one-third of a kilometre north-east of the Osireion (see Fig. 66, C), is smaller than Sety I's monument and somewhat less well preserved. The absence of the roof is perhaps fortunate here, for the reliefs that are seen in consequence are unsurpassed in delicacy by anything else in this king's considerable production. One may admire, to begin, the version of the Battle of Kadesh carved on the north and west exterior walls: less complete than in other versions at Luxor, the **Ramesseum or Abu Simbel (see above, p. 58), it surpasses them in the fineness of** detail possible in limestone relief. The same high standard is also seen in the calendar of yearly feasts carved on the south wall of the building, but is less evident in the chapel near the south-east corner of the temple (Fig. 69, A), which was added later.

Ramesses conceived his temple on less eccentric lines than his father's, so the building's interior arrangement resembles that of a contemporary mortuary temple at Thebes. A portal in red granite leads into an open court supported by Osiride pillars, and the walls of the cloister are carved with a striking procession (colours excellently preserved) of offering bearers, priests and other attendants. The beginning of the temple proper is marked by the portico at the court's west end, and here too we find the first of the small chapels grouped along the building's axis wherein the gods of Abydos and prominent guests were worshipped: among these were the deified Sety I (B), the royal ancestors (C), the Ennead (D), **Ramesses II (E), Onuris (F), Osiris, residing in**

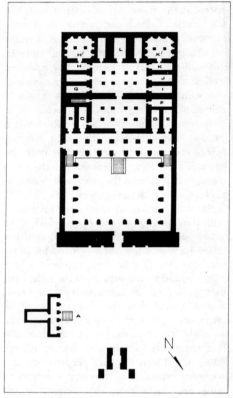

Fig. 69 **Ramesses II** *Temple*

this temple (G), the Theban Triad and their associates (H), Thoth (I), Min (J), and Osiris, 'Lord of Abydos', together with his circle (K). The gods of Thebes and of Abydos each have a suite of two rooms, the rear chamber being outfitted with statue niches that are lavishly decorated: especially fine is the humanoid Djed Pillar in the second Theban room (H'). The sanctuary (L) was also a splendid chamber, its limestone walls resting on sandstone bases, but it is now much ruined. A large alabaster stela has been set up before the entrance in modern times, while inside are the remains of a statue group in **grey granite, comprising Ramesses II, Sety I,** Amun and two goddesses.

NORTHERN OUTLYING SITES

The *Temple of Osiris* was situated about one kilometres north-east of the Ramesses II temple, near the present edge of the cultivation (see Fig. 66, D). Little remains of this ancient site (locally known as Kōm el-Sultan) beyond some mudbrick ramparts and the limestone portico built by Ramesses II in front of the temple. A number of mudbrick cenotaphs — small vaulted structures dedicated for private individuals — were preserved under the pavement just east of this, however, and thus stand as the clearest survivals of the popular cult of Osiris during ancient times.

Much more conspicuous is the *Second Dynasty enclosure* (Fig. 66, E) located one half-kilometre west, in the desert: its current name, Shūnet el-Zebīb or 'Storehouse of Dates', reflects a more recent use, and a similar structure even today is still occupied by a Coptic village, further north (Fig. 66, F). On closer inspection, it is seen to consist of two enclosures, the massive inner walls being surrounded by a lighter wall of mudbrick. The main ramparts — which display the niching characteristic of early mudbrick architecture — are about 12 m. high today, with an average thickness of over 5 m., and the entire complex has surface dimensions of about 135 × 78 m. Long referred to loosely as a fort, the 'Shūna' seems rather to be one of the several archaic funerary complexes located in this area. The *royal burials* — or cenotaphs — that went with them are located further out in the desert, some 3 km. east of the Sety I temple (Fig. 66, G). Identified as the tomb of Osiris during the New Kingdom, the place is today known as Umm el-Qa'ab, 'the Mother of Pots', on account of the vast number of votive jars scattered on the surface of the various graves. Little in the way of structural remains survive, however, so that — despite its historical importance — the site today is of no great interest to the average visitor.

SOUTHERN OUTLYING SITES AT ABYDOS

The area south of the Sety I temple, in which cenotaphs of the Middle and earlier New Kingdoms are found, is even more ravaged than the northern end of the site. Remains of a temple of Senwosret III are found at the edge of the desert, about 2 km. south of the centre (Fig. 66, H), with the king's cenotaph (now sanded up) a kilometre further west, at the nearest face of the cliffs (I). The pyramid of Ahmose (J) is a huge sandy mound, with a few brick walls indicating the site of the chapel at the east end, located about a kilometre south of the Senwosret temple.

From here, head west again, through the Muslim cemetery, to reach the ruined cenotaph of Queen Tetisheri, Ahmose's mother (K), and the king's own cenotaph and temple, a terraced building, poorly preserved, at the base of the cliffs (L). As there are no paved roads and hardly even a decent track in this locality, the visit should be made in vehicles possessing four-wheel drive.

DENDERA

The road through the desert from Nag Hammadi (west bank: 45 km.) passes Dendera, home of the goddess Hathor. The site can also be approached from the south by crossing the bridge at Qena and continuing a few kilometres to the north, but from either direction the view of the ruins from across the fields is a dramatic one. Apart from Philae, Dendera is the most extensive of the temple complexes that have survived from the Late Period. The site goes back, of course, into remote antiquity. Ruined tombs of the Old Kingdom abound in the desert behind the temple enclosure, and a limestone chapel of the Eleventh Dynasty found near the great temple resides today in the Cairo Museum (Chapter 10, p. 114). Basically, however, the buildings to be seen here date from the last years of Egyptian independence during the fourth century B.C. into the Roman period, over five centuries later.

The great shrines at Dendera were originally three, belonging to Hathor, her consort (Horus of Edfu), and their child, variously called Ihy or Harsomtus. Only the precinct of Hathor remains more or less intact: its massive columned hall, looming behind the mudbrick enclosure, dominates the surrounding countryside. The other temples were destroyed and their remains lie scattered over the rubbish heaps of the ancient town: the gateway leading to Ihy's precinct still stands, however, about a quarter of a kilometre south-east of the main enclosure.

The avenue leading to Hathor's precinct is flanked by two fountains, no doubt built in Roman times, where visitors could rest in the shade of their columned porches. Excess water was channelled into two pools to the south, where weary travellers might wash their feet or perform other ablutions in order to be 'pure' on entering the temple. Note, on passing through the gateway into the precinct, peg-holes for the veil that normally hid the figures of Hathor, Isis and the king on the left, marking this as a special place for popular worship. The ceiling of the passage still has beautifully painted figures of a winged disc and of the sacred beetle pushing the sun with its claws.

The entire precinct, like most temples, is located at right angles to the river: in local terms, the Nile is seen as running from south to north, but owing to the 'great bend' at Qena the river actually runs from east to west. The temple, oriented towards the local 'east', actually faces north. Once inside the enclosure, the visitor has two choices — to explore the immediately adjacent buildings or to forge on to the temple itself. We shall follow the second course, pausing only to examine the varied statues, sarcophagi

and reliefs piled at either side of the entrance: note especially the large figure of Bes, the bandy-legged god who protected women in childbirth, on the east.

The *Temple of Hathor* was apparently built in two stages: first came the cult chambers (everything behind Room Z: see Fig. 71), built and decorated under the later Ptolemies (the many blank cartouches reflecting the uncertainty of the times); then the columned hall (G') was added early in the first century A.D. by the Emperor Tiberius. The façade is characteristic for later Egyptianizing temples: instead of being completely enclosed, the front row of columns east and west of the entrance is linked with walls low enough to reveal the interior of the building. The resulting structure, which includes also the pronounced batter of the traditional pylon, is oddly graceless here, though undeniably imposing from the standpoint of sheer mass. Each pillar terminates in a four-sided capital carved to represent the emblem of Hathor — a woman's face with cow's ears, bearing the sacred sistrum on her head. All the faces on these capitals were vandalized in antiquity, but the reader may admire the figures on the astronomical ceiling in each nave, which are substantially undamaged: note the figure of the sky goddess Nūt (east side), as she swallows the winged disc at evening in order to give birth to it in the morning; or the familiar signs of the zodiac — Taurus, Sagittarius, Scorpio (west).

The second hypostyle hall was known also as the 'Hall of Appearances' (Z) because it was here that the goddess's statue first manifested itself on leaving the sanctuary during the great processional feasts. The ceiling is supported by two rows of Hathor columns (smaller than those in the front hall): as in most Egyptian temples, the floor rises progressively as the sanctuary is approached, the better to emphasize the mysteriousness of the inner chambers. Of the reliefs on

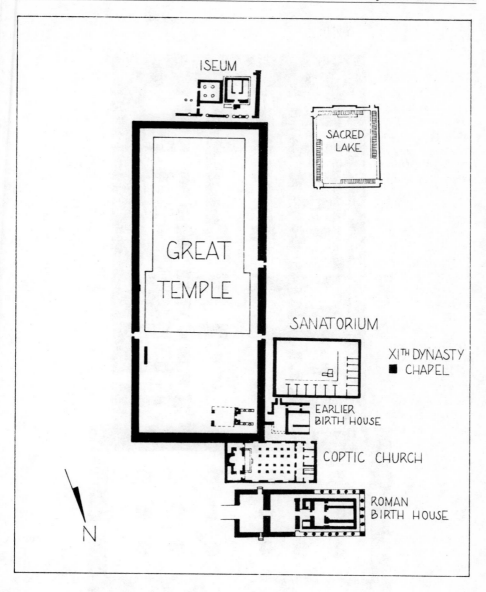

Fig. 70 **Dendera** *precinct of Hathor*

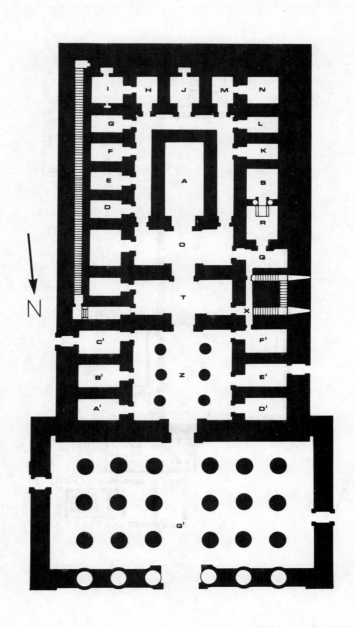

the walls, note the foundation ceremonies — for example, the king hoeing the earth and fashioning a brick (north-west corner) or sprinkling gypsum into the foundation trenches (east).

The six rooms at the sides of the hall were service chambers connected with the daily ritual. On the east side are the 'laboratories' (A'), where perfumes and unguents were consecrated for divine use; a magazine perhaps used for produce from temple properties, in which certain venerable statues were also kept (B'); and a passage through which food and other solid offerings entered the temple (C'). To the west we have the 'treasury' (D') and two more intermediate chambers — one leading out to the well that supplied the ritualists with water (E'), and a room (F') allowing access to the western stairway and the temple's interior without requiring that the great double doors to the sanctuary be opened.

The offering hall (T), where the goddess received the daily sacrifices, stands before the most sacred part of the temple — the sanctuaries of Hathor and her associated gods. The central shrine, or 'Great Seat' (A), is now empty: from the wall reliefs, however, we can see that it once contained the stone naos that housed the cult statue, and also the portable barques of Hathor and (perhaps) of Horus of Edfu, her consort. The chamber in front of this shrine is called the 'Hall of the Ennead' (O) because it was here that the statues of Hathor's divine colleagues assembled on feast days. It is also from here that we enter the shrines around Hathor's sanctuary in which associated divinities were housed. Included are the gods of the nome of Dendera (D), Isis (E), Sokar (F); Harsomtus and/or the serpent god 'Son of Earth' (G); the gods of Lower Egypt (H) and Hathor's sacred sistrum (I). Various

especially venerable statues of Hathor herself were kept in the shrine directly behind the sanctuary (J): a niche high up on the south wall contained an ancient squatting statue of the goddess (represented on its walls), and we shall see that the corresponding spot outside was an important cult focus for persons not admitted into the temple itself. West of this room is the suite dedicated to the falcon statue of the sun god Rē (M and N), followed by cult chambers for Hathor's *menat*-collar, with its heavy counterpoise (L) and for Ihy (K).

The most valuable of the temple's possessions — ancient papyri, statues, shrines, jewellery and magical paraphernalia — were kept in crypts, small chambers hidden under the floors and in the walls of the cult chambers behind the temple. Only one of them can be visited at present, but it conveys a fair impression of the type. At the bottom of the passage which is entered from the vestibule of the 'Throne of Rē' (M), are five narrow chambers, three to the east and two to the west of the entrance. Their former contents are displayed on the walls: the goddess's ceremonial rattles, statues of Hathor, sacred collars and images of the falcon god Harsomtus (east), as well as an ancient statue from the remote age of King Pepi I during the Sixth Dynasty, showing this king presenting the child Ihy to his mother (west).

The most important object kept in this crypt was the statue of the *Ba* or active essence of Hathor, an icon that played an important part in the New Year's feast. On the night before New Year's Day, priests would manoeuvre the shrine that housed the idol up the narrow passage from the crypt into Room M. In Room O, it joined the statues of the other gods from the chapels around the sanctuary, and together they

Fig. 71   Temple of Hathor, ground floor

proceeded through the passage (Q) into the open-air 'Court of the First Feast' (R). A sacrifice was now performed – note the piles of offerings displayed on the east and west walls – followed by the principal rite of vesting the goddess's statue. This ceremony took place inside the kiosk-like structure just south of the court known as the 'Pure Place' (S): note, on the ceiling, the enormous figure of the sky goddess Nūt giving birth to the sun whose rays fall upon the image of Hathor, poised, like the rising sun, between the two hills of the horizon.

This symbolic union with the solar disc is the purpose of the rite that follows: in the dead of night, the goddess's statue was next carried up the western staircase (X) to the roof. The walls are carved with figures of the participants – masked priests with standards, ritualists, and the king himself, turning back to cense the shrine as it is borne up by Hathor's clergy. (Note that a similar procession is inscribed on the opposite wall, going downstairs: the orientation is such that the visitor always has the parade moving with him at his right side.) The statue was placed inside the kiosk at the south-west corner of the roof (Fig. 72, A) to await the dawn. Gods' figures are placed along the wall beside the ruined stairway leading to the roof of the Roman hypostyle (Fig. 72, B: access to the top by an iron staircase), as if to watch for the break of day; and as the sun's first rays illuminated the statue, the *Ba* of Hathor was seen to have been united with the solar disc and thus revived for the coming year.

Hathor's role in the mystery of the divine birth of her own son Ihy gave her certain affinities with Isis, the 'mother of the god' Horus and wife of Osiris, lord of the dead. There are, accordingly, two sets of rooms on the roof which serve as mortuary suites for Osiris. On the west side, from the stairway, we enter first an open court (Fig.

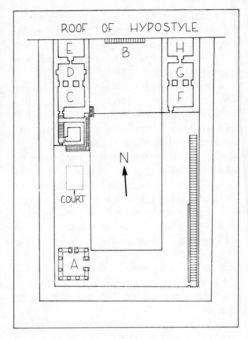

Fig. 72   Temple of Hathor, roof

72, C), with Isis and Nephthys bewailing the recumbent Osiris on the east and west walls. The other decoration has to do with spells for the divinities who guard the corpse of Osiris during the hours of night and day. Beyond is the vestibule (D), with knife-wielding chthonic deities and the gates of the Underworld depicted on its walls. The ceiling, once again, shows the sky goddess, under whom is a curiously doubled-up figure of the earth god Geb, apparently in the act of impregnating himself. The inner room (E) is the 'tomb' proper: the reconstituted body of Osiris is shown throughout lying on his bier, though he is occasionally revived by magical means. The crucial scenes are those in which the god brings himself to erection and impregnates Isis (pictured as a kite hovering above the bier) with the seed of Horus, future King of the living. On the ceiling is another Nūt figure, with various astronomical entities.

The eastern Osiris chapel is in some ways the more distinctive of the two. Its function may be guessed from a text carved on to the walls of the court (Fig. 72, F) which recounts how, during the lunar month of Khoiakh, an 'Osiris bed' of linen was filled with earth, sown with grain and watered daily until it sprouted, thus asserting the hope for life eternal in harmony with the rhythms of nature.[4] Inside (G), above the *Book of Hours*, with canopic jars and other grave goods for Osiris depicted on the walls, note the remarkable ceiling: over the central part of the room, between the two doorways, is an outstretched figure of Nūt, nude and carved in high relief; the goddess's usual bending figure, accompanied by astronomical imagery (boats, discs), is found on the east side; and on the west is a plaster cast of the famous zodiac which was carried off to Paris and sold to the French government early in the nineteenth century. The inner room (H), again, has scenes of Osiris on his couch mixed with other vignettes of cosmic significance, for instance, the night- and day-barques of the sun.

The New Year's procession left the roof by means of the eastern stairway, with its descending file of priests. Outside the temple, walk along the west wall to the back, noticing the great lion-headed spouts which drew off rainwater from the roof. On the back (= south) wall of the building, the historically minded may wish to recognize the royal figures as Cleopatra VII with Caesarion, her son by Julius Caesar, whom she made her co-regent before the Romans came. The main attraction, however, is the 'false door', with its gigantic Hathor emblem carved behind the goddess's central niche inside (see Fig. 71, J): visitors who could not enter the temple proper were allowed to address their prayers to this figure, which literally 'touched' the icon indoors. Countless generations of piety have left their mark, for the area has been so thoroughly gouged by pilgrims seeking to take some of the precious dust home with them that much of the emblem is now destroyed.

Immediately behind the temple of Hathor is the *Iseum*, a chapel dedicated to Isis (Fig. 70). The sanctuary, built by Augustus, is oriented towards the north, like the temple itself. The stairway, running along the north side of the building, is mostly gone, but the visitor can enter through the ruined northwest corner. The plan is simple: two side chapels flank the sanctuary, on the back wall of which is a niche containing a statue of Osiris (destroyed) protecting a small figure of Isis: note that the arms of the relief figures of Isis and Nephthys at either side are modelled in the round as they extend their arms into the niche to support Osiris.

The external development of the temple, which should have been on the axis of the sanctuary, was impeded by the proximity of the Hathor temple, so the front chambers were placed against the east wall, in line with the gate through the eastern enclosure. They consist of a columned forecourt, a pillared hall (with remains of an earlier sanctuary, all built by Nectanebo I), and a Ptolemaic girdle wall around the entire temple: these elements are much reduced today, and were probably in ruins when Augustus rebuilt the sanctuary. The focus of this processional way is the false door on the sanctuary's east wall, which served a similar function in the popular cult of Isis as the corresponding feature on the back wall of Hathor's temple.

4. An example, found in the tomb of Tutankhamun, is exhibited in the Cairo Museum: see Chapter 10, p. 120.

On the Hathor temple's west side, near the south corner, is the *sacred lake*: nearly perfectly preserved, it has a sunken terrace built into the south end so that visitors could observe the rituals enacted on the water during the Feast of Osiris (above, p. 73). The gateway that now stands free a short way north of the lake was connected to this precinct in a manner as yet not clear, as were two small chapels nearby — both of them reduced to ground level, but with remains of emplacements for statues. Beyond is the *well*, a staircase cut in the rock down to the water level, which supplied the temple's daily requirements.

It is easy to think of the temple enclosure as a divine estate sealed off from the community around it. The mudbrick building situated at the north-west corner of Hathor's temple, however, was a *sanatorium*. Diseased persons rested in the chambers built around the sides of the building, awaiting the dreams that brought divine prescriptions for their recovery. The central area was given over to magical 'water cures': divine statues, mounted on pedestals inscribed with magical texts, communicated their power to the waters poured over them (one such pedestal still lies in the ruins). This holy water was then collected in basins (remains are to be seen at the west end) and was drunk or used for the immersion of the sick. Other great temples must have housed similar institutions, but only the isolated location of Dendera has preserved this rare place of pilgrimage.

The stone enclosure wall which the Romans built around the Hathor Temple runs through the next building to the north, the birth house or *mamissi of Nectanebo I.* Such buildings, which are indispensable in temple complexes of the Late Period, celebrated the divine birth of a young god (in this case, the child of Hathor and Horus of Edfu) who, by analogy, represented also the living king. Birth reliefs in certain New Kingdom temples (cf. Chapter 17, p. 237) no doubt played a similar part in ensuring the continued vitality of the ruler, and study of the scenes in the later mamissis reveal undisputed points of contact with these Theban prototypes.

The columned approach to the mamissi lies to the east of the Roman wall, with the vestibule and cult chambers preserved on the other side. Passing the finely painted patterns in the passage (known as the 'shadow of the door', against which the doorleaves rested when they were open) we enter the remains of a broad hall decorated with offering scenes: note particularly the relief at the top of the east wall, showing one of the Ptolemies in the act of pouring out streams of powdered gold before Hathor, 'the Golden One'. A staircase at the back of the southern side chamber leads to the roof, from which there is an excellent view of the sanatorium and other adjoining buildings. The birth room proper is the central chamber downstairs: note the scenes showing Amun with the goddess, the modelling of the child's figure by the ram god Khnum, and the conducting of Hathor to her confinement by Khnum and the frog goddess Heket (north wall, top, left to right). On the back wall, Hathor suckles her child in the presence of the gods, including Amun, Montu, Thoth and the Theban Ennead.

Immediately north of Nectanebo's mamissi is a *Christian church* (c. fifth century A.D.) built out of well-dressed sandstone blocks taken from the tumbled-down buildings of the precinct. Entrances on the north and south sides of the building (near the west end) lead into a narthex: at the south end is the baptistry, its lintel carved with leaves enclosing a cross, and with the figure of the dove in the half-shell niche inside, over the font. A stairway at the north end of the narthex led perhaps to an upper gallery which in most

Egyptian churches today accommodates the women of the congregation. The main floor, east of the narthex, must have been a lofty hall: it is now much reduced, but the statue niches in the side walls convey some of its original flavour. At either side of the main altar are chapels which, again, in modern churches are used by the different sexes when they receive communion.

The Roman enclosure wall destroyed the usefulness of the mamissi of Nectanebo, necessitating its replacement by the *Roman mamissi*, north of the church. Mounting on to the temple platform, note traces of the Christian church erected on this site: the plan has been incised on the blocks of the pavement. Several broken statues of the naked young god Harsomtus, in polished black granite, are lying here as well. Around the mamissi proper is an ambulatory formed by columns linked by low curtain walls: note the reliefs carved on the exterior south walls, where the Emperor Trajan is shown offering to Hathor in reliefs that are the finest of their type in Egypt. The columns are also worth noting, with their graceful floral capitals supported by abaci carved with relief figures of the god Bes (above, p. 214), while on the architrave we see repeated figures of Bes and the hippopotamus goddess Taweret worshipping Harsomtus (pictured as a child crouching on a lotus flower). This decoration falls off rapidly on the back of the building: the column capitals are left as undressed blocks of stone, as are the projecting blocks to be carved into the solar discs that surmount each of the intercolumnar walls. Unattractive though the west and north sides of the building consequently are, they supply many precious details about the Egyptians' way with stone-working.

The mamissi's entrance is flanked by two wings, with the stairway that led to the roof on the north side: as in the Hathor temple, the walls of the passage are carved with ascending and descending priests, suggesting that a similar 'union with the sun's disc' was performed on the statue kept in the birth house. On the south side there is a small guardian's room and also, on an upper level, a hidden chamber — a crypt? — which can be seen owing to the destruction of the masonry over the passage leading to the ambulatory on the south side.

The interior of the birth house is similar to that of the earlier building of Nectanebo. First there is a vestibule filled with offering scenes, communicating with three chapels. Inside the sanctuary (middle) we find the usual farrago of birth scenes, as well as repeated episodes wherein the child is presented to or suckled by various deities. The scenes are not carved in sequence, so that the important episodes, for instance, the divine birth itself (south wall, west end, third register), adjoin the main cult spot on the back wall. Here we find a false door surmounted by a niche, protected by the standards of Hathor, from which a ruined statue of Hathor and her child emerges. Before leaving the building, the visitor should look into the two side chambers where, lit through slits high up on the back wall, remains of the statuary that once graced the temple are found.

QENA TO THE RED SEA

Permission from the military authorities is no longer needed by foreigners venturing out to the Red Sea. The road through the Wadi Qena to Safaga branches off the main road a few kilometres north of the city. A guide who knows the area will be able to direct you to the unmarked turning that leads to the *Mons Claudianus*. The marble found here was mostly ignored by Pharaonic builders, but the site was heavily exploited by the Romans who staffed the quarries with felons condemned to penal servitude. Remains of their activities lie strewn about in such profusion that the site is known locally as Umm Digal, 'Mother of Columns', and the visitor will also be able to explore the ruined village where the workers were confined.

From Safaga (160 km. from Qena), the coast road runs north another 85 km. to the nearly abandoned port of Abu Sha'ar (the Myos Hormos of the ancients). A number of desert tracks branch off from here, leading eventually to Qena. The services of a guide, or a good map, will once again be needed for a visit to the *Mons Porphyrites*, another Roman site. Located at the foot of the Gebel Dokhan (*c.* 50 km. from Abu Sha'ar), the quarries were a major source of porphyry. In addition to the usual remains left of the stone works, there is also a ruined temple built by Trajan and Hadrian.

COPTOS AND THE WADI HAMMAMAT

The main Pharaonic highway to the Red Sea departed from *Coptos* (modern Qift), 23 km. south of Qena. In addition to its commercial importance, the town was also the home of Min, god of fertility, and though it is virtually destroyed today, the traveller may wish to spend a short time at the ruins. Turn off the main road, going east through the town a short distance until a clearing is reached; then follow the main street north, then east again until you arrive at the great open space where the temples lay. The entrance to the site is marked by the foundations of Christian churches, where a number of fragments re-used from the pagan buildings can be seen. The main temple of Min and Isis lies due east, and though the site is ruinous and overgrown, some idea of its scale can be had by wandering through the three pylons (note the double processional way) to the broad steps that led on to the temple platform. The Middle Temple to

the south still boasts a gateway built by Thutmose III, but it is otherwise ruinous and of note chiefly because the so-called 'Coptos Decrees' were found under the floor (see Chapter 10, p. 109). More substantial remains are seen at the south temple of Geb. Even here, however, there is only a ruined portico, but the small chapel of Cleopatra repays inspection: facing south, towards the gate that led out to the city's necropoleis, it was a popular oracle, and the visitor will see not only the 'priest's hole' at the back, but also the façade of the inner shrine – a cross-section of a sacred barque, with its hull mounted on five carrying-poles, all carved in stone so that the god might be permanently 'in residence' for his worshippers!

The road to Quseir on the Red Sea branches off the main highway just south of Qift. The entrance to the ancient road is at Lagheita (49 km.) which in Roman times was a watering place for travellers. The ancients travelled this route not only on trading missions but also in search of stone, leaving innumerable graffiti – prehistoric rock drawings, hieroglyphic texts and inscriptions in Greek and Latin – on the way. The greatest concentration of ancient graffiti is in the *Wadi Hammamat* (83 km.), mostly on the south side of the road: note the prominent role given to Min, lord of the desert tracks. At *Bir Fawakhir* (108 km.), the only settlement on the desert road, travellers may stop for a cup of tea and then visit the wadi immediately north of the village, where – stretching as far as the eye can see – are the stone huts of the Roman gold-miners' camp. Roman watch-towers are frequently seen along the road and, beyond Fawakhir, be on the alert for the ruined stone enclosures that mark the sites of ancient caravanserais. This route to the Red Sea is longer than that through the Wadi Qena (200 km. to Quseir), but scenically it is more dramatic and of greater historic importance.

MEDAMŪD

If time permits, the traveller may make yet another side-trip before entering Luxor. Turn west, off the main road (31.5 km. south of Qift) and proceed another 1.5 km. to the village of Medamūd. The Roman temple is just behind the houses, having been rebuilt on the site of the Pharaonic sanctuaries. The temple's entrance is actually a triple portal, each one preceded by a kiosk, with an 'audience hall' situated at the south-west end of the façade. Behind is the large courtyard of Antoninus Pius, the graceful columns of which constitute the most substantial remains inside the temple proper. The interior of the building is extremely denuded, although we can still see how the late architects took the trouble to conserve *in situ* a doorway built in an earlier version of the temple by Amenhotep II. The foundations of the rear temple, the precinct of the sacred bull who was Montu incarnate, are barely visible today, although a relief of the Pharaoh worshipping the sacred bull on the south exterior wall marks the spot at which oracles were delivered. Outside the temple, a processional avenue leads east, through a portal dating to the reign of Tiberius, and on to the quay, from which a canal once conveyed worshippers to and from the precinct of Montu at Karnak.

17. Luxor, East Bank

Luxor is the site of ancient Thebes — home of the Twelfth and Eighteenth Dynasties and headquarters of the 'Estate of Amun', a vast clerical corporation that at its height owned land all over Egypt. The city itself was on the east bank and has been so thoroughly swallowed up by the modern towns and fields that only the temples remain. The west bank was the city of the dead, reserved for the tombs and cult spots of deceased kings and the burials of their followers.

KARNAK, PRECINCT OF AMUN

Amun's state temple is located 3 km. north of the large hotels at the centre of town, near Luxor Temple. At the end of the paved corniche, the visitor will turn east on to an access road that runs over the ancient canal from the river. At the end, in front of the great mass of Karnak itself, is Ramesses II's rectangular quay (Fig. 73, A) from which the god's river barge departed for Luxor or the west bank. The avenue that leads from here to the temple is lined with crio-sphinxes, fantastic beasts having the body of a lion with the head of a ram (the animal who represented, perhaps, Amun's divine 'awesomeness'): each of these crouching figures holds between its paws a statuette of the king — originally Ramesses II, though most of these statues were usurped during the Twenty-first Dynasty by Pinedjem I. South of the avenue are later constructions, notably ramps leading down to the river-

bank and built during Dynasty XXV to provide water for the daily services; and a sandstone shrine (B) dating to the Twenty-ninth Dynasty, which accommodated the barque of Amun before it left or re-entered the temple grounds.

The First Pylon (C) rears up enormously at the end of the avenue, linking the mudbrick ramparts that surround the entire precinct. The pylon itself is unfinished — note the undressed blocks that project from its walls — and scholars differ on the date of its construction: the simplest solution would place it in the reign of Nectanebo I (Dynasty XXX), who did build the enclosure wall and who may have demolished an earlier pylon placed hypothetically on this site. In any case, this is an impressive building, measuring 113 m. wide, 15 m. thick and originally some 40 m. high, with four niches in each tower to hold the flagstaffs whose tops would have shot above the level of the roof. High on the north thickness of the gate — possibly an earlier structure, as its masonry is not bonded to the pylon and its blocks are smoothly dressed — note the inscription left by members of the Napoleonic expedition.

Grasping the totality of Karnak will be simpler if one remembers that the building expanded outwards from a central core. The oldest part of the temple lies near the middle of the main axis (L), with the rest having been built as elaborations or annexes to the basic plan. The first court at Karnak (constructed early in Dynasty XXII) thus

The remaining obelisk of Tuthmosis I at Karnak

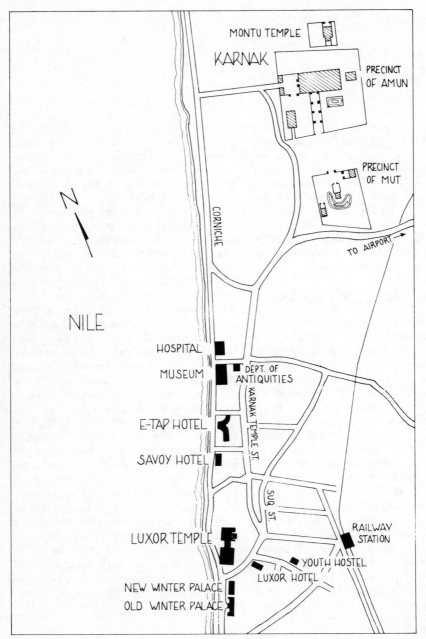

**Luxor,
East Bank**

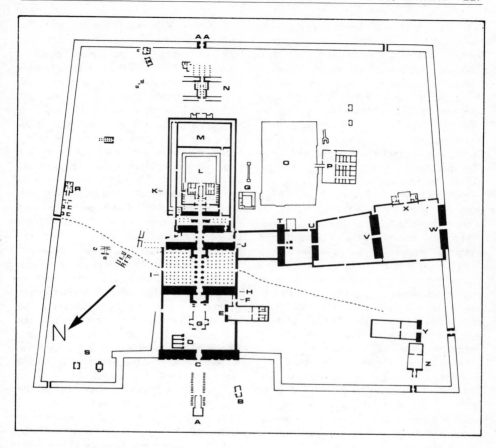

Fig. 73 **Karnak** *precinct of Amun*

embraces a number of elements that lay outside the temple proper: at the south end, for example — beyond the mudbrick ramp used to build the First Pylon and which was, inexplicably, never removed — and also on the north side of the court, we find rows of crio-sphinxes which were evidently moved out of the way when the area was enclosed and the processional avenue abbreviated.

The first court also contains a number of 'way stations' in which the members of the Theban Triad rested during welcoming or departing rites at their processional feasts each year. On the left as one enters the court is the chapel of Sety II (D), a simple shrine with three rooms for the barques of Amun (centre), Mut (left) and Khonsu (right). The niches sunk in the walls once held royal statues. A more elaborate form of the same sort of building is located at the south-east corner of the court, where two royal colossi guard the entrance to Ramesses III's temple

(E). Not satisfied with a mere way station, the king built a functioning temple in miniature. The front court is conceived as a festival hall, the sides being lined with large pillars carved into mummiform statues of Ramesses III: compare the second court of the king's mortuary temple at Medinet Habu (Chapter 18, p. 271). Festival scenes and texts cover the side walls – note especially (west wall) those illustrating the yearly progress of the ithyphallic form of Amun, who was related to the god Min of Coptos and represented the principle of exuberant fertility in nature. Beyond the courtyard, the temple is equipped with the usual portico and hypostyle hall, and the barque shrines of Amun, Mut and Khonsu are at the back of the building. It is dark inside the temple, but the exterior walls are covered with relief that can be seen all day long: particularly impressive is an immense version of the water procession to Luxor which fills the west wall. (To reach these, exit through the western side door in the court and turn left, into the clearing that goes around the temple.)

Next to the temple of Ramesses III is the Bubastite Portal[1] (F), a gateway covered with inscriptions and with ritual scenes carved mostly during the early Twenty-second Dynasty. Step just outside to examine the important historical document carved on the south face – a scene in which Amun presides over the ceremonial slaughter of captives by King Shoshenq I. The texts in the small name-rings behind Amun are place-names of localities in Palestine, and the entire scene is thus a primary source for the raid of 'Shishak, king of Egypt' that is described in the Bible (I Kings 14:25–26).[2]

The most striking monument in the first court, however, is the gigantic ruined kiosk at its centre (G): standing directly before the entrance to the great hypostyle hall, it was built by Taharqa, later usurped by Psamtik II (Dynasties XXV–XXVI), and restored under the Ptolemies. It consists simply of ten great papyrus columns, arranged in two rows and linked by low curtain walls. The building was open at both its east and west ends. Only one of the great columns is standing today, and the building's sole furnishing is a huge rectangular block of alabaster. A recent analysis of the building's architecture rejects the supposition that the building was roofed, with wood or any other substance, and suggests it lay open to the sky, perhaps with divine images placed at the tops of the columns. Although the kiosk is generally viewed as yet another way station for the divine barques, both its layout and position are quite unlike those of other known barque shrines. An alternative suggestion is that the climactic rites of the New Year's festival (see above, Chapter 16, pp. 217–19) took place here, and that offerings were piled on the alabaster altar after the statue of Amun had been 'united with the solar disc'.

The Second Pylon (H) stands behind the kiosk of Taharqa. Owing to its poor standard of construction, the building had to be consolidated even to its present ruinous state: it is best preserved around the vestibule, which bears the original Nineteenth Dynasty decoration on the side walls, but the Ptolemaic 'renewal' on the east face. Two striding colossi of Ramesses II flank the pylon's gateway, with a third royal statue – a king who grasps the crook and flail of his office, with his queen (at a smaller scale) standing between his legs – on the north side: this last piece, perhaps dedicated late in Ramesses II's reign, was subsequently

1. This conventional name reflects the supposed origin of the Twenty-second Dynasty in the Delta town of Bubastis.

2. The king's figure, unfinished and carved lightly in plaster (now gone), is nearly invisible.

usurped by Ramesses VI and finally by the High Priest of Amun and 'king', Pinedjem I.

The passage through the Second Pylon takes us into the great hypostyle hall (I), which was built early in the Nineteenth Dynasty by closing off the space between the Second and Third Pylons with transverse walls (the joints are best seen where they connect to the Second Pylon, in the north-west and south-west corners). A romantic ruin to early travellers, the hypostyle hall was restored after several columns in the north-east corner collapsed in 1899. Originally there were 134: 12 'open' columns, 22 m. high, along the central aisle, and 122 of the smaller 'closed' or 'bundle' papyrus columns (nearly 15 m. high) in the rest of the hall. The entire structure was roofed with stone slabs, light being admitted through clerestory windows that ran along the nave at the centre of the hall: the west walls, belonging to the Second Pylon, were re-inscribed: traces of the erased decoration can still be seen, especially on the north wing. On the east side, new walls were built against the Eighteenth Dynasty pylon and vestibule. These have been disengaged on the north side and the Third Pylon moved back slightly to reveal the flagstaff niches of the original façade.

The decoration of the hypostyle hall was begun by Sety I and completed by his successor, Ramesses II: the fine raised relief of Sety's work can be seen in the northern half, contrasting with the cruder, but still graceful, sunk relief of his son in the rest of the hall. The choice of material in the two sections is complementary to some extent: the river barge of Amun appears on the north and south halves of the west wall (bottom register); and on both north and south walls we see the portable barque of Amun borne in procession (west) and at rest in the sanctuary (east). But the whole of the decorative scheme is by no means sym-metrical: thus the scenes from the daily offering ritual (east wall, north half) are not paralleled elsewhere in the hall. Fine individual touches abound: note the depiction of Sety I seated inside the sacred Persea Tree while Thoth, scribe of the gods, inscribes his name on one of the leaves (north wall, east half, second register); or (south wall, east half, second register) Ramesses II enthroned between Edjo and Nekhbet, with Horus and Thoth steadying the crowns on his head. This last composition has unusual fluidity and movement, given the generally static conventions of Egyptian art.

Few of the statues that once thronged the hypostyle hall remain today. An exception is the large alabaster group showing Amun and the king just north of the western entrance. On the opposite side, against the wall of the Second Pylon, note the alabaster 'station' of Ramesses I, with the Nine Bows — symbols of Egypt's traditional enemies — inscribed on the floor where the king's image rested. The three red quartzite statues elsewhere in the hall — belonging to the Nineteenth Dynasty usurper Amenmesse and re-inscribed for Sety II — were placed here later.

The north exterior wall of the hypostyle hall is covered by the battle reliefs of Sety I. Stereotyped scenes of ritual massacre before Amun, with ranks of name-rings (cf. p. 268), flank the doorways. Beyond, however, the characteristics of different foreign groups are sensitively drawn: contrast the scrawny Bedouin (west side, bottom) with the sleek Palestinian chieftains (east side, top; east side, top), or with the grim, clean-shaven Hittites (west side, bottom). Certain episodes transcend the genre as well: note the Palestinian herdsman who drives his cattle into the forest (west side, top right); or the almost surrealistic battle, with the king then binding his prisoners and bundling them, like so many pillows, into his chariot (east side, top left). Ramesses II's battle scenes, carved on the south exterior wall over a poorly erased version of the Battle of Kadesh (see Chapter 4, p. 58), verge on parody when compared with the splendid work of his predecessor. The suppression of the earlier reliefs may owe something to Ramesses' well-publicized treaty with the Hittites, for a copy of this document was carved on a tablet in the centre of the transverse wall, now flanked by later reliefs of Merneptah's 'Israelite' campaign (see Chapter 10, p. 115).

Amenhotep III planned the Third Pylon (J) on a monumental scale, a fit gateway to Amun's temple. Today the building is a shell, shorn of its upper courses and hollow: the blocks from earlier structures dismantled to make room for the pylon and packed into its interior have all been removed and now stand − sometimes reconstituted into their original buildings − in the area north of the first court (see pp. 236−7 below). All that is left to admire here is the boldness of what remains of the relief, and also the emplacements for two sets of obelisks that once stood behind the building.

Much of the inner temple owes its existence to Thutmose I, so it is fitting that the one standing obelisk in front of the Fourth Pylon (Fig. 74, A) belongs to him. The space between the Third and Fourth Pylons was also the focal point of the avenue leading through the transverse axis of Amun's temple from the precinct of Mut (see below, pp. 237−8), but we will continue for the present down the main axis, to the sanctuary.

The area immediately behind the Fourth Pylon (Fig. 74, B) is congested with later additions. Apparently it was once a columned hall − note the column drum preserved below the foundation of the later hypostyle hall in the south half. After Thutmose I built the Fourth Pylon, he − or one of his successors − introduced the row of tall, Osiride statues that line the sides of the hall.

Inevitably, though, the space between the Fourth and Fifth Pylons is dominated by the colossal obelisks of Queen Hatshepsut: only the northern monument remains intact (C), although the top of the southern obelisk is now lying on its side near the sacred lake (Fig. 73, O). The enormous labour of transporting these monoliths from their quarry at Aswan and erecting them in the temple of Amun was accomplished in connection with Hatshepsut's Jubilee; their progress north is shown in the south wing of the lowest colonnade in Hatshepsut's mortuary temple at Deir el-Bahri. They fell victim, however, to Thutmose III's campaign against his aunt's memory, for in his later reign they were enclosed within masonry sheaths that permitted only the pinnacles to stand free − a fate, ironically, that preserved them from the worst of the iconoclastic vandalism during Akhenaten's reign and which probably accounts, in part, for the preservation of the northern obelisk today.

Passing beyond Thutmose I's Fifth Pylon (Fig. 74, D) and the Sixth Pylon (E) of Thutmose III, we reach the courtyard in front of the sanctuary. This was the holy of holies − the place where Amun dwelt, and where the great god revealed himself in the course of every day. The symbolism of the two heraldic columns in front of the sanctuary − carved with the Lower Egyptian lotus (north) and the papyrus of Upper Egypt (south), thus expressing the union of the Two Lands before Amun − is surely deliberate. Note also, at the north end of the court, two large statues of Amun and his consort, which were dedicated by Tutankhamun when he restored the full panoply of the old religion following the Atenist heresy.

The granite shrine of Amun (Fig. 74, F) was built in the name of Philip Arrhidaeus, the half-brother of Alexander the Great who was acknowledged as king of Egypt between Alexander's death and Ptolemy I's

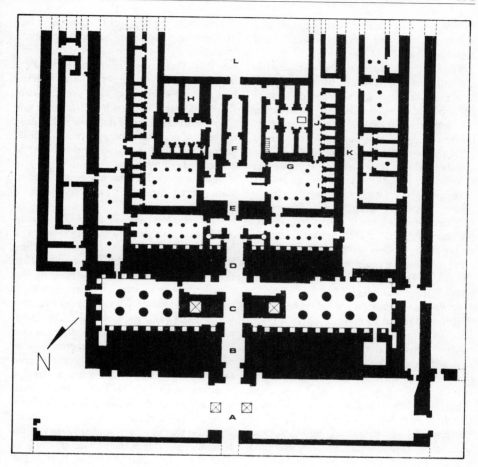

Fig. 74   Temple of Amun, central part

final seizure of power. Replacing an earlier shrine of Thutmose III, it is internally divided into two rooms: the front was the shrine proper, where the god's statue was kept and where the daily offering ritual took place. The portable barque of the god rested on the pedestal in the inner chamber. The walls are covered with scenes illustrating episodes of the offering rite, with Amun appearing in his usual anthropomorphic guise and also in the ithyphallic form he shares with Min, the god of fertility. The exterior walls of the sanctuary are brightly painted (especially on the south side): from the suite of rooms just south of the sanctuary it is possible to see the full sequence of scenes showing the progress of the rituals during the annual feasts. Note also, on the offering scenes to the right, that the painted grid used to place the texts and figures on the wall before carving is still preserved.

The sandstone chambers that surround the granite shrine were built by Hatshepsut: note, in the south wing, the splendid alabaster statue placed there later, showing Amenhotep II wearing the elaborate *Atef*-crown (contrast the rendering of this feature in the round with the version carved in relief on the granite shrine). The walls of the passage around the granite shrine were added by Thutmose III: especially noteworthy is the offering scene on the north wall, wherein the king dedicates an array of ceremonial vessels (including two obelisks) to Amun. The lower part of this and other walls in the ambulatory are covered with inscriptions, the so-called 'Annals' of Thutmose III, which describes the king's foreign victories.

In altering the appearance of these rooms, Thutmose III had to erase or cover a good deal of Hatshepsut's original decoration. The contrast between the exposed, later vandalized and subsequently restored material (on the one hand) and the pristine quality of the hidden relief can be appreciated in a small room just north of the granite shrine (Fig. 74, H). On the north wall is the original work of Hatshepsut – her names and figures hacked out, but otherwise intact, brightly coloured and spared even the malice of the Atenists. On the south wall, Thutmose III has entirely removed his aunt's figures from the scenes (substituting offering tables or bouquets) and, in the cartouches, he has inserted the names of his father or grandfather, as if to re-date the relief to their reigns: the effect – with the royal names floating, as it seems, in empty space – is ludicrous, and the figures of Amun have undergone the usual damage during the Amarna Period, with a careless restoration during the Nineteenth Dynasty.

The granite shrine and its associated suites are themselves surrounded by small chapels dedicated to the kings of the past who had left their monuments at Karnak. In the south court (see Fig. 74, I) are votive pieces dedicated by Thutmose III himself, including a large false door (see Fig. 74, G) on which the figures were once inlaid with precious substances. The row of chapels on the south side (I) are dedicated by Thutmose III jointly for himself and Amenhotep I, whose earlier shrines he thus replaced and whom he acknowledged with an unusual display of Pharaonic modesty. Note the headless royal statue of red granite still preserved in one of these rooms.

The corridor between the south chapels and Hatshepsut's southern suite (Fig. 74, J) brings us into the devastated space on which the oldest part of the temple once stood (L in Figs. 73 and 74). This limestone building was quarried away in late antiquity, leaving a confused tangle of pavements as evidence for its doubtless complex history. The visitor may now notice three granite doorsills that lead, at the east end of the court, to an alabaster pedestal on which the shrine containing the god's statue once stood. The two retaining walls (Fig. 73, K) that once closed off the back of the building have also been destroyed, and because of this we now face a structure that was not originally part of the temple at all: this is the memorial temple of Thutmose III, called the 'Most Splendid of Monuments' (M).

The entrance to this building is at its south-east corner, at the end of the avenue (Figs. 73, 75) between the two retaining walls. Flanked by two large statues of the king in Jubilee dress (only one survives complete), the portal opens on to an antechamber (Fig. 75, A) from which the south passage leads to a row of magazines set against the building's south end. The floor of the passage has, for the most part, collapsed, exposing the foundations of these elevated chambers: their interiors are decorated with

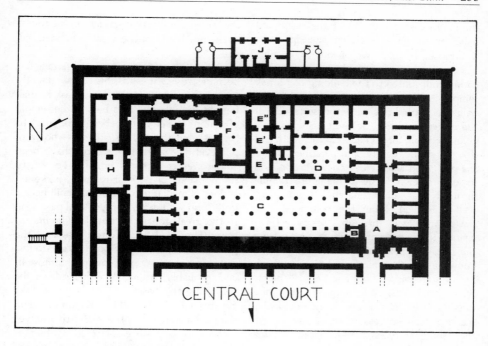

Fig. 75   Temple of Amun, eastern part

painted offering scenes, and on the north wall of the passage are carved episodes from Thutmose III's Jubilee.

Returning to the anteroom, we take the left-hand turning into the great columned hall (Fig. 75, C). Note that while the outer sections of the room are supported by square pillars, the inner aisles are graced by curiously shaped columns that imitate ancient tent-pegs: as with many ancient buildings, the prototype of this stone structure is to be found in the temporary booth-like shrines of Egypt's high antiquity. During the early Christian era the hall was re-used as a church, and crude paintings of holy men can still be made out at the tops of the tent-

peg columns near the centre of the room. The walls that once enclosed the hall are much reduced today, but some of the painted relief on the architraves still survives with something approaching its pristine brilliance.

The memorial temple encompasses a number of features − Jubilee reliefs, suites dedicated to chthonic and solar deities, chapels for ancestor worship − that are normally found in shrines dedicated to the cult of the ruler, particularly the kings' mortuary temples. While the building's ruined condition obscures the purpose of some of its parts, we can call attention to some of its more important features. The 'Chamber of the Ancestors', for instance, is located at

3. The inscribed walls of this chamber were removed in 1843 and are now in the Louvre Museum, Paris. A cast of the reliefs has recently been installed in their place.

the south-east corner (B) of the columned hall:[3] on its walls, receiving offerings from Thutmose III, are rows of kings who perhaps represent a selection of rulers who had earlier contributed to the building of Karnak temple. A doorway at the south end of the columned hall leads into the suite (D) of the underworld god Sokar: consisting of a columned hall, three chapels at the south end (for the statue, barque and paraphernalia of the god), and three elevated storerooms on its east side, it forms a miniature temple in itself that, unfortunately, is not very well preserved. From the columned hall, the visitor passes through a series of three chapels (E) to enter the suite of Amun from the rear. The columned vestibule (F) is also known as the 'botanical garden' because on its walls are carved flora and fauna — 'plants which his Majesty encountered in the land of Syria-Palestine'. These exotica evidently made a deep impression on the king: 'All these things truly exist,' he declares, '. . . [and] my Majesty has made this [chamber] so that they may be allowed to be in the presence of my father Amun.' Note that on the west wall some zealous follower of Akhenaten defaced the image of a goose, presumably because the animal was sacred to Amun; but otherwise the relief is in good condition, recalling the varieties of nature shown in the sun temple of Niuserrē at Abu Ghurob (see Chapter 12, pp. 158–9). From the 'botanical garden' one enters the sanctuary of Amun himself (G), dominated at its north end by an immense pedestal of quartzite set into a niche: the naos that held the god's statue once stood on this dais, and offerings were made on the massive offering table that lies in front of it.

The rooms at the north-east end of the building are severely damaged. Notable for its preservation is the upper room (H), reached by a staircase, doubtless part of the suite dedicated to the rising sun. Note also

the remains of massive statuary in the rooms at the north end of the great columned hall (I).

Since the back of the memorial temple has been destroyed, it is possible to pass directly across the outer retaining wall of Karnak temple and into the area behind the temple of Amun. The city of Thebes lay beyond, to the east, but most of its citizens (who were not even lay priests) would not have been able to enter Amun's temple. To satisfy the demands of popular religion, however, shrines of mediating deities were built here — gods who would 'hear prayer' and pass it on to the great god in his temple. The first of these (Fig. 75, J) is set directly against the girdle wall and centres on a large double statue in alabaster, representing Thutmose III and (probably) Amun. At either side of the shrine are the bases for the huge obelisks Hatshepsut set up behind the temple of Amun during her reign, but the shafts themselves have been long since shattered. Further to the east lies a later temple, 'Temple of the Hearing Ear', built by Ramesses II (Fig. 73, N) — a building of halls and colonnades dominated at the back, by the base for a single obelisk (probably the one which now stands in the piazza before the Church of St John Lateran in Rome). Afficionados of the heretic Pharaoh Akhenaten will want to know that one of his temples lay just outside the gate of Nectanebo I (AA) at the edge of Amun's precinct, but they are warned that there is virtually nothing left to see today.

From the eastern chapels it is only a short walk south to the sacred lake. This rectangular pool (O), its contents maintained by the water table, is today overlooked by the seating used during the *Son et Lumière* show in the evenings: under this structure are remains of priests' houses excavated before the seats were built. The far side of the lake is mostly unexcavated, but one can see the course of the stone tunnel through which the domesticated birds belonging to Amun were driven from their fowl-yard (P) into the lake each day. At the north-west corner of the lake, visitors will pass the curious building of Taharqa (Q), the underground rooms of which are inscribed with texts relating to the sun god's nightly journey and his rebirth each morning as a scarab beetle. The supposition that this myth was ritually enacted on the waters of the sacred lake would explain not only the function of the Taharqa building, but also the significance of the large scarab statue (brought from Amenhotep III's mortuary temple in West Thebes) which, together with the pyramidion from Hatshepsut's southern obelisk, graces this corner of the sacred lake.

We next pass into the first court before the transverse axis, facing the Seventh Pylon (T). Although the pylon is the work of Thutmose III, the court's side walls were added during the Nineteenth Dynasty: note the relief showing King Merneptah as a child protected by the ram of Amun (east side, north end). The court's archaeological interest lies in the deposit of 751 stone statues and stelae, along with over 17,000 bronzes, which were excavated from beneath the pavement. This find, the mainstay of the collection of Egyptian sculpture in the Cairo Museum, was probably buried early in the Ptolemaic Period, perhaps to dispose of those relics of the past that had outlasted their usefulness. A few examples of the monumental sculpture in this cache are set against the side of the Seventh Pylon.

The way through the transverse axis is now blocked by work in progress, but the visitor can follow the path along the west edge of the complex. Note, between the Seventh and Eighth Pylons, the earthworks employed to remove one of the obelisks to Constantinople during the fourth century A.D. It now stands in the Atmeidan ('Horse Square') in Istanbul, leaving its eastern companion – now a mere fragment – *in situ*.

The Eighth Pylon (U), built during the reign of Hatshepsut, was adapted by Thutmose III and completed (south face) by Amenhotep II. The southern approach is enhanced by six colossal statues ranging in date from Amenhotep I down to Amenhotep II, so it appears that some of these statues originally stood in front of an earlier pylon that was demolished in the middle of the Eighteenth Dynasty. The remainder of the transverse axis is in poor condition, consisting of two more pylons – the Ninth (V) and Tenth (W) – which Horemheb built. Blocks from the local Atenist temples were used to fill their interiors, and it is planned to consolidate these buildings, once their contents have been removed. Two limestone colossi (probably of Horemheb) flank the gate that leads out, towards the precinct of Mut. On the east side of the court is a small building (X), ostensibly a chapel commemorating Amenhotep II's Jubilee, restored after the Amarna Period by Sety I.

The south-west corner of Amun's precinct is reserved for the temple of Khonsu, a moon god who forms the third member of the Theban Triad. The interest of this building (Y) lies partly in its state of preservation, for it is a good example of a smaller temple of the late New Kingdom. But it also reflects some of the conflicts that brought an end to the Ramesside age. The pylon was decorated during the pontificate of the High Priest, later 'King' Pinedjem I, in a style that only stops short of claiming royal status for its author. The columned court inside is earlier, dating to the reign of 'King' Herihor, who officiates in countless offering scenes in conventionally royal fashion. The hypostyle hall beyond dates to a previous stage of Herihor's career, when he was still only High Priest of Amun under Ramesses XI: the protagonist in most of the scenes in this hall is the king, but Herihor appears in two important reliefs flanking the doorway on the north wall, in which he usurps the king's place in making offerings before the barque of the Theban Triad.

The rooms further inside the temple are still earlier in date, but were renewed in some cases under the Romans: particularly interesting is a chamber in the north-east corner, in which the Ramesside painted relief is preserved virtually intact. A contemporary pedestal for the barque of Khonsu stands nearby, in the columned hall at the back of the temple. The barque shrine itself lies just in front of this, and from the south-east corner of the corridor surrounding this chapel, the visitor may ascend to the sun chapel on the roof, thereby gaining a good overall view of the temple of Amun.

The Ptolemaic gateway in front of the Khonsu Temple opens on to the northern end of the avenue of sphinxes that led, in antiquity, to Luxor (see below, pp. 239 ff.). Before leaving the area, though, one may visit the curiously proportioned Temple of Opet (Z). The goddess worshipped here (not to be confused with the god of 'Opet', Luxor) was a hippopotamus deity who assisted women in childbearing. Her temple, however, was pre-eminently dedicated to the cult of Amun who, by the Graeco-Roman Period, had absorbed most of Osiris's characteristics: it is thus Amun's death and resurrection that is commemorated in the temple's various rooms. Turning to the building itself, we pass through the south-west doorway from the Khonsu temple forecourt and through the back door of the Opet temple, over the deepest of its several crypts (an easy matter), through the sanctuary and into the offering hall. The preservation of the interior is good, though the reliefs are smoke-blackened, but it is difficult for the novice to decipher the role played by the various parts of the building in the funeral rites of Osiris. Note, however, that the temple has its own gateway through the mudbrick enclosure wall of the precinct of Amun: since the cult of the Opet temple has much in common with that of Luxor and of the small temple at Medinet Habu (see below, p. 238, and Chapter 18, pp. 273–4), this special entrance may have been designed to facilitate the frequent comings and goings of the image kept in the Opet temple.

The visitor now returns to the north end of the precinct, walking back through the great hypostyle hall and following the path north to the main enclosure wall. Instead of continuing north, through the gate of the Montu precinct,[4] turn right for a visit to the temple of Ptah (R). Just as Amun possessed temples throughout the Nile Valley, so did the lord of Memphis receive worship in the state temple of his main rival. The temple is oriented from west to east, with the visitor proceeding through six gateways (late Pharaonic, Ptolemaic and Roman) into a small columned hall, behind which are three chapels dedicated to Ptah (north and centre) and to Hathor (south): a headless statue of Ptah stands in the central room, but in the south chapel a statue of the lion goddess Sekhmet is found instead of Hathor, no doubt because this goddess was in the god's northern entourage as 'the beloved of Ptah'.

The Montu precinct itself and the other small buildings (mostly Osiris chapels) in the northern half of Karnak will probably seem too badly ruined or too scattered to appeal to most visitors. If time permits, however, and if permission can be obtained from the Chief Inspector of Karnak, it is worthwhile to visit the open-air museum (S) located just

---

4. Montu, 'Lord of Thebes', originally a falcon god residing in Armant, lost his status as the 'great god' of the Theban Nome to Amun, remaining nonetheless a popular deity.

north of the first court, where blocks found packed inside the Third Pylon or sunk in the floor of the court before the Seventh are stored. Study of the fragments is still in progress, but three, more or less complete, buildings should be mentioned.

First, to the left of the entrance, are blocks from the sanctuary of the temple of Amun built by Hatshepsut, a red quartzite building resting on a bed of black granite. Although the queen's image was hacked out in several instances, she is more often seen officiating before various deities or in procession, followed by her junior co-regent, Thutmose III, with the barque of Amun.

The other two buildings have been reconstructed in the north-west corner of the precinct. First is the limestone barque shrine of Senwosret I, a delicate, airy structure on a raised platform, its roof supported by square pillars on which are carved scenes and hieroglyphs of surpassing fineness. It appears that this 'White Chapel', in which Amun appears in both his anthropoid and ithyphallic forms, was a 'way station' built on the occasion of the king's Jubilee. Nearby is the equally fine alabaster barque chapel of Amenhotep I: this is a very different, much simpler conception, being a spare rectangular structure, open at both ends. Inside, the king is shown in various attitudes, offering to the barque and to the statues of the god. This building too seems to have been made ready for the king's Jubilee, but Amenhotep I died before it was completed, leaving the south wall to be carved by his successor, Thutmose I. The rest of the area is filled with smaller fragments, mostly of limestone. The delicacy of this material and the splendid carvings suggest a temple less monumental, but more finely grained, than what survives of the present structure. Taken together, these stones are a precious link with the past, a tantalizing glimpse into what the temple of Amun once was, and the artistic glory of

Karnak. One hopes it will be more accessible with the passing years.

KARNAK, PRECINCT OF MUT

The avenue of ram-headed sphinxes that begins at the Tenth Pylon of the Temple of Amun leads to the precinct of Amun's consort, Mut. The site is in much worse condition than its neighbour, but it is also eerier, more deserted and wilder in aspect, and is worth a quick visit. North of the entrance, note the ruins of the temple of the ithyphallic god 'Bull-of-his-Mother' (Fig. 76, A) and foundations of a barque sanctuary of the usual type dating to the early reign of Thutmose III (B). Inside the enclosure wall, turn east, past the massive alabaster shrine fragments re-used here during the later New Kingdom, and pass into the temple of Khonsu-the-Child (D): constructed largely of re-used New Kingdom blocks, it has some lively variants of the normal birth and circumcision scenes on its north walls. Another temple, virtually unexcavated and of unclear purpose, is found next to this one, on the hill above the main temple of Mut.

The Mut temple (C) lies on the main axis, between the entrance and the sacred lake. Considerably rebuilt during the Late Period, it nonetheless retains its New Kingdom foundations (especially near the back) and is notable for the profusion of statues in the form of the lioness-headed Sekhmet found in its overgrown courts. Behind the temple is the kidney-shaped sacred lake, on the west side of which (E) one may visit the temple of Ramesses III, with its headless colossi of the king before the main entrance and its fragmentary military scenes carved on the outer walls.

TEMPLE OF LUXOR

The back road into Luxor adjoins the west side of the complex of Mut, allowing the

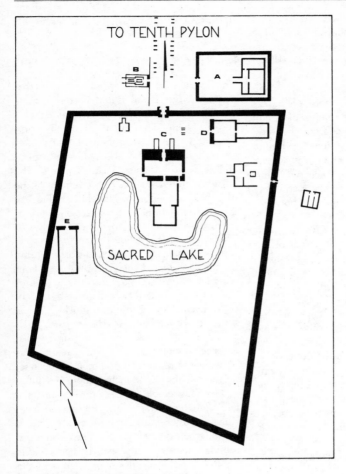

TO TENTH PYLON

SACRED LAKE

N

Fig. 76 **Karnak** *precinct of Mut*

traveller to follow, at least part of the way, the course of the ancient avenue of sphinxes (mostly ruined and buried today) to the south. Once a year, Amun of Karnak left his temple and journeyed about 3 km. south to visit his counterpart, a mysterious manifestation of Amun who resided in the 'private apartments of the south' at Luxor Temple. This Amun, usually seen in the god's ithyphallic form, was a dynamic entity who may

originally have represented the inexhaustible fertility in the earth. This characteristic linked him with the cult of death and resurrection celebrated on the west bank of Thebes. The Amun of Luxor thus crossed the river every ten days to rest in the small temple at Medinet Habu, where certain rituals were performed around him.

The popularity of Luxor's god and his temple persisted down to the end of paganism in Egypt, even after the sacred precinct was invaded by a Roman camp later in the third century A.D.: traces of its massive stone avenues and pillared streets can be seen on the visitor's right as he enters the modern enclosure (Fig. 77, *a*), while slender columns of even later Christian churches rise up beyond. A modern stairway leads down to the court before the temple, from which one may visit the first 200 metres of the avenue of sphinxes that once stretched from here to the south gate of Karnak Temple: the sphinxes seen here were erected, as a renewal of the avenue, by Nectanebo I some time in the fourth century B.C. (*b*). Most of the small chapels that lay along the avenue of sphinxes have disappeared, but a Roman shrine, with a headless statue of Isis in the Hellenizing style still inside, can be seen in the north-west corner of the court (*c*).

The temple's pylon (*d*), fronted by obelisks and colossal statues, is the work of Ramesses II: the western obelisk was removed in 1833 and is now set up in the Place de la Concorde, Paris. The morning sun or the illumination of the temple in the evening offer the best conditions for studying the Battle of Kadish reliefs on the pylon's outer face (see Chapter 4, p. 58). Inside, on the south face of the east tower, amid scenes from the festival of ithyphallic Amun, is a representation of the pylon when it was first built, before the addition of the standing colossi. The other wing has in front of it a chapel (*e*) built out of sandstone, but having columns and other elements of granite built into it, features which belonged to an earlier building of Hatshepsut rebuilt by Ramesses II: it was here, in this triple shrine, that the barques of Amun and his two companions rested during the opening ceremonies of the Opet Feast at Luxor Temple.

The Ramesside plan for this part of the temple conceived of a columned court, with large statues placed at strategic intervals

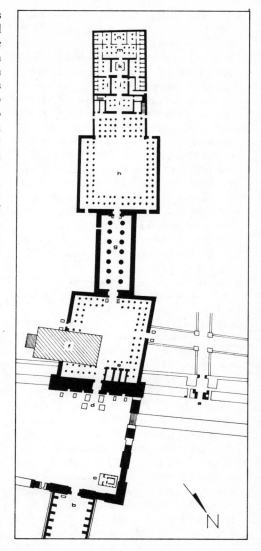

Fig. 77   Temple of Luxor

along the colonnade; but the symmetry has been compromised, first by the introduction of a Christian basilica in the north-east corner, then by the building of a more permanent mosque dedicated to a local saint, Abu'l Hagag (*f*): during the annual feast of Abu'l Hagag (which rotates, according to the phases of the lunar calendar) the saint's portable barque is dragged in procession through the town, illustrating the persistence of some ancient rites when adapted to new contexts. Note especially the reliefs in the south-west corner of the court, showing the festal procession of sacrificial animals at the Opet Feast brought by the king's sons and other officials to the door of Luxor temple (this time with the addition of the standing colossi). The statues in the south-west corner are especially well preserved, and one Greek tourist so admired the lissom Queen Nefertari who stands beside the king's leg that, on the column adjoining, he carved a figure of a huntsman with its name, 'Paris' — a delicate compliment — above its head.

One now enters the processional colonnade (*g*), noticing for the first time a definite bend in the temple's axis. Since, as with most ancient buildings, Luxor Temple grew outwards from a core structure, the most probable explanation is that the temple (being somewhat removed from the avenue of sphinxes) was only approximately oriented towards it, and that a greater degree of correction was required as the later forecourts approached the avenue's entrance. The processional colonnade was itself a later addition by Amenhotep III to the body of his temple: unfinished at his death, it was abandoned during the reign of Akhenaten, and the decoration was only resumed after the end of the Amarna Period. Two fine portraits of Tutankhamun grace the doorjambs on the north wall, while both west and

east walls have sequences of relief depicting the journey of the Theban Triad to and from Luxor Temple during the Opet Feast.

The voyage south from Karnak is shown on the west wall, with the return — almost a mirror image — on the east side of the colonnade. The sequence begins at the northwest corner, where King Tutankhamun[5] is shown offering sacrifice before the barques shrines of Amun (top), Mut and Khonsu (bottom right) within the sanctuary at Karnak; the barque of the living king (bottom left) also takes part in this ritual. Next, the barques are placed on carrying poles and borne out of the temple on the shoulders of the priests. We see them emerging from the gate in the Third Pylon, which was the façade of Karnak Temple at this time: the artist has successfully conveyed the rough, knotty texture of the tall flagstaffs that stand in the niches flanking the entrance, as well as the offering scenes carved on the gate between the two towers. A troupe of musicians (including a drummer) marches before the procession as it reaches the river bank.

The next episode (badly preserved here) shows the river barges of the Theban Triad as they are towed up the Nile to Luxor. Since the procession moves against the current, the tugboats use their sails (preserved on the boat in front of the barque of Mut, on the right);[6] and they are helped along by ropes pulled by the enthusiastic throng on the shore, which includes assorted officials, soldiers (carrying spears, hatchets and various standards), chantresses, Nubian dancers and charioteers. On arrival, the portable barques are again shouldered by the

5. The king's names have been altered to those of Horemheb throughout. The scenes at the south end of the east and west walls, showing the king in the sanctuary at Luxor, were apparently left executed in paint during the late Eighteenth Dynasty, for they were carved in the name of Sety I (early in Dynasty XIX).

6. A better preserved example of the water procession to Luxor is found on the south exterior wall of the temple of Ramesses III in the first court at Karnak (see above, p. 228).

priests and carried into the temple: at the head of this procession are dancing girls who execute astounding backward bends, while in the lower register butchers are seen dismembering cattle and piling the fresh meat, bread and other offerings in tiny kiosks for the welcoming sacrifice — this being illustrated by the fragmentary scene at the south end, of which only the barques of Mut and Khonsu, along with their laden offering tables, are preserved.

The east wall has a similar programme of reliefs illustrating the gods' return to Karnak. Better preserved than the western sequence, it also contains elements that are either striking in themselves or which are missing on the west side. Note in particular the musicians who accompany the river procession, below the barge of Mut (north of the intrusive doorway, bottom) and the river barges of Amun and Mut, with their fleet of escorting tugboats.

The temple of Luxor proper begins at Amenhotep III's graceful columned court (*h*). Processions would have moved across it to a portico, at the sides of which are found shrines for the barques of Mut and Khonsu when they visited Luxor Temple. Directly on the axis, though, is a curiously anachronistic structure: originally a columned hall, the room (*i*) was transformed into a chapel of the Roman legion that took up residence around the temple late in the third century A.D. The Pharaonic reliefs were covered with plaster and painted with the figures of court officials, and the portal into the temple was closed off by a niche-shaped shrine[7] flanked by Corinthian columns. Inside the niche are painted figures of the two reigning Augusti — Diocletian and Maximian — along with their two Caesars, Constantius Chlorus and Galerius. The insignia of the legion were also venerated here, and — far from having been

used as a church, as earlier scholars thought — it was probably here that local Christians were offered the choice between martyrdom and sacrificing to the imperial cult.

The room behind the Roman chapel was the offering hall in Amenhotep III's temple (*j*). The sacrifices presented to the god were assembled here, and on the side walls we see the divine barques being carried into the sanctuary along with such implements as boxes, small jars and large vases, statuettes, etc., to be used in the rites. Note, on the west wall, the small figure of the 'God's Wife' accompanying the king in procession — perhaps, as we shall see, to play an important part in the rites of the Opet Feast.

Directly beyond is the barque shrine — or, rather, shrines, since inside Amenhotep III's large room is a free-standing chapel, built in the name of Alexander the Great, to contain the barque of Amun (*k*). The walls of this later shrine are decorated with offering scenes in which the king — very much the Egyptian 'Pharaoh' — appears before Amun in his ithyphallic form. The original chapel of Amenhotep III was a simpler building, its roof supported by four huge columns, the drums of which can still be seen in the floor of the present structure. Its walls are more conventionally decorated in the style of the Eighteenth Dynasty, with reliefs showing the king before the god's barque.

From the barque shrine we move through the eastern doorway (widened, perhaps, by the Romans to provide an alternative way into the temple's interior?) and into the 'Birth Room' (*l*) — so called because of the sequence of scenes illustrating the divine birth of Amenhotep III, on the west wall. Earlier counterparts of these reliefs are found in the lower colonnade, north side, of Hatshepsut's temple at Deir el-Bahri (see Chapter 18, pp. 258–9), where they are somewhat easier to

7. The present doorway through the niche is a modern expedient.

see than in the dark, cramped confines of the 'Birth Room' at Luxor. The scenes on the bottom register move from right to left: the queen is embraced by Hathor, then Amun is shown leaving the presence of Thoth on his way to the palace; Amun and Queen Mutemwia are next seen sitting on a bed, and then (the union having been consummated) Amun instructs the ram-headed Khnum, god of potters, who fashions the baby Amenhotep III with his Ka on a potter's wheel. The upper two registers are read from left to right. In the second register, Thoth appears before the queen, who is next led to the Birth Room by Khnum and Hathor. Once there, Mutemwia delivers while seated on a block throne in the presence of three sub-registers of jubilating divinities; the new-born Ka, with the king's name positioned above its head, is seen held by an attendant at the right side of the scene. Hathor next presents the child to his father, Amun, who kisses him while Mut and Hathor look on. In the top register, the baby is suckled by thirteen goddesses in turn (including two divine cows) as Mutemwia watches. Young Amenhotep III and his Ka are next conveyed out by the gods of magic and the Nile and are presented to Amun by Horus, as an assemblage of gods determines the future king's length of reign. The myth of the divine birth is thus incorporated into normal royal propaganda (more so than at Deir el-Bahri, where it is tied to a specific plea for the legitimacy of 'King' Hatshepsut). Perhaps it reflects a ritual 'sacred marriage' performed here by the king and his queen, the 'God's Wife', during the Opet Feast, to secure the continued vitality of the ruler. If so, it is no wonder that this rite was celebrated deep inside the temple and was not portrayed along with the festival's exoteric ceremonies.

The suite of rooms behind the barque shrine[8] was the unit which gave the temple its name: this was the *opet*, 'private apartment' or 'hareem' (in the Arabic sense of the word, the intimate family quarters). It consists of a broad columned hall (*m*) opening on to a number of smaller rooms, of which the central chamber (*n*) was the holy of holies: note the remains of the pedestal on which the god's image rested. Other deities were represented by statues that stood in the niched rooms off the central hall. The separation of this sanctuary complex from the rest of the temple, while not unparalleled, is unusual; and it may have been dictated by the mysterious nature of this god and by the secret rites that took place in the temple. A hint of some cosmic significance embodied in the building itself is suggested by the columned hall (*n*), which has twelve columns — one for each hour of the day — standing between representations of the day- and night-barques of the sun located at the east and west ends of the room respectively.

THE LUXOR MUSEUM

Open only since 1975, the Luxor Museum contains a relatively small collection of pieces which, nonetheless, are well chosen and superbly exhibited: on these grounds alone, it lays claim to being the best museum in Egypt, and visitors who find the prodigality of the Cairo Museum bewildering will see some fine examples of Egyptian art displayed here to full advantage.

Hours: Daily, from 4 p.m. to 9 p.m. (winter) and from 5 p.m. to 10 p.m. (summer).

GROUND FLOOR
In the foyer, note on the left side a tomb painting (from Theban Tomb 226) showing

8. The doorway, again, is modern, for these rooms did not communicate directly with the barque shrine.

the erased figure of the deceased in the presence of the young Amenhotep III and his mother, Mutemwia. On the opposite side of the room is a gigantic red granite head of the same king from his mortuary temple in West Thebes; and in the rotunda is the first of several pieces from the tomb of Tutankhamun, a wood and gilt head of a cow believed to represent the goddess Hathor.

We now pass up a short flight of steps into the museum's lower gallery (see Fig. 78). First encountered is the red granite head from a statue of Senwosret III (1), with its strongly modelled features. Nearby (2) are a pair of headless statues depicting the Twelfth Dynasty vizier Montuhotep as a scribe: the plastic moulding of the torso is notable, as is the socket left for the head, which was made separately and attached to the finished piece. Between these two statues is a red quartzite block from the barque sanctuary of Hatshepsut (see above, p. 237) on

which the queen is seen presenting two obelisks to Amun (3). A small obelisk of red granite (4), dated to Ramesses III, is next, followed by the upper half of a statue of Amenhotep II (5). The succeeding piece of the first of the many objects in this museum coming from Su-menu, a town on the west bank of the Nile near Armant where a crocodile cult was popular. The mayor of this town, one Maya – his figure preserved from the waist down – is seen kneeling as he presents a pedestal with the image of Sobek, Lord of Su-menu (6: black granite statue). Next we come to one of the treasures of the museum, the fine basalt statue of King Thutmose III (7), which is followed by a limestone sphinx of New Kingdom date, the beard, eye and brows of which were once inlaid (8). Beyond the painted sandstone statue of an official of the Eighteenth Dynasty (9) are two blocks from the Deir el-Bahri temple of Thutmose III, represent-

Fig. 78   Luxor Museum

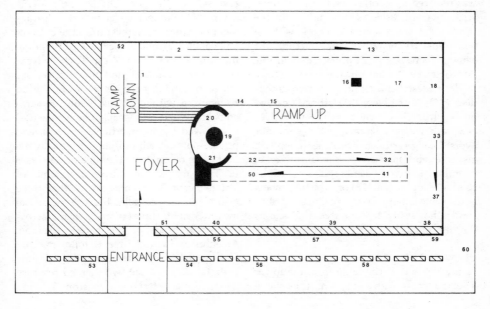

ing painted low relief at its finest (10). These are followed by the grey granite block statue of Thutmose III's chief herald, Yamunedjeh (11) and a curious 'beggar' block statue of the troop captain Amenemōne – a pathetic balding figure, crouched with his hand cupped under his chin and a Hathor standard between his legs, as he beseeches offerings from passers-by (12: limestone statue). The upper part of a statue of the lion-goddess Sekhmet, from the Temple of Mut (13), rounds off the display of pieces set against the east wall of the gallery.

Returning along the west side of the room, we encounter the great stela of King Kamose (14), describing the conclusion of a successful raid against the Hyksos rulers in the north. Nearby is a seated statue of Amenhotep III in black granite (15), but the impact of this piece is lessened by the imposing dyad in crystalline limestone in the centre of the hall (16), showing Amenhotep III protected by the crocodile god Sobek: the snout of the animal, damaged in antiquity, was replaced by another, carved in a somewhat different fashion from the rest of the statue, and the original inscriptions have been replaced by rather crude hieroglyphs naming Ramesses II. A private demonstration of piety is found in the next piece, a model pedestal surmounted by two crocodiles (17): an emblem of Hathor is carved on the front face, while on the two sides and back we find figures of the dedicator (worshipping cartouches of Amenhotep III), his wife and mother. A similar piece, in intention at any rate, is the stela set into the south wall of the hall (18) on which members of the same family are seen offering to Sobek and Hathor seated under a tree (top) and to the enthroned crocodile god alone (bottom).

UPPER FLOOR

Facing the end of the ramp from the lower level is a recess, with a grey sandstone statue of an early Middle Kingdom ruler in the guise of Osiris in front (19). Inside the recess, which overlooks the foyer, are two cases in which various small objects are exhibited. In the first (20), we find first a collection of articles found at the mortuary temple of Mentuhotep-Nebhepetrē at Deir el-Bahri, including a set of blue glazed cups, stands and model instruments and also some bronze chisels and hatchets. Next are four stoppers for canopic jars, all of them with human features, followed by an array of amulets and jewellery. Further on is a group of silver dishes, and also the metal top of a box decorated with figures of three gods, headed by Sobek. Finally, a painted wooden *Shawabti*-figure is set above a porphyry mortar and a set of basalt weights. In the next case (21), we see first a collection of bronze and silver Ptolemaic coins; a series of small votive stelae in limestone, together with two trial pieces of royal heads; and an assortment of bronze vessels and statuettes.

The next group of objects is found on the east side of the large display case in the centre of the upper gallery. First is a fragment of rather crude relief from the tomb of Unis-ankh (22), one of the few Old Kingdom monuments found in West Thebes. Next (23), we see a sandstone lion and a curious image of Amun, depicted as a ram's head rising from within a lotus bloom. A small embalming bed of crystalline limestone (24) is followed by an assortment of royal and private statue-heads (25): note especially the bust of an official from the time of Ramesses II. Two model boats from the tomb of Tutankhamun are seen next (26), then three *talattat* blocks – so called because their usual measurement is three (= *talatta*) hands across – bearing heads of the heretic Pharaoh, Amenhotep IV (27). Next, following the black granite crocodile mounted on its low pedestal (28), we see two painted funerary papyri displayed above two stone offering tables (29): note the schematic display of offerings carved on the upper sides, as well as the runnel to carry off liquids. The exhibits on this side conclude with a pink granite statue of a Ramesside High Priest of Khonsu (30), a large limestone offering table (31), and a display of three votive stelae dedicated to Osiris, Sobek (no fewer than ten crocodiles are represented) and the deified Amenhotep I, patron of Deir el-Medina (32).

Larger pieces of statuary and relief are grouped along the south wall. First is the well-known statue of Amenhotep, Son of Hapu, with the sage represented as a scribe (33). Another block from the barque chapel of Hatshepsut at Karnak (34) shows dancers and musicians greeting Amun (not shown) at his entry into the temple. A remarkably preserved royal head of painted sandstone, dated to the early Eighteenth Dynasty (35), is next, followed by a limestone block statue of the Twenty-sixth Dynasty vizier Espekashuty (36) and the upper part of a black granite statue of the lion goddess Sekhmet (37) from the precinct of Mut at Karnak.

Two fragmentary statues of Akhenaten (38 and 40) frame what is surely the outstanding exhibit in this museum: the reconstructed wall of *talattat* blocks from a temple of Amenhotep IV/Akhenaten at Thebes (39). On the left we see various figures of the king officiating inside the temple, while the sun's rays stream over all. Further right are offering bearers, together with scenes of daily life on the Estate of the Aton: men are seen receiving grain from the piles in front of the granary, and feeding cattle in their stalls. Next are scenes of industries and cooking — weighing metal, making and decorating pottery, and brewing beer in front of a storehouse crammed with jars, boxes and ingots of metal (top). Below we see men making collars, cutting up meat, baking bread and making furniture: note

the distribution of round loaves from one of the magazines nearby. The extreme left of the scene is taken up with the outer rooms of the temple, where custodians are busily sweeping up and sprinkling water against the dust.

The exhibits on the west side of the display case are widely varied. First (41) is an assortment of prehistoric pottery — only a few pieces, but fine. Next (42) is a limestone stela on which the dedicator offers a brazier to Sobek, below which we see a red granite offering table. A collection of bronze candlesticks from the Roman Period (43) and an assortment of brightly painted and glazed Islamic pottery (44) precedes the display of arrows from the tomb of Tutankhamun, one of them blunted for practice (45). The exhibition next zig-zags chronologically, between the Old Kingdom stone vessels (46) and the Eighteenth Dynasty statue head of Amun (47). Gilded bronze studs from the pall of Tutankhamun are next seen above two pairs of the king's sandals (48). A display of the ancient Egyptian art of basketry — a stool and a low chair, baskets and a bag, all plaited with reeds — comes next (49), followed by a sample burial: first a mummy, still encased in its brightly painted cartonage covering, and then four canopic jars — each stopper having the head of one of the sons of Horus — set inside a wooden canopic box (50).

The head and torso of a large sandstone Osiride figure of Senwosret I (51) looks sombrely over the ramp that leads down again to the lower level. On the left wall of the ramp we see several Coptic stelae, with displays of birds and animals, crosses and model façades of buildings. At the bottom of the first ramp (52), beneath a limestone baptistry niche, there is a charming piece — probably once part of a fountain — showing a rather corpulent man reclining on a couch and clutching a bunch of grapes: a relief figure of a serpent (perhaps the 'Agathodaimon'? See

Alexandria Museum, Room 11) is carved below the sculptures.

GARDEN

A few large objects are pleasingly displayed on the lawn of the museum or set against its front wall. North of the entrance is a large pink granite slab (53) showing King Nebhepetrē-Mentuhotep enthroned between Horus and Seth with two female deities. Opposite (54) is the famous relief, also in granite, showing the sportsman King Amenhotep II shooting arrows through a copper target. The other pieces on exhibit here are less distinctive: most of them royal statues, seated or standing, which bear Ramesside cartouches but may well date originally to the Eighteenth Dynasty (55, 56, 58, 60). Note, however, the upper part of an Osiride statue in limestone that belonged originally to Thutmose IV, but has been re-inscribed for Ramesses II (57); and, at the south corner of the building, a block from a destroyed building of Amenhotep III showing this king in the presence of the ithyphallic Amun (59): the style of this relief, which is bold and detailed in content, stands in marked contrast to the more delicate carvings seen in the Luxor Temple.

18. Luxor, West Bank: Royal Monuments

Visitors to the west bank may cross the Nile from Luxor by using either the tourists' or the local ferry. Once on the other side, however, all tickets must be purchased at the tourist kiosk at the river bank, as no admissions will be sold at the sites themselves. Individual admissions are sold for most of the attractions (for example, Valley of the Kings), and travellers should buy only what they are confident of seeing in one day, for the tickets may not be used on any other.

THE VALLEY OF THE KINGS

The rulers of the New Kingdom chose to be buried at the end of a remote wadi at the north end of the cemetery (see Map, below). The most direct route is over the Theban hills, for the site is virtually behind the bay of Deir el-Bahri. Nearly all travellers, however, will follow the path taken by the royal cortèges, past the north end of Dra-abu'l-Nagga and snaking off to the south. Not all

Luxor, West Bank

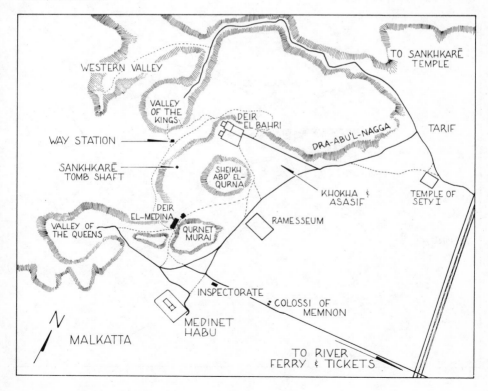

the decorated tombs are open to the visitor, but those which are accessible can give the visitor a reasonably complete impression of the styles employed during the four centuries in which the royal cemetery was in use. The principal tombs (whether or not they occur in this itinerary) are shown in Fig. 79, in order to facilitate any wider rambling.

The *tomb of Thutmose III*, the earliest of those which can be visited, is situated in a cleft at the south end of the Valley of the Kings. An iron staircase leads one up to the entrance, near the top of the cliff. The first distinctive feature to be encountered after the several descending corridors is the well (Fig. 80, A), a deep shaft designed either as a trap for rainwater, as an obstacle to grave robbers, to symbolize the tomb of the god Sokar as it appears in the *Book of What is in the Netherworld* — or possibly, in varying degrees at different times, with all three purposes in mind. The sides of the well are uniformly decorated with a simple decorative frieze along the top: the entrance pushed into the tomb through the far wall was surely sealed after the funeral. The walls of the vestibule that follows (B) are covered with representations of the divinities who will appear in the mortuary composition painted on the walls of the burial chamber (C). That room's oval shape is reminiscent of a royal cartouche, with small chambers cut into the sides to accommodate the objects buried with the king. The quartzite sarcophagus —

Fig. 79 **The Valley of the Kings**

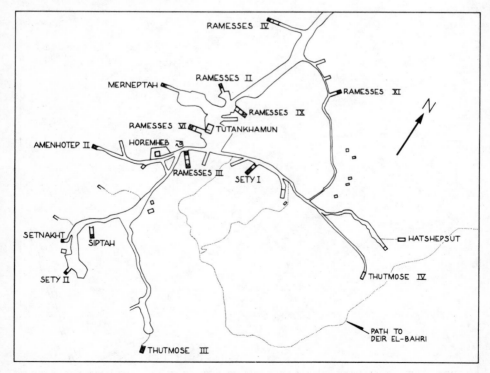

of surprisingly modest dimensions — is still *in situ*, resting on the cracked limestone podium: note the image of the sky goddess Nūt, carved both on the bottom of the lid and on the box, protecting the king's limbs. The style of the painting on the walls deliberately imitates that of a papyrus manuscript. Especially charming are two scenes on the north face of the west pillar: one showing the king with female members of his family, the other representing him receiving milk from the breasts of a tree goddess.

The *tomb of Amenhotep II* is similar in plan, though laid out in a more regular fashion. The painting in the well (Fig. 81, A) is identical with that of the previous tomb, but for some reason it was left unfinished. The

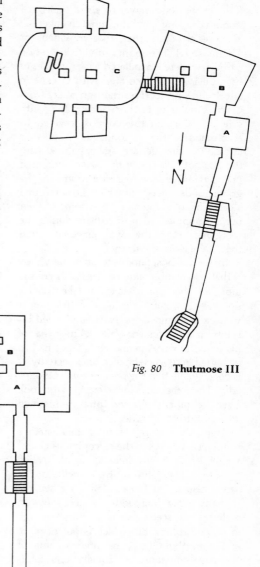

Fig. 80   **Thutmose III**

Fig. 81   **Amenhotep II**

vestibule (B) is even more incomplete – the walls of the room never received their final smooth dressing – but the burial chamber (C) is more elaborate than that provided for Thutmose III. The room is divided into two parts: first there is a 'pillared hall', the faces of each pillar being decorated with a scene in which the king receives the sign of life from Osiris, Anubis or Hathor; and on the south side of the room the floor is lowered to accommodate the sarcophagus. The walls around the chamber are, again, painted with the *Book of What is in the Netherworld*, and once again there are four side-rooms for the grave goods – in one of which (D) was found a cache of royal mummies and some of their burial equipment, deposited here during the reorganization of the royal cemetery during the Twenty-first Dynasty.

By far the most famous tomb in the Valley is that of *Tutankhamun*. His treasures are the glory of the Cairo Museum (Chapter 10, pp. 118–21), but his tomb will strike most visitors as cramped: perhaps he planned his tomb for the 'Western Valley',[1] near that of his grandfather, Amenhotep III, but had to be buried here when he died unexpectedly. It is conceivable that the present tomb belonged to Tutankhamun's minister, Ay, who took over the initially planned tomb on his own accession to the throne.

The sole decoration in Tutankhamun's tomb (Fig. 82) lies in the sarcophagus chamber, which itself was almost completely filled by the gilded shrines that enclosed the sarcophagus. On the east wall we see the mummy being dragged to the necropolis on a sledge – a scene that is common enough in private tombs, but which is out of place in the mythologically oriented scheme of the royal monuments. Equally unusual is the next scene, on the north wall, in which King Ay is seen performing the 'Opening of

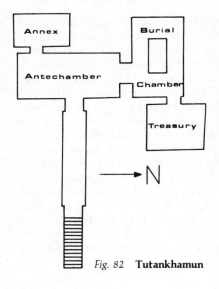

Fig. 82   **Tutankhamun**

the Mouth' ceremony before Tutankhamun's mummy (see Chapter 6, pp. 74–5): it occurs here because Ay was not legally entitled to succeed Tutankhamun, but could establish his claim to the throne by burying him. The other scenes are less remarkable: Tutankhamun is greeted by Nūt and, with his Ka, embraces Osiris (north wall); a vignette from the *Book of What is in the Netherworld* (west); and Tutankhamun, followed by Anubis, before Hathor (south). The figures are rather curiously proportioned, but are brightly coloured against a dull gold background. Note the niches for magical bricks, providing protection for the burial, in the corners. The centre of the room is occupied by the sandstone sarcophagus, with its protecting goddesses at the four corners. The king's body is still enclosed within the gilt wood sarcophagus inside.

More characteristic of the transitional style is the *tomb of Horemheb*. The customary descending corridors lead down to

1. The entrance is at the west side of the road leading to the main valley, shortly before reaching the latter.

the well room, on the walls of which the king appears, offering to various gods (Fig. 83, A): the figures are brightly coloured, set against a blue-grey background. The doorway to the room beyond was evidently blocked up, covered with a coat of plaster and decorated like the rest of the well room: remains of this scene remain at the sides of the doorway. The chamber that follows (B) was no doubt meant to mislead robbers into believing they had broken into an uncompleted burial chamber. They succeeded, however, in discovering the stairway sunk into the floor that leads down to the actual burial. The antechamber (C) is the stylistic duplicate of the well room above, with similar scenes showing the king offering to and being embraced by the gods. The burial chamber that follows (D), while spacious, is unfinished. Episodes of the *Book of Gates* were drawn on the walls in paint, but the final carving had only been sporadically accomplished, enabling the visitor to discern the various steps in the process with unusual clarity. Horemheb's sarcophagus, similar to that of Tutankhamun but not so finely carved, is still *in situ*. A number of side chambers open off the burial chamber, in one of which (E) is found a pleasingly painted figure of Osiris.

It is with the *tomb of Sety I* that the hypogea of the kings' valley reach their full development. The mortuary *Books* crowd its walls with their mysterious protagonists, and the decoration expands out of its customary localities on to virtually every surface in the tomb. The scenes here are carved in delicate raised relief, beautifully painted, but it is to be regretted that the often superb carvings have been dulled by the questing fingers of too many tourists. Readers of this book are encouraged not to follow their example.

The first scene on the left on entering the tomb is one that will become standard in all later tombs in the Valley: Sety I offers to

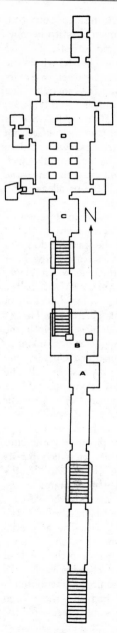

Fig. 83   **Horemheb**

Rē-Harakhti, the falcon-headed sun god. Beyond is another element soon to become traditional – the sun god in both his aged and nascent form (ram and beetle) within the solar disc, which is placed between two of its enemies, the serpent and the crocodile. The remaining decoration in this room (Fig. 84, A) is the text of the 'Litany of Rē'. Scenes from the *Book of What is in the Netherworld* appear on the walls of the next two corridors (B and C), while on the walls of the well room (D) the visitor will recognize the same offering scenes found at the parallel spot in the tomb of Horemheb.

The two rooms beyond, as in Horemheb's tomb, were meant to deceive any potential violators of the tomb: the staircase down to the lower tomb, again, is sunk in the floor and the decoration of the inner room (F) was merely sketched. On the south wall of the front chamber (E), note a fine depiction of Osiris, enthroned in his palace with Hathor behind him, as the king is led into the presence by Horus. The races of mankind – Egyptian, Asiatic, Nubian and Libyan – are shown at the bottom of the eastern wall. The main decoration of these rooms are the *Book of Gates* (E) and *Book of What is in the Netherworld* (F).

The next two corridors (G and H) are decorated with scenes illustrating the rites before the king's statue, in which priests perform the 'Opening of the Mouth', the offering list ritual and various litanies: note in particular the 'Iunmutef' priest, with his characteristic sidelock of hair, who takes the part of the deceased's son. The anteroom before the burial chamber (I) is, once again, a duplicate of the same room in the tomb of Horemheb. In the burial chamber itself (J–K) we step back into the tomb of Amenhotep II for the antecedents of the plan – the pillared hall in front, with the sunken recess for the sarcophagus beyond. The king's alabaster

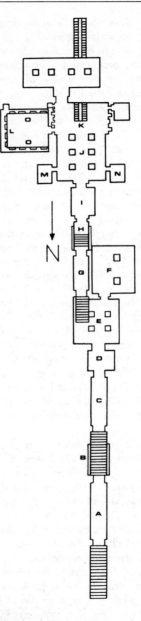

Fig. 84 **Sety I**

box was removed by Belzoni in 1817 and now rests in the Soane Museum, London. The chamber, for the most part decorated with scenes from a condensed version of the *Book of What is in the Netherworld*, has on its ceiling a map showing the principal stars and constellations (sarcophagus room). Note, in the south wall of the recess, an opening (locked at present) to a staircase that plunged into the bowels of the earth for a great distance before being given up.

The burial chamber is surrounded, once again, with a number of side rooms, most of which are rather strikingly decorated. The largest (L) is notable less for its main decoration (*Book of What is in the Underworld*) than for painted representations of tomb furniture – shrines, amulets, animal couches – on the base, below the ledge on which some of the king's grave goods once rested. The *Book of Gates* is the substance of another of these rooms (M), on the south wall of which are vivid evocations of the furnaces of the damned. The chamber on the west side (N) is inscribed with the figure and 'Book' of the Heavenly Cow, bringing to a close one of the richest repositories of mythological lore in all of Egypt.

Royal tomb design was radically simplified under *Merneptah*, grandson of Sety I, who reorganized the basic elements of the plan along a corridor that plunged straight down into the burial chamber. Much of the decoration was destroyed when the tomb was flooded, but the structure's immensity commands respect and the painting in the 'false burial chamber' (Fig. 85, A) survives intact. Note, at a lower level (B), the remains of an immense outer sarcophagus of granite, which was never carried all the way into the tomb. The king's anthropoid sarcophagus, still resting in the burial chamber (C), is all the more evocative in the gloomy ruin of its setting.

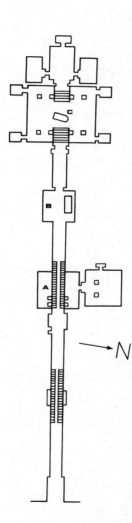

Fig. 85   **Merneptah**

A similar resting place had been planned, no doubt, for Sethnakht, founder of the Twentieth Dynasty, but his hypogeum ran into the adjoining tomb of Amenmesse and was abandoned. It was later adapted for *Ramesses III*, who avoided any further interference from neighbouring tombs by relocating the axis at the end of a sharp bend to the right (see Fig. 86, A). Structurally, this tomb is in poor condition, but visitors may wish to admire the fine and unusual paintings in the many side-chambers along the corridors — particularly the sailing boats (B), Nile gods (C), the blind harpist (D), and the representations of luxury products, including beds, furniture, vases (some of them imported from the islands of the Aegean), weapons, baskets and skins (E).

The large number of mortuary compositions in the *tomb of Ramesses VI*, along with its great size, make it one of the great attractions in the royal valley. Much visited in the Graeco-Roman era, it has the additional distinction of having concealed the tomb of Tutankhamun under the rubble thrown out when it was being built. On the outer lintel we see the goddesses Isis and Nephthys, who are kneeling at either side of the solar disc. The good preservation of the interior may encourage closer attention to the changes, shown here, that actually occurred as of the reign of Merneptah. Note that the well room (Fig. 87, A) is architecturally only a vestige of its former self. The similarity to earlier plans emerges, however, in the 'false burial chamber' (B), with its splendid double scene showing the king before Osiris above the corridor into the lower tomb. Note also the arrangement of corridors leading down to the 'second vestibule' (C) and the burial chamber proper (D). The decoration throughout is of a simple elegance, with polychrome painted figures in sunk relief against a creamy background. In the burial chamber are the remains of the

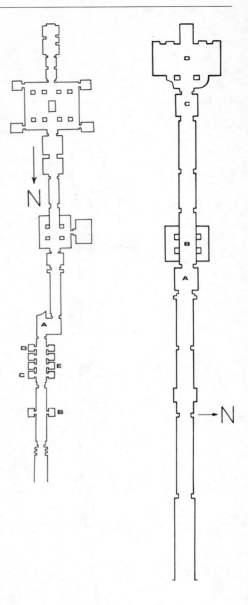

Fig. 86 **Ramesses III**   *Fig. 87* **Ramesses VI**

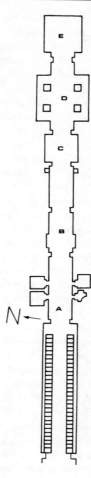

Fig. 88 **Ramesses IX**

black granite sarcophagus: its once splendid appearance was noted by a Greek traveller who, by his own account, was impressed with nothing else in the tomb; but it was broken up by treasure seekers hunting for the gold they believed was hidden inside it.

The *tomb of Ramesses IX* was never finished: a glance at the plan shows that the corridor (Fig. 88, E) beyond the 'false burial chamber' (D) was hastily adapted to receive the sarcophagus. Only the first three corridors were completely decorated by the time of the king's death, beyond which only the east doorway of the well room (C) is inscribed with priestly figures bearing implements for the 'Opening of the Mouth' ceremony. Most of this and the subsequent room was left unfinished, while the burial chamber (E), with its mythological vignettes and astronomical ceiling, is painted in a style that compares unfavourably with the rest.

Artistically, the tomb represents a continuation of the style found in Ramesses VI's monument. The painting, however, is far more opulent than before, and a greater individuality emerges from the royal portraits here than is found elsewhere. The selection of mythological scenes, moreover, is hardly conventional. On the south wall of the first corridor (A), for instance, the king is seen sacrificing before a four-headed form of Amun-Rē-Harakhti and to the necropolis goddess Meretseger, 'She who loves Silence'. Further in, on the south wall of the third corridor (B), the king appears with his arms stretched above his head, lying within a hillock. The skin of the figure is black and it was originally represented as ithyphallic before its member was hacked out by one of the tomb's more prudish visitors. The sacred beetle appears above the hillock, pushing the solar disc across the sky. The king's resurrection is thus presented by analogy with a basic cycle of nature: as the sun's rays revive the dormant living forces in the earth, symbolized by the dark god Sokar, so does the king benefit from the sun's warmth in order to extend his own influence into the realm of men in the role of Osiris, who is the lord of the grain crop as well as ruler of the dead. The king's place in the hereafter and his relationship with the community of the living are concisely expressed in this one richly symbolic composition, itself a supreme example of a technique used often in Egyptian religious art.

DEIR EL-BAHRI

The oldest mortuary temples at Thebes are located at the back of a deep 'bay' called Deir el-Bahri (see Fig. 89). Here, side by side, are two imposing buildings, the southern and more ancient of which belonged to *King Nebhepetrē-Mentuhotep I* of the Eleventh Dynasty. Though smaller and less well preserved than its neighbour, it is of interest both for the similarities and points of difference it displays in comparison with the more famous structure at its side.

Unlike the later New Kingdom mortuary temples at Thebes, the complex of Nebhepetrē functioned also as a royal tomb. In approaching the monument, the visitor will pass a deep trench cut into the floor of the esplanade before the temple: the unfinished rooms at the bottom of the shaft (now choked by debris) contained an empty coffin and the seated statue of the king now in the Cairo Museum (Chapter 10, p. 112), wrapped in fine linen: it is believed that this shaft, originally designed as the royal tomb itself, was converted into a cenotaph dedicated to the Osirian resurrection of the king when the site of the temple was moved back against the cliff.

The approach to the temple proper is graced by an avenue, its entrance marked by two seated statues of the king and its sides lined with standing figures, all of which have had their heads removed and now lie scattered before the temple. At either side of the ramp leading to the upper terrace are remains of a colonnade of square pillars, curiously slender and inscribed with the names of the king. The outer enclosure wall, built of small limestone blocks, is best preserved on the north side, being damaged only where it was interrupted by the causeway that led to Thutmose III's destroyed temple high on the hill between the two preserved buildings, and now also cut off by the Hathor chapel of Hatshepsut's temple (see below, p. 262).

The upper terrace also has a pillared façade that surrounds, on three sides, an enclosure. Inside, a forest of octagonal columns surrounds a solid core structure that for many years was interpreted as the base of a pyramid, but which now seems to have been a squat, mastaba-type building that projected above the level of the colonnades around it (Fig. 89, A): this was a full-scale model of the superstructure of the royal tomb, which itself is located further back inside the temple. Note, on the west side of the core structure, a restoration inscription of King Siptah (kneeling) and his minister, Chancellor Baï. The western edge of the enclosure is badly ruined: six chapels serving the cult of Nebhepetrē's wives and family stood here, with shafts leading to their burials placed behind the enclosure's west wall. Note that the rock at the north-west side of the terrace (B) is cut back: this was done during the Eighteenth Dynasty to accommodate the painted chapel of Hathor which, together with the statue of the cow goddess found inside, has been removed to the Cairo Museum (Chapter 10, p. 112).

The western end of the temple consists, first, of a columned courtyard (C) whose pavement would have concealed the entrance to the royal tomb; and a hypostyle hall, in the midst of which we find the

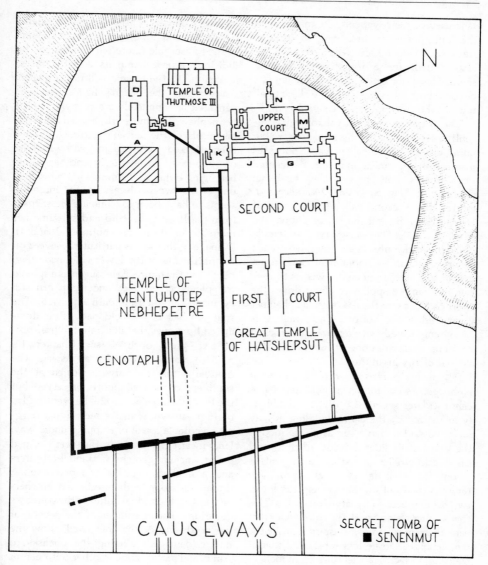

Fig. 89 **Deir el-Bahri** *Temples*

sanctuary of the royal cult (D). Inside, note the limestone altar, ascending in inclined steps to a summit on which there is an emplacement for a round-based offering stand. The shrine of the royal statue lay just beyond, built into the side of the cliff, but all trace of the cult spot itself has vanished.

The entrance to the royal tomb has recently been outfitted with a steel door, so the burial chamber is for all practical purposes inaccessible. A similar monument executed on a smaller scale, however, is the burial chamber of *King Sankhkarē Mentuhotep II*, located in the second valley to the south of Deir el-Bahri, behind the hill of Qurna (see Map, p. 247). The causeway and temple platform had only been roughly graded before work on the monument came to an abrupt halt, but anyone who wishes to seek out this remote spot may climb down the short corridor into the red quartzite chamber assembled at the bottom. The structure is nicely engineered, with a pointing corbelled roof but, apart from one or two graffiti, it is devoid of any inscription.

The *temple of Hatshepsut*, to the north of Nebhepetrē's complex, was built about five centuries later (see Fig. 89). While undoubtedly influenced by the earlier building, it may fairly be said to have surpassed its model: the grace of its lines is justly admired, and the fine low relief carved on to its walls is among the most delicate in all Egypt. The temple is laid out on three levels, the lower two being preceded by large forecourts. This spaciousness, along with the colonnades that flank the central ramps, conspire to make the temple appear to be less substantial than it really is. In fact, Hatshepsut's monument is a masterful example of terrain shrewdly chosen and of masonry artfully deployed. It withstood the rock slides endemic to the area far better than its neighbours, the temples of Nebhepetrē and of Thutmose III (see below, p. 263), and the consolidation effected by

members of the Polish National Academy of Sciences will not only protect the building in the foreseeable future but emphasizes, by judicious reconstruction, its salient features.

Visitors to the temple will notice that in many places the queen's figure has been damaged or completely erased by agents of her nephew, Thutmose III. When this has not taken place, the queen's cartouches have been attacked — either damaged by hacking or suppressed in favour of another name, belonging either to Thutmose III himself or one of his two predecessors: the intention seems to have been to eliminate Hatshepsut from the historical record and subsume her reign under those of Thutmose I and II. Damage of this sort is particularly severe on the north side of the lower colonnade (Fig. 89, E), but the figure of the queen as a sphinx, trampling her enemies underfoot, can still be made out on the south end wall. The southern half of the colonnade (F) is dominated by scenes that illustrate the transport of two great obelisks (see Chapter 17, p. 230) from the quarries at Aswan. The monoliths rest on barges, located at the south end of the wall (poorly preserved, but the tip of the obelisk can still be seen), pulled by tugboats whose masts and rigging suggest a veritable forest of shipping under way. Underneath the scene is the fleet's armed escort, including archers, standard bearers and a military band (a trumpeter and a drummer), along with priests and butchers performing their ritual duties at the convoy's departure. The remainder of the scenes, at the north end of the west wall, show the queen (damaged) offering the obelisks to Amun and participating in other cultic acts at their dedication.

The second terrace is reached by means of a ramp, the side walls of which terminate at the bottom in the crouching figure of a lion. The walls of the northern colonnade (G) establish the queen's right to rule by illustrating her purported parentage by Amun-Rē and her coronation in the presence of her earthly father, Thutmose I.[2] The birth scenes proper are in the lower register: Amun appears before the Ennead (south wall), then (west wall), after conferring with Thoth, proceeds into the palace to confront the queen mother, Ahmose. Their union takes place on a lion couch, with Amun discreetly presenting his consort with the sign of life. He then confers with the ram god Khnum, who fashions the bodies of the queen and her Ka on a potter's wheel. Thoth then summons the queen mother to the birth room: Ahmose is led in by Heket, the frog goddess who presides over childbearing, and Khnum, and delivers, seated on a high-backed chair, in the presence of jubilating divinities: note the bandy-legged god Bes at the bottom right. The child is then presented to Amun, who accepts it as his own, and it is then suckled by its mother and a number of other deities, being subsequently presented to other gods and then again to Amun. In the final episode (north wall) the child's destiny and length of reign are established by Seshat, goddess of writing, and by Hapi, lord of the Nile.

The coronation of Hatshepsut is shown in the upper register. The queen is first purified by Rē-Harakhti and Amun and is formally presented by the latter to the gods of north and south (south wall). Then (west wall) Hatshepsut proceeds with various deities into the presence of Thutmose I. After several other ceremonies, she is crowned (north wall) by Horus and Seth and, preceded by the standards of her tutelary gods, emerges in triumph.

The north-west corner of the upper terrace is occupied by the shrine of Anubis (H). In front is a hypostyle hall, excellently preserved with its original colours intact, except where Hatshepsut's figure has been removed: on its walls the queen and her nephew, Thutmose III, present offerings to Amun, Anubis and other mortuary gods. A narrow corridor in the west wall leads to an equally confining sanctuary with a painted statue niche at the far end. Other gods of the Underworld would perhaps have been venerated in the statue niches set at the back of the colonnade north-east of Anubis's shrine (I), but this part of the temple was never finished.

In the southern colonnade (J) we find the reliefs that commemorate Hatshepsut's famous expedition to Punt (c. 1496 B.C.). As we have seen (Chapter 16, p. 222), caravans had to leave the Nile Valley near the town of Qift (Coptos) in Upper Egypt, crossing the Eastern Desert through the Wadi Hammamat and departing by ship from one of the Red Sea ports. The Egyptians' delight in natural observation is reflected in Hatshepsut's reliefs, for the carved band of water under the ships is well stocked with squid, sharks, turtles and other denizens of the deep. Commercial transactions in Punt are shown on the south wall: the chieftain of Punt, with his grotesquely fat wife,[3] are shown bringing their products – particularly incense trees – to the Egyptian envoy who stands, with his armed retinue, on the right. Note the domed Puntite houses, mounted on stilts, on the left (bottom register). Moving on to the east wall, we see the Egyptian flotilla – large sailing vessels, elaborately rigged – being laden for departure: bales of produce and incense trees in pots are carried on board, while in one instance a consignment of baboons has escaped and is seen capering aloft. Finally, the fleet is under

OVERLEAF The mortuary temple of 'King' Hatshepsut at Deir el-Bahri (Luxor, West Bank)

2. Virtually the same sequence is found in Luxor Temple (Chapter 17, pp. 241–2).

3. This is a cast of the original, which is now in the Cairo Museum (p. 54).

way, and in the next episode we see the transplanted incense trees flourishing in the garden of Amun at Karnak. State employees are hard at work, shovelling the imported incense into piles for disposal, and the cargo of the expedition is finally marshalled, weighed and presented by the queen to Amun – for whom, according to the polite fiction, the expedition had been devised.

Just to the south, balancing the northern chapel of Anubis, is the shrine of Hathor (K). On the façade of the building we find large reliefs showing the goddess in the form of a cow, licking Hatshepsut's hand: the same scene, along with another showing the queen being suckled by Hathor, is found on the north wall of the vestibule inside. The processional way at the centre of the hall is lined with pillars bearing, on top, sculpted Hathor heads facing into the avenue. The columns that otherwise filled the chamber had full-scale Hathor-headed capitals which depicted the goddess's female complexion along with her cow's ears, and with the sacred sistrum mounted on her head. Beyond the vestibule is a small hypostyle hall: note in particular the delicacy of the carving in the festive navigation of the goddess on the north wall, with its dancing Libyans and elaborately carved standards. The west walls, flanking the doorway, again show the Hathor cow licking Hatshepsut's hand.

The chapel proper is cut into the side of the mountain. In the first chamber we see Hatshepsut or Thutmose III offering to Hathor and other deities: note the curious ritual shown north of the east doorway, in which the king prepares to strike a ball (representing the eye of the demon Apophis) with a twisted stick, while two priests hold other balls in readiness. The four niches were probably meant for statues of other deities

associated with Hathor at this spot. The western doorway leads into the sanctuary, each side being flanked by two slender Hathor columns carved into the masonry. The decoration, once more, is done jointly by Thutmose III and Hatshepsut. The inner room has the usual scenes showing the young queen suckled by the Hathor cow (side walls), but is dominated by the queen's apotheosis on the west wall: Hatshepsut is here embraced by Hathor, 'Mistress of the Western Mountain' and Lady of the Deir el-Bahri area, and receives life from Amun, pre-eminent in Thebes. Note, on the inner walls of the two west niches, where the doorleaves would have covered them, small figures of Hatshepsut's architect Senenmut, who thus took advantage of her permission to conceal himself by her side for eternity (see below, pp. 263–4).

The pillars fronting the upper terrace have the additional duty of providing support for large Osiride statues of the queen which face outwards. Passing into the upper court through a massive portal of granite,[4] the visitor enters a columned court. The east wall, north and south of the doorway, is inscribed with scenes illustrating the ceremonial navigation of boats carrying statues of Hatshepsut and of Thutmose I, II and III. On the north wall are scenes from the Feast of the Valley (second register): the barques of the Theban Triad are welcomed by the co-regents Thutmose III and Hatshepsut, with their accompanying priests, torch-bearers, singers, dancers and attendants bringing royal statues. The queen next offers public sacrifice before the barque of Amun, then repeats the ritual in private. Damage to the wall makes the subsequent rites unclear, but the sequence apparently concludes with the triumphant emergence of Hatshepsut, sig-

---

4. Admission to this area may be restricted, owing to work in progress.

nalling a beginning to the sacred processions through the private tombs (see Chapter 6, pp. 64, 75).

The rooms south of the central court were dedicated to the mortuary cult (L). A door in the south wall leads into a vestibule with two chapels on the west side: the larger of these, to the south, belonged to Hatshepsut, the other to her father, Thutmose I, whom the queen had also buried in her own tomb. The decoration of both chambers is similar, with rows of offering bringers and lists of supplies dedicated to the sustenance of the deceased on the side walls. The end walls accommodated stelae which served as false doors, permitting the deceased's spirit to enter from the tomb or wherever else it might be: Hatshepsut's stela was spirited away by her enemies, while that of Thutmose I is in the Louvre Museum, Paris.

The suite of rooms north of the court (M) is dominated by the two open-air chambers dedicated to the sun god. Two niches, one in the vestibule and the other in the inner hall, contained statues, the inner one certainly of Hatshepsut herself. In front of this niche is the great altar on which sacrifices to the sun god were exposed to its rays. A small chapel to Anubis, dedicated to the use of Thutmose I and his mother, is set into the north wall of the sun court. A separate room west of this complex is dedicated to Amun who, as noted above, played an important part in the cult of the royal dead: Senenmut is here, behind the doors as usual, and the necessary rituals are performed both by the queen and by her co-regent, Thutmose III – who later hacked out his aunt's names and figures without completely destroying either.

The west wall of the central court is lined with small niches that contained statues of Hatshepsut, alternatively in the wrappings of Osiris and enthroned. The sanctuary inside (N) consisted originally of two rooms, on the walls of which Hatshepsut, Thutmose III

and Princess Nefrurē, Hatshepsut's daughter, worshipped the gods, among them their own deified predecessors. A third chamber was added in the second century B.C. by Ptolemy VIII Euergetes II in honour of Imhotep and Amenhotep, Son of Hapu, the celebrated officials of Djoser and of Amenhotep III, who were worshipped in the later Pharaonic age. It is oddly fitting that these two 'saints', renowned for their builders' skills, should have as their cult spot the architectural masterpiece that is Queen Hatshepsut's temple.

The outcropping of rock between the temples of Mentuhotep-Nebhepetrē and Hatshepsut was utilized by *Thutmose III* for his own temple at Deir el-Bahri (Fig. 89). Although it is the highest point in the bay, the site was poorly chosen in that it was most vulnerable to rock slides from the cliff behind, and it was in fact destroyed by just such a collapse in antiquity. Visitors who are energetic enough to scramble up the hill from the south side of the Hathor Chapel of Hatshepsut (not recommended by the authorities) will find only a few truncated columns to reward their efforts. Remains of the ramp that led to the building can be seen below, between the Eleventh Dynasty temple and Hatshepsut's second terrace, and also near the cultivation, just east of the main road (where the Eleventh Dynasty ramp is also found). Painted relief from the temple is exhibited in the Luxor Museum (Chapter 17, p. 244).

Before leaving Deir el-Bahri, ask the guard for the keys to one of the more overweening monuments to private ambition, the *secret tomb of Senenmut*. As steward of Amun, architect of Hatshepsut's Deir el-Bahri temple and tutor to the royal children, Senenmut already possessed a fine tomb at the north end of Qurna (Th. 71), but he apparently received permission to build another, located east of the temple's first court, a bit north of the road from the valley. The modest entrance admits the visitor into a long stairway: note, where the stone was smoothed to accommodate a round-topped stela near the bottom (right side), the sketched head and shoulders of the tomb owner – the 'Overseer of the Estate of Amun, Senenmut' – which conveys well the ageing yet alert features of the man. At the bottom of the stairway lies a small chamber, its walls inscribed with extracts from the *Book of the Dead*: note the carved panels beside the door, on which the tomb owner is shown saluting the cartouches of Hatshepsut. Opposite the doorway is the deceased's false door, with Senenmut himself shown offering to his parents in the entablature. The most remarkable decoration in the tomb, however, is the astronomical ceiling, the earliest of its kind found so far: the great stars and constellations of the northern and southern skies appear in corresponding parts of this chart, along with the great monthly festivals, rendered as twelve circles with twenty-four hourly compartments.

Senenmut's tomb was never finished: a stairway at the south end of the first room leads down to two other chambers, both incompletely carved. Most of Senenmut's figures in the tomb have been defaced by hacking, no doubt when he fell from power late in Hatshepsut's reign. His image survived behind the shrine doors in the queen's temple (see above, p. 262), however, and his tomb rested undisturbed until this century, both attesting to what was surely one of the most remarkable careers in Egyptian history.

THE MORTUARY TEMPLE OF SETY I

Similarities between Hatshepsut's monument and the mortuary temples of later kings can best be appreciated by returning to the north end of Dra-abu'l-Nagga and turning east, to reach the temple of Sety I (the so-called 'Qurna Temple': see Map, p. 247). The pylons and front courts have mostly been destroyed, so the visitor will enter the temple from the portico, left incomplete on Sety's death and finished by Ramesses II. The hypostyle hall inside was decorated jointly during the two kings' co-regency, but the fine raised relief which is the hallmark of Sety's workmanship is apparent throughout. At the sides of the hall are cult chapels dedicated to the Theban and Osirian circle of gods and to the deified Sety I: note (Fig. 90, A) scenes of the Iunmutef priest purifying the king, followed by a female personification of the temple; and of Sety making

Fig. 90 **Sety I** *Mortuary Temple*

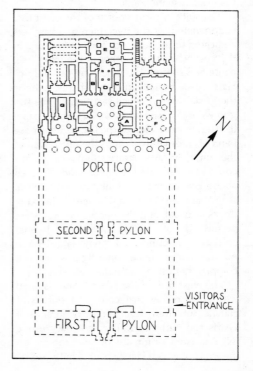

PORTICO

SECOND PYLON

VISITORS' ENTRANCE

FIRST PYLON

libation to Amun, with whom, as the god of his mortuary temple, he was identified. At the back of the hypostyle hall are the barque shrines of Mut (B), Khonsu (C) and Amun (D) — the latter still having its low barque pedestal in place, along with the scenes of the king offering before the sacred barque on the walls. Behind Amun's chapel is the holy-of-holies (E), with remains of the king's false door set against the west wall.

The chambers of the solar cult, as in Hatshepsut's temple, are located at the north end of the building: the great open sun court (F), carved in the dull, flat relief of Ramesses II's maturity, is dominated by the large altar in the centre. Among the ruined elements in the back on the west side, note the remains of the staircase that led to a sanctuary on the roof. Separate entrances from the portico lead into the rooms of the solar cult and also into a suite, south of the hypostyle hall, dedicated to the deceased Ramesses I: this king, Sety's father, reigned for too short a time to build his own mortuary temple, so a chapel was provided for him in his son's monument. Note, on the north wall of the hypostyle, a scene purporting to show the coronation of Ramesses II in the presence of the Theban Triad and of Sety I. The sanctuary of this chapel (G) is graced by a superbly preserved false door set into the back wall.

THE RAMESSEUM

Ramesses II's mortuary temple, a sprawling building of enormous proportions known as *the Ramesseum* (see Map, p. 247) has suffered severely from time and man. It is nonetheless the most romantic ruin in West Thebes, being particularly atmospheric at sunset. The visitors' entrance leads directly into the second court: the nearly collapsed mass of the first pylon (Fig. 91) can be seen a short distance to the east. Enormous pillars with engaged Osiride statues of the king dominate the second court: behind, on the east side, on what is left of the second pylon, we see remains from the yearly festival of Min, god of fertility (top), and a portion of the Battle of Kadesh (bottom). The remains of the pylon's south wing are partially covered by the upper part of a tumbled colossal statue of the king in granite: its base is still to be found in the first court. This behemoth, measuring 7 m. from shoulder to shoulder and with an estimated height of over 17 m. when complete, has the distinction of having inspired Shelley's poem, 'Ozymandias'.[5] Two smaller colossi stood flanking the doorway into the temple: the head of one, in black granite, rests on the ground near the stairway leading to the hypostyle hall.

Of the 48 columns originally in the hypostyle hall, only 29 are still standing. The walls are similarly denuded: of importance is the scene on the east wall, south half, showing the king with his army and his sons attacking the fortress of Dapūr. On the west wall, flanking the doorway out of the hall, is a double procession of Ramesses II's sons, appearing by order of seniority. Merneptah, Ramesses' eventual successor, appears as the thirteenth figure on the north side, being set apart from the others by the addition of his royal cartouche and of a long robe about his figure.

The second hypostyle hall is sometimes referred to as the 'Astronomical Room', because of the astronomical 'map' carved on its ceiling. It is distinguished on the eastern side by representations of the barques of the Theban Triad and other deities, including Ramesses II. Note, particularly, a fine large-scale relief on the west wall north of the doorway, showing the king seated in front of

5. A Greek version of Ramesses II's throne name, 'Userma'atrē'.

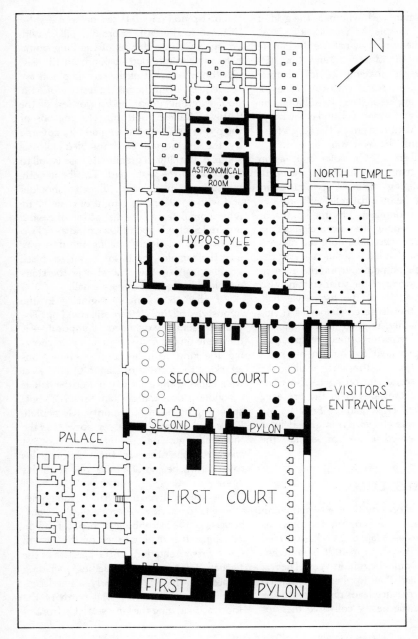

N

NORTH TEMPLE

ASTRONOMICAL ROOM

HYPOSTYLE

SECOND COURT

VISITORS' ENTRANCE

PALACE

SECOND PYLON

FIRST COURT

FIRST PYLON

Fig. 91
The Ramesseum

the sacred Persea Tree while Thoth, Atum and Sefkhet-'abwy write his name on the leaves: the presence of this last-named goddess, the 'mistress of writing', has suggested to some scholars that the library mentioned by Diodorus Siculus' *History* (I, 49) was located in this room; but such an institution would surely have been found elsewhere in the complex and not in the temple itself.

The rest of the temple is, for the most part, destroyed, but the vandals who quarried away its walls were not interested in the mudbrick magazines seen at the back of the complex. A number of these structures still have their vaulted roofs, and in one chamber in the north-west quarter one may see the remains of mudbrick statue groups – perhaps in the chapel of the scribal school that appears to have been located here. Note also, north of Ramesses' temple and adjoining the building, the foundations of another, smaller temple that appears to have been dedicated to the king's mother.

COLOSSI OF MEMNON

No visitor to West Thebes will be able to miss the immense statues (see Map, p. 247) which are the most conspicuous extant remains of Amenhotep III's mortuary temple: these seated figures of the king, flanked by figures of the queen mother and the king's wife, Tiyi, are nearly 18 m. high, and would have stood before the main entrance to the temple. As a result of an earthquake in 27 B.C., the northern colossus was damaged in such a manner that, according to Strabo, it began to emit a soft, bell-like sound at dawn. Greek tourists were attracted by stories of this phenomenon and they accordingly identified this statue with Memnon, the son of Aurora, but the 'singing' stopped early in the third century A.D. when Septimius Severus repaired the upper part of the statue in the crude fashion visible today. The greater part

of the temple had already been destroyed, having been used as a quarry from the time of the late New Kingdom: a number of statues and fragmentary columns can be discerned further back, along with a large quartzite stela, describing the king's building works, which has been re-erected on the site.

MEDINET HABU

The south end of the necropolis area is occupied by the temples of Medinet Habu (see Map, p. 247). Originally occupied solely by the small temple to Amun built by Hatshepsut and Thutmose III, the site is now dominated by the great mortuary temple of Ramesses III. The thick retaining wall of mudbrick still harbours crumbling houses from the Coptic town of Djēme, which was abandoned in about the ninth century A.D. Up until that time, and for much of the past two millennia, it was the most defensible spot in West Thebes – a factor that probably has much to do with the relatively good preservation of the Pharaonic remains.

Visitors to Medinet Habu enter the complex through its eastern gate: note the two guardhouses flanking the entrance. Inside is an enormous model of a fortified gate, (Fig. 92, A) inscribed with reliefs that show the Pharaoh vanquishing the enemies of Egypt. The holiness of the grounds inside is emphasized by the icon of Ptah 'who hears prayer' found on the south wall of the passage: persons who could not gain admittance to the temple made their petitions to this veiled and inlaid figure, who would then transmit them to the 'great god', the Amun of Ramesses III's temple.

The upper chambers of the high gate served as a retreat for the king and his intimates during royal visits to the temple. Ascending the modern staircase to the upper level, the visitor enters the tower and can gaze over the temple grounds from its broad windows. From here, too, one can examine the painted consoles of prisoners' heads that face out into the eastern passage. The wooden floors of the upper levels have collapsed, permitting us to examine the sculpted walls throughout the building, where the king is shown at play – playing draughts or bestowing ornaments – with lissom young females. It was probably while taking his ease here, in the upper chambers of the high gate, that Ramesses III was assassinated. No such bloody memories remain, however, to haunt the airy solitude of this royal retreat.

The space between the high gate and the temple of Ramesses III is occupied by the small Eighteenth Dynasty temple (north side), which had been incorporated into Ramesses' precinct and possessed its own separate enclosure; and, on the south side (B) by two of the four chapels built there during the Twenty-fifth and Twenty-sixth Dynasties. These buildings served the mortuary cult of the 'Divine Adoratrices of Amun', daughters of the reigning king who symbolically 'wed' the god of Thebes and ruled by proxy for the king in the north and the local officials who in fact governed the Thebaid. That on the east side belonged to Amenirdis I, daughter of the Nubian 'Pharaoh' Kashta. It consists of a columned forecourt, with its offering table still in place, and a large inner chamber inside which the princess's mortuary chapel is placed: the deceased was buried in the crypt under the floor. The reliefs are for the most part incised with great care and have an elegance that is not matched by the hasty, cruder work in the adjoining chapel to the west. This building (constructed for Shepenwepet II, last of the Nubian incumbents, by her success-

or Nitocris, daughter of Psamtik I) has three chapels behind its entrance courtyard: the central room belongs to Shepenwepet; those on the left and right, added later, belong to Nitocris and to her mother, whose chapel contains motifs considerably different from those in the rooms dedicated to the three divine adoratrices buried here.

The pylons of Ramesses III's temple are inscribed with the usual scenes of the king massacring captives before the gods: note the rows of 'name-rings' with human heads and bound arms, each inscribed with the name of a foreign country, that symbolize the extent of the Egyptian empire. Details of the king's prowess are revealed in the battle reliefs found on the temple's outer walls, to the north. The morning light is best for viewing these records which, owing to their liveliness and importance, will be described in the following paragraphs.

The first onslaught came in the fifth year of the king's reign, when Libyan tribes – in need of living space and resentful of Pharaonic interference in their affairs – launched an invasion. On the back wall of the building (sc. 4)[6] the king is shown within the temple of Amun, receiving the sickle-sword of victory from the god in the presence of Thoth and Khonsu. Next (sc. 5), he leaves the temple, escorted by the war god, Montu, and by priests carrying the standards of Wepwawet, the jackal who acts as 'Opener of the Ways', and of the Theban gods, which he will carry into battle; and (sc. 6) mounts his chariot, as a bugler calls the army to attention. Turning to the north wall (sc. 1), we see Ramesses III setting out to meet the enemy: the ram-headed standard of Amun rides in the front chariot, while the

Fig. 92 **Medinet Habu**

---

6. The first three scenes deal with an unimportant Nubian war, probably fought earlier in the reign.

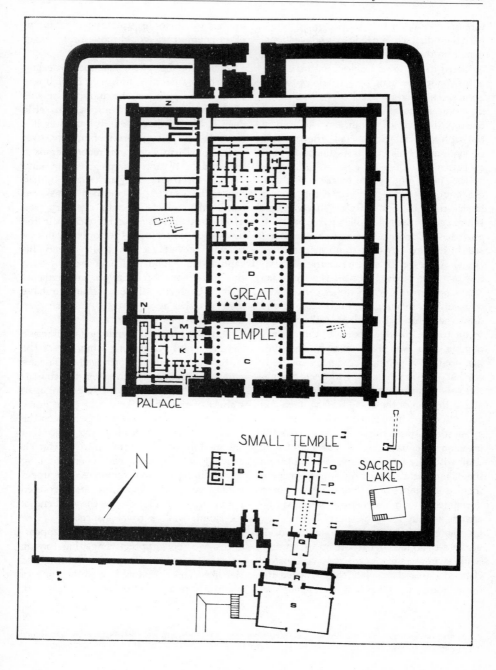

foreign contingents of the Egyptian army, with their distinctive headgear and weapons, march on the lower left. The battle (sc. 2) is rendered in the usual fashion, with the king in his chariot charging into a welter of fallen bodies. The victory is celebrated before an Egyptian fortress: the king stands on a balcony, receiving the officers who lead in the captives, while scribes tally the numbers of hands and phalli from the slain, brought in by common soldiers for a reward (sc. 3).

The next, and even more formidable, challenge came in regnal year eight, when a fresh group of 'Sea Peoples' threw themselves against the Nile Valley (see Chapter 4, pp. 58–9). The invaders came by land and sea. In the first episode from this campaign (sc. 4), Ramesses III supervises the distribution of arms to his people. The Egyptian forces next march across the eastern border to meet the invading land force (sc. 5) and draw them into battle (sc. 6). Although this scene too is conventionalized, there are a number of realistic vignettes showing Egyptian soldiers engaging the enemy in single combat. The Sea Peoples, with their distinctive robes and helmets, are vividly rendered, and at the top of the scene their women and children cower in wagons drawn by oxen.

Although this action effectively broke the invasion, the naval force remained to be dealt with: the Egyptian fleet sailed out from the Nile mouths to meet the enemy, keeping them at a distance until their crews had been decimated by the withering fire Egyptian archers kept up from the shore. Then (sc. 8), grappling hooks were thrown and the survivors were subdued in hand-to-hand fighting, while swimmers from capsized vessels were clapped into fetters when they reached the shore. Ramesses III might well enjoy his

triumph (sc. 9), for his strategy had rid Egypt of an enemy that would move on to easier prospects and trouble her no more.

While the Egyptians had been dealing with the Sea Peoples, however, the Libyans were once again on the move. Elements of the Meshwesh tribe contrived to settle deep inside the Delta and, in Ramesses III's eleventh year, a large body of emigrants set out to join them. The scenic record begins in the middle of this campaign:[7] the king pursues the fleeing Libyans (whom he had tricked into laying down their arms) and carries their chiefs off into captivity (scs. 1–2). He then celebrates his victory in the field (sc. 3), is greeted at the border by priests bearing flowers (sc. 4), and presents his captives to Amun and Mut (sc. 5). Such themes are common in Egyptian monuments – but Ramesses III could claim to have 'defended Ma'at' to greater purpose than many of his predecessors.

A bellicose note is maintained even inside the first court (C), where a number of the battle scenes from the north wall outside are repeated. Structurally, however, the court is dominated by pillars with huge engaged statues of the divine king along the north side, all facing the columned portico to the south: this was the façade of the palace that adjoined the temple, at the centre of which is a 'window of appearances' where the king stood during public ceremonies. The upper panels, beside the doorways, are decorated with martial scenes: note, on the west end of the south wall, a royal inspection of the cavalry. Just below the window of appearances, we see Egyptians engaging foreign adversaries in wrestling, stick-fighting and the like. This, no doubt, was the tone of many a formal occasion held in the court,

---

7. These scenes begin on the first pylon (west face), continuing on the north wall, between the first and second pylons (lower register). The upper register has scenes from an apparently fictitious set of Asiatic campaigns.

with princes, officials and members of the diplomatic corps in attendance, as they are here.[8]

The second court of Ramesses III's temple (D) was converted during the Christian era into the 'Holy Church of Djēme'. The Copts destroyed the large Osiride statues of the king engaged to the pillars, but the coat of whitewash they applied to the walls helped to preserve the colours on the festival scenes in the upper registers. On the north wall we see the Feast of the fertility god, Min: the king is borne out of the palace in a carrying chair with his retinue (west end), and sacrifices to Min in his shrine. He then escorts the god forth in procession: Min's statue is borne aloft on carrying poles which are draped in a red pall worked with metal studs. Attendants carry his heraldic lettuce plants — regarded by the Egyptians as an aphrodisiac — behind him in a planter's box, while in front are the king and queen, a white bull who plays an obscure part in the proceedings and a row of priests carrying standards.

The order of the subsequent rites (east wall, north side) has been sacrificed to artistic considerations: the king first cuts a sheaf of emmer (middle) which is then presented by a priest to the god (not shown) in the company of the queen, the white bull and statues of the royal ancestors (middle/right). The god's blessing on the harvest having been thus obtained, the king releases four sparrows, representing the four sons of Horus (left), so they may carry the news to the gods of the four quarters of the universe. Min is then returned to his shrine, where there is a final sacrifice (right) before the celebration comes to an end.

The upper register on the south side of the court is taken up with the Feast of Sokar, the dark god of the earth's potency who, in a curious sense, is Min's counterpart in the underworld. In the first two scenes (beginning on the south wall, west end) the king offers sacrifice to Sokar-Osiris (hawk-headed) and to three of his associates, including the ram-headed Khnum. He then offers incense over the barque of Sokar, reciting the names by which the god was worshipped in different parts of Egypt, and escorts the barque out of the sanctuary. Although the texts tell us that the barque was dragged in public on the traditional archaic sledge, this is not shown (for reasons of space); instead, we see officials drawing the tow-ropes which are held by the king, as they enjoy the privilege of pulling Sokar (not shown here) around the walls of the temple. The procession also includes the fetish of Nefertem — a plumed lotus-blossom mounted on a pole, which is borne in an ornamental sling. Other standards and divine barques (east wall) join the procession as it wends its way through the necropolis, celebrating the enduring potency for life in the inert soil. This, by analogy, expresses the Egyptian hope for the dead in the cemetery. In conjunction, moreover, the feasts of Sokar and Min reflect the processes of resurrection that will apply for the king in his mortuary temple.

A short ramp leads from the second court to the portico (E), on the back wall of which is a carved procession of the sons and daughters of Ramesses III. Behind, the first hypostyle hall (F) is sadly reduced, as are most of the rooms on the central axis in this

---

8. Note that the block directly under the 'window' bears the name, not of Ramesses III, but of Ramesses II! Apparently, it was brought from the Ramesseum (where it occupied an analogous position) in late antiquity, and was re-used in the modern consolidation of the temple with only a slight discrepancy in style and scale. Both the Medinet Habu temple and the Ramesseum were laid out on very similar lines, and the ruins of the latter may well be more comprehensible after a visit to Ramesses III's monument.

part of the temple. On the south side is the temple treasury: its doorway, once disguised to resemble a continuation of the adjoining relief, opens on to a suite of five rooms that housed the prized ritual implements of the temple (some of which are shown on the walls inside). The obviousness of its location, despite the efforts to conceal the entrance, suggests that its presence on this spot was to some extent a ritual rather than a practical decision. Beside the treasury (south wall, west end) is the barque chapel of the deified Ramesses II, a king on whom Ramesses III modelled much of his public manner. The five chapels on the north side (from east to west) are shrines of the living king, Ptah, the divine standards, and of Sokar, with the ritual 'slaughter-house' in the two-room suite at the west end: the butchering scene carved on the east wall of the first room is particularly lively. Flanking the central axis are the chapels of Montu (south) and the portable barque shrines of the deified Ramesses III, the god of the Medinet Habu temple (north).

The second hypostyle hall (G) gives access to a pair of suites familiar from earlier mortuary temples. On the north side is the solar chapel, with its staircase leading to the roof and its open courtyard: note, on the architrave in this enclosure, that the king worships the barque of the sun in the company of baboons, animals regarded as devoted to the rising sun because of their howling at daybreak. To the south of the hypostyle is the 'contiguous temple' of Osiris, where the dead king received the god's sovereign power over the realm of the dead. After the vestibule (in which the king is seen enthroned and receiving an offering list from the Iunmutef priest on its east wall) we enter a small hypostyle, where the king is presented to the various gods who will confirm his right to rule. Beyond the vestibule that follows are two chapels that served, perhaps, as a cenotaph. That on the south

side consists of two small rooms inscribed with extracts from the *Book of the Dead*, including vignettes of the king tilling the soil in the next world. The other chapel, to the north, has a vaulted ceiling carved with an astronomical chart – an almost exact copy, as it happens, of that found in the second hypostyle hall at the Ramesseum. The king is seen offering to Osiris and his circle of gods on the side walls, while at the back is a false door, through which the dead king might enter to receive the worship performed here for his benefit.

Most of the other chapels in the temple are too poorly preserved to tell us much about their function. The nine niches found in one suite north of the third hypostyle (H) strongly suggest that it was dedicated to the gods of the Ennead. The sanctuary of Amun lies at the focus of the central axis (I), flanked by the shrines of the other members of the Theban Triad, Mut (south) and Khonsu (north). Behind Amun's chapel, in the broad hallway at the back, are the remains of another false door, this one for the use of 'Amun-Rē "United with Eternity" ', the god of Medinet Habu (i.e., Ramesses III). At the very back of the building are two narrow rooms with low, easily concealed entrances. Since a visitor who was in ignorance of the rooms behind might easily mistake the back wall of the sanctuary for that of the temple, it is possible that these were the treasuries in which truly valuable articles were kept.

On leaving the temple, turn south, going around the pylon tower to visit the ruins of the palace. A small building, doubtless this is not a full-fledged residence, but probably served as a rest house whenever royalty visited Medinet Habu. Most of the time it was a 'dummy' palace for the king's spirit, and possessed, like the temple, a false door. Built out of mudbrick, the palace was decorated with stone features and other decoration, e.g. glazed tiles, that have been removed in part to the Cairo Museum (Chapter 10, pp. 116, 126 = Rooms 15, 20, 44). Careful excavation has permitted recovery of the ground plan, however, and this has been built up to give visitors some idea of the place.

The normal means of entry into the palace was through a doorway in the brick wall built against the temple's first pylon, now vanished: this led into a reception room (Fig. 92, J). A more imposing set of vestibules adjoined the double staircase and other doorways that gave Pharaoh access to the Balcony of Appearances in the first court's south wall, and into the temple proper. Processions on these occasions probably formed in the columned hall just behind (K), while semi-public audiences could be given in the suite next door: petitioners could stand in the front hall (M) and transact their business with the king, who sat on a throne dais in the next room; a 'window of appearances' apparently connected the two rooms. The king's private suite was apparently behind the main hall: a passage gave on to a bathroom on the right side, and into the sovereign's living-room (L) and bedroom to the left. Behind the reception area a doorway leads into a passage serving three suites (N), no doubt for members of the king's family.

The upper storeys of the palace, being of mudbrick, have not survived, though the beam holes that supported the roof can be clearly seen in the south wall of the temple. The remainder of the south wall is occupied by an important, but visually monotonous, calendar of offerings for the yearly feasts celebrated at the temple. Note, however, two opulent scenes carved on the back wall of the first pylon, near the north-east corner of the palace, in which the Pharaoh is shown hunting wild asses and cattle in the desert. Other buildings in this quarter — mostly barracks and workshops for temple

employees — are in ruinous condition. A memorial of the troubled times near the end of the eleventh century, when the population of West Thebes fled behind the temple's walls from Libyan marauders, can be seen, however, in the house of the necropolis scribe Butehamun, the front part of which — with its slender columns — survives near the south-west corner of the temple (Z). Some time later, the temple was besieged and captured: the invaders destroyed the western high gate so thoroughly that it was never rebuilt, and lies in fragments today.

We now move back to the east half of the enclosure, to a building that kept its religious significance long after the great temple of Ramesses III had ceased to function. This is the so-called 'small temple' at the north-east corner of the precinct. The visitor's entrance is near the back of the building, allowing a sequential view of its development. In its initial stage, the monument consisted of a pillared cloister surrounding the barque chapel of Amun, with a number of small rooms in the back. This sanctuary area (O) is divided into two parts: at the north end is the single chamber dedicated to the cult of Thutmose III; the five chambers to the south are the god's own sanctuary. The pillared offering hall in front gives access to three small, dark chambers, the one in the north-west corner containing a large naos that was introduced during the Late Period by dismantling the back wall. The decoration was originally in the name of Hatshepsut and Thutmose III, but the latter has suppressed his aunt's name throughout in favour of her predecessors, Thutmose I and II.

Outside, on the barque chapel (P), note in particular the reliefs carved on its outer face, especially on the north exterior wall, where foundation ceremonies are depicted: first (west end), the king and Sefkhet-'abwy 'stretch the cord' to determine the dimensions of the temple on the ground; next, the king pours gypsum into the foundation trenches, hacks at the soil with a large hoe, moulds a brick, and then offers wine and sacrificial victims before Amun. The interior of the chapel was renovated under Ptolemy VIII, who re-carved its contents in the graceless, congested style of the later age. The two wings at the north-east and south-east corners of the cloister were added by Hakoris in the Twenty-ninth Dynasty: note the modern travellers' inscriptions in the south room.

The succeeding eighteen centuries brought extensive changes to this rather modest building. The formal entrance of the New Kingdom was swept away, and in its place was built a pylon (dedicated by the Nubian Pharaoh Shabaka and usurped by his nephew Taharqa), connected to the earlier cloister by a colonnade (Q) that reached its final form during the Ptolemaic period. The small gateway and columned vestibule in front were built during the Twenty-sixth Dynasty and usurped by Nectanebo I during the Twenty-ninth. A more impressive façade was devised by the Ptolemies, who built a mudbrick pylon (now destroyed) with an outer facing of stone (R) and a massive gateway. Many re-used blocks can be seen in the masonry of the pylon, most of them from the Ramesseum. The outer lintel of the gateway, carved with the emblem of the winged disc, retains its original colour and makes a brilliant effect. The last and most ambitious of the additions made to the small temple was begun by Antoninus Pius: his columned portico and courtyard (S) were never completed, however, and within a few centuries the pagan temples were abandoned and engulfed by the Christian town. Fortunately, they escaped destruction and survive to offer a priceless glimpse of the ancient history of West Thebes.

MALKATTA

The palace complex of Amenhotep III was at Malkatta, south of Medinet Habu. Its most outstanding feature (clearly visible from any height in the Theban Hills) is the enormous T-shaped harbour which is still visible because of the high levees left by the excavation of the basin: these mounds are now occupied, for the most part, by villages, and the basin itself lies within the cultivation.

The palaces and the Temple of Amun also remain — at least, their foundations. The guards on the site will be able to show you a few of the decaying murals left in situ (most, fortunately, were removed to museums). But while many illuminating details can emerge from a walk through these ruins, they will appeal most to persons possessing background knowledge or interest in the site itself.

THE VALLEY OF THE QUEENS

The queens' valley (see Map, p. 247) is located roughly 1 km. south-west of Medinet Habu. Only three of its tombs are kept open to the public, none of them having an exceptional interest. The setting, however, is splendid, commanding from the back of the amphitheatre a view of the Colossi of Memnon, and it is unspoiled by the modern excrescences that have robbed so much of the atmosphere from the Valley of the Kings.

The first tomb to be visited belonged to *Queen Titi*, an otherwise unknown princess of the Twentieth Dynasty. The first corridor (Fig. 93, A) is reminiscent in style of a royal tomb, executed on a smaller scale. The queen appears before a variety of gods, the scenes being carved in lightly sunk relief and delicately coloured against a white background. In contrast, the scenes in the room that

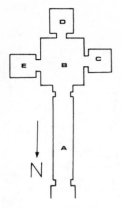

Fig. 93 **Queen Titi**

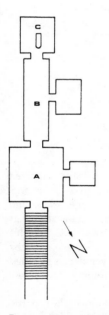

Fig. 94 **Prince Amenhikhopeshef**

follows (B) are painted against a gold background. The protagonists are the mythological beings that populate the Egyptian netherworld: note the solar barques of the day and the night flanking the doorway on the south wall. The queen is also represented here, rattling the sistra and presenting royal standards before the four sons of Horus; but she is also seen more informally, squatting on a cushion on the north wall, west corner.

The three side-rooms housed the grave goods, with the canopic chest apparently placed on the west side (C): the four jars, at least, are shown on the south wall along with three demons, one of them with a serpent's head. On the west wall, the queen appears before the tree goddess in the necropolis, behind whom the cow goddess Hathor emerges from her mountain in the West. The central chamber (D) can be regarded as the sanctuary: the queen offers to the deities seated at offering tables on the side walls, while at the back of the room is shown the court of Osiris: the god is enthroned, attended by Neith and Selkis (front) and Isis, Nephthys and Thoth (back) — the four goddesses traditionally assigned to protect the corpse of the deceased. The east room (E) is less well preserved than the others: an array of mythological beings appears on the walls, and the floor has collapsed into the shaft which is now choked with rubble.

A short distance further west is the *tomb of Prince Amenhikhopeshef*, a son of Ramesses III who was in line to inherit the throne before his premature death. Once again, the standard of workmanship is high, the scenes being nicely carved and painted against a blue-grey background. In the first corridor (Fig. 94, A) the prince is represented several times following his father, who greets a number of divinities on his behalf: the young man carries a slender fan, symbolic of his honorific office, 'Fanbearer on the right side of the King'. The second corridor (B) is decorated in a similar style with episodes from the *Book of Gates*. The burial chamber (C) was not completed and contains a modestly scaled sarcophagus in red granite. A foetus found in the tomb is exhibited in the south-west corner: it cannot represent the prince himself, who attained a number of important posts before his death, but may have been one of his stillborn children.

Back in the south-east corner of the valley is the *tomb of Khaemwēse*, eldest son of Rameses III who apparently died before he could be placed in the line of succession. The decoration is similar to that found in Amenhikhopeshef's tomb, but the plan is more elaborate. In the first corridor (Fig. 95, A), again, the prince appears in the company of his father as the latter offers to various gods. At either side of this corridor are side rooms (B, C) in which the prince offers to mortuary deities – the four sons of Horus, Anubis – on the side walls, with Isis and Nephthys greeting Osiris (or Sokar) on the back wall. The second corridor, once again, is inscribed with extracts from the *Book of Gates* (D). The burial chamber (E) is immediately beyond: painted with a gold background, it is virtually identical with the corresponding chamber in Queen Titi's tomb, although the protagonist in all the offering scenes is the king. The back wall resembles that in Titi's sanctuary chamber, with Ramesses III appearing with the usual protecting goddesses before Osiris: note the four sons of Horus, tiny figures perched upon a lotus bloom in front of Osiris's throne.

The most elaborate tomb in the Valley of the Queens belonged to *Queen Nefertari*, wife of Ramesses II. The lowest tomb in the Valley, it is severely affected by the extrusion of mineral salts thrust out of the very walls, an effect of the rising water table

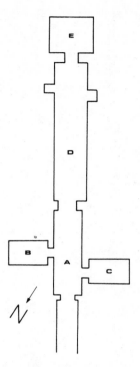

Fig. 95 **Prince Khaemwēse**

at Thebes. The reliefs (mostly executed on plaster covering the native limestone) are thus being pushed off the walls, and the Egyptian Antiquities Organization has decreed a moratorium on visits to this tomb until a solution to the problem can be found. The description given here is supplied against the day that the tomb will be accessible once more.

The fame of this monument lies in the perfection of the draftsmanship and the vividness of the colours preserved. At the bottom of a stairway, with a ramp down the middle

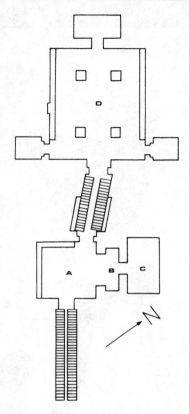

Fig. 96   **Queen Nefertari**

for dragging heavy objects into the tomb, is the offering hall (Fig. 96, A), with its stone shelves projecting from the north and west walls: offerings were no doubt placed on these ledges, with shrines and other ritual objects fitted into the niches below. East of the doorway, on the south wall, the queen worships Osiris, while on the west side she participates in vignettes from the *Book of Gates*: Nefertari plays draughts while seated in a booth, her *Ba* perched on the shrine in front; then, kneeling, she adores the gods who appear above the shelves on the west

and north walls. The two lions of the horizon are seen first, along with the phoenix and also the two kites, Isis and Nephthys, who stand guard over the bier of Osiris (west). On the north wall the four sons of Horus are seen watching the shrine of Anubis.

The east wall of the first room communicates with two other chambers. In the vestibule (B) the queen is led by Isis into the presence of the beetle-headed Khepri, symbol of the rising sun (north side) and by Horus into the presence of Rē-Harakhti and Hathor, Mistress of the West. The back wall of the inner chamber (C) contains a double scene, showing the queen offering a hecatomb to Osiris (left) and Atum, lord of Heliopolis (right). Other scenes show Nefertari in the presence of the ibis god Thoth, offering cloth to Ptah (north), and worshipping a bull with seven cows, together with the steering oars of the four corners of heaven; behind, Isis and Nephthys protect the mummiform figure of the sun god in his aged ram's-headed form (south).

Another stairway, inscribed with funerary texts and scenes of Nefertari offering to various deities, brings us down into the burial chamber (D). The walls are mostly decorated with extracts from the *Book of Gates*: the queen appears before each of these portals, which are guarded by a variety of deities wielding knives. Finally (north wall, east side) she appears in triumph before the gods of the Underworld, Osiris, Hathor and Anubis. The pillars are all decorated with similar scenes, showing the officiating priest (Iunmutef, or 'Horus, Protector of his Father'); Osiris in his shrine; the queen receiving life from Isis, Hathor or Anubis; and the Djed Pillar, symbol of Osiris and of life eternal. The side rooms have remains of brightly painted vignettes of mythological beings, but they are poorly preserved in comparison with the tomb's principal chambers.

19. Luxor, West Bank: Private Monuments

Behind the royal mortuary temples, in the hills edging the high desert, are the private tombs of Thebes. The road from the river-bank (where tickets to the 'tombs of the nobles' have been purchased) goes through the fields, past the village of 'New Qurna' and the Colossi of Memnon, and reaches the desert's edge at the south end of the necropolis. In this itinerary we will temporarily ignore the main road, which turns north and runs along the edge of the cemetery, and proceed along the left fork, to the branch that leads to the village of Deir el-Medina (see Map, p. 247).

DEIR EL-MEDINA

The workmen's village of Deir el-Medina, with its cemeteries and temples (see Chapter 2, pp. 35–6), is located in a little valley behind the hill of Qurnet Murai, at the south end of the Theban necropolis (see Fig. 97). The town itself – reduced to its foundations – lies in the middle of the depression, with the tombs in the hills surrounding (mostly on the west side) and the temples at the north end. Most visitors, especially those travelling in groups, seldom linger here, confining themselves to visiting one or two of the tombs. Travellers with more time are urged to spend some of it here, for few other spots convey more of the totality of life in ancient Egypt.

To explore the village, walk to the north end of the valley and enter the enclosure at its north-east corner (Fig. 97, A). The narrow street that runs towards the south is some-times barely a metre wide, and the houses are wedged tightly together, almost every one sharing the common wall that separates it from its neighbour. Each house, as a rule, fills the space between the enclosure wall and the street. Parts of the town where this does not apply were later additions to the plan, and the houses are reached by side streets (B). The end of the main north–south street, after about 85 m. (C), marks the limit of the town during the Eighteenth Dynasty. Here the main street turns sharply to the west and then, after about 12 m., south again, into the later quarter (D).

The houses, small by modern standards, were in some cases further reduced by parti-tioning. In the north-east quarter we may visit two neighbouring houses. The first (E) which is quite narrow, owing to its sub-division in antiquity, has a vestibule and a main chamber behind: a column supported the roof, and against the west wall is a divan of mudbrick where family members took their ease. The passage to the cellar opens on to the middle of this room. Before the kitchen, with emplacements for the oven and two mortars still visible on the floor, are the remains of the stairway that led to the roof. The importance of the upper storeys as living and storage space has been shown in the representations of private houses found in the tombs, so we may be sure that the plan of this house reveals only a fraction of the space actually available to the owner in ancient times.

The house to the north (F) is larger, also having the unusual feature of its kitchen at

Grain harvest, with vignette of quarrelling girls, tomb of Menna (Luxor, West Bank)

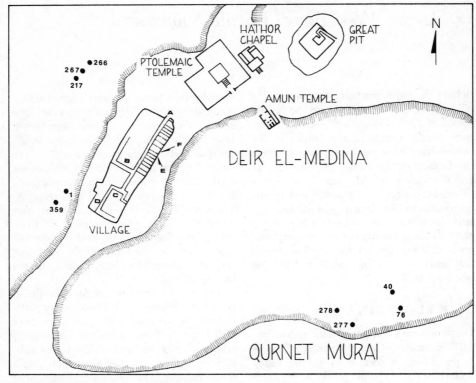

Fig. 97 **Deir el-Medina and Qurnet Murai**

the front, just south of the entrance vestibule. The bakery, with its two ovens, is separated from the rest of the cooking area by a curtain wall. Both the two reception rooms and the kitchen lead, each by their separate way, into a large living-room, with the owner's divan against the back wall. Behind this is a back room with a rectangular storage crib, while the stairway down to the cellar is off the north end of the divan. The stairway to the roof, once again, is against the north wall, though this is not invariably the arrangement in all houses in the village. The column that supported the roof of the living-room identifies the owner as the 'chief of the crew, Kaha'. Status and residential

comfort apparently went hand-in-hand at Deir el-Medina.

The hills that rise to the west and north of the town are covered with the private tombs of the workmen who lived here, but at the north-east corner of the valley a cleft cuts through the hillside, out to the rest of the Theban necropolis. This area is now dominated by the mudbrick enclosure wall of a temple built by the Ptolemies. During the town's heyday, however, this was the temple quarter *par excellence*. We can see the remains of two of these structures just north of the Ptolemaic enclosure: the two buildings that rise up in terraces are the temple of Amenhotep I (upper) and the temple to

Hathor built by Sety I (lower). Opposite the Ptolemaic temple, on the eastern hillside, are the remains of a temple to Amun built by Ramesses II. Between the Ptolemaic enclosure and the town, there are poorly preserved vestiges of smaller chapels dedicated by the state and by private donors to various deities worshipped by the villagers.

The Ptolemaic enclosure was built over the remains of several New Kingdom religious structures. The temple itself is dedicated to Hathor and, apart from being well preserved, is unremarkable. The front doorway leads into a columned hall which is also served by two side-entrances. From here, a narrow portico separates the visitor from the three sanctuaries at the back of the building. A stairway on the south-east side of the portico leads up to the roof. The reliefs in the temple pay special attention, not only to Hathor, but also to the members of the Theban Triad, Amun, Mut and Khonsu. In this, however, they merely conform to Theban usage, for the three great local gods would have had their main cult in the ruined Amun temple across the way.

If from Deir el-Medina the visitor wishes to continue to the other private tombs, the path at the north-east corner should be used. Beyond the Ptolemaic temple, at the very edge of the little valley's border, is found the last of the local 'sights' — a gigantic pit, which seems to have been excavated in Graeco-Roman times in an attempt to supply the nearby temple with well water. Beyond, to the north-east, lies the hill of Sheikh-Abd'el-Qurna, with its cemetery (see below, pp. 283–93) and the Ramesseum, or with the path running behind to Deir el-Bahri, passing Sankhkarē's unfinished tomb (see Chapter 18, p. 258) on the left.

Innumerable tracks wind through the hills to the various sites where villagers of Deir el-Medina plied their craft. The main path leaves the village at its south-west corner, mounting high above the valley before branching off in two directions. The south branch goes to the Valley of the Queens, passing the so-called '*Sanctuary of Ptah*' on the way — this being a series of small shrines and votive stelae dedicated on behalf of the kings and high officials in the Nineteenth and Twentieth Dynasties. Modest these monuments may be, but in the utter quietude of their setting they are powerfully evocative. The other branch continues into the hills to the north and finally arrives — on an eminence that commands a stunning view both of the river valley and the Valley of the Kings — at the *camp* used by the workmen during their 'weekly' labour. The way station itself is unspectacular, consisting of mere huts and lean-to's built of undressed local stone. Visitors who follow the path that skirts the cliff behind the royal valley, however, will see another dimension of this settlement in the innumerable tiny shrines which dot the hillside facing the shrine. These rough shelters, simply made by propping up limestone flakes, contained the workers' memorial stelae, and a few of these were still *in situ* when the site was first visited in the nineteenth century. All have since vanished, into museums or private hands, but the 'high place' remains, a mute witness to the piety of the men who built the great tombs in the valley below.

Selected tombs at Deir el-Medina:[1] *1*, 217, 359**

The tombs, arranged in terraces on the hills north and west of the village, date mostly

1. A star attached to a tomb number at Thebes will indicate that the tomb is open to visitors. Many of the most interesting are closed, unfortunately, although it is hoped that a happier medium between security and accessibility will be reached in the future. Most visitors to Thebes can form at least a fair impression of the various styles on the basis of the open tombs. Persons with special interests should acquire permission for specific tombs from the Egyptian Antiquities Organization in Cairo.

Fig. 98 **Sennedjem*** *Servant in the Place of Truth*

(Th 1)   *Dynasty XIX*

1 Deceased adores Atum (outer lintel), horizon deities (left thickness), Ished Tree with cat slaying serpent (right thickness), deceased adoring horizon disc held by Nūt (inner soffit).
2 Mummy on couch, with Isis and Nephthys as hawks; family of deceased below.
3 Deceased with wife adore Underworld gods.
4 Anubis tends mummy on couch, deceased squats before Osiris, deceased led by Anubis.
5 Baboons adore barque of Rē (top), with scenes of deceased in Fields of Iaru below.
6 Deceased and wife adore guardians of gates, with relatives below.

* *Brightly painted tomb chamber, in almost perfect condition.*

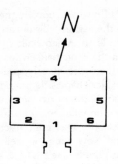

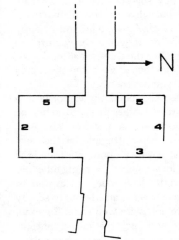

Fig. 99 **Ipuy** *Sculptor**

(Th 217)

1 Deceased rewarded by king from palace window; funeral procession to tomb; house and garden of deceased; procession of sacred barques, and laundry scenes.
2 Deceased and family.
3 Agricultural scenes; herding animals; market scenes; wine press and vintage scenes; marsh scenes.
4 Felling tree, making tomb- and cult-furniture, fishing.
5 Deceased and family offer to Underworld gods.

* *Damaged and now locked, but containing a wealth of imaginative detail.*

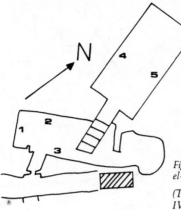

Fig. 100   **Inherkhau** *Foreman (of 'Crew' at Deir el-Medina)**

(Th 359)   Dynasty XX (Ramesses III–Ramesses IV)

1   *Book of Gates* scenes.
2   Scenes from *Book of the Dead*, including playing *senet*; relatives offer to deceased and wife.
3   Deceased and wife offer to past kings and queens.
4   Scenes in Underworld.
5   Deceased before various mythological beings, including Ba on pylon, hawk god opening mouth of mummy, and priest presenting Osiris statue and *shawabti* box to family.

* *Burial chamber, almost as well preserved as Sennedjem's.*

to the Ramesside period, though there are a few from the settlement's earliest period of occupation in the Eighteenth Dynasty. The best examples are close to the bottom and are noted both for their exquisite painting and lively rendering of subjects sacred and profane.

QURNET MURAI

The hill east of Deir el-Medina, known as Qurnet Murai, is the first of the private cemeteries found along the main road (see Map, p. 280). The German Institute's expedition house (at the top of the road) marks its northern limit, while ruins of a Coptic monastery crown the summit. The tombs

(see Fig. 97) are small and date from the later Eighteenth Dynasty into the Ramesside period. Some of the officials buried here served the kings of the late Eighteenth Dynasty (e.g., the viceroy of Nubia, Huy, and the later deified sage, Amenhotep, Son of Hapu, whose ruined tomb has recently been discovered) or were employed in their mortuary temples nearby. By this time, however, the tombs of crown servants were not necessarily located in the vicinity of their masters' mortuary complexes, but were often built some distance away at sites offering a better view or superior quality of limestone.

Selected Tombs at Qurnet Murai: 40, 277.

Fig. 101 **Amenhotep** called **Huy** *Viceroy of Nubia**

(Th 40) Late Dynasty XVIII (Tutankhamun)

1 Deceased receives produce on barge, with offering bearers, sailors, dancers and musicians.
2 Deceased inspects freight ships.
3 Deceased arrives from Nubia with tribute ships.
4 Deceased marshals Nubian tribute and envoys.
5 Deceased presents Nubian tribute to king.
6 Deceased appointed to office by king, with sub-scenes of registering animals in Nubia (?).
7 Deceased with Syrian tribute before king.

* *Lively subject-matter and elaborate painting.*

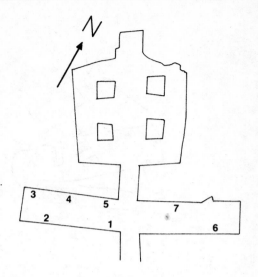

Fig. 102 **Amenemōnet** *God's Father in the Mansion of Amenhotep III**

(Th 277) Ramesside

1–2 Procession with statues of Amenhotep III and Tiyi, rites before Mentuhotep I and queen; rites before deceased's tomb and funeral procession.
3 Deceased and wife adore Osiris and Isis, Shu and Tefnut.
4 Deceased adores Osiris and Ma'at (double scene).
5 Deceased adores Horus.
6 Offering incense and libation to Amenhotep III and Tiyi.
7 Niche (with offering table inside) and shrine: deceased adoring Osiris and Anubis.

* *i.e., priest in mortuary temple of Amenhotep III.*

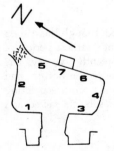

SHEIKH ABD'EL-QURNA

A narrow plain opens up to the north of Qurnet Murai and Deir el-Medina, wedged between the cultivation and the cliffs of the western desert. In the centre of this plain rises a large, rambling hill that extends to the north: this is *Sheikh Abd'el-Qurna*, named after a Muslim saint whose brightly painted tomb chapel rests on the summit, near the northern end. The ancient tombs below this

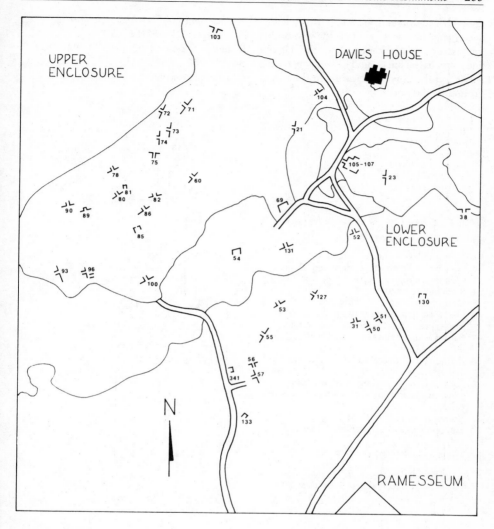

Fig. 103 **Sheikh Abd'el-Qurna**

shrine are particularly worth visiting because they have kept their external features to an extent unparalleled elsewhere in this area and, in the silent and unpopulated environment of the locality, evoke a glimpse of what the necropolis was like in its heyday (see Chapter 6, pp. 69–70). The open tombs lie lower, amid the houses of 'Old Qurna' village to the south (see Fig. 103). For the visitor's convenience, this cemetery may be divided into three main areas: the village, occupying the low ground north-west of the Ramesseum (see Chapter 18); the Upper Enclosure in the hill behind the village, to the west; and the Lower Enclosure, in the rising ground to the north.

Selected tombs of Sheikh Abd'el-Qurna:
A. *Village:* 52*, 55*, 56*, 57*.
B. *Upper Enclosure:* 60, 69*, 71, 74, 78, 81, 86, 90, 96*, 100*, 103*.
C. *Lower Enclosure:* 23, 38, 107*.

Fig. 104 **Tchay** *Royal Scribe of the Dispatches**

(Th 23)   Dynasty XIX (Merneptah)

1 Tree goddess scene.
2 Pharaoh's foreign office; deceased's house.
3 Offering bringers, preparing mummies.
4 Rites before mummy.
5 Deceased rewarded by king.
6 Deceased dedicates offerings; tree goddess scene; priest before deceased and family.
7 Baboons adore sun barque, with king adoring Atum (above doorway).
8 *Book of Gates;* deceased before Amenhotep I and Ahmose-Nofretari.
9 *Book of Gates,* including lutist with song.
10 Feast of Sokar (top), with funeral procession below.
11 Scenes from *Book of Gates.*
12 Sarcophagus Room: scenes of deceased before gods.
13 Statues of deceased and family.

* *Although this tomb is normally closed to visitors, the reliefs in the open courtyard may be seen without official permission.*

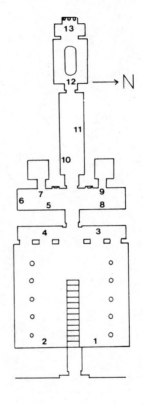

Fig. 105 **Djeserkarēsonb** *Scribe, Grain counter of the Granary of the Divine Offerings of Amun*

(Th 38)   Dynasty XVIII (Thutmose IV)

1 Deceased with family consecrates offerings.
2 Agricultural scenes.
3 Offerings to deceased.
4 Deceased and wife offer on braziers, with offering bringers.
5 Banquet.

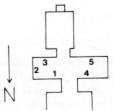

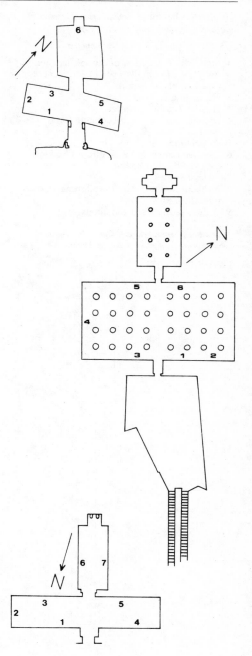

Fig. 106   **Nakht** *Astronomer of Amun**

(Th 52)   Dynasty XVIII (Thutmose IV?)

1 Agricultural scenes.
2 False door, with sub-scene of tree goddess.
3 Banquet.
4 Offering bringers and priests before deceased.
5 Marshland scene.
6 Statue niche (statuette removed, lost at sea).

* *Superb paintings of lively subjects.*

Fig. 107   **Ramose** *Vizier**

*(Th 55)   Dynasty XVIII (Amenhotep III–
Amenhotep IV)*

1 Deceased and wife consecrate offerings.
2 Statue of deceased purified, deceased in
  offering list ritual.
3 Banquet.
4 Funeral procession.
5 Deceased before Amenhotep IV and Ma'at
  (conventional style).
6 Deceased before Amenhotep IV and Nefertiti,
  receiving foreign delegates (revolutionary
  style).

* *Ramose is a transitional figure in the reign of Amenhotep
IV, who is seen in this tomb both in the conventional
Theban style and in the later, more naturalistic manner he
adopted as he became increasingly dissatisfied with the old
religion. He had not changed his name to Akhenaten by the
time Ramose died (5–6). In the banquet scenes (2, 3)
Ramose advertises his prominent connections, including the
sage Amenhotep, Son of Hapu.*

Fig. 108   **Userhēt** *Royal scribe, Child of the
Nursery**

(Th 56)   Dynasty XVIII (Amenhotep II)

1 Inspecting cattle (top), agricultural scenes
  (bottom).
2 Stela, with statue purified (left) and Opening
  of the Mouth (right).
3 Banquet.
4 Deceased and wife offering.
5 Storehouse scene; registering recruits;
  barbers.
6 Military escort and hunt in desert; marshland
  scenes and viticulture.
7 Funeral procession.

* *Title indicating that its possessor was brought up with
the young king. The tomb itself is worth seeing for its
range of subjects and unusual paintings.*

Fig. 109 **Khaemhēt** *Royal Scribe, Overseer of Granaries of Upper and Lower Egypt**

(Th 57) Dynasty XVIII (Amenhotep III)

1 Stela with illustration of canopic jars and shrine; stela with illustrated instruments for Opening of the Mouth.
2 Harvesting scenes.
3 Freight ships and market.
4 Men bringing cattle before king (original head in Berlin).
5 Agricultural scenes.
6 Deceased rewarded with officials by king (original head in Berlin).
7 Funeral scenes.
8 Fields of Iaru and Abydos pilgrimage, with offering scenes.
9 Statues of deceased and family.

* *Carved in superb raised relief, but with a range of subjects more usually seen in painted tombs.*

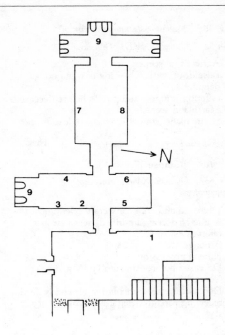

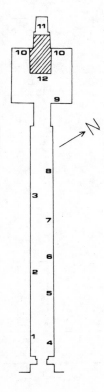

Fig. 110 **Antefoker** *Vizier**

(Th 60) Dynasty XII (Sesostris I)

1 Gardening and picking grapes, dancers and tumblers, filling granary.
2 Abydos pilgrimage.
3 Funeral procession.
4 Agricultural scenes.
5 Marsh scenes, with sub-scene of agriculture.
6 Hunt in desert.
7 Butchers, bakers, brewers, cooks.
8 Inspecting New Year's gifts.
9 Musicians, offering bringers, butchers.
10 False doors.
11 Shrine of wife.
12 Statue of wife (found in shaft).

* *One of the seminal tombs of the Theban necropolis: see it if you possibly can.*

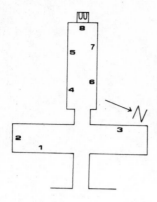

Fig. 111 **Menna** *Scribe of Royal Fields**

(Th 69) *Dynasty XVIII (Thutmose IV?)*

1 Agricultural scenes.
2 Deceased and wife before Osiris.
3 Banquet (top), with offering list ritual below.
4 Funeral procession.
5 Weighing scene.
6 Abydos pilgrimage, rites before mummy.
7 Marshland scenes.
8 Statue niche.

* Superb painting, comparable to Nakht's tomb (p. 287).

Fig. 112 **Senenmut** *Chief Steward of Queen Hatshepsut*

(Th 71) *Dynasty XVIII (Hatshepsut)*

1 Remains of Cretan offering bearers.*
2 Ruined hall, with name stones of deceased.
3 Statue niche with remains of statue.

* Except for the paintings at (1), the tomb is open: see above, Chapter 6, pp. 69–70.

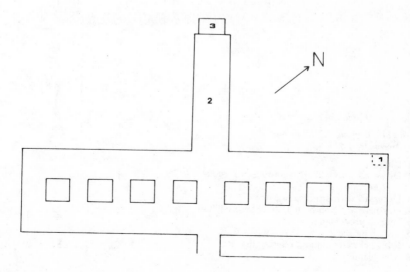

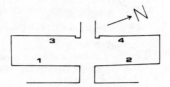

Fig. 113 **Tchanuny** *Royal scribe, Commander of Soldiery*

(Th 74) *Dynasty XVIII (Thutmose IV)*

1–2 Offering scenes; deceased and family
before Osiris.
3 Military parade.
4 Deceased inspects recording of recruits and
horses.

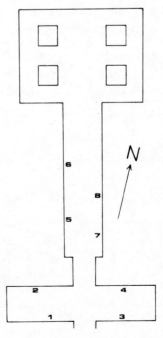

Fig. 114 **Horemheb** *Scribe of Recruits*

(Th 78) *Dynasty XVIII (Thutmose III–
Amenhotep III)*

1 Banquet.
2 Deceased before king; recording provisions
at storehouse.
3 Deceased with princess on knee.
4 Northern and Southern Tribute before [king].
5 Funeral procession.
6 Weighing scene.
7 Rites before mummies, offering list, etc.
8 Marshland scenes.

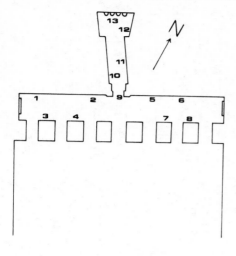

Fig. 115 **Ineni** *Overseer of the Granary of Amun*

(Th 81)   Dynasty XVIII (Amenhotep I – Hatshepsut)

1 Produce brought for temple.
2 Northern and Southern tribute.
3 Hunt in desert.
4 House of deceased.
5 Inspecting animals and fowl.
6 [Fowling] and fishing, with sub-scene of vintage.
7 Agriculture (sowing, etc.).
8 Agriculture (harvest).
9 Rites before mummies.
10 Funeral procession.
11 Offering list ritual.
12 Banquet.
13 Statues of deceased and family.

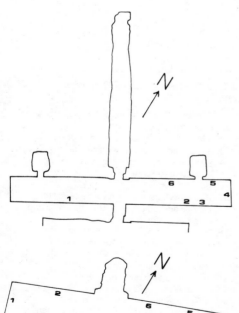

Fig. 116 **Menkheperrēsonb** *First Prophet of Amun*

(Th 86)   Dynasty XVIII (Thutmose III)

1 Agricultural scenes.
2 Bringing animals, produce, fowl.
3 Inspecting temple workshops.
4 Deceased receiving produce of Coptos and Lower Nubia.
5 Viticulture (top), with bringing produce and animals (below).
6 Deceased presents Northern tribute to king.

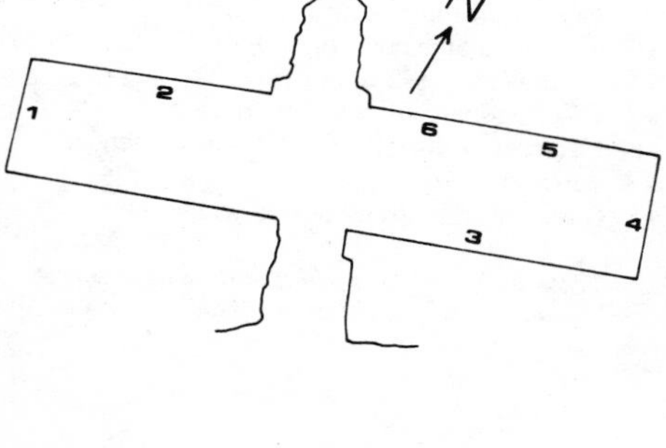

Fig. 117 **Nebamun** *Captain of police troops in West Thebes*

(Th 90)   Dynasty XVIII (Thutmose IV– Amenhotep III)

1 Chariot and [king] in royal barge.
2 Appointment to office by [king].
3 Deceased and wife offering; banquet.
4 Stela, with ritual scenes at sides.
5 Viticulture; cattle branded and recorded.
6 Presenting Syrian tribute to [king].

Fig. 118 **Sennefer** *Mayor of the Southern City (= Thebes)**

(Th 96) Dynasty XVIII (Amenhotep II)

1 Hathor and Osiris with deceased, and funeral procession.
2 Abydos pilgrimage.
3 Mummy on couch tended by Anubis, and *Ba* between Isis and Nephthys.
4 Tree goddess scene.
5 Deceased and wife under tree.
6 Deceased purified by four priests.
7, 8 Wife offers flowers to tomb owner.

Ceiling Painted vines and grape clusters.

* Burial chamber only; the upper tomb is used as a magazine and is inaccessible, but the fine quality of the paintings here displayed is ample reward.

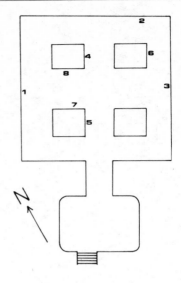

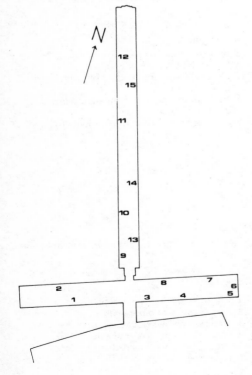

Fig. 119 **Rekhmirē** *Vizier**

(Th 100) Dynasty XVIII (Thutmose III–Amenhotep II)

1 [Deceased] in judgement hall collecting taxes from Upper Egypt.
2 [Deceased] inspects foreign tribute.
3 [Deceased] inspects taxing of Lower Egypt.
4 [Deceased] inspects temple workshops.
5 Agricultural scenes.
6 Banquet.
7 [Deceased] inspects products of eastern border and marshes, with viticulture and bringing animals.
8 [Deceased] hunting in desert and fowling.
9 Preparing food and storing produce in temple storehouses, distributing rations to slaves, bringing various products.
10 Industries and building scenes.
11 Funeral procession and rites.
12 Offerings and offering list ritual.
13 Deceased returning from royal audience.
14 Banquet.
15 Rites before statues of deceased.

* Malicious damage to some figures of the tomb owner is noted in square brackets. The paintings are of unrivalled subtlety.

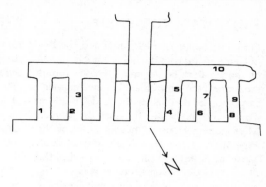

Fig. 120 **Dagi** *Vizier**

(Th 103) End of Dynasty XI

1 Gardening and picking grapes.
2 Preparing reeds for weaving.
3 Crossing water in canoe.
4–5 Abydos pilgrimage.
6 Women spinning and weaving.
7 Storing grain in granary.
8 Brewing and cooking.
9 Baking.
10 Industrial scenes.

* *Tomb is accessible, exposed to the open air; scenes damaged, but interesting.*

Fig. 121 **Nefersekheru** *Steward of the Palace of Amenhotep III**

(Th 107) Dynasty XVIII (Amenhotep III)

1 Offering list ritual before statue of deceased.
2 Statue of deceased purified by priests.

* *Portico of tomb accessible, carved in sunk relief of exquisite quality. Interior unfinished, filled with debris.*

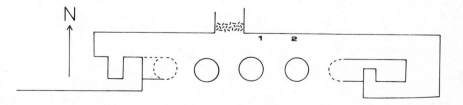

KHOKHA AND ASASIF

Between Sheikh Abd'el-Qurna and the bay of Deir el-Bahri rises the hill of Khokha. Some of the greatest Eighteenth Dynasty tombs are found here, as well as the few fragmentary rock-cut burials of the Old Kingdom. To the north, below the majestic domed Metropolitan House – headquarters of the expedition of the New York Metropolitan Museum of Art in years gone by – lies the plain of Asasif, which stretches between the cultivation to the back of the amphitheatre of Deir el-Bahri (see Fig. 122). Many tombs of the later period (Dynasties XXII–XXVI) are found on the Asasif, as well as a few dating to the Eleventh Dynasty. Although the late tombs are locked, one may wander through the plain to admire the imposing mudbrick pylons of Montuemhēt (Th. 34) and Pabasa (Th. 279), as well as the great open sun court of Montuemhēt's tomb, which can be seen but not entered. Important tombs of the Eleventh Dynasty are found ranged along the hills on the north side of the bay, but these too are inaccessible.

Selected tombs of Khokha: 49*, 181, 188, 192*, 296, 409*.
Asasif: 34, 279, 414.

Fig. 122 **Khokha** *and* **Asasif**

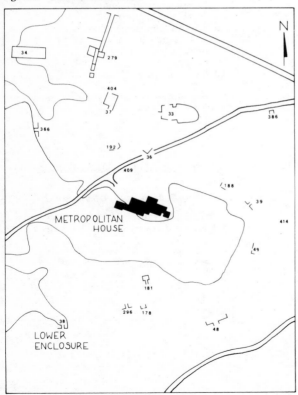

Fig. 123   **Neferhotep** *Chief Scribe of Amun**

(Th 49)   Late Dynasty XVIII (Ay)

1 Funeral procession.
2 Wife honoured by queen from balcony;
  deceased returning to horse and chariot;
  banquet, with scenes in garden, musicians.
3 Deceased rewarded by king.
4 Funeral procession.
5 Deceased with Osiris and Hathor; wife with
  priests and offering bringers.
6 Tree goddess scene (mostly destroyed).
7 Deceased receives bouquet of Amun at
  temple, with industrial, herding and
  gardening scenes.
8 Deceased before Osiris and Anubis.
9 Deceased offers to Western Goddess; stela.
10 Statue room.

* *Worth seeing for its unusual range of subjects.*

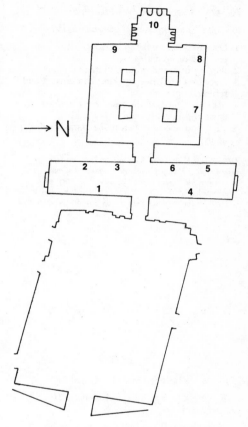

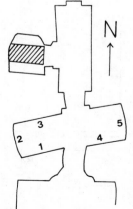

Fig. 124   **Nebamun** and **Ipuky** *Sculptors**

(Th 181)   Dynasty XVIII (Amenhotep III)

1 Ipuky leaving and returning to tomb;
  banquet scene.
2–3 Funeral procession to tomb.
4 Ipuky adores Amenhotep I and Ahmose-
  Nefertari; Nebamun inspects workshops.
5 Ipuky adores Osiris and four sons of Horus;
  two tomb owners before parents (double
  scene).

* *The tomb is decorated on behalf of both men, who were
married to the same woman; but it is not certain which
one of them was senior to the other. Superb paintings of
conventional subjects are to be seen in this tomb.*

Fig. 125 **Parennefer** *Royal Butler, Steward**

(Th 188) Dynasty XVIII (Amenhotep IV)

1 Deceased before [king] in kiosk, recording produce of granaries.
2 Picking fruit and grapes, vintage scene.
3 Deceased rewarded by [king and queen], and returns home.
4 Various figures of deceased offer bouquets to [king and queen].
5 King and deceased before Rē-Harakhti at altar.

* The deceased also owned a tomb at El Amarna, built after the king changed his name to Akhenaten and established his capital in the new city. The reliefs and paintings in the tomb are not well preserved, but are of interest for their subject-matter and their transitional style.

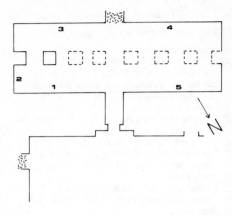

Fig. 126 **Kheruef** *Steward of Queen Tiyi**

(Th 192) Dynasty XVIII (Amenhotep III–Amenhotep IV)

1 Amenhotep IV and mother, Tiyi, before Atum and Rē-Harakhti (lintel, double scene).
2 Amenhotep IV before Rē-Harakhti and before parents.
3 Deceased before Amenhotep III, Hathor and Tiyi inside kiosk.
4 King and queen leave palace for jubilee rites, with courtiers, dancers and clappers.
5 King and queen navigate on lake at conclusion of jubilee.
6 Deceased before Amenhotep III in kiosk.
7–8 Amenhotep III erects and adores Djed Pillar (right and left), with sub-scenes of men driving cattle, fishing, and stick-fighting.
9 Columned hall (collapsed).

* A good example of an elaborate tomb of the later Eighteenth Dynasty, it contains unusual scenes from the royal jubilee carved in raised relief of exquisite quality.

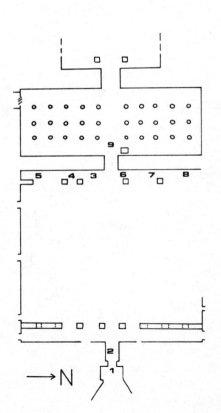

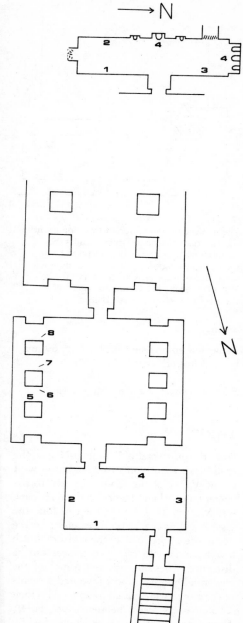

Fig. 127   **Nefersekheru** Scribe of the Divine Offerings of all the Gods, Treasury official in the Southern City*

(Th 296)   Ramesside

1 Book of Gates, including playing senet, weighing scene, drinking from pool, deceased before Amenhotep I and Ahmose-Nofretari.
2 Funerary scenes, including harpist, and deceased before Osiris and Harsiēse with mummiform Isis.
3 Book of Gates, including deceased with Thoth before Osiris and Ma'at; funeral procession to tomb, including Hathor cow emerging from mountain.
4 Statues.

* The lively paintings and the life-size statues of the deceased and his family are both well preserved.

Montuemhēt Mayor of Thebes, Fourth Prophet of Amun

(Th 34)   Late Dynasty XXV–Early Dynasty XXVI

Although the tomb is formally closed, visitors who wander about the Plain of Asasif may examine the large mudbrick pylon which dominates the landscape, and look down into the enormous sun-court, with its statues of Montuemhēt and other sculptured features carved out of the native limestone along its walls (see above, Chapter 6, p. 70).

Fig. 128   **Pabasa** Steward of the Divine Votaress

(Th 279)   Dynasty XXVI (Psamtik I)

1–2 Deceased receives offerings, with sub-scene of Abydos procession (below).
3–4 Deceased receives offerings, with sub-scene of funeral procession (below).
5 Scenes showing bedroom prepared.
6 Spinning, cleaning and netting fish.
7 Bee-keeping, capturing birds, picking fruit.
8 Viticulture.

Fig. 129 **Sa-Mut** called **Kiki** *Chief Cattle Counter of the Estate of Amun**

(Th 409)   Dynasty XIX (Ramesses II)

1 Stelae.
2 Lutanist before deceased and wife.
3 Agricultural scenes; deceased worships Mut and receives offerings.
4 Deceased offers to various divinities, including Amun-Rē (note figures of Ramesses II worshipping the god on the sides of his kiosk).
5 *Book of Gates*; deceased inspects cattle.
6 Banquet; funeral procession.
7 Judgement scene.
8 Raising Djeh Pillar, and tree goddess scene (both unfinished).
9 Mummy on couch, with masked mourners.
10 Statues of deceased and family.

* *Nicely painted and accessible Ramesside tomb. The deceased appears to have been an unusual character, boasting in texts at (3) that he disinherited his family in order to bequeath his property to the goddess Mut.*

Ankh-Hor *Chief Steward of the Divine Votaress of Amun; Overseer of Upper Egypt*

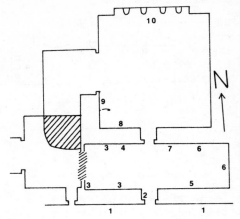

(Th 414)   Dynasty XXVI (Psamtik II–Apries)
The meticulous restoration of this monument by the Austrian mission in Egypt permits the essential features of this type of tomb to be seen, even though little of the decoration is preserved (see above, Chapter 6, p. 70). Visits can be made by prior arrangement with the chief inspector of West Thebes.

DRA-ABU'L-NAGGA

The range of hills known today as Dra-abu'l-Nagga (see Map, p. 299) extends for over 1 km. north of the bay of Deir el-Bahri. Modern occupation is quite heavy near the south end but falls off as one proceeds northwards, so that the far end presents a scene of utter desolation, broken only by the large domed houses that stand on the hill opposite the cemetery and which are occupied today by foreign missions and members of the Egyptian Antiquities Service. The area has suffered heavily from spoliation and unscientific excavation – a pity, for some of the earliest and latest tombs built at Thebes during the New Kingdom were found here. The royal necropolis of the Seventeenth Dynasty has disappeared today and none of the tombs are kept open for visitors, but the mudbrick pyramid shrines of the great

Ramesside tomb (see Chapter 6, p. 69) may be seen from the road (Fig. 130).

Selected tomb at Dra-abu'l-Nagga: 15.

TARIF

From the north end of Dra-abu'l-Nagga, the road bends sharply in two directions – west to the Valley of the Kings, and east to the irrigation canal and thence to the river bank (see Map, p. 247). Taking the east fork, the visitor will pass a Muslim cemetery on the north side of the road, in the midst of which low mounds with carved entrances can be discerned. These are the *saff* tombs of the Eleventh Dynasty, where favoured servants of the crown were buried together with their royal masters (see Chapter 6, pp. 68–9). These 'row' burials are now all engulfed by the cemetery and the village of Tarif. The tombs themselves − long plundered and innocent of any decorative attraction − will be unrewarding for most visitors, and foreigners are advised not to wander through this area without a guide who is on good terms with the inhabitants.

At the canal, the paved road turns south. If you take the unpaved north turning, however, another 500 m. will bring you to two mudbrick mastabas, completely devoid of decoration, but having on their south-east sides the primitive offering niche of the earlier Old Kingdom. Excavated early in the 1970s by the German Archaeological Institute, they are among the most recently found, and yet the oldest monuments that the visitor is likely to see in West Thebes.

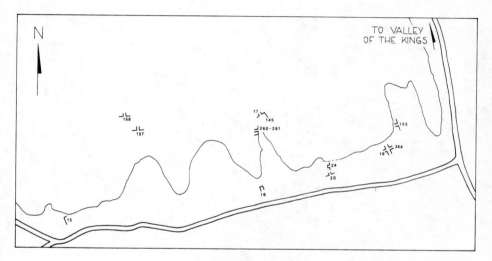

Fig. 130 **Dra-abu'l-Nagga**

Fig. 131 **Tetaky** *King's Son,* * *Mayor of the Southern City*

(Th 15)   *Early Dynasty XVIII*

1 Queen Ahmose-Nefertari before Hathor cow.†
2 Funeral procession.
3 Deceased with wife seated under tree, with agricultural scenes beyond.
4 Banquet.
5 Deceased with butcher offers to Osiris.
6 Shrine, offering scenes, with man picking grapes (left wall).

* *Honorific title, perhaps connected with the deceased's office as Mayor of Thebes.*
† *Note the simulated wooden beam painted along the length of the ceiling in this chamber.*

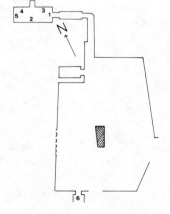

20. Luxor to Aswan

The main road through Upper Egypt continues south from Luxor on the east bank. Bridges at Esna and Edfu will allow you to reach all major sites on the west bank except for the monuments at Gebel Silsila West (see below). A poor but passable country road runs along the west bank as far as Edfu: most visitors, however, will not have the specialized interest to make worthwhile a visit to *Nagada* (between Qena and Luxor), *Armant* and *Gebelein* (between Luxor and Esna), or *Hieraconpolis* (between Esna and Edfu), although these sites are of considerable importance.

The first stop south of Thebes on the east bank is at *Tod*: at Armant Station (21 km. south of Luxor) turn east, across the tracks, and proceed inland about 6 km. before coming to the village at the cultivation's edge. Depending on the tracks followed, one will arrive either at the front or back of the temple: this itinerary will proceed from the front, on the west side. The inevitable quay leads down to an avenue of sphinxes, with the temple at the east end. Before reaching it, turn off the north side of the avenue to visit a small ambulatory 'way station', presumably for the barque of Montu, built during the reign of Thutmose III. The columned court and the rooms of the main temple were built during the Ptolemaic and Roman periods to connect with a temple of the Middle Kingdom behind. Only the front wall of this earlier building survives, but the visitor will be able to see how the original decoration was either usurped or reworked in later antiquity. A silver hoard found under the floor in one of the rooms of the Middle Kingdom temple is now on display in the Cairo Museum (see Chapter 10, p. 121). The denuded rear of the Graeco-Roman building also allows one to inspect the treasury, a hidden room located above the chapel at the south side of the hall. Blocks from earlier building phases, as far back as the Fifth Dynasty, are stored in an open-air magazine on the hill south-east of the temple.

The provincial cemetery of *Moalla* is located about 15 km. south of Armant Station, on the east side of the road. Of the two decorated tombs found here, the more important belongs to Ankhtify, whose career has been sketched above (Chapter 3, pp. 48–9) and whose funerary monument itself possesses considerable interest. The architect has eschewed straight lines in order to follow the stronger veins in the rock, giving the tomb an irregular but oddly graceful appearance. Moreover, the paintings on the walls have a wealth of incident and also a force sometimes lacking in the more refined work found in major Old Kingdom cemeteries. A few metres north of Ankhtify's tomb is the smaller chapel of Sobekhotep which, though roughly executed and not well preserved, has some unusual features.

At *Esna* (55 km. south of Luxor) turn west and cross the river. The remains of the temple are in the centre of town, at the bottom of a deep pit formed by the accumulation of rubbish

Statue of the falcon god Horus in the forecourt of his temple at Edfu

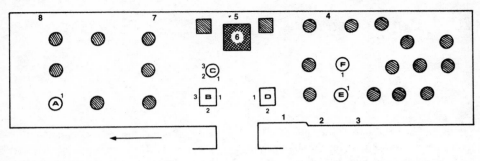

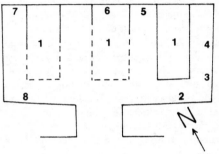

Fig. 132 Ankhtify

(M 1) Dynasty IX

1 Deceased and family fishing and fowling in the marsh; note how the wife seizes an unfortunate fowl by its beak.
2 Deceased spears and reels in fish: details of fish in water are worth studying.
3 Deceased supervises butchers.
4 Sub-scene: rows of cattle (some with braided hair) and other animals.
5 Deceased and wife seated (from false door).
6 Shaft.
7 Remains of banquet: ladies seated, butchers preparing meat.
8 Rows of huntsmen carrying bows and sheaves of arrows, with hunting dogs.
7–8 Sub-scene: rows of donkeys carrying grain.

Column A (1) Industries, including making of door and bed.
Column B (1) Man carrying piebald calf; (2) man bringing gazelle; (3) piebald cattle.
Column C (1) Deceased facing door of tomb, holding staff and flower; (2) men bringing small cattle and rabbits to cooks; (3) men roasting and boiling meat.
Column D (1) Deceased with staff and sceptre faces into tomb, three dogs beside him; remains of butchery below; (2) remains of baking and brewing.
Column E (1) Remains of seeding, ploughing.
Column F (1) Choir of women, holding hands.

Fig. 133 Sobekhotep

(M 2) First Intermediate Period

1 Emplacements for burials.
2 Men filling storehouse.
3 Remains of funeral: deceased lying on bed.
4 Deceased faces wife and son.
3–4 Sub-scene: remains of industries.
5–7 Top: hunt in desert.
5–6 Bottom: bringing animals and produce.
7 Bottom: two rows of men and women approaching deceased and wife.
8 Offering bearers before deceased and wife.

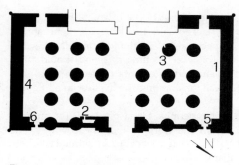

Fig. 134 **Esna** *Temple of Khnum*

from settlements since ancient times. Only the first hypostyle hall is left of a monument that was no doubt constructed along lines similar to those of the Dendera or Edfu temples. As at Edfu (below, p. 311), the lofty hall is supported by columns having wonderfully varied floral capitals, and the relief on the walls has a certain elegance as well: note, for example, the netting of fowl and other beings (representing hostile spirits) on the north wall (Fig. 134, 1). The back wall of the building is the façade of the destroyed Ptolemaic temple, to which the hypostyle was added by the Romans. The regularity of the present plan is disrupted only on the south side of the east wall, with the introduction of a small engaged room – a glorified closet – which we shall see repeated in structures such as the Edfu temple (2).

Space prevents even a summary of the religious scenes and inscriptions that crowd the walls at Esna. The influence of classical Western art may be seen in one scene on a column (3) where the king offers a laurel wreath to the gods. The offering scenes on the south wall (4) were carved under

Septimius Severus and his sons, Caracalla and Geta, the latter of whom was erased following his assassination by his elder brother in A.D. 212. Finally, the visitor may gain some sense of the fantastically esoteric uses to which the hieroglyphic script could be put from two texts, where the signs are almost exclusively crocodiles (5) and rams (6).

Returning to the east bank, we drive south through a subtly changing countryside: the limestone rock-bed characteristic of the northern Nile Valley begins to give way to Nubian sandstone, but the change – though it is most pronounced at Es-Sebaiya (between Esna and Edfu: see Chapter 1, p. 15) – is not strongly marked. Presently (32 km. south of Esna), the fields become narrower, hugging the river, and the traveller will see the mudbrick ramparts of *El Kab* rising up on his right. Nekheb, as it was known in antiquity, is one of the most historic sites in Egypt. Home of the vulture goddess Nekhbet (one of the 'Two Goddesses' who extended protection over the king from earliest times), it was somewhat eclipsed by its sister city Hieraconpolis, which lies directly across the river. By the time of the New Kingdom, however, the tables had been reversed, and El Kab had a certain additional importance as the northern limit of the area under the jurisdiction of the Viceroy of Nubia (see Chapter 4, pp. 56–8).

The present town probably dates to the later Pharaonic period (the north-east corner lying over part of the Old Kingdom cemetery). The ramparts are its most impressive feature, being over twelve metres thick and equipped with generous interior defences: the visitor can pass through the best preserved of the city gates, on the east side (see Fig. 135) and then ascend the wall, either by an inner staircase to the north or a broad ramp south of the entrance. Inside the enclosure, all is overgrown and desolate: the houses in the south-west quarter of the town date to the Graeco-Roman Period and are reduced to their foundations, so the visitor may press on to the temples, which are surrounded by their own enclosure wall (Fig. 135, insert). The older of the two present structures, the Temple of Thoth, was built by Ramesses II and is partly cut off by the rebuilding of the adjoining Temple of Nekhbet during the Late Period: many re-used blocks of New and even Middle Kingdom date can be seen in the foundations of both buildings. Those who seek the measure of a civilization in its plumbing will find part of the Nekhbet Temple's drainage system exposed in front of its second pylon. On leaving the divine precinct, pass the malodorous pond that was once the sacred lake and follow what archaeologists believe to be the remains of a circular double wall, dating to the Second Dynasty, in the north-west quarter of the town.

The most important of El Kab's antiquities are the rock-cut tombs ranged along the hill, north-east of the town. At present they are locked and the keys are kept at the Inspectorate of Antiquities in Edfu, but the visitor who has time to spend should make advance arrangements to see these tombs, which rank among the liveliest in all Egypt.

If time permits, try also to visit the antiquities in the wadi east of the town – 'The Valley', as it was called in antiquity, where many Nubian gods are also worshipped. About 2.5 km. from the road, on the north side (Fig. 135) is a temple built by Ptolemies VIII–X, probably on the site of an earlier structure: a staircase ascends from the desert floor, reaching two columned vestibules before a sanctuary carved into the rock. At the base of the cliff, south of the Ptolemaic structure, is a small box-like chapel (referred to locally as *El Hammam*, 'the Bath'), which was built by Setau, Viceroy of Nubia under Ramesses II (and not to be confused with the owner of EK 4); the keys to the interior must be secured beforehand at Edfu, but the reliefs inside – roughly carved and poorly preserved – are worth no great trouble. Far more interesting is a large crag, further out, in the centre of the wadi: known as 'Vulture Rock' because of its suggestive shape, it is covered with drawings and inscriptions dating from prehistoric times down to the late Old Kingdom. Finally, on the south side, about 4 km. from the main road, is a small chapel of Amenhotep III, apparently a resting place for the barque of Nekhbet when the goddess visited her 'valley' (the keys, again, are kept in Edfu). Inside, on the west wall, flanking the entrance, the king appears enthroned with his father, Thutmose IV, under whom the chapel was begun. The rest of the single room contains ritual scenes, brightly painted by the restorers of the building in late antiquity. A number of graffiti, carved on the walls by early European visitors to the site, are also worth examining.

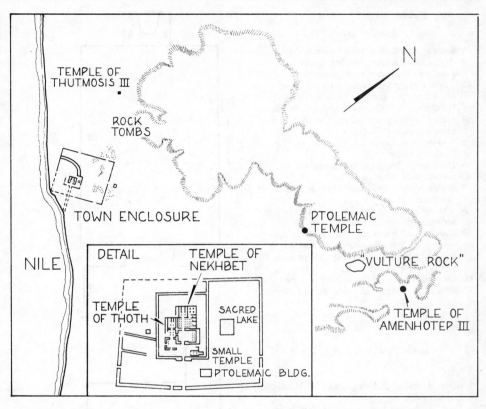

Fig. 135   **El Kab** *cemeteries and temples*

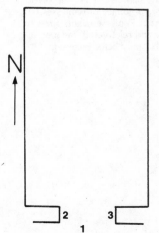

Fig. 136   **Ahmose Pennekhbet** *Overseer of the Seal*

(EK 2)   Early Dynasty XVIII

1 Lintel: priests with censer, and titles of deceased.
2 Biographical text; deceased with brother and [son].
3 Biographical text; deceased with [son] and another couple.

Fig. 137 **Paheri** *Mayor of El Kab*

(EK 3) Early to Middle Dynasty XVIII

1 Deceased kneeling, with hymn to Nekhbet.
2 Agricultural scenes; loading boats with produce; herdsmen with swine.
3 Top: offering bringers before deceased with prince on lap; vintage; bottom: offering bringers before deceased and wife in kiosk.
4 Funeral procession and rites, with deceased kneeling before Osiris.
5 Son offers to deceased and wife, with relatives below.
6 Deceased offers to two princes, and to parents with siblings below.
7 Statue of deceased, flanked by wife and mother.
8 Son with offering list and wife; brother as scribe, with servants below.
9 Banquet, with servants and musicians: one serving man speaks sharply to the lady in front of him and receives an angry look from another guest to his left.
10 Deceased with family worship before offerings; offering bringers and butchers below.

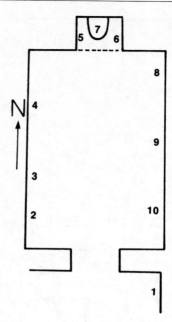

Fig. 138 **Setau** *First Prophet of Nekhbet*

(EK 4) Dynasty XX

1 Stela: deceased and wife adore Rē-Harakhti and Khepri.
2 Boats (including barque of Nekhbet) before [king] with tests of jubilee of Ramesses III.
3 Son-in-law, vizier Ramessesnakht, offers to deceased, wife and relatives at banquet.
4 Deceased with family before offerings.

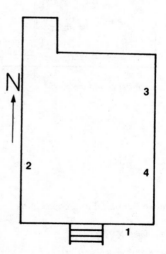

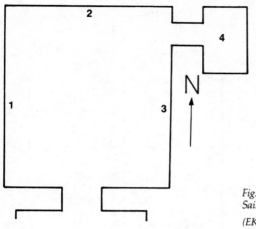

Fig. 139   **Ahmose, Son of Ebana*** *Chief of Sailors*

(EK 5)   Early Dynasty XVIII

1 Deceased's descendants before him, with relatives.
2 Grandson and relatives offer to deceased and wife (unfinished) and to parents of deceased.
3 Deceased with grandson Paheri, with text of war against Hyksos on right and Paheri's dedication text on left.
4 Burial chamber.

* *Grandfather of Paheri (EK 3), who built tomb for Ahmose.*

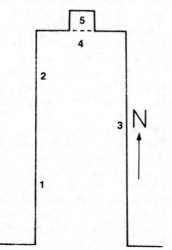

Fig. 140   **Renni** *Mayor of El Kab, Overseer of Priests*

(EK 7)   Amenhotep I

1 Agricultural scenes, counting cattle and swine, loading boats with produce, all before deceased.
2 Banquet, with musicians.
3 Funeral scenes, and banquet before father and wife.
4 Lintel: deceased before cartouche of Amenhotep I.
5 Remains of deceased's statue with jackals on either side.

Fig. 141 **Sobeknakht** *Overseer of Priests**

(EK 10)   Dynasty XIII

1 Above door: remains of filling granary;
   craftsmen below.
2 Top: funeral procession, with wheeled
   catafalque; bottom: fishing and fowling in
   marshes.
3 Five registers: chief craftsman before Ptah,
   carpenters, men hanging meat, etc.
4 Five registers: Osiris; man and woman with
   offering text; man weaving; man and boy
   with bows and arrows, etc.
5 Deceased with attendants, and long text.
6 Relatives before deceased and wife.
7 Hunt in desert.
8 Burial chamber.

* *This tomb is at present inaccessible.*

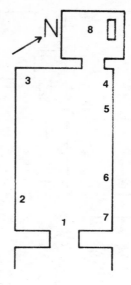

Half an hour's drive beyond the ruins of El Kab brings us to the eastern extension of Edfu (train stop). Before crossing the bridge, however, the visitor interested in the byways of Egypt may wish to visit some of the desert wadis east of the town: to do this, follow the main road east on the north side of the settlement. This road, which today ends at Mersa Alam on the Red Sea, was well travelled in antiquity, for it led to the rich goldmining district of Barramiya. Its importance is witnessed by the area's principal monument, the rock temple in the Wadi Mia, which Sety I built in memory of his re-opening of the old road: previously impassable for lack of water, it was given a new lease on life when the king dug new wells for the miners who worked in this forbidding district. The temple, 50 km. from Edfu, is on the south side of the main road. Graffiti and more formal votive inscriptions by the site's ancient visitors are found nearby.

Returning to Edfu East, cross the river to visit the great Temple of Horus at the edge of town. Though the pylons of the building can be seen for miles from any direction in the surrounding countryside, the approach to the building itself is a disappointment: the modern town presses against it to the south and east, so that visitors are obliged to enter the precinct from the rear. To the west, beyond the enclosure wall, lies the mound of the ancient city. But for the great temple and the mamissi, however, the structures in the cult centre of Horus have vanished.

Building inscriptions scattered through the *Temple of Edfu* give us a surprisingly detailed overview of its history. The present structure was begun in 237 B.C. under Ptolemy III, and completed (exclusive of the first hypostyle, the court and the pylon) in 212. The decoration of the walls took six years, being finished in 207, when the great door was set in its place; but the painting, furnishing and general outfitting of the temple could not be accomplished (owing to revolts in Upper Egypt) until 142 B.C. It was then that the formal dedication took place, though work on the interior was not actually finished until two years later. The hypostyle hall was next added, being finished in 122, and the forecourt and the pylons were finally completed in 57 B.C., just over 180 years following the foundation of the new building.

Visitors today are first confronted by the face of the enclosure wall. The figures in the scenes carved on the sides — Ptolemies offering to various deities — were deliberately vandalized by Christian zealots, but along the base remain the repeated images of Nekhbet, the vulture of El Kab, and the falcon Horus (often rendered also as a hawk-headed sphinx protecting the ruler's cartouche). In the reliefs of the lowest register — and even below, in the marginal inscriptions — note that the gods' figures are surrounded by peg-holes for the veils that shielded these icons from view: what inducements, one wonders, persuaded the temple's guardians to lift these covers for pilgrims who were denied access to the building itself?

The New Kingdom Temple of Edfu was oriented towards the river, facing east. When the Ptolemaic temple (oriented south to north) was built, it was nevertheless decided to retain what was left of the old pylon (Fig. 142, V) on the east side of the first court, where it is to be seen — even more reduced — today. Marginal inscriptions dating to the Nineteenth and Twentieth Dynasties are preserved *in situ*, but the building may well be even older, going back into the Eighteenth Dynasty.

Before entering the great temple, we continue south — passing through the portal that frames the processional way — and turn west into the mamissi. Built along the same lines as the Roman mamissi at Dendera (which was modelled after this building), it preserves more of the forward structure — for instance, the 'colonnade' with its low curtain walls between the columns and the curious blend of Pharaonic and foreign motifs in the reliefs: note, on the east side the Pharaoh leaving his palace, followed by small figures of a horse and groom. As at Dendera, the birth-room is surrounded by an ambulatory composed of columns linked by low walls: most of these were inexplicably cut down in antiquity; but, though the carving lacks the finish found at Dendera, there are charming details — on the north side, for instance, where the king presents fields, including a date-palm heavy with fruit, the ripe clusters being suggested by red painted dots. Some of the vivid colour on the column capitals and the wall reliefs is preserved on the south side of the building, which otherwise resembles its counterpart at Dendera in the relief figures of Bes on the abaci and in the pattern on the architraves, where the infant Harsomtus is worshipped by different pairs of deities.

Two wings, containing the guardian's quarters (south) and the stairway to the roof (north) stand before the single chamber of the birth-house itself. The upper two registers on the north and south walls contain the birth reliefs, along with repeated scenes showing the infant Harsomtus being suckled by a variety of goddesses. In the lower register, we find offering scenes featuring the reigning monarch (Ptolemy VIII) officiating, leading the goddesses of the Two Lands (north) and the gods of Upper and Lower Egypt (south) into the presence of Hathor and her child. The mystic union of Hathor and Horus, held in the mamissi during the 'Feast of the Beautiful Meeting' (see above, Chapter 5, p. 63), is evoked by the depiction of the sacred barques — Hathor (north) and Horus (south) — at the west end of the first register. The sympathetic relationship of this divine union with the stability of the royal line is suggested in another scene (south wall, middle) wherein

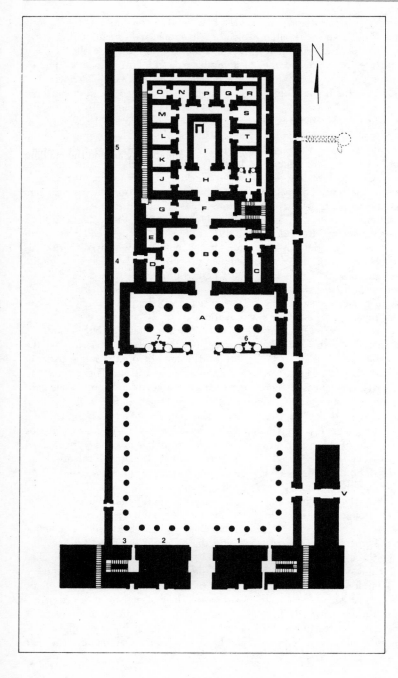

Fig. 142
Edfu *Temple of Horus*

Thoth establishes the reign of Ptolemy VIII, followed by his mother, wife and young son, underneath a similar scene in which Seshat performs the same function for the child Harsomtus.

We are now ready for the temple proper, the massive façade of which is best viewed from the mamissi's roof. Each of the pylons is inscribed with a large scene showing the king smiting the enemies of Egypt — a traditional scene not improved either by the staleness of its rendering nor by the curiously sway-backed draftsmanship of the figures. The offering scenes above are occasionally interrupted by windows, placed to hold the clamps that supported the gigantic flagpoles set inside the niches. Two mismatched statues of Horus flank the portal, completing an ensemble that achieves grandeur through sheer size rather than any finesse in execution.

Inside is the courtyard, its columned porches relieving the oppressive vastness of the enclosure. Most of the reliefs carved on the walls and columns are the usual cultic scenes — king presenting offerings, slaying serpent, purified, crowned, etc. — but at the base of the side walls, at either side of the doorway, are reliefs illustrating the 'Feast of the Beautiful Meeting'. On the east side (Fig. 142, 1), the barge of Horus tows the Hathor barque with its escort along the course of a canal leading to the temple. After the flotilla's reception, the cult image of Horus is made ready in the sanctuary, the god's portable barque is carried forth and both gods come to rest inside the sanctuary. The west side (2) shows us the end of the festival: the gods' barques are borne out of the temple and placed on board their river barges, proceeding by water to the border of the nome of Edfu, where they will part: since the ships are moving downstream, with the current, note that on this side they do not use their sails. Final ceremonies — men danc-

ing and women shaking rattles — are seen west of the doorway into the pylon (3).

The interior of the pylon — several chambers connected by a tortuous staircase — offers little of interest, though the views from the summit and from the top of the colonnades along the sides of the court are worthwhile. At the end of the west colonnade we pass through a doorway between the side of the temple and the enclosure wall, gaining the ambulatory around the building. The scenes — well carved in sunk relief — stand out despite the Christian hacking of the figures. A number of episodes offer more than the usual gestures: note, for example, the scene on the outer wall (Fig. 142, 4) where the king and the gods pull shut a clapnet confining evil spirits in the shapes of birds, men and other beings. Beyond, also on the west wall (5), are the famous episodes of the 'Triumph of Horus', a ritual play enacted each year at Edfu: in the vignettes illustrated here we see Horus — and his living image, the reigning king — repelling the forces of evil embodied in the hippopotamus, symbol of his enemy, Seth. Other reliefs carved on the enclosure wall and the sides of the temple are more conventional: unlike Dendera or Kom Ombo, however, the Temple of Horus lacks an external cult focus (hence, perhaps, all the 'popular' images on the outer side of the enclosure wall). Note, on the sides of the temple, the lion-headed waterspouts for rainwater, a feature shared with Dendera. And, on the east side of the building, a staircase in the pavement leads down to the well that supplied daily requirements to the temple.

The first hypostyle hall (A), its ceiling supported by lofty columns, is of a type that visitors to Esna and even Dendera will recognize. Dendera's fine astronomical ceilings are not matched, however, for the ceiling blocks at Edfu were never decorated. Among the usual offering scenes we find episodes from the foundation ceremonies — stretching the cord, pouring sand, hacking the ground, strewing gypsum, making bricks, and the rest. These scenes are duplicated to some extent on the east and west walls, and also on the façade of the second hypostyle (which was built earlier). Note also the two small chambers built on to the south wall — the 'library' (6) on the east, in which copies of important religious texts were kept; and, on the west, the 'robing room' (7) wherein the chief officiant was vested for the ceremonies to be held in the temple.

The resemblance between Edfu and Dendera increases as the inner rooms of Edfu Temple are explored. The second hypostyle (B), less lofty than the first, also has a number of side chambers and doorways communicating with the ambulatory. The eastern doorway led out to the well, the liquid offerings being kept in the small room off the passage (C). The entrance and repository for solid offerings is on the west side (D), which is also where we find the 'laboratory' (E), with recipes for incense and other concoctions inscribed on the walls. The hall itself also functioned as a place where the god formally 'appeared' on his way out of the building — in token of which we see the barques of Horus and Hathor displayed flanking the doorway on the north wall.

We now pass into the most sacred part of the temple, crossing the offering hall (F) and the vestibule (H) to enter the sanctuary (I). Two remnants of the ancient furnishings are found inside. First is the low pedestal on which the god's portable barque rested — sometimes joined by the barque of Hathor, if the reliefs on the side walls are to be believed, when the goddess visited Edfu. More immediately striking is the great granite naos in which the god's statue 'lived': dedicated by Nectanebo II, it is the oldest element in the present temple and was undoubtedly saved from the wreckage of the earlier building to connect this new foundation with the old. Each morning the high priest would unseal the doors of the shrine (now lost) to reveal the statue during the daily offering rites: the effect, with sunlight streaming into the sanctuary through the open portals of the temple, must have been very similar to conditions seen today in its present abandoned state.

The vestibule before the sanctuary communicates, as at Dendera, with a number of chapels surrounding the holy-of-holies. Beginning on the west side, we enter the chapel of Min (J), the ithyphallic fertility god, with eight other chambers opening into the corridor around the sanctuary. The 'Chamber of the Linen' (K) and 'Chamber of the Throne of the Gods' (L) are both decorated with offering scenes showing Horus of Edfu with his circle of gods. Next is the equivalent of the Osiris rooms at Dendera: the 'Chamber of Osiris' (M) and a double chapel comprising the 'tomb of Osiris' (N) and the 'Chamber of the West' (O), in all of which the lord of Abydos is the protagonist. The next room (P), directly behind the sanctuary, is called the 'Chamber of the Victor', i.e., Horus. There is no statue niche set high in the back wall, as at Dendera, but as if to compensate, a full-scale model of the barque of Horus looms out of the dusk: it was built early in this century for E. A. E. Weigall, sometime Chief Inspector of Antiquities in Upper Egypt, who used it in a re-enactment of the divine ritual at Edfu.

Another double chapel, belonging to Khonsu (Q) and Hathor (R), comes next: note the crescent under the disc atop the moon god's head, though otherwise he resembles the falcon lord of Edfu. The following room, called the 'Chapel of the Throne of Rē' (S), commemorates the coronation of the divine king: on the north wall we see Horus of Edfu worshipped along with a number of serpent deities (bottom), while in the corresponding scene on the south wall the king is joined by the monkeys whose howling greets the rebirth of the sun at dawn. At the top of both side walls, note the king inside the sacred tree receiving a long reign from the gods. And finally, in the 'Chapel of the Spread Wings' (T), we see the deities who protect the ways on which the soul travels towards resurrection in the netherworld – notably the lion goddess Mehit, whose barque is represented on the north side of the room.

None of the crypts reached from these chambers was decorated in antiquity, and thus all are inaccessible to the public. As at Dendera, however, we may imagine that the statues and ritual paraphernalia were brought from there into the vestibule (H) at the Festival of the New Year. The procession next moved into the open-air offering court (U), with its kiosk-like shrine behind: the court's side walls are much reduced, permitting a view into the passage that led into the crypt on the east side. On the ceiling of the kiosk is the expected figure of the sky goddess, though without the additional features that make the example from Dendera so interesting.

From the offering court the procession moved into the first vestibule (F) and up the stairs to the roof. Priests and standard-bearers are seen on the walls of both stairways, but only from the west side (G) can the upper level be reached at present (the other entrance is blocked). The roof terraces are much less interesting than at Dendera, however: the kiosk, if there ever was one, has disappeared, and in place of the Osiris rooms are undecorated magazines, with a number of hidden chambers opening in or beside them. From the roof one may still gain an excellent view of the surroundings – of the mamissi; of the immense mound of ruins still

awaiting excavation to the west; and of the hills beyond, where the tombs of the lords of Edfu still remain to be fully explored.

A few kilometres south of Edfu, we begin our descent into the ancient marsh known as the Kom Ombo basin. At Gebel Silsila the desert, which has hitherto skirted the broad fields at the river's edge, sweeps down and fastens on the bank. The narrowest part of the Nile before Aswan, it is also rich in fine sandstone and was extensively quarried. The impressiveness of these stone workings, together with the historical and religious significance of the monuments, should make the effort spent in visiting the site worthwhile.

Some of the commercial Nile cruises include *Gebel Silsila West* in their itineraries. Otherwise,[1] proceed south from Edfu to the village of Kajūj (41 km.). Once there, you will note a broad track that goes through the fields towards the river (this is located a short distance north of the local railway station): there, negotiate with a boatman for the trip to the western side. If possible, have your party taken to the Nile shrines (Fig. 143, P), about 2 km. south, and either arrange to have the boat bring you by river to the speos (K) or have the boatman meet you there if you wish to cover the distance on foot.

The approach to the shrines is marked by a gigantic pillar of rock (O), on the top of which rests a huge boulder: this landmark is known as the 'Capstan', so called because of a local legend that a chain once ran between the east and west banks. In fact, the shaft was formed by ancient quarrymen who thus exploited the surrounding rock without having to dislodge the useless boulder on top.

The three shrines (P) were built, from north to south, by Merneptah, Ramesses II and Sety I (the latter's having been wrenched in two by an earthquake that also destroyed

1. Security clearance may not be necessary for a brief visit; if in doubt, see a travel agent.

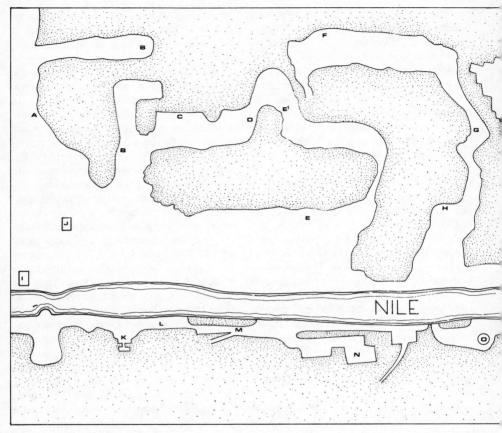

Fig. 143 **Gebel Silsila** *quarries*

the quay in front of the shrines). In addition, a stela of Ramesses III dominates the north end of the clearing, and several private *ex votos* are carved on the rock between the shrines. Here, at the start of the calendric Inundation season, the Nile was offered yearly sacrifices to ensure Egypt's wellbeing for the coming year. The onrush of the river at its height through the narrow channel must have been an impressive spectacle, perhaps explaining the location of a cult of the Nile at this spot during the New Kingdom.

Further north, we find greater evidence of quarrying and the first private memorials, although these southern shrines are not easily entered now. The path is soon interrupted by a large quarry, which can be avoided by crossing a gully slightly inland and next descending, via an ancient staircase hewn in the rock, to the bed of the main quarry (N) where masons' marks and evidence of past work abound. The most accessible group of shrines lies just beyond (M): many of these were also damaged by later quarrying or earthquakes, so one of the more

N

had been content with private chapels which often acknowledged the ruler under whom they worked, these later functionaries have converted the speos to their own use with scant respect for its original sponsor. Royal memorials still predominate, but officials' *ex votos* and their claim to a personal relationship with the gods are stressed here beyond all previously acceptable standards.

The most northerly monument of Gebel Silsila West is also the least ancient, being a tablet (located a short distance north of the speos) showing several registers of divinities. The texts were never carved, but the style of the figures is of the Graeco-Roman Period.

Although the most attractive monuments are on the west bank, _Gebel Silsila East_ offers the more spectacular quarries. The approach is best made on foot, along the northern side of the mountain where, after passing a series of bat-infested grottos (Fig. 143, B) we reach the stela of Amenhotep IV (A) on which this king is shown — incongruously, given his later history — worshipping Amun. Other grottos (B, C) illustrate the Egyptians' techniques of extracting stone from enclosed areas: the latter (C) being especially notable for the preservation of a beautifully painted, but uninscribed stela on its façade. Ruined shrines (D), some of them quite massive, even in their fragmented state, attest to the piety of one of Amenhotep III's viziers, who left them on the site as *ex votos*. A number of unfinished sphinxes (E), having both rams' and humans' heads, are scattered around the site. Near the unfinished crio-sphinxes (E') a path leads up an incline into another, higher cleft where stelae of Amenhotep III (F) are found. Further along the same road is a stela of Sety I (G), and near the end, approaching the river bank, is another stela, this one belonging to Pharaoh Apries of the Twenty-sixth Dynasty (H).

elaborate chapels is now entered through the fissure that divides it in two.

Stelae of Ramesses V, Shoshenq I and Ramesses III (L) mark the northern limit of the quarry itself, bringing us to the speos (K). This rock-cut chapel, begun by Horemheb late in the Eighteenth Dynasty, was left unfinished at his death and was taken over for the Ramesside kings by their officials, who left memorials here while exploiting the quarry. The hallmarks of the new age are vividly embodied in this monument: while powerful officials of the Eighteenth Dynasty

The open quarries (Fig. 143, I–IV) lie to

the south of these monuments. Anyone wishing for some impression at a glance of the enormity of the Pharaohs' works in stone can do no better than to wander through these workings, observing the enormous shelves left by the removal of blocks, the numerous quarry marks and drawings left by the artisans. The quarries' entrances are formally blocked by iron gates, and although there are alternative entrances, visitors are not encouraged to walk around the site without having first notified the inspector at Aswan. On leaving, on his way to the modern pump station (I), the visitor may pass over the ruins of Ramesses II's temple (J) without having been aware of having done it, so thorough is the destruction of this building.

The industrial town of *Kom Ombo*, 59 km. south of Edfu, is removed in both site and spirit from its ancient counterpart. Located originally to the west, closer to the river, it was the home of two gods — Harwer or 'Horus the Elder', and the crocodile deity Sobek — who, together with their associated gods, formed the two triads worshipped here in antiquity. The temple, 3 km. out of town, stands on a promontory overlooking the river: its situation, one of the most magnificent throughout the Nile Valley, is due to the eastward shift of the river, which was also responsible for sweeping away a number of the temple's outbuildings. Modern control over the waters has checked this threat, and the vigilance of the Antiquities Department similarly prevents the sand and debris of the adjoining mound (the ancient town site) from engulfing the temple.

Visitors enter the temple through what is left of the Ptolemaic portal at the southeast corner of the precinct. Beyond and to the right are small chapels, one of which — formerly dedicated to Hathor — is now filled with crocodile mummies and their clay coffins. Ruins of the birth house are found near the south-west corner of the temple: little remains from the assault of the river, but on the high wall facing west is a fine scene, carved with great delicacy and attention to detail, showing the king in a reed boat with two Nile gods, fowling in the marshes. A large well, which in ancient times supplied the temple with water, is situated to the west of the building, while nearby is a pool in which, it is believed, young crocodiles were raised.

We now pass into the temple's forecourt (Fig. 144, A), which is the first of the cult chambers to be shared between the two lords of Kom Ombo. Sobek's share is on the east side, while Harwer 'owns' the western half; otherwise, the layout of the temple is very similar to Dendera or Edfu. The remnant of the columned portico around the forecourt (built by the Romans) still retains much of its original paint — and one column, in the south-east corner, is notable for the inlay (now gone) that once stood in the eye and facial markings of the falcon god Horus. In the centre of the court is an altar base, with a small granite basin sunk into the pavement at either side — perhaps to catch the libations that flowed during ceremonies held during the great processional feasts each year.

The temple proper dates to the Ptolemaic age; and though it is considerably reduced in many places, the elegant proportions observed throughout stand in admirable contrast to the giantism and the cramped reliefs found in many contemporary structures. As in other late temples, the columns of the first hypostyle hall are to be seen above the curtain walls that form the façade of the building. Inside (B), one may admire the ingenuity of the column capitals (some of them unfinished), as well as the exceptional carving of the scenes: note that the decoration is divided between Sobek (east) and Harwer (west). Ritual scenes of a similar

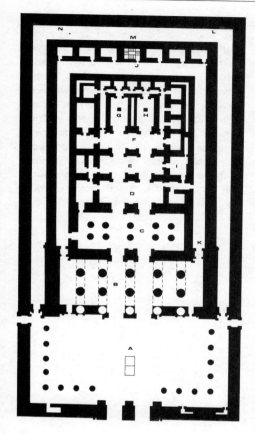

Fig. 144 **Kom Ombo** *Great Temple*

double sanctuary of Harwer (G) and Sobek (H). Service rooms and cult chambers radiate off this central area, as at Edfu and Dendera; similarly, too, the stairway to the roof proceeded from the chamber at the east side of the second vestibule (I). The sanctuaries, though denuded of nearly all features beside the pedestals for the divine barques, reveal in their reduced condition the presence of a chamber hidden between the two rooms: reached by a tunnel that runs beneath the floor to one of the rooms behind, this space was quite literally a 'priest hole', enabling the local clergy to deliver oracles or to overhear petitions submitted by pilgrims in the holy-of-holies. This part of the temple, in fact, contains a veritable warren of secret passages which the visitor, if so inclined, may explore if they are not choked with rubbish.

Extensions of the outer walls of the first hypostyle hall form a corridor around the temple — a feature unparalleled at Dendera or Edfu — which the visitor may now reach by climbing over the ruined back-walls of the chapels behind the sanctuary. At the back of this inner corridor are six small rooms, three at either side of a stairwell leading to the roof (J). Reliefs inside these rooms were left in various stages of incompleteness, yielding a great deal of information on the sequence of decoration in buildings of the later Ptolemaic age.

Proceeding again towards the front of the temple, we enter the outer corridor, formed by the enclosure wall and the outer mass of the temple. On the south-east side (K), note the remains of the traditional massacre scene, with the king's tamed lion rending captives. On entering the north corridor, attention is drawn to the crude relief added to the neater work of the Antonine emperors by Macrinus and his son Diadumenianus in about A.D. 217 (L). Of greater interest are the remains of a much-discussed scene (N) in which the king offers up a table laden with what have

nature dominate the second hypostyle (C) which, though less well preserved than the first, retains over the western gateway on the north side a Greek inscription recording the contribution of the troops stationed in the area to the cult of Harwer on behalf of Ptolemy VI and his queen, Cleopatra II.

A series of three vestibules (D, E, F), in more or less ruinous condition, precede the been interpreted as surgical instruments, but which are more probably to be seen as implements used during the ritual. The most striking feature, however, is found at the centre of the back wall of the temple (M), where the false door required by the popular cult undergoes a further modification. Figures of Sobek (left: head damaged) and Harwer (right), each with their signs of power – a lion-headed wand for Sobek and curiously legged knife for Harwer – stand at either side. Between them is a small niche that once held a cult figure, flanked by carved amulets – 'hearing ears' for the pilgrims' prayers, and also sacred eyes, symbolic of the wholeness and health to be achieved thereby. The cosmic aspect of the two great gods – a theme developed in the double hymn carved between them – is emphasized by the presence above the niche of the four winds – a winged lion, a falcon, a bull, and the remains of a many-headed snake – along with the winged goddess Ma'at who holds up the sky. The humble visitors who worshipped here thus paid their respects to an icon that contained within itself more than a single hint concerning the esoteric powers held by the lords of ancient Kom Ombo.

21. Aswan

Our arrival in the Aswan region is heralded
long before the first majestic view of the
town. Ochreous iron deposits lend a reddish
tinge to the desert hills, and whitewashed
Nubian houses replace the drab mudbrick
villages of Upper Egypt. Aswan was the
southern border of the Pharaonic land of
Egypt, and it is still something of a frontier
today. Nubians, many of them resettled
following the drowning of their homes by
the Aswan High Dam, are a conspicuous part
of the population, and anyone wishing to
travel south to Abu Simbel or the Sudan
must make special arrangements to do so.
Ancient legend situated the wellsprings of
the Nile at Aswan, and here too was the hard
granite of many hues so prized by Egyptian
builders. It is not surprising that local monuments span the full length of Egyptian
history.

The visitor should allow at least three
days to savour all that Aswan has to offer.
The scattered ruins on the east bank can be
disposed of quickly, leaving the remainder of
the first day for a visit to the island of
Elephantine, its museum and its ruins. The
tombs at Qubbet el-Hawwa will occupy a
full morning, with the balance of the day to
spend at the Aga Khan's tomb and the
monastery of St Simeon, which are also on
the west bank. The third day may be spent
visiting Sehêl by boat or the High Dam,
along with the Nubian temples that have
been relocated on an island south-west of
the dam. The temples of Philae, dismantled
and now rebuilt on the neighbouring island
of Agilkia, should also be visited. Even when
all the antiquities have been seen, however,

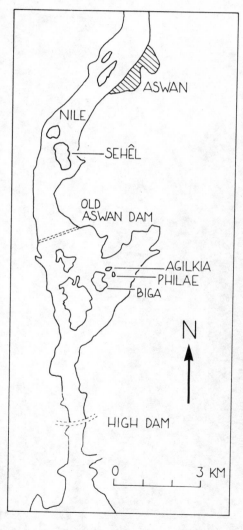

Fig. 145   **Aswan region**

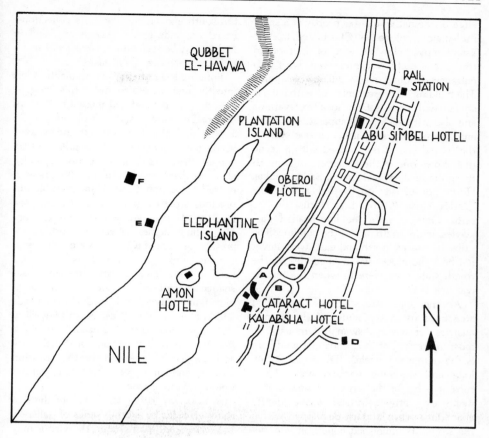

Fig. 146   Town of Aswan, monuments

Aswan remains a pleasant place in which to linger: the botanical gardens on Plantation (formerly 'Kitchener's') Island, the splendid corniche, the public gardens by the river, and the colourful marketplace (*suq*) are all beguiling in their different ways. This visitor, at least, has always wished for more time in Aswan than he had at his disposal.

The southern part of Aswan town was originally a quarry and many rock inscriptions remain to evoke this period: some

pleasing examples are to be seen in the public gardens just north of the big hotels (Fig. 146, A), while another large relief, located in a field east of the Kalabsha and New Cataract hotels (B), shows the chief sculptors Men and Bek standing before a statue of Amenhotep III and a destroyed figure of Akhenaten respectively: this relief faces south-east, so it is best seen in early morning or afternoon, when the sun's rays rake diagonally across its surface. At the

The second pylon of the temple of Isis on Philae (prior to the temple's removal to the island of Agilkia)

edge of the native quarter nearby is a small Ptolemaic temple to Isis (C): situated, like the Esna temple, below the level of the modern town, it is quite well preserved, with two entrances leading into a pillared vestibule. The building, at present infested with bats, is stuffed with objects from local excavations and also with such cultic apparatus as altars and fragmentary statuary. The rear wall of the central chapel is inscribed with a scene that shows one of the Ptolemies offering to the gods of Aswan (Khnum, Satis, Anukis, Horus Son-of-Isis) on the left and to the Osiride circle (Osiris, Isis, Horus) on the right. Outside, note the lion-headed gargoyles on the south face of the building. The other two faces (north and east) were never finished, the blocks having been left in the rough state they were in when the temple was first built.

Another kilometre south of the settled area finds us in the midst of the granite quarries for which Aswan is famous. The most impressive of the remnants found here is the unfinished obelisk (D): about 42 m. long and weighing approximately 1,197 tons, it is by far the largest of such monuments ever attempted and was evidently abandoned when a crack developed within the stone. Its unfinished condition is nonetheless a boon to archaeologists, enabling them to reconstruct the way in which the Egyptians managed, without the aid of hard metal tools, to extract such behemoths from their bed of granite.[1]

The local ferry crosses to Elephantine Island from a mooring just north of the public gardens (Fig. 146, A), depositing the visitor on the beach in front of the museum (Fig. 147, A). Since visitors must pass this building on their way to the monuments on the south end of the island, its collections, based on finds in the Aswan area and in Nubia, may be seen now. (*Admission charged; closed on Mondays and holidays.*)

Entering the museum's vestibule, turn left into the first of two rooms in this wing. A collection of painted and incised pottery of the pre-Dynastic period is displayed in Case 5. Note also objects of stone (grinders, axe-heads, palettes, mace-heads, spindle whorls), copper (hatchets, chisels, harpoon heads), alabaster dishes, and even ostrich eggs with incised decoration (Case 6); and an exhibit of precious stones and ivories in Case 7 (see Fig. 148, 1). Proceeding into the next room (2), we find a somewhat earlier assortment of pre-Dynastic pots (Case 1), slate palettes of various shapes and sizes (Case 2), ivory combs, knife handles and needles, disc-shaped mace-heads of stone from Lower Nubia, flint knives, sickle blades, arrowheads and 'fishtail' scrapers (Case 3), and jewellery — strings of glazed steatite beads, cornelians, garnets — as well as amulets of stone, ivory and copper (note especially the scorpion charms), and game pieces, both spherical and oblong, made of stone (Case 4).

A doorway in the south wall of the first room (1) leads to another series of galleries. From the south-east corner, the visitor may pass down a flight of steps into the basement, a patio lit from above by a skylight (3). In the centre is one of the mummified sacred rams that were found in the tombs beside the Temple of Khnum (see below): the head and neck are covered by a gilded mask and pectoral made out of cartonage, and the creature's divine aspect is highlighted by the plumed crown on its head. Mummies and coffins — for the most part very crude — fill the remainder of the room.

---

1. This apparently combined laborious pounding with dolerite balls and an artificially induced widening of fissures in the rock: see Labid Habachi, *The Obelisks of Egypt: Skyscrapers of the Past* (New York: Charles Scribner's Sons, 1977), pp. 15–37.

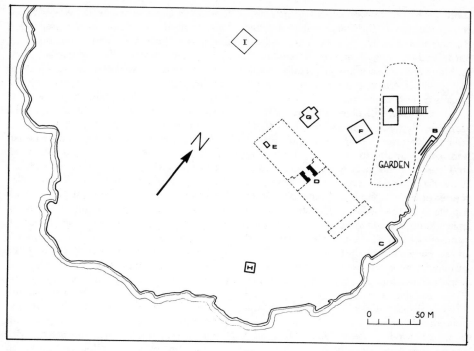

Fig. 147   Monuments on Elephantine

Fig. 148   Aswan Museum

Returning to the upper level, pass into the last of the back rooms (4) where a number of statues from the sanctuary of Hekayib (see below) are displayed: note especially the seated statue of the Governor Ameny, with its remarkable depiction of the man's stern, ageing features (south wall). On the east side of the room, there is a curious seated statue of another dignitary, his left hand crossed over his chest and his head, oddly proportioned as to the rest of his body and tilted at a quizzical angle. Beside this is the serenely elegant statue of Khema, son of Sarenput. All these statues were placed as votive offerings in the shrine of Hekayib, who himself appears against the north wall as a kneeling statue, offering wine.

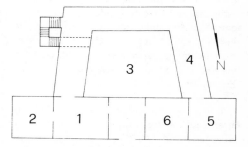

From the ambulatory we pass to the inner room in the museum's west wing (5). The objects are from the later periods, mixing pagan and Christian motifs. In Case 13 we find Nubian and Byzantine pottery and jewellery, a beadwork shroud with its heart scarab (both Ptolemaic) and censers of bronze and terracotta used in Christian worship. In Case 12 there is a display of Ptolemaic glass, spear- and arrowheads of iron, bronze bowls and jars, and also a large shepherd's crook, along with metal bowls and heavy bronze anklets from Meroitic Nubia.

An assortment of objects, many of them from the New Kingdom, is seen in the next room (6). Bronzes – mirrors, dagger-blades and other utilitarian items – are found in Case 10, and nearby are Middle and New Kingdom pottery vessels, terracotta figures of animals and broad-hipped 'Mother Goddess' figures (Case 8): note also the collection of armlets in the same case. Case 9 is dominated by a reconstructed board used in the game of *senet*, but has an interesting display of miniature mummy masks and of imported Mediterranean pottery. Jewellery (Case 11) and a collection of scarabs and votive plaques (Case 12) round out the contents of the room.

Before leaving the museum, note the seated statue of Merneptah in full regalia (pink granite) against the back wall. Other statues and larger pieces are displayed on the porch of the museum (note the dyads of Amenhotep III with a goddess flanking the entrance), and still others can be found in the lush and well-kept garden to the east, where the visitor may spend a few quiet minutes before visiting the other monuments on Elephantine.

On leaving the museum, turn right and after a few metres you will see the famous Nilometer of Aswan (Fig. 147, B) – a steeply graded staircase that plunges down the side of the island into the river. Belonging in ancient times to the temple of Satet (now mostly destroyed), its ninety steps helped men measure the rate of the river's annual rising. As recently as 1870 a modern gauge (remains still to be seen in the plaques inserted in the staircase walls) was installed here, though the ending of the inundation during the 1960s now renders this obsolete. A few steps beyond the Nilometer looms the imposing mass of the Roman quay of the temple of Khnum (C): blocks of the dilapidated New Kingdom structures that preceded it can be seen built into the northern face.

Further south, oriented from east to west, was the temple of the lord of the Nile flood, the ram god Khnum. The pavement which is the only substantial remnant of the building's front section is a late restoration, built up around the still-standing columns of Ramesses II's structure, which can be seen set into a floor at a lower level. Note, where a cross-section of the floor is revealed at the north end, how blocks of earlier buildings were packed under the present pavement. The columns that supported the roof were painted in crude but vivid colours by the Romans: several fragmentary examples, ranged along the north side of the pavement together with several altars with inscriptions in Greek, can give an idea of the effect.

The entrance to the temple proper is marked by the only standing feature of any substance, the granite gateway of the younger Alexander (D). The area behind it is a fascinating tangle of remains in several layers, evidence of the temple's development over the millennia: this area today is badly ruined, but the visitor will find a large granite naos (E) begun under Nectanebo II (preliminary designs in paint) and never finished during the seven centuries thereafter during which the building was used.

To the north of the temple are remains of the vaulted mudbrick tombs of the sacred rams (Late Period): sarcophagi and other remains are grouped nearby, and the visitor will have already seen the ram mummy in the museum. Beyond, near the back of the museum, was the temple of Satis, consort of

Khnum: the New Kingdom temple is now being rebuilt by the German Archaeological Institute, and under this building the visitor will also be able to examine the earlier phases of the temple as revealed by excavation (F). Slightly north-west (G) is the shrine of Hekayib, deified governor of Aswan, whose tomb at Qubbet el-Hawwa will also be visited (see below, p. 328). This building was dedicated to Hekayib's cult during the Middle Kingdom and yielded a rich cache of statues, some of which have already been seen in the museum. Although both the Satet temple and Hekayib's shrine are now closed to the public, they will undoubtedly be opened, once work in the area has been completed. Beyond, to the east of this structure, is another witness to the activity of the earliest Pharaohs at Aswan: a stepped pyramid built of granite. The architectural features of this building (I) date it to the late Third Dynasty, but its purpose remains unknown.

Finally, at the south end of the island (H) there is a small chapel, reconstructed from blocks built into the Roman temple of Kalabsha and revealed when it was dismantled prior to its removal to higher ground (see Chapter 22, pp. 337–8). The single chamber that forms the sanctuary, built by the Ptolemies, received additional decoration on behalf of the Nubian 'Pharaoh' Arkamani

Fig. 149 **Qubbet el-Hawwa**

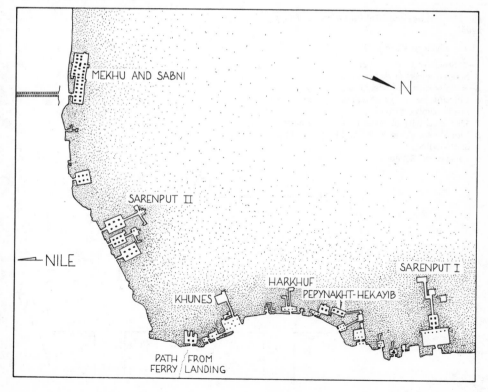

(third century B.C.), and was completed by the Romans shortly before it was destroyed, to make way for a more ambitious project. Note the reliefs on the outer walls, naming Caesar Augustus with the unusual soubriquet *Hromys* or 'The Roman'. Fragments from the vestibule (not reconstructed) are laid out on the ground a short distance in front of the chapel.

The tombs of the governors of Aswan during the Old and Middle Kingdoms are located on a bluff opposite the north end of town (see Figs. 146, 149). Originally named after the owner of the Muslim tomb at the hill's summit, it is now known simply as *Qubbet el-Hawwa*, 'Dome of the Wind'. A local ferry, which departs from the east bank a short distance north of the Abu Simbel Hotel, leaves passengers on the beach just north of the cemetery, and a pleasant walk, along palm-shaded irrigation channels, brings one to the base of the hill: the path here is noticeably gentler than the sharply graded causeways of the tombs themselves. From the point of arrival in the middle of the necropolis, the tombs may be visited in several sequences. This itinerary − which covers only tombs in the upper level, most others being closed − will, for simplicity's sake, proceed from south to north.

Fig. 150 **Sabni** and **Mekhu** *Overseers of Upper Egypt*

(A 1) *Dynasty VI (Pepy II)*

1−2 Stelae of tomb owners.
3 Small obelisks at doorways.
4−5 False doors of Mekhu and family.
6 Offering table (?) of Mekhu (*n.b.*: columns inside tomb omitted).
7 Deceased with attendants receiving animals.
8 Double scene, deceased and family fishing and fowling.
9 False door of Sabni.

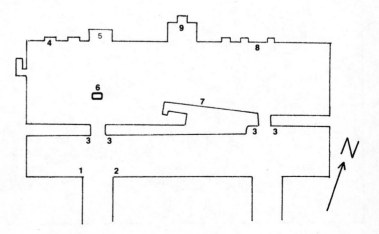

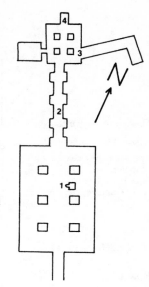

Fig. 151 **Sarenput II** *Overseer of Priests of Khnum, Commander of the Frontier Garrison of the Southern Lands*

(A 3)   Dynasty XII (Amenemhēt II)

1 Offering table.
2 Hall, with mummiform statues of deceased.
3 Shaft (*n.b.*: slippery, dangerous).
4 Niche: son (rear wall), deceased with wife and son (left), and mother (right), with offerings.

Fig. 152 **Khunes** *Lector Priest, Chancellor*

(A 6)   Dynasty VI

1 Side room (Coptic cell), with door left leading to adjoining tomb.
2 Top: Scribe and offering bringers, scene of fowling and fishing; bottom: offering bringers, ploughing, bringing a bull.
3 Top: deceased and son before wife and offering tables; bottom: two registers of butchers and cooks.
4 Top: bringing cattle, and fowling with draw-net; bottom: preparing food and beer.
5 Burial chamber.
6 Upper-level chamber: serdab.

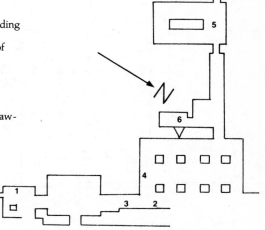

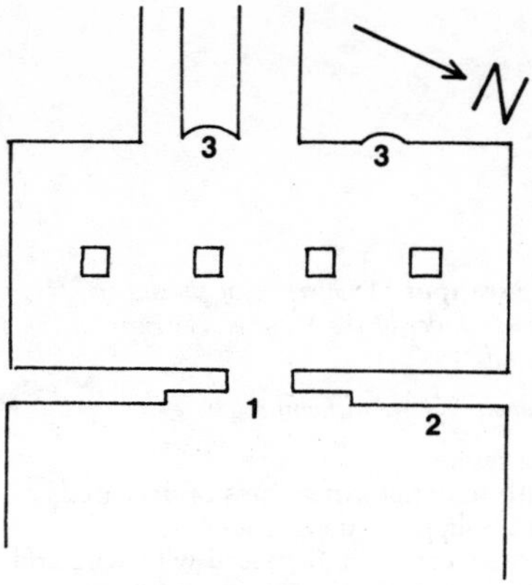

Fig. 153 **Harkhuf** *Overseer of Foreign Soldiers*

(A 8)   Dynasty VI (Pepy I, Mernerē, Pepy II)

1 Jambs: scene with priests and deceased with offerings, and biographical text.
2 Text of letter of Pepy II to deceased, requesting delivery of a dancing pygmy.
3 False door.

Fig. 154 **Pepynakht** called **Hekayib*** *Overseer of Foreign Troops*

(A 9)   Dynasty VI (Pepy II)

1–2 Jambs: figure of deceased with biographical text.
3 Deceased officiating.
4 Offering bringers.
5 Passage to neighbouring tomb.

* Hekayib owns the two tombs on the east (= left) side, the second of which runs into the tomb of his son, the governor Sabni.

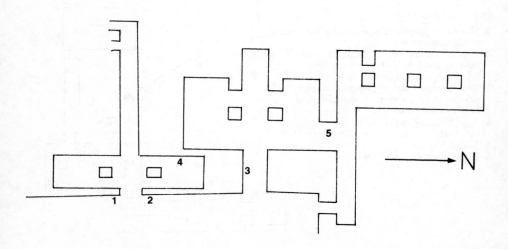

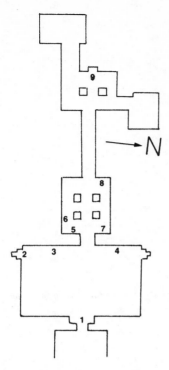

Fig. 155 **Sarenput I** *Mayor, Overseer of the Priests of Satis*

(A 11) Dynasty XII (Senwosret I)

1 Entrance: fine limestone reliefs and texts.
2 West niche: deceased receiving offerings (side and rear walls).
3 Three scenes: bulls fighting before deceased; deceased in canoe spearing fish; deceased with attendant and dog.
4 Three scenes: deceased with attendant and dog; four women before deceased (top); men playing board game (bottom).
5 Top: women and girl near kiosk; bottom: fowling with large net.
6 Top: two women playing game; bottom: men laundering (?).
7 Biographical text (note fine painted hieroglyphs).
8 Boating scene (remains).
9 False door (with mummies at centre of room).

The tomb of the Aga Khan, which rises on the promontory opposite the south end of town (Fig. 146, E), is the grandest and most recent of those Islamic saints' tombs that dot the west bank of Aswan. The majesty achieved in the transformation of a simple design to elephantine proportions is one of the reasons why it is a great tourist attraction, the other being that the climb leads also to the path to the monastery of St Simeon (F). The longish walk from the Aga Khan's mausoleum can be pleasant, depending on the weather, but camels and donkeys are also available for hire.

St Simeon's monastery (known also as 'Amba Hadra') is a relatively late foundation, and its community was dispersed shortly after the Arab conquest. The ruins survive in considerable detail, however, presenting us with as complete a picture of monastic life in Egypt as we are likely to find. Like its prototypes in the Wadi Natrûn, it was built with an eye to invasion from the outside: stout mudbrick walls girdle the precinct and, taking advantage of a rise in the desert, the complex is split down the middle, with the monks' living quarters and storerooms kept on the more defensible eminence at the west side.

Visitors enter through a vestibule on the east side of the enclosure (Fig. 156, a). Turn left, passing the cells that lodged visitors to the monastery (b), and you come to a stair that leads to the upper rooms from which a guard kept watch over the desert (c). Nearby is a kiln (d) and, on re-crossing the courtyard, the visitor will note the fosse (e) that perhaps entombed the remains of a revered

N

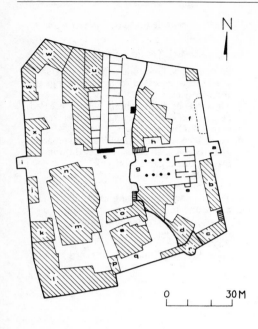

0   30 M

Fig. 156   Monastery of St Simeon

forefather. North of the entrance (a) is a broad court with a large mudbrick bench built into its eastern wall (f): this area perhaps served the monks for recreation or could have accommodated visitors who had to sleep in the open air.

Next to the church (g) we find the single staircase that connected the upper to the lower level (h). This upper floor is divided into several discrete units, among which we may note the western entrance (i) and the adjoining stables (j). The stable-hands were presumably quartered in a building nearby (k) that gave on to the first of the monastery's working areas, containing ovens, water cooling systems and even a winepress (l). Other magazines are found on the north side of the court (m), with several rooms devoted to the extraction of salt (n).

At the south-east corner, passing the mill (o), we enter a corridor that leads to the monks' bathhouse (p) and privies (q). Another lookout's quarters are found here as well (r), and the central building houses, among other work-rooms, a water filtration system (s).

The monks' living quarters are on the north side of the compound (t): the vestibule leads into a long corridor, on either side of which the monks' cells can be seen. The refectory (u) is a large room with a number of shallow stone basins set in the floor: it was around the edges of these that monks presumably sat, while the centres were filled with wooden tables that have since disappeared. Kitchens and water supplies occupy the rest of the building (v), while the adjoining buildings are granaries

(w) and workshops, with weaving perhaps having been practised in the area (x).

Most visitors to Aswan will want to visit the High Dam and also the temples on Philae. Before doing this, however, a few pleasant hours can be spent in taking a felucca upriver to the island of Sehêl (Fig. 145). A climb to the summit of either of the two hills at the south end of the island (particularly on the west) reveals a superb view of the cataract region. The rocks are covered with inscriptions of officials who visited the place in pursuance of their duties, and on the top of the east hill is the so-called 'Famine Stela' – a Ptolemaic inscription artificially dated to the reign of King Djoser in the Third Dynasty, describing the effects of a catastrophic famine and its relief by favour of the cataract god Khnum. The priests, making propaganda on their patron's behalf in order to keep or expand their property, gave their appeal a greater stamp of authority by disguising it as a document of such hoary antiquity that it could not be denied, and placed it in the heart of the cataract area, under the protection of Khnum himself.

Special permission (easily obtained by tour guides) is needed to visit the Aswan High Dam. Constructed between 1960 and 1969, it created a reservoir, called Lake Nasser, that in its 500 kilometres' length is the largest in the world after the Kariba reservoir on the Zambezi River. The High Dam ended the yearly inundation season in Egypt, which had still to be reckoned with when the first Aswan Dam had been in operation. This earlier dam was built in 1902 and heightened twice, in 1907 and 1933. Located 7 km. downstream from the High Dam, it can be seen in connection with a visit to the monuments of Philae.

The special sanctity attached to the island of *Philae* and its neighbours came relatively late in antiquity. Graffiti on the nearby islands of Biga and Konosso record occasional visits by high officials during the New Kingdom, but regular cult buildings do not seem to antedate the Twenty-fifth Dynasty. The mystique of the area seems to have developed by the start of the Graeco-Roman Period: it was at that time that the source of the Nile came to be regarded as a cavern deep under Biga island, on which was also the 'sacred mound' where part of the dismembered Osiris had been buried. A special shrine was built on Biga, endowed with an elaborate ritual and hedged about with restrictions. No music might be played, no hunting was allowed, nor might any man penetrate the sacred precinct: hence it was known in Greek as the 'Abaton', the forbidden, unenterable place. This dread holiness, along with the roughness of the terrain on Biga, may have allowed the development of Philae, just opposite, as the main cult centre in the area. Worshippers from the farthest corners of the Roman Empire thronged to the 'island of Isis': so important was it to the Blemmyes, inhabitants of Nubia during the early Christian era, that the temples were kept open for their benefit long after the official fall of paganism. Closed finally by Justinian in 551, the island shortly thereafter passed under the protection of its new patrons, St Stephen and Mary, the Blessed Mother.

Philae has not fared well in the last century. The building of the Aswan barrage (1898–1902) and its subsequent enlargement (1907–12) resulted in seasonal flooding of the island: generations of tourists have viewed the half-submerged temples from rowing boats throughout most of the year, or waited until the waters receded during August and September. Since 1964, when the creation of the vast reservoir known as Lake Nasser threatened the temples with permanent extinction, the necessity of more drastic action has finally been accepted. The principal monuments have finally been moved to the nearby island of Agilkia, where they will be permanently accessible all the year round.

Before visiting the monuments of Philae itself, the traveller may wish to stop at the *island of Biga*. Little is left of the Ptolemaic temple — the vestibule and remains of the pronaos are all that survive — and the exact site of the Abaton is lost. Tourists with the time and inclination to search for the New Kingdom graffiti will find them concentrated at the south-east corner of the island, though a massive cliff-face on the eastern side preserves large-scale inscriptions of Khaemwēse, son of Ramesses II, commemorating his father's jubilees; and (further south) cartouches of King Apries. Mudbrick ruins of a Christian monastery can be seen near the summit of the south hill on the island.

The earliest of the temples left standing on Philae is the *kiosk of Nectanebo I*, at the south-west corner of the island (Fig. 157, A).[2] This building, an airy structure of columns linked by screen walls, lies east of a quay which in ancient times could be reached from the river by two stairways. In front, to the north, is the processional way to the Temple of Isis. The *western colonnade* (B) is the more complete of the two, having thirty-one columns with wonderfully varied capitals. The back wall, decorated with ritual scenes, is pierced at intervals by windows that faced (originally) the island of Biga. Between the twelfth and thirteenth columns from the south is a well or 'Nilometer' descending along the cliff to the water below.

The *east colonnade* (C) was never finished, but it abuts several important buildings. At the south end is the *Temple of Arensnuphis* (D), belonging to an obscure god of the later ages of paganism who was worshipped on Philae as the 'goodly companion' of Isis. The building, consisting of a kiosk-like forecourt and enclosure wall surrounding the three vestibules and the sanctuary, is almost entirely destroyed. Other structures stand behind the east colonnade and are reached through doorways in the back wall. Of these, note only the ruined *chapel of Mandulis* at the south end (E) and the more substantial *temple of Imhotep* to the north (F): Ptolemy IV is seen before the deified sage, along with Khnum, Satis, Anukis, Osiris and Isis on the walls of the forecourt. The building's interior was never decorated.

The present temple of Isis dates to the late Ptolemaic and early Roman periods: previously, one suspects, the buildings had been arranged differently, and a survival of this early precinct is the *gate of Ptolemy II* (G) which stands at right angles to the west tower of the later pylon. The *first pylon* itself (H), built by Ptolemy XII and decorated in the accepted Egyptian style with scenes of massacre and divine offering, had to be adapted to the existing buildings behind: in addition to the main portal (which is earlier than the towers that adjoin, having been built under Nectanebo I and containing on its east wall an inscription by members of the French army who passed through in 1799), there is a passage through the east wing that communicates with the birth house (I). The sides of this passage are covered with scenes showing Ptolemy VI before the gods who will figure in the rites of the mamissi or (bottom) leading the personified districts of Nubia into the temple. Note the two undecorated guardrooms that are sunk into either side of the passage.

---

2. The following discussion, with its map, refers to the monuments as they were situated on Philae. Their disposition on Agilkia is nearly the same although Biga now lies off the southern tip of the island.

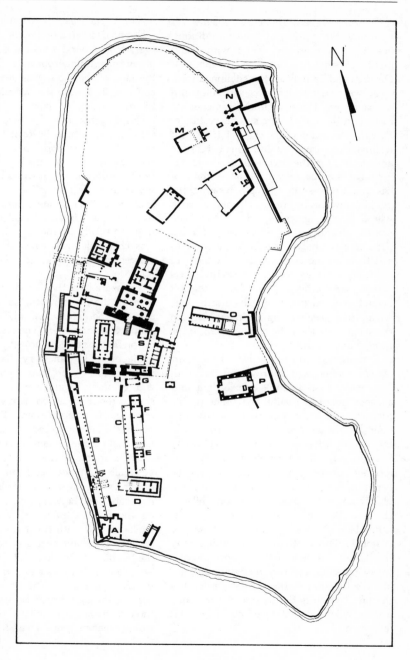

Fig. 157
Philae *Temples*

The *birth house* (I), built by Ptolemy VI, with later Ptolemaic and Roman additions, has its own character, albeit with many points of similarity with the buildings at Dendera and Edfu. From the columned forecourt we pass through two vestibules into the sanctuary. The standard birth-scenes are carved on the walls of the second vestibule: note the modelling of the child's figure (west wall) and the usual presentations before the gods (east). On the back wall of the sanctuary we see the falcon Horus — child of Isis and Osiris — in triumph, wearing the double crown as he emerges from the marsh where, according to legend, he had been reared. Outside, as at Dendera and Edfu, there is an ambulatory formed by columns and their linking screen-walls. The surfaces are covered with ritual or mythological scenes: note especially the lower register behind the sanctuary, on the north wall, where Isis is seen nursing the infant Horus in the swamp — a thematic counterpoint to the triumphant Horus inside.

Turning now to the east half of the court (where we find two doorways in the north face of the first pylon — one leading into another guardian's suite, the other to the roof) we reach the eastern colonnade (R). Built (like the ambulatory of the birth house) by Ptolemy VIII, its reliefs were executed by Ptolemy XII, showing the king in the performance of such ritual acts as dragging the barque of Sokar in procession. A granite altar of Taharqa — the oldest object on Philae — stands at the south-west corner of the colonnade, behind which we find five service chambers. The fourth from the south, clearly the 'library', is dedicated to Thoth alternatively in his ibis- and baboon-manifestations, but the function of the others (particularly the fifth, which is the largest of the group and has a separate entrance from the east) is unknown.

The *second pylon* (also built by Ptolemy VIII and decorated by Ptolemy XII) is seemingly built around a natural outcropping of granite protruding from under the east tower: the face of the stone was smoothed down and used to record the donation of land to Isis by Ptolemy VI; but no other season for preserving this curious feature — still less for the chapel (S) which the Romans later built in front of it — is apparent. Ascending the stairway, we pass into the hypostyle hall, the front portion of which was left open to the sky. The noble proportions of the building and the unusually fine column capitals remain to be admired, but much of the decoration (especially on the east side of the hall) was chiselled away when the temple was converted into a Christian church in about A.D. 553.

Compared to the labyrinthine development of the Dendera and Edfu temples, the plan of the interior of Philae may seem simple and anomalous. The essential features of the familiar design, however, may still be made out. The sanctuary, flanked by two side-chambers with their crypts, lies at the end of three vestibules: the two granite shrines that once stood here were long ago removed to Florence and Paris, but the pedestal that supported the goddess's processional barque remains *in situ*. An offering court is found to the east of the second vestibule and is reached from either the first or third, while the staircase leading to the roof is situated on the west side of the building, off the first vestibule. All these chambers are decorated with ritual and mythological scenes which have been seen, *grosso modo*, in the temples at Dendera and Edfu.

Further similarities and surprises await us on the upper level. The stairway ends by passing through a chamber sunk by nearly three metres below the level of the roof — a curious feature found at all four corners of the area behind the hypostyle hall. Of these, the north-east tank is void of inscriptions and the south-east corner has collapsed, but at the south-west corner we find a counterpart of the Osiris rooms seen in just this position at Dendera. Note, in the vestibule, scenes of the gods bewailing the dead Osiris or offering to the triad of Isis, Nephthys and Osiris-Wenennefer. The inner room is inscribed with scenes having to do with the collection of the limbs of Osiris after his assassination by Seth and with the posthumous generation of Horus. Another stairway at the back of the chamber leads to the roof of the hypostyle hall and, finally, to the top of the second pylon.

The scenes carved on the exterior walls of the Temple of Isis (by Augustus and Tiberius) do not have any special interest, but may be examined before visiting the area to the west. A *gateway of the Emperor Hadrian* (J) is the principal standing monument. A stairway to the east led down to the river, and the gate itself opens on to a single chamber that is inscribed with a number of highly interesting reliefs. On the south side, for instance, Isis stands outside her temple watching a crocodile bear the corpse of Osiris across the water to a rocky promontory that must represent the island of Biga; above, inside the disc that rises between the hills of the horizon, we see Osiris enthroned with his heir, Horus the Child, all under a canopy of stars framed by the sun and the moon. A corresponding relief on the north side shows a number of deities, including Isis and Nephthys, adoring the young falcon as he rises from his marsh; behind lies the stony mass of Biga, with the Nile god buried in a cave which is protected by a serpent who bites its tail.

Other monuments in the vicinity of Hadrian's gateway are the ruined *Temple of Horus the Avenger* (K) to the north, and a *nilometer* (L) near the front of the Ptolemaic mamissi. The Roman town spread out north and east of the Temple of Isis — or did before the yearly flooding destroyed the mudbrick buildings. Near the north end of the island, visitors will still find the much reduced *Temple of Augustus* (M) and also an imposing *quay and gateway* built by Diocletian (N). Further south, on the east side of the island, are substantial remains of the *Temple of Hathor* (O). Built jointly by Ptolemies VI and VIII, it too is much destroyed; but on the north and south walls of the forecourt are found festive scenes that pertain to this goddess's patronage of revelry and music: Bes beats on a tambourine, dances or plays the harp, an ape strums a guitar-like instrument, and the king rattles the sistra in the presence of the lion-goddess Sekhmet. The reliefs in the hall behind were never finished, and the sanctuary area behind has been reduced down to its pavement. Finally, the visitor's attention will be drawn to the lofty *kiosk of Trajan* (P) on the east end of the island. Known locally as 'Pharaoh's Bed', this is a rectangular structure, having fourteen columns, linked by screen walls, to support the architraves: the roof, presumably of wood, has disappeared. Wide doorways open from the quay to the east and then out on to the island to the west. Only a few ritual scenes were ever carved inside this building, which once served as the formal gateway into the temple precinct from the river, and which makes its effect today by the sheer massiveness of its basically simple design.

Visitors may also wish to see the Nubian temples moved to the vicinity in the 1960s (see below, Chapter 22, pp. 337–8). Permission may be obtained from the Department of Nubian Antiquities in Aswan.

22. Beyond the Borders

In Chapter 4 we saw some of the ways in which Egypt's foreign relations were reflected in her monuments. It remains here to explore the edges of the Nile Valley, to search out traces of Egyptian influence where it prevailed. Visitors to Egypt will find that this is easier said than done. As of the summer of 1982, Egypt's southern and western borders remain out of reach for most tourists. Access to the Nubian temples and to Siwa Oasis is limited at best, although travellers should now be able to visit such sites in the Sinai as the monastery of St Catherine or the turquoise mining area.[1] Changes in this situation cannot be predicted with any certainty. At the time of writing, however, most of the oases in the western desert and at least some of the Nubian temples may be visited, although special arrangements must be made to do so. The full description in these pages is given against the day on which all these sites will be open once more.

NUBIA

The Nubian monuments rescued during the salvage operations of the 1960s have been earmarked for re-erection at four locations along the shores of Lake Nasser. At present, only those in the vicinity of Aswan and Abu Simbel may be visited, but the Ministry of Tourism in conjunction with the Egyptian Antiquities Organization has ambitious plans for the development of the area, and it may be expected that Egyptian Nubia will be increasingly accessible with the passing years.

The temples of *Kalabsha*, *Qertassi* and *Beit el-Wali* have been relocated on an island a few kilometres south-west of the Aswan High Dam. Special permission is required to visit the site, but this is easily obtained through the Department for Nubian Antiquities in Aswan. Visitors disembark along the quay of the Kalabsha Temple (Fig. 158, A: originally situated about 40 km. upstream). The present building (B) is Roman in date, but worship at Kalabasha went back at least into the mid-Eighteenth Dynasty: the resident god was Merwel (better known in Greek as Mandulis), a Nubian solar deity. The panorama of the temple's new position can be surveyed from the roof of the pylon. Its layout is familiar enough: the open court in front is followed by a hypostyle hall, the walls decorated with religious scenes involving Min, Khnum and other gods of the area. Among the Greek and Meroitic inscriptions, a decree of Aurelius Besarion, commander of Ombos about A.D. 250, commands the expulsion of all pigs from the town of Kalabsha for religious reasons. The sanctuary area consists of three rooms (later converted into a

OPPOSITE Detail of a colossal statue of Ramesses II (Great Temple at Abu Simbel)

1. Some of the most historic inscriptions from the mining area have been removed to the Cairo Museum (see Chapter 10, p. 110); but many others, as well as the rock-cut Temple of Hathor, are still *in situ*.

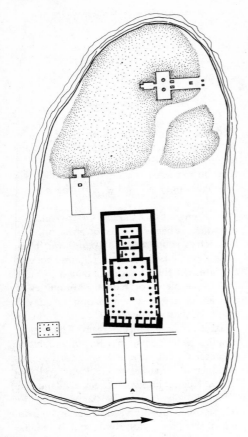

Fig. 158 **Kalabsha, Qertassi** *and* **Beit el-Wali**

A little to the south is the tiny Roman kiosk from *Qertassi* (C: originally located 30 km. upriver). The four slender papyrus columns inside, along with the two Hathor columns at the entrance, conspire to lend an uncommonly graceful air to what is left of the building.

The temple of *Beit el-Wali* (Fig. 158, E) is found on the island's north-west shore. Originally situated close to the site of Kalabsha, it was fashioned during the reign of Ramesses II and, unlike its neighbours, is entirely carved out of its native mountainside. The inner chambers are preceded by a narrow court, on the side walls of which are carved contemporary battle scenes. On the left, we see the king, together with his eldest sons, riding in their chariots to battle against Nubian tribesmen: as usual, the battle is a rout, with the enemy fleeing pell-mell to their camp and the women and children seen in attitudes expressive of woe. Next is the obligatory triumph scene, this one being notable for the detail with which the various spoils — gold rings, ivory and exotic animals (including monkeys and giraffes) — are mustered into the royal presence. Especially prominent is the Viceroy of Nubia, who probably led the campaign in person and is seen being rewarded by the king. On the right side are other, more generalized scenes of battle against Libyans and Asiatics, the prisoners being dragged into the king's presence by his sons. Inside, the temple is particularly fortunate in the preservation of the painted relief. The statues in the sanctuary (mutilated during the early Christian era) include the gods of Lower Nubia — Horus of Buhen and Isis — as well as Khnum, Satis and Anukis, local deities of Aswan.

Christian church), on the walls of which the 'Pharaoh' Augustus offers before various divinities — especially Mandulis, who is set apart by his tall composite crown. Finally, the visitor may stroll around the temple in the passage formed by the stone wall bonded to the pylon (cf. the temples of Edfu and Kom Ombo, Chapter 20, pp. 309–13, 316–18). The granite chapel of Dedwen (D) also found at Kalabsha has been re-erected south-west of the temple.

The temples of *Dakka, Maharraka* and *Wadi es-Sebua* are grouped on the west side of the new lake, about 140 km. south of the Aswan High Dam. The Wadi es-Sebua Temple (Fig.

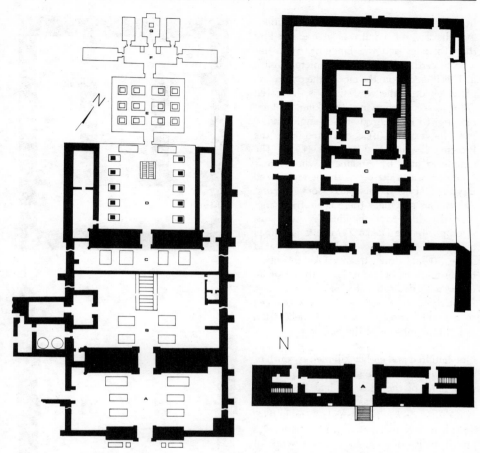

Fig. 159   **Es-Sebua** *Temple of Amun and
Rē-Harakhti*

Fig. 160   **Dakka** *Temple of Thoth of Pnubs*

159: now 2 km. north-west of its former site)
is approached down an avenue of sphinxes
and through two outer courts (A, B). Two
colossi of its builder, Ramesses II, stand
before the stone pylon (C), and engaged
standing statues of the king are displayed
against the pillars of the court inside (D). The
interior of the temple is carved directly into
the rock: proceeding through the vestibule
(E), with its twelve columns, and the antechamber (F), we reach the sanctuary, where

the central niche shows the king (carved on
the jambs) facing in and offering to what
should have been the two gods of the temple
(G). Owing to the temple's conversion into a
Christian church, however, we find Ramesses
II adoring St Peter instead of Amun-Rē and
Rē-Harakhti!

The temple of *Dakka* (Fig. 160: originally
located 40 km. downstream) has a curious
history: begun (D) by the Meroitic King
Arkamani (*c.* 220 B.C.), who used materials

from earlier Middle and New Kingdom buildings that lay at hand, it was later adapted by the Ptolemies and the Emperor Augustus, who nevertheless did not completely finish it. This is clear from the face of the pylon (A), of which only the west wing is decorated with a scene showing the king making offerings to Thoth (god of the temple) and to Isis. The vestibule (B), constructed under the Ptolemies, abuts the pronaos (C) of the temple as built by Arkamani, whose work inside contrasts sharply with the Hellenized Egyptian style of his successors. Beyond Arkamani's sanctuary there is another sanctuary (E) added to the building by Augustus.

Opposite the Dakka Temple is the small temple of *Maharraka* (originally situated some 30 km. downstream). Like the other building, it is incomplete, dating from Roman times and dedicated to Serapis and Isis. Formerly more extensive, it is now reduced to a small hypostyle hall, with decoration only in the interior of the building.

One hundred and eighty kilometres south of the High Dam, on the site of Amada, on the west bank of the lake, we find the *temples of Amada and Derr*, as well as *the tomb of Pennē from Aniba*. The Amada Temple (Fig. 161) had only to be moved back about 2.6 km. from its original location. A work of the mid-Eighteenth Dynasty, it is entered through a portal (A), on the sides of which are seen *ex votos* of rulers and officials of the later Nineteenth Dynasty. The building itself was jointly built and decorated by Thutmose III and his son, Amenhotep II, while the pillared court in front (B) was added by the latter's successor, Thutmose IV. The interior of the temple preserves much of the original painted relief, despite the excision of Amun's name by the Atenists and its subsequent restoration during the Nineteenth Dynasty.

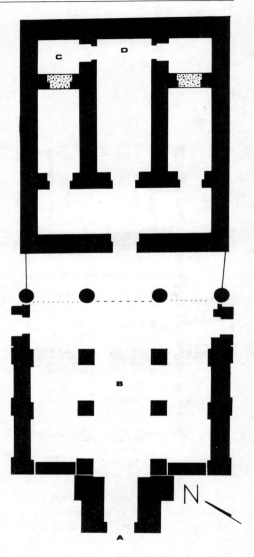

Fig. 161   **Amada** *Temple of Amun-Rē and Rē-Harakhti*

Especially interesting are the foundation ceremonies shown on the walls of the north-side chapel (C) — the ritual of 'stretching the cord' to delimit the building's dimensions, the strewing of gypsum in the foundation trenches, moulding the first brick, and finally 'presenting the house to its lord'. The stela on the back wall of the central shrine (D) recounts the temple's establishment and its formal dedication later, during the reign of Amenhotep II.

The temple of *Derr* (Fig. 162), another of the Nubian rock-cut shrines, was originally located 11 km. upstream. Dedicated to the great gods of the Egyptian pantheon — Amun-Rē and Rē-Harakhti — it was used as a church by the Christians. The damage is greatest in the first (A) of the two pillared halls: enough of the decoration remains to show the themes of battle and triumph illustrated here, as well as a short procession of the king's children at the base of the wall. Note also the four Osiride statues engaged to the third row of pillars inside the room. In the second pillared hall (B), the painted relief is much better preserved: the king presents flowers to the portable barque shrine of Amun-Rē, offers wine to the gods, and has his name recorded on the leaves of the sacred Persea Tree (east wall); escorts the sacred barque, and receives jubilees from Amun-Rē and Mut (west wall). The back of the temple is occupied by three chapels, of which the main shrine (C) in the centre preserved four statues of divinities: Ptah, Amun-Rē, the deified Ramesses II and Rē-Harakhti.

The tomb of Pennē, Viceroy of Nubia under Ramesses VI, was originally located at Aniba, 40 km. upstream, and was completely removed from the rock in which it was carved (Fig. 163). Its interest lies in the handling of traditional themes in this, the best preserved of the viceroys' tombs built on Nubian soil.

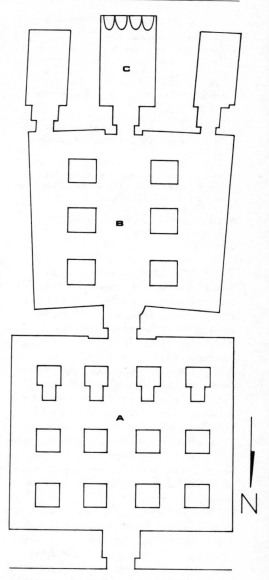

Fig. 162 **Derr** *Temple of Rē-Harakhti*

342

*Fig. 163   Tomb of **Pennē** (formerly at Aniba)*

1 Deceased and wife adoring.
2 Top: judgement scene in the Underworld; bottom: funeral procession and Opening of the Mouth at the tomb.
3 Top: deceased and wife led to Osiris by Horus, with mummy on bier; bottom: Fields of Iaru.
4 Top: adoring Hathor cow in mountain; bottom: two scenes of deceased before gods.
5 Text for endowment of statue of Ramesses VI.
6 Top: decoration of deceased; deceased and steward adoring statue of Ramesses VI, and before Ramesses VI inside kiosk; bottom: offering scenes with relatives.
7 Offering scenes, relatives.
8 Three statues of divinities (mutilated).

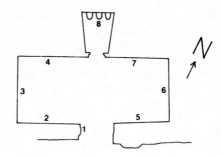

The widely publicized salvage of the great rock temples of *Abu Simbel* has come to be regarded as one of the wonders of the modern world. This work – the disengagement of the temples from their native hills, dismantling them into blocks whose weight reached as much as thirty tons apiece, transferring the numbered blocks to their new positions, and building an artificial hill to house the temples anew – was carried out between January 1966 and September 1968, with finishing touches added as late as 1972. In their new environment, they remain one of the great attractions for the tourist in Egypt, and it takes a trained eye to detect any trace of the process they underwent during their rescue.

The Great Temple (Fig. 164) is dedicated equally to the deified Ramesses II and to the gods of state: a statue of the falcon-headed sun god appears in a niche above the doorway, with incised figures of the king worshipping at either side, while a frieze of smaller baboon statues stands at the top of the wall, as if to greet the rising sun. But the façade is really dominated by the four seated colossi of the king under whom, at the base

of the supporting balustrade, are kneeling Negroes (south) and Asiatic captives (north). Statues of the king's favourite children stand at the feet of these immense figures, which are each about twenty metres high. Of the later visitors' inscriptions carved on the colossi, note especially one in Greek on the most destroyed of the four, left by mercenaries in the service of King Psamtik II in about 591 B.C.

At the north end of the terrace on which the colossi stand, note the remains of a covered court (A) dedicated to the worship of the sun by Ramesses II. A number of large stelae are found at the opposite end – among them, a commemoration of the king's military exploits, a private dedication to Amun-Rē, and the famous Marriage Stela, relating how the daughter of the King of the Hittites arrived in Egypt to wed the Pharaoh following the peace between their two nations.

The scale of the inner rooms becomes progressively smaller as the sanctuary is approached, and the level of the floor rises gradually. This convention of temple building is particularly noticeable here, and serves to focus the building's axis towards the holy-of-holies, where the god of the temple dwells. The first pillared hall is still, however, on a grand scale, with eight Osiride statues of Ramesses II engaged to the pillars that support the roof. The walls are covered with scenes dwelling on the king's prowess in battle. Two scenes showing the slaughter of captives in the presence of Amun-Rē (B)

and of Rē-Harakhti (C) flank the eastern doorway, while on the north wall (D) is represented the great Battle of Kadesh (see Chapter 4, p. 58). More generalized scenes, showing the king engaged in single combat and attacking a Syrian town, are seen on the opposite wall (E), while on the west wall (F, G) are stereotyped reliefs showing the presentation of prisoners before the gods.

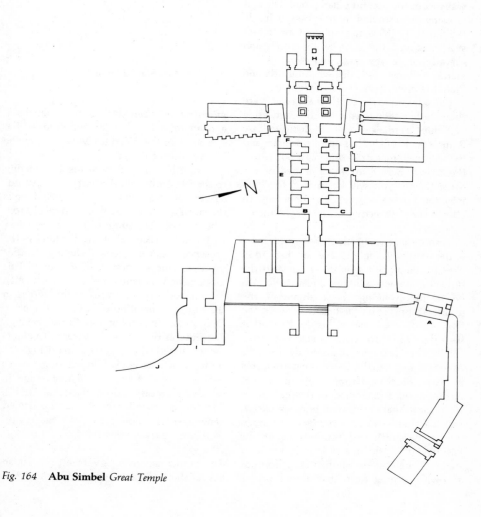

Fig. 164 **Abu Simbel** *Great Temple*

After exploring the temple's magazines, the doors to which open on to the first pillared hall, we pass through a second room, supported by four large pillars and decorated with offering and ritual scenes, into the vestibule before the holy-of-holies. Some sanctity was evidently attached to the use of the main axis, for the two side-chambers (which were themselves storerooms for cult objects) could be reached by their own doorways from the second pillared hall, without crossing the restricted central passage. Inside the sanctuary (H) is an altar and four statues seated against the back of the room and carved out of the rock, representing Rē-Harakhti, Ramesses II deified, Amun-Rē and Ptah, the divine patrons of the temple.

Outside and to the south of the temple are found other monuments of the Ramesside age: first a small chapel (I) dedicated by Ramesses II to Thoth, god of learning; and five stelae (J) memorializing high officials of the crown. Before leaving the area of the great temple you will be invited to climb into the bowels of the new mountain, to admire the engineering of the reconstructed monument.

A short distance north of the great temple is the smaller Temple to Hathor (Fig. 165). This building, in a special way, is also the domain of Ramesses II's first queen, Nefertari: her statue, wearing the costume of the goddess, appears on the façade between the two standing colossi of her husband that flank the main entrance, with statues of their children beside them (A). Inside, on the walls of the pillared hall (B), the queen participates in divine ritual in the same capacity as her husband. The arrangement of the rear rooms is similar to that in the great temples, except that the chambers beside the sanctuary open on to the north and south walls of the vestibule (C). Inside the shrine (D), we see a statue of the goddess Hathor in the form of a cow, emerging from the interior of the

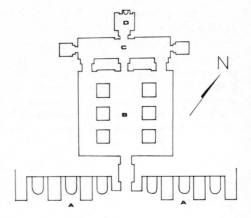

Fig. 165 **Abu Simbel** *Small Temple*

mountain between two Hathor columns — a form reflecting her identification as the patroness of the 'Western Mountain' in the Necropoleis of Egypt.

Two other small monuments, both dating to the late Eighteenth Dynasty, will eventually be set up at Abu Simbel as well. One is the small rock-cut chapel of Horemheb from Abu Hoda (1 km. south of the present site), with painted reliefs showing the king in the presence of several gods, including the four forms of Horus worshipped in Nubia. This monument was converted into a Christian church, so there are traces of this re-use in the form of a painting of St George and the Dragon (south wall) and of Christ (ceiling). The other is the tomb of a Viceroy of Nubia named Paser who served under King Ay, both of whom appear in offering scenes before local divinities: note one scene in which the deceased adores the jackal Anubis, Sobek (the crocodile god) and the deified Senwosret III, whose activities in the region won him a posthumous cult.

The border between Egypt and the Sudan lies a short distance upstream from Abu

Simbel, at Wadi Halfa. There is still much of the ancient kingdom of the Nile to be seen beyond this frontier, and the Egyptianizing monuments of Meroitic Nubia abound on their home soil. Regrettably, difficulties both formal and practical[2] make it impossible for these monuments to be seen by many tourists. Reasons of space similarly oblige their exclusion from this guide.

THE OASES

The road to Kharga and Dakhla Oases leaves the main highway in the Nile Valley some 6 km. north of Assiūt, on the west side of the river. The road is excellent and the distance — 228 km. — may easily be covered in a day. The descent into the depression of the *Kharga Oasis*, when the expanse of the canyon suddenly opens up, and the road winds along the side of the cliff until reaching the bottom, is breathtaking. Of course, the oasis is considerably reduced from its original dimensions, and signs of life are slow in appearing: a few scraggly bushes, heralding the occasional palm tree, gradually multiply to form the characteristically dense vegetation of the oasis, although this is rather less spectacular than might have been expected.

The principal monuments lie 2.5 km. north of Kharga City, and may be seen before

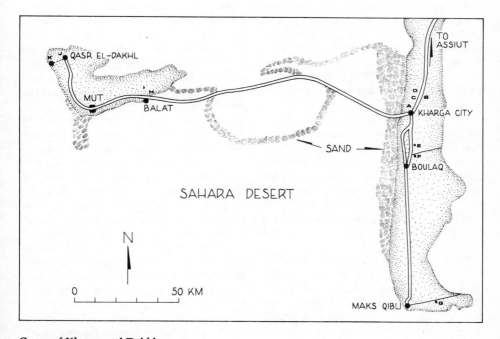

Oases of Kharga and Dakhla

2. Those undeterred by the above will find much useful information in the chapter by Alain Fouquet in the newest edition of the *Guide bleu* for Egypt: D. Meeks and C. Favard, *Égypte, le Nil égyptien et soudanais du delta à Khartoum* (Paris: Hachette, 1976), pp. 685–808.

going into town. Of the Pharaonic remains, the most significant is the *Temple of Hibis* (as the place was known in antiquity), which was begun during the reign of the Persian King Darius (fifth century B.C.) and completed under Nectanebo II, with Graeco-Roman additions (see Map, p. 345, A). Built out of the curiously speckled sandstone of the locality, it was excavated and restored by the expedition of the New York Metropolitan Museum of Art early this century and is currently undergoing new repairs by the Egyptian Antiquities Service. The temple's setting is picturesque, with its surrounding groves of palm trees and the remains of a once-extensive lake in front. Behind the quay and avenue of sphinxes, leading to a free-standing portal, lies the temple proper. Visitors familiar with the layout of Egyptian temples in the Nile Valley will find few surprises in its arrangement, but the reliefs display a bold, unusual style that may well reflect the influence of local artists. The scenes on the roof – particularly one sequence on the burial of Osiris – are easiest to see, but note the groups of deities on the walls of the sanctuary, and also a relief on the north wall of the hypostyle hall, wherein a winged figure of Seth (so often maligned in the Nile Valley) overcomes the serpent Apophis: Seth was the protector of the fertility of the oasis, and some authorities regard this icon as a precursor of the popular theme of St George and the Dragon in Christian mythology.

Opposite the Hibis Temple, on the hill of *Nadura* (see Map, p. 345, B), 2 km. to the south-east, are remains of a Roman temple, along with the mudbrick buildings attached to it. Although the ruins are unimpressive, the site commands a fine view of the countryside, particularly the uneasy border between the oasis and the sand dunes that are ever encroaching on it.

Less than a kilometre north of the Hibis Temple is the Christian cemetery of Bagawat (C). This is a true city of the dead: those who have already seen the later Theban tombs, and also the Hellenistic cemetery of Tuna el-Gebel (see Chapter 15, pp. 202–3), will best appreciate the continuity from earlier usages found here. The tombs consist of mud-brick chapels, with cupolas, false windows, and often elaborate moulded decoration on their façades. Most have only a single room, under which the deceased was buried, but a number also have a side chapel. Several family tombs, with open courts serving as the focus of the tomb's several parts, display even greater complexity. A few tombs also possess notable painted decoration (for example, one notable scene of Daniel in the Lion's Den): these are locked, but they will be opened by the local inspector for the Department of Antiquities if advance notice is given. Only traces of the church that occupied the middle of the necropolis remain; but anyone wishing to walk another kilometre north of Bagawat will find the ruins of a fortified monastery, locally called *Qasr Ain Mustafa Kashif* (D). The 'keep' of this fortress, which sheltered the monks from attack by hostile Bedouin, is preserved north of the entrance, while monastic buildings several storeys high can be seen on the west side of the compound.[3]

If two days or more can be spent in Kharga Oasis, the monuments at the south end of the oasis may be visited as well. Since Kharga is the largest of the oases, being nearly 100 km. in length, a full day should be allowed for the journey and the return to Kharga City. At *Qasr el-Ghueita*, about 25 km. south, there is a stone temple (E)

3. For better-preserved examples, see the Monastery of St Simeon at Aswan (Chapter 21, pp. 329–30) and the functioning monasteries of the Wadi Natrūn (Chapter 11, p. 133).

surrounded by mudbrick service buildings and dedicated to the Theban Triad: like the Hibis Temple, it has a long history, having been begun by the Nubian rulers of the Twenty-fifth Dynasty and finished during the Ptolemaic era. About 5 km. beyond, at *Qasr el-Zaiyan* (F), another temple to Amun from the Graeco-Roman Period may be seen. And at the far end of the oasis (85 km. south of Kharga City), at *Qasr Dush* (G), is a Roman temple to Isis and Serapis.

The road to *Dakhala Oasis* (see Map, p. 345), though mostly of the same quality as that from the Nile Valley to Kharga, must be travelled cautiously for the first twenty kilometres, as it is likely to be covered by shifting sand dunes: these can usually be avoided by using the emergency by-ways constructed by the local authorities, but it is sometimes necessary to go around the edge of a dune on the compacted desert floor. The first significant monuments appear at *Balat*, some 135 km. from Kharga: it was here (H) that the governors of the oases had their capital during the Old Kingdom, and 500 m. north of the road (before the town is reached) looms a large *mastaba*, the best preserved found in the cemetery once located on this spot. The ancient town, now being excavated, is located several kilometres to the north-west, at *'Aïn Asul* (I). Since there is no suitable road for any but the most rugged vehicle, this distance must be covered by foot or on a pack animal if the remains, such as they are today, must be seen.

After the town of Mut (about 165 km.), the capital of Dakhla Oasis, the road begins to deteriorate until it ends at Qasr el-Dakhl (197 km.); but the difficulties are worth enduring for the monuments found here. First, at *El Mazauwaka* (see Map, p. 345, J) we find two brightly painted tombs of the Hellenistic period: native and classical styles blend in lively fashion, and the larger tomb

(which belonged to one Petosiris) has a wealth of mythological scenes, including a zodiac on the ceiling of the front chamber. A few kilometres beyond is the Roman temple at *Deir el-Hajar* (K): built in the first century A.D., its unrestored tumble-down aspect evokes more than many other sites in the Nile Valley those 'romantic ruins' pictured in the earliest travellers' prints of the Egyptian monuments.

The road to the two northern oases leaves from Cairo and is of good quality for the 334 km. to *Bahriya* (Fig. 166). Most of the ancient monuments are found in the vicinity of *El Qasr*, the capital, which is at the northern end of the oasis. In and about the town one may visit the ruined temple of the Twenty-sixth Dynasty, with the still-preserved chapel of King Apries; and also the remains of a Roman triumphal arch, which was the principal sight in the area before its destruction in the mid-nineteenth century. Three kilometres south, at *Qarat Hilwa*, there is a tomb of one

Fig. 166 **Bahriya Oasis**

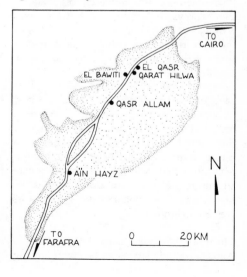

Amenhotep, governor of Bahriya during the later Eighteenth or early Nineteenth Dynasty, which reveals the principles of Egyptian tomb decoration flourishing in this remote outpost. The later Pharaonic necropolis is found at *El Bawiti*, 5 km. south of El Qasr: the tombs (nearly all of Twenty-sixth Dynasty date) are located at two sites nearby, namely *Qarat es-Subi* and *Qarat Qasr Salim*; and an especially notable tomb in the latter group, belonging to one Bannentiu, displays paintings of some refinement depicting the journeys of the solar and lunar barques through the sky. An ibis catacomb, with a decorated forecourt, is also found at El Bawiti (*temp.* Dynasty XXVI; cf. the similar catacomb at Tuna el-Gebel in the Nile Valley [Chapter 15, p. 203]). Sixteen kilometres south of El Qasr, at *Qasr Allam*, there is a substantial stone chapel of Alexander the Great, with priests' houses, offices and magazines, all enclosed within a temenos wall: this site is known locally as *Qasr el Migysbah*. Finally, if time permits the fifty-kilometre journey to *'Ain Haïz* (which itself was classed as a separate oasis in antiquity), there are interesting post-Pharaonic remains — a church, originally in two storeys, dating to the fifth or sixth century B.C.; a military camp; and, between the two, remains of contemporary houses, some of them imposing and decorated with Christian motifs.

Farafra Oasis, known in antiquity as 'The Land of the Cow', is set within the largest of the ancient depressions in the western desert. The monuments, clustered around the capital at Qasr el-Farafra, near the centre of the oasis, are insignificant and not well excavated, so only the most resolute adventurer need push on, along the 170 km. of dirt track that separates Bahriya from its western neighbour.

The oasis of *Siwa* is situated 593 km. west of Alexandria and may be reached by following the road that leads through the resort town of Mersa Matruh: the paved road ends 130 km. out of Siwa, but resumes for the final 30 km. to the oasis. The most important sites are located near the town of Siwa itself. About 4 km. east of the modern centre rises the rock of Aghurmi, around which the medieval Siwans built their stronghold (abandoned today). On top of the rock is the famed 'Temple of the Oracle', already a recognized foundation in the Mediterranean world before Alexander the Great visited it in 331 B.C. and was greeted there by the god Amun as his son. The building is surprisingly well preserved: its façade, in the plainest Egyptian style, was augmented during the Ptolemaic era with half-columns of the Doric order, giving it the appearance of a Greek temple. Inside, we proceed through two courts and an antechamber into the sanctuary, which is the only part of the temple to be decorated in the Egyptian manner: although the inscriptions are worn, it appears that the king under whom the present building was dedicated was Ahmose II (Twenty-Sixth Dynasty). Note, on the east side of the sanctuary, a short corridor with three niches carved into the wall adjoining the sanctuary and with two small apertures near the ceiling: hidden chambers are also found in such temples as Kom Ombo (Chapter 20, p. 317) and the Khonsu Temple at Karnak (Chapter 17, pp. 235–6), and some scholars believe that it was from hiding-places such as these that the oracles were called out by the priests. Outside the temple, across the courtyard on the south-west side, is a deep well from which pure water for the ritual was drawn in antiquity.

A second temple to Amun once stood amidst groves of palm trees on the plain below the rock of Aghurmi; but the temple of Umm Ubayda was blown up in 1897 by a local official, so only one standing wall and a few blocks remain of this once picturesque site. Nearby is the 'Aïn el-Gubah, the 'Spring of the Sun', which the ancients believed grew cold during the day and waxed furiously hot at night — a story still told by Siwans today, though it is not to be taken seriously.

About 1.5 km. north-east of the modern town of Siwa lies the ancient cemetery. Known locally as Gebel el-Mawta, 'Hill of the Dead' (also as Qaret el-Mussaberīn, or 'Ridge of the Mummified'), its tombs date from Dynasty XXVI into Roman times. Of the four decorated tombs located here, the most important belonged to an official of the Graeco-Roman Period named Siamun, being beautifully painted in a mixed Egyptian and Hellenizing style.

Apart from the ancient monuments, visitors will find Siwa to be the most exotic of the oases. The old walled towns of the Siwans (e.g., Aghurmi) are of considerable interest, as are the plantations of palm and fruit trees that are the chief source of livelihood in the oasis. Although constantly in contact with Arab civilization and governed by Egypt since the last century, Siwa retains its own cultural identity: the inhabitants prefer to speak their own Berber-based language and their old traditions are still very much a part of daily life. Increasing contact with the outside world will surely wear down these individualities in succeeding generations. An educated Siwan a thousand years hence may well look on his forefathers with the same blend of detachment and recognition with which we today view the ancient inhabitants of the Nile Valley.

Appendix
Capsule King List and History of Ancient Egypt

Archaic Period (c. 3150–2686 B.C.)*

Dynasty '0' (c. 3150–3050)
King Scorpion
Horus Narmer

The essential steps leading to the unification of Egypt took place at this time. A semi-mythical King 'Menes', credited with founding the Egyptian state, is frequently identified by scholars as the Horus Narmer but may represent an amalgam of several kings. The new capital was fixed at Memphis, near the border between Upper and Lower Egypt.

Dynasty I (c. 3050–2890)
Horus Aha
Horus Djer
Horus Djet
Horus Den

The basis for the historic administration of Egypt was developed, with the division of the country into districts (the nomes) and the creation of the bureaucracy. But, while the kings functioned as rulers over a united Egypt, their identity as kings over the separate parts of the Two Lands appears to have been maintained.

Dynasty II (c. 2890–2686)
Horus Hotepsekhemwy
Seth Peribsen
Horus-and-Seth Khasekhemwy

Consolidation of the united kingdom continued in the earlier part of the dynasty. The latter half was dominated by an obscure disruption in which the god Seth joined (or displaced?) Horus as the divine patron of royalty. We may never know what factors lay behind this so-called 'Seth rebellion', but the problem appears to have been resolved with the adoption of the double 'Horus and Seth' name by the last king of the dynasty.

The Old Kingdom (c. 2686–2181 B.C.)

Dynasty III (c. 2686–2613)
Nebka (c. 2686–2668)
Djoser = Horus Netcherykhet (c. 2668–2649)
Horus Sekhemkhet (c. 2649–2643)
Horus Khaba (c. 2643–2637)
Huni (c. 2637–2613)

The first monumental stone structure – Djoser's step pyramid at Saqqara – epitomizes the emergence of the Egyptian state in its classic form. Leaving behind the problems of the late Second Dynasty, the country was governed by an effective civil service that acknowledged the absolute power of the god-king.

Dynasty IV (c. 2613–2498)
Snefru (c. 2613–2589)
Khufu (c. 2589–2566)
Djedefrë (c. 2566–2558)
Khafrë (c. 2558–2532)
Menkaurë (c. 2532–2504)
Shepseskaf (c. 2504–2500)

The reign of Snefru, who established definitive Egyptian control over Lower Nubia, inaugurated this 'Pyramid Age', the apogee of the Old Kingdom. The splendour of contemporary royal tombs, however, could not mask persistent difficulties within the royal family (for instance, in the succession of Khufu by the intruder Djedefrë) that eventually brought an end to the dynasty.

Dynasty V (c. 2498–2345)
Userkaf (2498–2491)
Sahurë (2491–2477)
Neferirkarë-Kakai (2477–2467)
Neferefrë (c. 2460–2453)
Niuserrë (c. 2453–2422)
Djedkarë-Isesi (c. 2414–2375)
Unis (c. 2375–2345)

---

* While the broad outlines of Egyptian chronology are clear, details are in dispute. The dates given here are those that the author regards as most probable or (at worst) most convenient. Only the most important rulers, together with others who are named in the text above, are included in this listing.

Power seems to have passed to the new dynasty when Userkaf married Khenthawes, sister and widow (?) of Shepseskaf. Particularly notable during this period was the ascendant influence of the sun god Rē of Heliopolis. Some diminution in the status of royalty can be inferred from the dominance of the solar cult, the comparative poverty of the royal tombs, and the increasing importance of private families who held high office under, or married into, the royal house.

Dynasty VI (c. 2345–2181)
Teti (c. 2345–2333 B.C.)
Pepi I (c. 2332–2283)
Mernerē (c. 2283–2278)
Pepi II (c. 2278–2184)

Economic disorders, the collapse of Egyptian authority in Nubia, and aggrandizement of the nomarchs at the crown's expense are the hallmarks of this period. Stratagems, such as Pepi I's marriage alliances with powerful provincial families, only emphasize the current weakness of the royal house, and the dynasty ended ingloriously following the all-too-lengthy reign of Pepi II.

The First Intermediate Period (c. 2181–2040 B.C.)

Dynasties VII and VIII (c. 1281–2160)

Dynasty IX (c. 2160–2130)

The feeble kinglets who ruled from Memphis following the end of the Sixth Dynasty were supplanted by a more vigorous ruling house from Heracleopolis, near the modern town of Beni Suef. Most of the independent nomarchs were forced to acknowledge the suzerainty of this Ninth Dynasty, but the government of Egypt remained fragmented among numerous principalities.

Dynasty X (c. 2130–2040)

Dynasty XI/1 (2133–2060)
Horus Wahankh Antef II (2117–2069)

The dominance of the second Heracleopolitan Dynasty was successfully challenged by the nascent Eleventh Dynasty from Thebes. Efforts by the Heracleopolitans to form an anti-Theban coalition of nomarchs in Upper Egypt (including the renowned Ankhtify of Moalla) were eventually overcome, and the new dynasty made significant gains in Middle Egypt.

The Middle Kingdom (c. 2040–1782 B.C.)

Dynasty XI/2 (2060–1991)

Nebhepetrē Mentuhotep I (2060–2010)
Sankhkarē Mentuhotep II (2010–1998)
Nebtowyrē Mentuhotep III (1997–1991)

The final push against the Heracleopolitans and the reunification of the country was accomplished by Mentuhotep I, who is thus recognized in Egyptian records as the founder of the Middle Kingdom. The following reigns saw the rebuilding of a national government and the resumption of large-scale foreign trade.

Dynasty XII (1991–1782)
Amenemhēt I (1991–1962)
Senwosret I (1971–1928)
Amenemhēt II (1929–1895)
Senwosret II (1897–1878)
Senwosret III (1878–1841)
Amenemhēt III (1842–1797)
Amenemhēt IV (1798–1786)
Queen Sobeknofru (1785–1782)

The founder of the Twelfth Dynasty was a man from the southernmost nome in Egypt who may have served as vizier to the last king of the Eleventh Dynasty. Although the period overall was a prosperous one in Egypt, the dynasty was plagued by internal strife. Amenemhēt I found it politic to conciliate the still powerful nomarchs; they were finally suppressed by Senwosret III, who re-organized the country into large administrative districts governed by officers of the crown. Pressure on the royal house from within and without no doubt explains the frequent coregencies, whereby the senior monarch associated his heir on the throne before his death in order to secure the succession. Egyptian sovereignty over Lower Nubia was re-established under the Twelfth Dynasty, which also pursued landreclamation projects inside Egypt, notably in the Faiyūm.

The Second Intermediate Period (1782–1570 B.C.)

Dynasty XIII (1782–1650)
Auyibrē Hor (c. 1760)
Sekhemrē-Khutowy Sobekhotep II (c. 1750)
Khendjer (c. 1747)
Khasekhemrē Neferhotep I (1741–1730)
Khaneferrē Sobekhotep IV (1730–1720)

Little is known about this turbulent era and its mostly ephemeral rulers. Reigns were generally short, and real power in the land seems to have been held by court officials. Near the start of the seventeenth century, the central government was challenged by separatist movements in the Delta (known collectively as the Fourteenth Dynasty).

The Hyksos: Dynasty XV (c. 1663–1555)

A horde of invaders from Asia (known traditionally as the Hyksos, 'rulers of foreign countries') swept through the Delta, bringing to an end the tenuous sovereignty of the Thirteenth Dynasty. The Egyptian yoke in Nubia was thrown off at about the same time, and native princes in Egypt found themselves hemmed in by a hostile Nubian kingdom to the south and by the Hyksos state in the north. The Asiatic rulers set themselves up as rulers in the Egyptian mould and had no difficulty in imposing their suzerainty over the rest of the country, particularly over the 'lesser Hyksos' princes who formed the wholly artificial Sixteenth Dynasty in Egyptian records.

Dynasty XVII (c. 1663–1570)
Sankhenrē Mentuhotep VI (. 1633)
Sekenenrē Tao II (c. 1574)
Wadjkheperrē Kamose (c. 1573–1570)

Once again, it was a Theban family which led the way towards the eventual reunification of the country. Claiming descent from the Thirteenth Dynasty, its early rulers established a kingdom in Upper Egypt that could resist both the Hyksos and Nubian states allied against it. Most later rulers then acknowledged Hyksos suzerainty, but the last kings of the dynasty entered on a frankly expansionist policy. At first, the Hyksos succeeded in mustering a coalition of Egyptian princes to oppose the southerners: the mangled corpse of Sekenenrē, one of the prize exhibits of the Cairo Museum's mummy room, bears eloquent witness to this temporary setback for the Theban cause. The next king, Kamose, led an ambitious raid to the very outskirts of Avaris, the Hyksos capital in the Delta. By this time, both the Nubians and the Hyksos, together with their Egyptian allies, were reduced to a defensive posture against the waxing power of the Theban Dynasty.

The New Kingdom (c. 1570–1070 B.C.)

Dynasty XVIII (c. 1570–1293)
Ahmose I (c. 1570–1546)

Amenhotep I (c. 1551–1524)
Thutmose I (c. 1524–1518)
Thutmose II (c. 1518–1504)
Thutmose III (1504–1450)
Hatshepsut (c. 1498–1483)
Amenhotep II (c. 1453–1419)
Thutmose IV (c. 1419–1386)
Amenhotep III (c. 1386–1349)
Amenhotep IV/Akhenaten (c. 1350–1334)
Smenkhkarē (c. 1336–1334)
Tutankhamun (c. 1334–1325)
Ay (c. 1325–1321)
Horemheb (c. 1321–1293)

Kamose was succeeded by his brother, Ahmose I, to whom posterity granted the honour of inaugurating a glorious new period because he successfully expelled the Hyksos and reunified the Two Lands. The next century saw the establishment of the Egyptian 'empire' in Asia – really a number of nominally independent states which acknowledged Egyptian suzerainty – as well as the colonization of Nubia down to the Fifth Nile Cataract. Accommodation between the Egyptians and the neighbouring 'empire' of Mitanni in North Syria brought the Pharaohs recognition as the equals of the other 'great kings' of the Middle East, a position enhanced by Egyptian control of trade routes to southern Africa and of Nubian gold. At home, the early kings of the Eighteenth Dynasty crushed the supremacy of their last native challengers and built an administration that lasted, substantially unchanged, for the next five hundred years. The Pharaoh's central role in directing both domestic and military policy is one reason why the dynasty survived virtually unscathed the several crises – culminating in the usurpation and posthumous dishonouring of Queen Hatshepsut – that attended the replacement of Ahmose's family by the more vigorous Thutmoside line.

The later Eighteenth Dynasty was dominated by the crown's struggle with a power which owed its advancement to the royal house – the clergy. Religious establishments had profited greatly from their patronage of Egyptian expansion abroad, and in particular the wealth and influence of Amun's clergy threatened the authority of the monarchy. The revolution of Akhenaten, with its attempted diversion of resources into a cult that celebrated the king and the solar disc as exclusive representatives of the divine, ultimately failed, and it was left to his successors, particularly Horemheb, to rebuild the influence of the monarch along more traditional lines.

Dynasty XIX (c. 1293–1185)
Ramesses I (c. 1293–1291)
Sety I (c. 1291–1278)
Ramesses II (1279–1212)
Merneptah (c. 1212–1202)
Amenmesse (c. 1202–1199)
Sety II (c. 1199–1193)
Siptah (c. 1193–1187)
Twosret (c. 1187–1185)

Horemheb bequeathed his kingship to his vizier, Ramesses, whose family ruled Egypt for over a century as the Nineteenth Dynasty. The earlier part of this period was taken up with the struggle against the Hittites, a new power in Asia who had overthrown the Mittanian Empire during the reign of Akhenaten and were encroaching on Egypt's sphere of influence. The Battle of Kadesh (c. 1275), although militarily inconclusive, did maintain the credibility of Egyptian power in North Syria, and later in the reign of Rammesses II (c. 1259) a formal treaty of peace between the two powers was signed. The first of several threats to Egypt's security stemming from the movement of peoples at this time was checked during the reign of Merneptah (c. 1207) when an invasion by a combined force of Libyans and 'Peoples of the Sea' was repulsed. The closing years of the dynasty were turbulent, filled with obscure quarrels of rival branches of the family of Ramesses II manipulated by a 'grey eminence' of Syrian origin, Chancellor Bai.

Dynasty XX (c. 1185–1070)
Sethnakht (c. 1185–1182)
Ramesses III (c. 1182–1151)
Ramesses IV (c. 1151–1145)
Ramesses V (c. 1145–1141)
Ramesses VI (c. 1141–1133)
Ramesses IX (c. 1126–1108)
Ramesses XI (c. 1098–1070)
Herihor (c. 1080–1072)

Dynastic troubles came to an end when Sethnakht (perhaps a distant relative of the reigning house) took power with the consent of the country's civil authorities. The dynasty was firmly established by his son, Ramesses III, who in the first decade of his reign had to repel no fewer than three invasions by various groups of Libyans and 'Sea Peoples'. Late in his reign, however, we hear the first rumblings of the persistent economic difficulties that were typical for the remainder of the dynasty. The royal treasury was seriously overextended throughout this period, during which magnates such as the High Priest of Amun came

to exercise direct authority in governing various parts of Egypt. The tomb-robbery scandals at Thebes during the reigns of Ramesses IX and XI point both to the breakdown in law and order and to the economic depression of the times. Roving bands of Libyans made the country unsafe and in the reign of Ramesses XI the Thebaid was seized by the Viceroy of Nubia, who was himself next expelled by the general Herihor in the name of the king. At the end of the dynasty we find Herihor governing in Upper Egypt as High Priest of Amun (later as 'king'). The defeated Viceroy had successfully detached Nubia from Egyptian control, and in the northern capital at Tanis a certain Smendes was governing for an ineffectual Ramesses XI.

The Third Intermediate Period (c. 1069–525 B.C.)

Dynasty XXI (c. 1069–945)
Smendes (c. 1069–1063)
Psusennes I (c. 1059–1033)
Amenemōpe (c. 1033–981)

Thebes
High Priest /King Pinedjem I (1070–1026)

At the death of Ramesses XI, Smendes assumed the diadem in the north. His dynasty's authority was generally recognized at Thebes, but the south was effectively independent. By the end of this period the predominant power lay in the hands of the 'Great Chiefs of the Me(shwesh)-Libyans', commanders of a standing army largely descended from the prisoners whom Ramesses III had settled in military colonies throughout Egypt.

Dynasty XXII (c. 945–712)
Shoshenq I (c. 945–924)
Osorkon I (c. 924–889)
Shoshenq II (c. 890)
Osorkon II (c. 874–850)
Takelot II (c. 850–825)
Shoshenq III (c. 825–773)

Thebes
High Priest /King Harsiēse (c. 870–860)

At the demise of the last king of the Twenty-first Dynasty, the throne passed to the 'Great Chief of the Me', Shoshenq I. Although Thebes had been reunited with the kingdom, local magnates frequently resisted the ruling house and its agents, especially in the turbulent period following the accession of Shoshenq III.

Libyan Anarchy (c. 818–712): Dynasties XXIII and XXIV

Dynasty XXV/1 (c. 772–712)
Piankhy/Piyi (c. 753–713)

As Egypt fragmented into an increasing number of kingdoms and principalities, the Nubian state that had developed over the previous three centuries began to extend its authority over the north Nile Valley. Campaigns such as that of Piankhy (c. 734) stopped short of completely occupying the country, however, allowing resistance to flare up anew.

Dynasty XXV/2 (712–656)
Shabaka (713–698)
Taharqa (690–664)

Shabaka assumed control over the united kingdoms of Egypt and Nubia in 712. The allegiance of the perennially fractious Thebans was secured by allowing them a *de facto* independence, the royal presence being maintained by a princess who ruled in name as the 'divine votaress of Amun'. Attempts to manipulate the balance of power in Western Asia failed, however, resulting in the two Assyrian invasions (667/6 and 664/3) that devastated Thebes and drove the Twenty-fifth Dynasty back into its Nubian homeland.

Dynasty XXVI (664–525)
Psamtik I (664–610)
Necho (610–595)
Psamtik II (595–589)
Apries (589–570)
Ahmose II (570–526)
Psamtik III (526–525)

The principalities that re-emerged following the Assyrian invasions gradually acknowledged the suzerainty of the ruling house of Sais in the West Delta. Thebes also bowed to the new dynasty by accepting its candidate for the office of divine votaress. No small role in the Saite triumph was played by Greek and Carian mercenaries, who from now on made up an increasingly important part of the Egyptian army. The first significant settlement of Greeks in Egypt took place during this period, when they were granted the site of Naucratis in the West Delta. Egypt was now more open to influences from the northern Mediterranean, and the Saites' solicitude towards Egyptian commerce is evident from the construction of Necho's canal between the Delta and the Red Sea. In foreign affairs, the Twenty-sixth Dynasty kept a watchful eye on its borders. Nubia was chastised

in the reign of Psamtik II, and the country was secured from the successive Assyrian and Babylonian ambitions in Western Asia. The Saites' failure to establish an effective buffer between Egypt and the dominant Asiatic empire, however, laid it open to attack.

'Late' Period (525–332 B.C.)

First Persian Period: Dynasty XXVII (525–404)
Cambyses (525–522)
Darius I (521–486)
Xerxes (485–465)
Darius II (423–405)

Dynasty XXVIII (404–399)

Dynasty XXIX (399–380)
Hakoris (393–380)

Dynasty XXX (380–342)
Nectanebo I (380–362)
Teos (362–360)
Nectanebo II (360–342)

Second Persian Period: Dynasty XXXI (342–332)

The invasion of the Persian King Cambyses put an end to the Saite Dynasty, incorporating Egypt into the Achaemenid Empire. The earlier Persian kings adopted the Pharaonic style towards their Egyptian subjects, but their rule was never popular and the repression that followed a revolt (464–454) fanned resentment against the conquerors. Egyptian independence, regained by the Saite prince who constituted the Twenty-eighth Dynasty, lasted for six decades, as the Pharaohs encouraged Greek states against the Persians and enlisted Greek mercenaries: the installation of one of these as virtual governor of Egypt during the reign of Teos gave the Egyptians a foretaste of the rigours of Ptolemaic administration. The second period of Persian rule was turbulent and brief.

Graeco-Roman Period (332 B.C.–A.D. 323)

Alexander the Great (332–323)
Philip Arrhidaeus and Alexander II (323–305)

Ptolemaic Dynasty (305–30)
Ptolemy I Soter (323–282)
Ptolemy II Philadelphus (285–247/6)
Ptolemy III Euergetes (247/6–222/1)
Ptolemy IV Philopator (222/1–205)
Ptolemy V Epiphanes (205–180)
Ptolemy VI Philometer (180–164, 163–145)

Ptolemy VIII Euergetes II (170–163, 145–116)
Ptolemy IX Soter II (116–110, 109–107, 88–80)
Ptolemy X Alexander (110–109, 107–88)
Ptolemy XII Neos Dionysus (80–67, 55–51)
Cleopatra VII (51–30)
Ptolemy XV (Caesarion (36–30)

Alexander the Great became king of Egypt in 332 B.C., but the empire fell apart after his death. When the nominal rule of his successors came to an end in 305, Ptolemy Son of Lagos (who had been effectively ruling the country since 323) assumed the diadem as the founder of the Ptolemaic Dynasty. The rule of this house in Egypt is characterized by the displacement of Egyptians by Greeks in the ruling classes and the economic exploitation of the country by the royal exchequer. The Ptolemies were frequently at war with their neighbours, the other successor states, and the winning of a crucial victory at Raphia (217 B.C.) with the aid of native Egyptian troops brought about an upsurge of nationalist feeling, culminating in a lengthy rebellion in Upper Egypt (206–186). The latter half of the dynasty was plagued by family quarrels, and the kings fell increasingly under the influence of Rome, which finally took over the country following its victory over Cleopatra VII and Mark Antony.

Roman Emperors (30 B.C. – A.D. 323)
Augustus (30 B.C. – A.D. 14)
Tiberius (A.D. 14–37)
Claudius (41–54)
Nero (54–68)
Vespasian (69–79)
Titus (79–81)
Domitian (81–96)
Nerva (96–98)
Trajan (98–117)
Hadrian (117–138)
Antoninus Pius (138–161)
Marcus Aurelius (161–180)
Septimius Severus (193–211)
Geta (209–211)
Caracalla (209–217)
Diocletian (284–305)

Byzantine Period (A.D. 323–642)

Constantine (323–337)
Theodosius (379–395)
Justinian I (527–565)

Egypt remained a province of the Roman, later Byzantine Empire until the Arab invasion and the capitulation of imperial forces in A.D. 642.

Further Reading

CHAPTER 1

John Baines and Jaromir Malek, *Atlas of Ancient Egypt.* Oxford: Phaidon, 1980.
Karl W. Butzer, *Early Hydraulic Civilization in Egypt. A Study in Cultural Ecology.* Chicago: University of Chicago Press, 1976.
William C. Hayes, *Most Ancient Egypt.* Edited by Keith C. Seele. Chicago: University of Chicago Press, 1964.
Hermann Kees, *Ancient Egypt. A Cultural Topography.* Edited by T. G. H. James. Chicago: University of Chicago Press, 1961.

CHAPTER 2

Adolf Erman, *Life in Ancient Egypt.* Translated by H. M. Tirard. London: MacMillan and Co., 1894.
Pierre Montet, *Everyday Life in Egypt in the Days of Ramesses the Great.* Translated by A. R. Maxwell-Hyslop and Margaret S. Drower. London: Edward Arnold Ltd, 1958.
Sir J. Gardiner Wilkinson, *The Manners and Customs of the Ancient Egyptians.* 2nd edition revised and corrected by Samuel Birch. 3 volumes. London: John Murray, 1878.
A. Lucas, *Ancient Egyptian Materials and Industries.* 4th edition revised and enlarged by J. R. Harris. London: Edward Arnold Ltd, 1962.

CHAPTER 3

Henri Frankfort, *Kingship and the Gods.* Chicago: University of Chicago Press, 1948, 1978.
Sir Alan Gardiner, *Egypt of the Pharaohs.* Oxford: Oxford University Press, 1961.
John A. Wilson, *The Culture of Ancient Egypt.* Chicago: University of Chicago Press, 1956.

CHAPTER 4

William Y. Adams, *Nubia: Corridor to Africa.* Princeton: Princeton University Press, 1977.
Walter B. Emery, *Egypt in Nubia.* London: Hutchinson & Co. Ltd, 1965.

Ahmed Fakhry, *The Oases of Egypt:* Volume I: *Siwa Oasis;* Volume II: *Bahriyah and Farafra Oases.* Cairo: American University in Cairo Press, 1973–4.
Georg Steindorff, *When Egypt Ruled the East.* Revised by Keith C. Seele. Chicago: University of Chicago Press, 1957.

CHAPTER 5

E. A. Wallis Budge, *The Gods of the Egyptians, or Studies in Egyptian Mythology.* 2 Volumes. New York: Dover Publications, Inc., 1969.
Siegfried Morenz, *Egyptian Religion.* Translated by Ann E. Keep. London: Methuen and Co. Ltd, 1973.
Serge Sauneron, *The Priests of Ancient Egypt.* Translated by Ann Morissett. New York: Grove Press, 1960.
John A. Wilson, 'Egypt' in *Before Philosophy.* Harmondsworth: Penguin Books, 1949; pp. 37–133.

CHAPTER 6

E. A. Wallis Budge, *The Mummy: Chapters on Egyptian Funerary Archaeology.* 2nd edition. New York: Biblio and Tannen, 1964.
Jean-Philippe Lauer, *Saqqara, The Royal Cemetery of Memphis.* London: Thames and Hudson Ltd, 1976.
Charles F. Nims, *Thebes of the Pharaohs.* London: Elek Books, 1965.

CHAPTER 7

Christiane Desroches-Noblecourt, *Tutankhamen: the Life and Death of a Pharaoh.* London: The Connoisseur and Michael Joseph Ltd, 1963.
I. E. S. Edwards, *The Pyramids of Egypt.* Revised edition. Harmondsworth: Penguin Books, 1961.
W. B. Emery, *Archaic Egypt.* Harmondsworth: Penguin Books, 1961.
James E. Harris and Kent R. Weeks, *X-Raying the Pharaohs.* New York: Charles Scribner's Sons, 1973.

CHAPTER 8

H. Idris Bell, *Egypt from Alexander the Great to the Arab Conquest.* Oxford: Clarendon Press, 1948.

Edwyn Bevan, *A History of Egypt under the Ptolemaic Dynasty.* London: Methuen & Co., 1927.

Evaristo Breccia, *Alexandrea ad Aegyptum.* (English edition) Bergamo: Istituto Italiano d'arti grafiche, 1922.

E. M. Forster, *Alexandria.* 2nd edition. Garden City, N.Y.: Anchor Books, Doubleday & Co., 1961.

P. M. Fraser, *Ptolemaic Alexandria.* 3 volumes. Oxford: Clarendon Press, 1972.

J. Grafton Milne, *A History of Egypt under Roman Rule.* 3rd edition, revised. London: Methuen & Co., 1924.

W. W. Tarn, *Hellenistic Civilization.* London: Edward Arnold & Co., 1930.

CHAPTER 9

F. Gladstone Bratton, *A History of Egyptian Archaeology.* London: Robert Hale, 1967.

Leslie Greener, *The Discovery of Egypt.* London: Cassell and Co., 1966.

—, *High Dam Over Nubia.* New York: Viking Press, 1962.

J. R. Harris, ed., *The Legacy of Egypt.* 2nd edition. Oxford: Oxford University Press, 1971.

John A. Wilson, *Signs and Wonders Upon Pharaoh.* Chicago: University of Chicago Press, 1964.

General Index

Index of Localities

*Modern place names are printed in roman type,
ancient place names in italic.*